INDIA, CENTRAL ASIA AND RUSSIA

Three Millennia of Contacts

INDIA, CENTRAL ASIA AND RUSSIA

Three Millennia of Contacts

Chief Editor

D.N. TRIPATHI

Editors

R.C. AGRAWAL
P.K. SHUKLA

Indian Council of Historical Research

New Delhi

Aryan Books International

New Delhi

INDIA, CENTRAL ASIA AND RUSSIA

ISBN: 978-81-7305-294-1

First Published in **2013** by

Indian Council of Historical Research
35, Ferozeshah Road, New Delhi-110001

and

Aryan Books International
Pooja Apartments, 4B, Ansari Road, New Delhi-110 002 (India)
Tel.: 23287589, 23255799; Fax: 91-11-23270385
E-mail: aryanbooks@gmail.com
www.aryanbooks.co.in

Designed and Printed in India at
ABI Prints & Publishing Co., New Delhi

Dedicated

To

The Cherished Memories

of

Shri Baldev Raj Grover, Indian Council of Historical Research, New Delhi

&

Prof. G.G. Kotovsky, Moscow
Who took pains to activate
'The Cultural Exchange Programme' between
India and the Russian Federation

Preface

The present book includes most of the papers presented in the international seminar on "India, Central Asia and Russia: Three Millennia of Contacts" held in New Delhi on 6-8 November 2001. These papers have been meticulously edited by Dr. R.C. Agrawal and Dr. P.K. Shukla, former Member-Secretaries of the Indian Council of Historical Research, New Delhi. I am convinced that the papers included in this book are still relevant for any further study in this field.

The idea of Central Asia as a distinct region of the world was introduced in 1843 by the geographer Alexander von Humboldt. The borders of Central Asia are subject to multiple definitions, and no one definition is universally accepted. Despite this uncertainty in defining borders, it does have some important overall characteristics. For one, Central Asia has historically been closely tied to its nomadic peoples and the Silk Road. As a result, it has acted as crossroad for the movement of people, goods and ideas between Europe, West Asia, South Asia, and East Asia.

Central Asia is the core region of the Asian continent and stretches from the Caspian Sea in the west to China in the east and from Afghanistan in the south to Russia in the north. In the modern context, all definitions of Central Asia include five republics of the former Soviet Union: Kazakhstan, Kyrgyzstan, Tajikistan, Turkmenistan and Uzbekistan. Other areas included are Afghanistan, northern Iran, Mongolia, and sometimes Xinjiang in western China and southern Siberia in Russia.

Central Asia and the ancient Indian subcontinent have long traditions of social-cultural, religious, political and economic contact since remote antiquity. The two regions have common and contiguous borders, climatic continuity, similar geographical features and geo-cultural affinity. There has always been uninterrupted flow of people, material and ideas between the two regions.

So much so, some ancient literary sources trace common lineage for Indians, Pakistanis, Afghans, and other nationalities of Central Asia.

The archaeological excavations in the Amu valley in southern Uzbekistan, in Afrasiab on north-eastern edge of Samarkand and some other places in Uzbekistan, Turkmenistan, Kazakhstan and Tak-mak in Kyrghizstan provide evidence of the existence of links between ancient India and Central Asia since remote antiquity. Further, extensive excavations have been carried out with remarkable results at Kara Tepa, Fayaz Tepa, Dalverzin Tepa, Yer Kurgan, Ak-Beshin, Kranayerezka and Isyk-Ata. The discovery of manuscripts in Xinjiang (China) and many other valuable finds of excavation substantively establish that India and eastern Central Asian region of Xinjiang were also in extensive political, cultural and religious intercourse with each other. Dynasties of India came from Central Asia as invaders and dynasties of Indian origin also ruled in Khotan and other places in Central Asia. Quite recently, in Turkmenistan, a treasure of 1515 coins of Vasudeva, Kushana king (III-IV AD), have been found.

Immigration of peoples and tribes from Central Asia into India, as well as expansion of Central Asian empires into India, is a recurring theme in the history of the region—from the Bronze Age Indo-Aryan migration to the Iron Age Kushan Empire, the Indo-Scythians, the Indo-Greeks (via Bactria) and the medieval Islamic conquest of the Indian subcontinent. Intrusion is typically across the Hindukush, and influence of the intrusive population is first established in the Punjab and the Indus Valley, and sometimes further expanded into the Ganges Plains.

In the Neolithic epoch, most of the territory of Central Asia, Kazakhstan and northern India was part of a large area inhabited by agricultural cultures which were close to each other and went through similar processes of social development.

Comparable research of the Neolithic cultures of Kazakhstan, India and Central Asia allows us to review in detail the sources of the agricultural cultures of the south of Kazakhstan, Central Asia and the northern India, particularly to observe stages of development of pre-Harappan and Harappan settlements. Archaeological excavations in the north-western regions of India, in the centres of the Harappan Civilisation, display an existence of inter-tribal exchange of goods in the ancient times. From Central Asian towns the Harappan civilisation acquired gems. In turn, Harappan handicrafts have been discovered in Central Asia. These facts display that there were processes of different goods exchange in Central Asian and Indian regions in the third-fourth millennium BCE. The recent researches of archaeological relics point towards the existence of contacts between towns of Sindh River Valley and Central Asian and Kazakhstan settlements. These discoveries belong to the period of golden age of the Harappan culture. Some items are similar with those of the

Harappan culture (metal goods, beads made of faience, pottery, ivory). Handicrafts from India as well as the local items that had obvious signs of Indian influence were discovered in Central Asia.

There are extensive references to people of Central Asia in Indian literature like *Atharvaveda, Vamsa Brahmana of Samveda, Aitareya Brahmana, Satapatha Brahmana, Puranas, Manusmiriti, Ramayana, Mahabharata, Raghuvamsa, Brihat-Katha-Manjari, Katha-Saritsagara, Rajaratarangini, Mudrarakshasa, Kavyamimansa* and host of other old Sanskrit literature. In classical Indian tradition, clans of the *Shakas, Yavanas, Kambojas, Pahlavas, Paradas*, etc. are also attested to have been coming as invaders from Central Asia to India in pre-Christian times. They were all finally absorbed into the community of *Kshatriyas* of Indian society. The *Sakas* were formerly the inhabitants of trans-Hemodos region—the *Shakadvipa* of the Puranas or the Scythia of the classical writings. The *Kambojas* and *Pahlavas* are known to have their original settlements in the east Iranian regions in Central Asia. Some allege the existence of some of their settlements in post-Christian times in southwest/southern India also.

The Common Era saw more invaders such as the Kushanas, Hunas, Turks, Mongols and Pashtuns coming to the subcontinent. They have all been absorbed into various South Asian communities, leaving, in some cases, no sign of clear-cut identification.

The Silk Route, which connected China, Europe and India, passed through Central Asia. A lot of cities were established along the Silk Route. In those cities, Indians settled and lived their own life; they had their own social and political organisations, language, scripts, literature, art, architecture and religion. Discoveries from Central Asian sites include remains of hundreds of Buddhist shrines, stupas and monasteries of designs inspired by India; numerous Buddhist texts in Sanskrit, Prakrit or local languages, largely in the Indian scripts, Brahmi and Kharoshthi; Sanskrit dramas and texts on medicine, astronomy and astrology written in Brahmi; hundreds of documents of administrative, commercial, legal and miscellaneous kinds, drafted in Sanskrit, Prakrit or Central Asian dialects written in Indian scripts; and tablets of complete Brahmi script. Kharoshthi documents in Prakrit language on wooden tablets amounting 764 leather pieces and silk fragments throw much light on the social, religious and political conditions of the Central Asia during early centuries of the Christian era. Aurel Stein's collection from Xinxiang also included Central Asian art objects including paintings from 'Thousand Buddha Temple' in Tun-Huang.

Presence of many Buddhist temples and centres in Central Asia and Kazakhstan is a nice example of mutual contacts and gives evidences of the Buddhist tradition being spread over Central Asia and Kazakhstan under the Kushanas. Spreading of Buddhism in Central Asia under the Kushans was accompanied not by blind acceptance of the ideas of ancient Indian culture, but by their understanding and combination with local cultural traditions. The most interesting from archaeological discoveries are the Buddhist Sanskrit manuscripts written in Brahmi and Kharoshthi. Palaeographically they are close to Gilgit manuscripts of *Pragyanparmita* literature (Vinayapitaka) and dated approximately in ca. 7th-8th ACE.

According to the inscriptions discovered in Central Asia, in the Kushan and Gupta periods, Indians settled there built large temple complexes. There are also written evidences of the direct contact between Central Asia and India. These are Buddhist manuscripts on birch bark and palm leaves, which were found in Central Asia. Central Asian Kazakh Buddhist painting has an image of Indian heavenly body that is sun (Surya). We find a parallel to this in images of sun chariot in the sculpture of Bodha-Gaya (*c*.1st BCE) and in Bamian painting (*c*. 5th ACE). There are parallels of winged lions in the Indian art (e.g. sculptural disk from Bharhut).

India's relations with Central Asia in early medieval times correspond with the spread of Buddhist teaching and worship. This initiated one of the greatest cultural movements in history—the passage of Buddhist thought and philosophical ideas from one civilisation to another and also the movement of Buddhist missionaries. Researches of Central Asian scholars reveal that Central Asia knew different schools of Buddhism. For example, Kyrgyz researches say that Kyrgyz people knew Tibetan version of Buddhism—Lamaism. Lamaist terminology may be found in "Manas" epic. And nowadays, a section of Kyrgyzs in China confesses Lamaism. With introduction of Islam, Buddhism as religion disappeared from Central Asia. A vast amount of literature is now available in Russian and local Central Asian languages on Buddhist monuments in Central Asia. But there is still a great field for research on the theme: what legacy has Buddhism left on Central Asian peoples' thinking and local philosophical and moral thinking, and how much of this legacy have been included into Islamic thought in Central Asia? From the Soviet researches we know that in Tibetan culture *Jatakas* occupied very important role. They were not preserved in mummified form but were used as basic material by local writers and poets for illustrations of Lamaist dogmatics understandable to local people. The same was the case in the whole Central Asia also. With removal of Buddhism from the scene its ideas and thinking could not disappear from the minds of the people. Buddhist ideas and thoughts may be found in Central Asian epics, folklore and even fairy tales.

Indian links with Central Asia and vice versa has not been completely continuous, for some centuries they were interrupted, sometimes very intense, as in the case of Kushana period, and sometimes feeble. Zia ul-Din Nakhshabi, the author of *Tutinameh* ("Book of Parrot") was born in central Asia. Al-Beruni came here, learnt Sanskrit and wrote *Tarikh-i Hind*(The History of India). Abdurazzak Samarkandi also came here. Ibn Sina and Al-Khorezmi were acquainted with Indian scientific works. Two-way movements for trade and culture continued during Mughal rule and after. Alexander Burnes, the British agent, wrote that turbans of Punjabi white cloth were used by "whole of the natives of Bokhara and Toorkistan" during 1830s. There were about eight thousand Indian settlers in 19th and early 20th century in Central Asia. Every market and village had Hindu moneylender in Turkestan in 1860s according to an observer. Indians had monopoly of book trade there.

Another splash in relations between India and Central Asia was during the reign of Mahmood Ghaznavi and during the times of Delhi Sultanate. That was the time when Persian language and literature were introduced to India. And mostly it has been done through Central Asia. Central Asia was conquered by Islam not by military means, but the Islamic missionaries mostly from Persia introduced Islam in Central Asia. It was at that time when many Sufi scholars, poets and saints came from Central Asia and settled in Delhi, Kashmir and elsewhere in India. This coincided with the return of many Buddhist thoughts and ideas back to India. The Delhi sultanate was the beginning of intensive penetration of Turkic culture into India.

We may mention two way road of cultural exchange between India and Central Asia. It is connected with Temurlang and his successors. But there was difference between Temurlang and his successors. Temur brought to Delhi great disaster: many buildings were burnt and looted; thousands of people were killed, except craftsmen and masons. Temur came to India to conquer and get enormous wealth. He took with him back to Samarqand Indian masons where they should learn also Persian art of building. It is believed that they constructed world famous architectural treasure of Samarqand—Gur-Emir mausoleum and other monuments in Samarqand and Bukhara.

The empire of the Great Moguls emerged in the northern part of India in 1526. Emir of Ferghana Zahir ud-din Muhammad Babur (1526–1530) started this dynasty. Establishment of a strong and organised state in India governed by Turkic-Muslim dynasty intensified penetration of new traditions, which were connected with culture and art of Central Asia and Kazakhstan, into this region. The Great Moguls have returned their enriched skills back to India and these masons combined these two traditions and invented the higher skill that is now widely known to the world as Indian-Islamic architecture. During this period, great traditions of cultural intercourse and contacts of Central Asia and Great Mogul Empire existed. Central Asia played special role in promotion of Indian culture. From the beginning of the 16th century Indian merchants from northern India started trading in the north to Afghanistan, Iran, Central Asia and Kazakhstan. Temur came to India for some time, his successors came forever and presented to the world the epoch of the greatest splendour. Their royal court was filled with scientists, writers, musicians and poets.

And still there are about 250 manuscripts on history and literature of Central Asia, mostly in Arabic and Persian in the museums and libraries of India. Khuda Bakhsh Library, Patna, is very rich in this matter. Important information is available in written sources of Indian historiography such as *Bukharnama, Tarih-i-Rashidi, Akbarnama, Alamgirnama* and others. In this connection, it is necessary to pay attention to these manuscripts and archival materials, which are in custody of India and abroad, particularly in India Office in the Great Britain, which are yet to be studied properly. *Baburnama* and a book got compiled by Akbar has a lot of material on India and Central Asia. This is a great source for researches on Central Asian-Indian relations in medieval period.

Exactly under the Mogul Empire, India was dramatically affected by the Turkic culture and the Turkic people. The Turks promoted the golden age of Muslim culture in India. Literature and lyrics in the Persian developed, elements specific for the Muslim architecture appeared, and basis of the Indian miniature school were founded. From the time of the Turkic appearance under the leadership of Babur, Indian culture developed in absolutely different way.

Miniature painting of Central Asia developed as a secular art in the medieval period. By the time of emergence of the Mongolian school, miniatures of Central Asia had been developed and improved for a long time, and thus its influence on the Indian painting was natural. However, several decades later, it got an impulse for development from the Mongolian miniatures. There was fruitful process of mutual enrichment and renewal. Achievements of the Indian and Central Asian schools, each of them having its own old traditions, always were accepted creatively.

The slow Russian conquest of the heart of Central Asia began in the early 19th century. Until the 1870s, for the most part, Russian interference was minimal, leaving native ways of life intact and local government structures in place. With the conquest of Turkestan after 1865 and the consequent securing of the frontier, the Russians gradually expropriated large parts of the steppe and gave these lands to Russian farmers, who began to arrive in large numbers. This process was initially limited to the northern fringes of the steppe and it was only in the 1890s that significant numbers of Russians began to settle farther south. The main opposition to Russian expansion into Turkestan came from the British, who felt that Russia was growing too powerful and threatening the northwest frontiers of British India. This rivalry came to be known as' The Great Game', where both powers competed to advance their own interests in the region. It did little to slow the pace of conquest north of the Oxus, but did ensure that Afghanistan remained independent as a buffer state between the two Empires.

During the First World War, the Muslim exemption from conscription was removed by the Russians, sparking the Central Asian Revolt of 1916.

When the Russian Revolution of 1917 occurred, a provisional Government of Jadid Reformers, also known as the Turkestan Muslim Council, met in Kokand and declared Turkestan's autonomy. This new government was quickly crushed by the forces of the Tashkent Soviet, and the semi-autonomous states of Bukhara and Khiva were also invaded. The main independence forces were rapidly crushed, but guerrillas known as basmachi continued to fight the Communists until 1924. Mongolia was also swept up by the Russian Revolution and, though it never became a Soviet Republic, it became a communist People's Republic in 1924.

The Second World War sparked the widespread migration of Soviet citizens to the rear of the USSR. Much of this movement was directed to Soviet Central Asia. These migrations included official, state-organised evacuations and deportations as well as the non-sanctioned, panicked flight from the front by both general citizenry and important officials. The evacuation of Soviet citizens and industry during World War II was an essential element of their overall success in the war, and Central Asia served as a main destination for evacuees.

The Union of Soviet Socialist Republics (USSR) was formally dissolved on December 25, 1991. This left all fifteen republics of the Soviet Union as independent sovereign states. The dissolution of the world's largest communist state also marked an end to the Cold War. Between August and December, 10 republics declared their independence, largely out of fear of another coup. The final collapse of the USSR was one of the most sudden and dramatic territorial losses that has befallen any state in history. Between 1990 and 1992 Kremlin had lost direct government control over about one-third of Soviet territory—most of it acquired in the period between 1700 and 1945—which had about one-half of the Soviet population by the time of the dissolution. From 1988 to 1992, a free press and multiparty system developed in the Central Asian republics as perestroika pressured the local Communist parties to open up. What Svat Soucek calls the "Central Asian Spring" was very short-lived, as soon after independence former Communist Party officials recast themselves as local strongmen. Political stability in the region has mostly been maintained, with the major exception of the Tajik Civil War that lasted from 1992 to 1997. The year 2005 also saw the largely peaceful ousting of Kyrgyz President Askar Akayev in the Tulip Revolution and an outbreak of violence in Andijan, Uzbekistan.

The roots of ethnicity have assumed importance over the past three decades in Europe and Russia. Both the countries have been driven by ethnic rivalries of a kind, which we had all fervently hoped had disappeared forever with the end of the Second World War. In what for many years seemed the stable nation-state of Yugoslavia, we see today live hostilities in which atrocities are ceaselessly committed in the name of ethnic identity. Just as the National

Socialists developed ethnic theories about Aryans and Semites (where they drew distinctions mainly of a racial nature, in terms of genetic descent, supplemented by cultural and linguistic ones), so we see the so-called undertaking what they call "ethnic cleansing" in the name of an ethnic concept. Likewise, in the former Soviet Union we see different ethnic groups in conflict: in Georgia, Armenia, Azerbaijan. Again, the fighting parties are groups, each of which claims allegiance to an essentially ethnic cause.

My essential claim is that these ethnic groups are no impermeable entities whose roots go back far into the past. They are all constructs, some of them recent, some of them many centuries old. But they are not timeless and eternal. It is quite likely that the sort of fiercely self-identifying ethnicity, which we have seen re-awakened in Europe over the past few years, is something which first arose here during the "Iron Age", in the first millennium BC. With the Roman imperium it diminished to some extent, but re-emerged with the decline in Roman power in the fifth century AD. Many European "ethnicities" emerged in the millennium that followed. Their roots may go deep. Linguistic diversity may be the most important factor, with genetic diversity (despite the Nazi delusions) not being a very important one. Both are complicated by the religious diversity, which accompanies the conflicting claims of the world religions.

India has been closely related, both politically and culturally, with the newly carved out states of Soviet Central Asia. We have to study this problem seriously as regionalism is becoming an important issue day by day in the Indian political scenario.

Strictly speaking history knows no end. Every age rewrites its history. Every generation, beset with new issues, problems and questions, looks back to its history, reinterprets, and renews its past. As such, I am confident that the publication of this volume will not only add to the existing knowledge on the subject but also prove useful to researchers, academia and the policy makers interested in this area. I am grateful to Professor Sabyasachi Bhattacharya, former Chairman, ICHR and Dr. Ishrat Alam, Member Secretary, ICHR for their support and efforts to bring out this publication. A special apology is needed for the inadequate attention given to various areas of Central Asia because of the regrettable paucity of Indian specialists in the languages of those areas. While we own the shortfalls in the book, we regret to record that all papers could not be included in this publication for some compelling technical reasons.

D.N. Tripathi

Contents

Preface *vii*
Introduction *xix*
Introductory Note *xxxi*
List of Contributors *xxxv*

SECTION I
ANCIENT PERIOD

1. Convergence and Cross-Currents of Civilisation in and Around Central Asia 3
— *D.P. Chattopadhyaya*
2. Central Asia and Indo-Aryans 14
— *D.N. Tripathi*
3. South Asia, Central Asia and South Russia: The Saka Connection 30
— *A.K. Narain*
4. Advent of Buddhism in Central Asia 46
— *S.M. Haldhar*
5. Travelling Names to and from Central Asia and Beyond 55
— *Aloka Parasher-Sen*

SECTION II
MEDIEVAL PERIOD

6. Indo-Central Asian Contacts: A Turkoman Initiative in the Medieval Period 79
— *R.L. Hangloo*

7. Hospices and Hospitality En Route Khwarizm to Sind: Evidence of Ibn Battuta 96
— *G.D. Gulati*

8. Status of Sine Tables in India and Central Asia during Medieval Times 102
— *A.K. Bag*

9. Indo-Central Asian Trade Relations 110
— *Mansura Haidar*

10. Naqshbandiyya Sufi Order: A Link between India and Central Asia 131
— *Sheikh Saleem Ahmed*

11. Indo-Tajik Relations: A Curtain Raiser 138
— *K.N. Pandita*

SECTION III

MODERN PERIOD

12. Indian Image in the Military and Political Circles of Russia till the End of the Nineteenth Century 147
— *M.R. Ryjenkov*

13. Nana Sahib's Nephew in Russia 151
— *T.N. Zagorodnikova*

14. Muslims in Eastern Turkestan 1871: Diplomatic and Trade Relations with British India 161
— *Z.U. Malik*

15. Afghan Trade with India and Russia, 1880–1901 171
— *Bir Good Gill*

16. Central Asia in Indo-Russian Relations 180
— *Devendra Kaushik*

17. The Emirate of Bukhara and Its Relations with India and Russia of Nineteenth Century 195
— *Iqtidar Husain Siddiqui*

18. Kashmir and Russian Turkestan during the Nineteenth Century 201
— *K. Warikoo*

19. The Anglo-Russian Setting in the Pamirs 213
— *Sneh Mahajan*

20. Russia's Threat to British India: The Tibetan Dimension 221
— *T. Shaumian*

21. Indians in Central Asia in the First Two Decades of the Twentieth Century 231
— *Surendra Gopal*

SECTION IV
CONTEMPORARY PERIOD

22. India and Central Asia: An Overview of Relationship 245
— *Tabasum Firdaus*

23. A Secret Report by the First Soviet Ambassador: India's Early Years of Independence 251
— *V.P. Kashin*

24. Indo-Russian Trade: Soviet and Post-Soviet Trends 258
— *V.V. Chernovskaya*

25. Security Issues in New Central Asia: India's Concern, US Perception and International Perspectives 262
— *S.P. Singh*

26. Russian-Indian Strategic Partnership as a Historical Necessity 290
— *Andrei Volodin*

Bibliography 295
Index 325

Introduction

R.C. Agrawal and P.K. Shukla

The present book is an effort to look into the cultural, economic and political contacts Central Asia had for the last 3000 years with India, Russia and China to a certain extent. Chapters of this book view the matter and discuss the interaction between these countries from various perspectives. These form the papers presented in the international seminar on Central Asia held in New Delhi on 6-8 November 2001, under the Cultural Exchange Programme between India and Russia. Most of the papers presented at the seminar are included in this book.

The papers of the seminar are classified into four sections, based broadly on the period each author covers while dealing with the three millennia of contacts. The sections include: Section I: Ancient Period, Section II: Medieval Period, Section III: Modern Period, and Section IV: Contemporary Period. The last one carries papers covering the modern period, which deals with late twentieth century and the current period, and hence named 'contemporary', distinguishing it from the modern period.

Besides the Introductory Note by A.K. Damodaran, the volume has, in all, 26 papers divided into four sections, as mentioned above. As A.K. Damodaran remarked while inaugurating the seminar, the millennium before Common Era is full of nostalgia and memories, though details are lacking, as far as India and Russia are concerned. While the first millennium of the Common Era provided direct contacts between the two civilisations, the last millennium made the relationship continuous and intimate. According to A.K. Damodaran, twentieth century and particularly its second half coinciding with post-independent India, is of genuine interest to us. He reminds us of the prehistoric linguistic evidences, Buddhist influence, Orthodox Church, Sufism and Sikhism, the Great Game of British and Tsarist Empires, Soviet alliance with national movements, Gandhi's emulation of Tolstoy, and Tashkent agreement.

Section I begins with D.P. Chattopadhyaya's paper titled 'Convergence and Cross-currents of Civilisation in and around Central Asia'. Chattopadhyaya considers the territory between China in the east and the Fertile Crescent (around the Euphrates and the Tigris) in the west and beyond comprising the extended Hellenic World, Russia and Ukraine in the north, and Pakistan and India in the south as a Eurasian cultural continuum. Since time immemorial, the peoples of these countries have been moving to and from different directions. While talking about the cultural cross-currents and intellectual exchanges, the author takes into account their contributions in the field as well as researches in different areas such as archaeology, iconography, maritime studies, astronomy and mathematics.

In his paper, 'Central Asia and Indo-Aryans', D.N. Tripathi discusses the continuously disputed issue of the homeland of Aryans. After giving a broad history of the debate, by dwelling into references about the people in the Vedic and Puranic literature, as well as through Western scholarship on the subject, he pinpoints the discussion on the question whether Aryans are from Central Asia or from India itself. Giving a thorough consideration of Aryans as Indo-Europeans, Indo-Iranians and Indo-Aryans, he finally concludes them as autochthonous to the Sapta-Sindhu region and argues that the Rigvedic culture reflecting their life 'has to be placed at least in Chalcolithic phase, if not earlier'.

The contacts between South Asia and Central Asia go much beyond three millennia; it is difficult to cross this limit if we include Russia. To be more precise, as A.K. Narain thinks, one cannot go beyond eighth-seventh centuries BC and the earliest contacts are related to the movements of the Sakas or the Scythians, the names by which they were known in the eastern and western world, respectively. Many scholars in the fields of Indo-European linguistics and antiquities tend now to look at South Russia either as the homeland of the Iranian speaking peoples, or as the secondary centre of their migrations, and more and more scholars now consider the Cimmerians as one of the Iranian speaking peoples. In the extreme form, Diakonow, considered the Cimmerians only as an individual tribal group within the vast Scythian ethnic groups. Khazanov, who finds this opinion cautious and acceptable, think that the Scythian invasion from Asia in the eighteenth century BC was apparently not the first appearance of the Iranian element in Europe, but only one of the movements of Northern Iranian nomadic tribes. Such movements repeatedly also took place later on. However, they did not result in drastic changes of population.

There is no doubt in respect of the ritual drinking, or revering, of *haoma* or *soma* by these Sakas. Offering of *hoama* was evidently of great importance in the pagan Iran. So was the offering of *soma* of Vedic religion. Together with animal and human sacrifices, it played an integral role in the development of their ideology and culture. There is ample evidence to indicate a link between the pre-Zoroastrian Daeva worship of the pagan Iranians and the Vedic religious beliefs and rituals. The linguistic closeness between the Rigveda and the *Gathas* is now a recognized fact. Disagreeing with B.K. Thapar, Narain is of the view that certain features of the Swat Grave Culture and related information about the region from various sources are sufficient to point at the Saka presence and their participation in the early phases of Vedic society and rituals. The *soma*-drinking Sakas, though eclipsed in between by the Mauryas and Indo-Greeks, were a continuity of Vedic culture.

Bamiyan Buddhas destroyed by the Taliban in Afghanistan reminds one, even without any substantial historical grasp, of the advent of Buddhism in Central Asia. S.M. Haldhar traces its history in Afghanistan, Bactria and Parthia. The author agrees with other writers that Buddhism lost to Zoroastrianism in Persia. The Kushana Empire stimulated the spread of Buddhism in Central Asia. Kubha (Kabul) had a strong presence of Buddhist intellectuals, including Vimalaksha and Kumarajiva.

Aloka Parasher-Sen enters into a discussion on the people who travelled around a millennium ago, out of necessities of life, across the upper Indus Valley, where three mountains meet the Western Himalayas, the Karakorum and the Hindukush. The sources are the rock art and inscriptions discovered in Pakistan, and these cover both Buddhist and Islamic periods (after prehistory).

The section on medieval period starts with R.L. Hangloo's paper, 'Indo-Central Asian Contacts: A Turkoman Initiative in the Medieval Period'. The exchange of people's ideas, epitomised by the millennia of contacts, produced and reproduced the cultures of India and Central Asia from time to time and is now too strong to be broken, according to R.L. Hangloo. The process of medieval Indian state formation owes much to Central Asian politics and its origin has to be sought partly in response to the developments in Central Asia. India also had to adopt its political organisation according to the exigencies of Central Asian influence. For example, in introducing Persian as the official language, the Delhi Sultanate, the Bahmani Sultanate in Deccan, and the Shahmir Sultanate in Kashmir, underlined the enduring importance of Central Asian culture to Indian states and also highlighted the central position of Indian relationship with Central Asia.

From very early times, Indian culture was acting at the popular level as an autonomous entity, expanding, contracting and submitting to outside influences. Under the Turkomans, it was again subjected to a process of reconstruction. Therefore, the Indians also saw the onset of thirteenth century as part of the continuous process that had been going on from early Bronze Age. But in the process, this time the Central Asians including the Turkomans felt themselves unquestionably superior to the caste-based society at popular level. They blended Central Asian military, administrative, technological, and cultural expertise of their heritage and Sufism with principles of peaceful coexistence of Indian religious systems.

Outside Central Asia and particularly in India, the Central Asians in general and Turkomans in particular proved themselves a desirable cultural asset representing skill and strength for shaping the Sultanate, which was the ultimate product of the convergence of these contacts. When a relationship lasts for such a long time, it is bound to encourage a process of acculturation. In India, this process of acculturation appeared in so many forms and one needs to be selective because the different aspects of polity, society, economy, history and culture are so deftly interwoven that it becomes difficult to separate one from the other.

G.D. Gulati's presentation narrates in a nutshell the hospices and hospitality that Ibn Battuta witnessed during his travels through Central Asia. Caravan serais and hospices (small lodging facilities), and the hospitality en route had impressed the Arab (Moroccan) traveller. Ibn Battuta visited the Turkish city, Khwarizm (modern Khiva), Bukhara, Nakhshab (Nafa), which is 100 miles southeast of Bukhara, Samarkand, Tirmidh, Balkh (in Khurasan), Herat, al-Jam, Tus, Sarakhs, Zawa, Naiasabur, Bistan, Hindukhir (Andakhuih, 100 miles west of Balkh), Qunduz, Baghlan, Andar (Andarab), Parwan (45 miles north of Kabul), al-Charkh, Ghazni, Kabul, Karmash, Shashnagar (Hashtnagar) and reached Indus River from where he, along with his party, was taken to the court of Muhammad-bin-Tughluq.

A.K. Bag deals on the status of Sine Tables in India and Central Asia during medieval times. Among the Arabic astronomers, al-Fazari (AD 796), Abu'l-Hasan al-Ahwazi (AD 771), Umar ibn al Farrukhan al-Tabari (died in AD 815), al-Khwarizmi (AD 825), Abu Ma'shar al-Balkhi (AD 886), Al-Biruni (died in AD 1050), al-Zarkali (Toledan Tables, *c.* AD 1080) and many others, became more or less acquainted with the sine-cosine concepts, sine table and astronomical theories of the Indians. The Greek work, *Almagest* of Ptolemy was also translated into Arabic during the reign of Caliph Harun al-Rashid (AD 786–808) and became well known during the reign of Caliph al-Mamum (AD 813–33). The Greeks used chord in a half-circle taking 180 degrees arc as the basis whereas Indians used half-chord (known as *jya*) in a quarter-circle taking 90 degrees arc as the basis. Indian process was much more simpler and of course had a natural advantage. Nallino, the great historian of Arabic history, states that the Arabs learnt from the Indian works the calculation of the movement of the stars and other matters of astronomical importance. Michio Yano, who has studied both Greek and Indian sine tables, remarked about 'the far greater convenience of the latter' in geometrical calculations.

The terms, sine and cosine, are derived from two Sanskrit technical words, *jya* and *kojya* (complementary to *jya*), respectively. Many Indian astronomers give the shadow tables of different places on equinoctial day for gnomon of 12 *angulas*. David Pingree has traced five such tables in the Sanskrit collections of America and Europe, which according to him, were mainly used for finding latitude of places, preparation of local *pancangas*, etc. The shadow tables for gnomon are also found in many medieval Central-Asian astrolabes of fifteenth and sixteenth century AD. As an example, the reverse of the Muhammad Muqim's astrolabe contains shadow lengths for 7 feet (Greek tradition) and 12 *angula* gnomon (Indian tradition).

While analyzing Indo-Central Asian trade relations, Mansura Haider describes also the pattern of trade between Russia and Central Asia. Central Asia, which had earlier been one of the important regions on the old 'Silk Road', is said to have become commercially a 'subdued phenomenon' during the sixteenth century. European travellers observed with dismay that in sixteenth century there was no hope of good trade in any part of the country, and that trade in Persia and Tartaria alike was of 'little utterance and small profit'. To the early medieval Persian chronicler, Ibni Hauqal, however, the brisk commercial transactions at various entrepots of Central Asia seemed to show no decline.

In Babur's time, there were two trade marts on the land routes between India and Khurasan, namely, Kabul and Kandahar. The caravans came to Kabul from Kashgar, Farghana, Turkestan, Bukhara, Samarkand, Balkh, Hesar and Badakshan, and the merchants made big profits in Kabul, as it was an excellent trading centre. Clavijo says that from India were brought to Samarkand the costly spices of the kind such as nutmeg, cloves, mace and cinnamon. Every year the caravans of ten, fifteen or twenty thousand heads of houses bringing slaves, white cloth, sugar candy, refined and common sugars and aromatic roots came to Kabul from Hindustan and many traders were not content with a profit of 30 or 40 on 10 (i.e., 300 to 400 per cent).

The privileges granted to English merchants in 1569 by Tsar authorized them 'to be and abide freely, to barter and bargain freely all wares of sale without custom of people' not only in Russia but also to pass through its land to Boghar, Persia, Caspian and other countries. The trading communities in Central Asia were Sarts, Tajiks and Jews. In later centuries, the Bukhara Jews held the wholesale trade in silkworms in the *Khanates*. Although the existence of credit operations, letters of credit (*suftan* or *suftaja*) pay order within a time and *khatti sarraf* (cheques for local transactions) in the form of 'dumb bartering' are mentioned in the sources, no detailed information about the working of these is available.

Sheikh Saleem Ahmed discusses the Naqshbandiyya Sufi order and its link between India and Central Asia. Naqshbandiyya constitutes one of the leading Sufi order in the Muslim world. Its history dates back to the fourteenth century Bukhara in Khurasan. Kh. Mohammed Bahauddin Naqshbandi (1318–1389) was considered its founder. By the sixteenth century Naqshbandiyya became a worldwide organisation spreading over major areas of Sunni Muslim world like Western and Central Asia, Ottoman Society, Indian subcontinent and China.

Bahauddin Naqshbandi and Abdul Khaliq Gujdwani were the early leading personalities who formulated rules for the order and made efforts to establish its centres in the whole of Central Asia, Herat, Balkh, Badakshan and India. The conquest of India by Babur in 1526 gave considerable impetus to the development of the Naqshbandi order in India. Many Sufis like Aziz Koka, harem's women like Gulrukh Begum and Salima Sultan, and Babur sought allegiance to Mohammad Naqshband or Khwaja Ahrar because they too belonged to their ancestral homeland.

Khwaja Baqi Billah (1564–1603) who was a disciple of Khwaja Ahrar came to India during the time of Akbar. He established Naqshbandi order in India. Sheikh Ahmed Sirhindi (1564–1624) entitled Mujaddid Alfsani, was an original thinker, known for his wisdom and learning. He was also involved in the social and political affairs of his times. Sheikh Ahmed Sirhindi felt uncomfortable to see the increasing alien, non-Muslim and Shia influence in the Muslim society of India. His concern was the supremacy of pure and pristine Islam and he wanted to revive the period of Khulfae Rashidin (first four caliphs).

When he came to know about the new invention in the field of physics being carried out in the West, he remarked that physics was not helpful in our religious affairs. Sirhindi expressed his dislike about modern sciences in his letters too and one of his friends ridiculed algebra. All the orthodox revivalist movements of eighteenth and nineteenth centuries, whether it was the declaration of India as *darul harb* by Shah Abdul Aziz or Wahabi movement of Syed Ahmed Shaheed and Shah Ishmael, author of *Taqwiatul Iman* or *Jamat-e-Islami*, *Tabiligh-i-Jamat* or *Deoband Seminary*, all owe their origin to Mujaddid thoughts.

K.N. Pandita discusses the Indo-Tajik relations from a medieval context. He says that travellers from Bukhara coming to India in medieval times often carried with them excellent copies of important treatises on theology, medicine, veterinary science, astronomy and exegesis, which were copied and distributed among local scholars. India, therefore, owes much to Bukhara in the proliferation of Islamic sciences. Besides, the contribution of Bukharans in the fields of music, particularly Sufiana music, architecture, laying of gardens and other aspects is commendable. The construction of dome, a speciality of the Mughal architecture was adopted from the Bukhara dome architecture. The double dome model of Taj Mahal is precisely the one we find in the dome of the Samanid king, Nasr bin Ahmad in Bukhara.

It should be remembered that at the Mughal court, there were more nobles and grandees of Central Asian, meaning Tajik, extraction than of

Iranian extraction. The word *velayat* for the Mughals meant Central Asia and not Iran. They did not use Tajikistan as a geographical entity though they did use Tajiks as a people. Therefore, when we speak of Indo-Tajik relations, we have to take into account all those people in Central Asia who have affinity to Indo-Aryan stock.

Section III dwells on the Modern Period. M.R. Ryjenkov studies the image of India and Indians in the Russian perception, as part of the Russo-Indian relations. From eleventh to nineteenth century, India was understood as a country of 'treasures, miracles and natural fertility'. In Tsar Paul's design to plunder India (which did not materialize, as he was assassinated), the treasures were to be rewarded to the Cossacks. The military and political authority during Tsar Alexander I believed in India's deep conviction in the invincibility of British fleet. Strangely, this was just before the 1857 mutiny in India. The Crown Prince Nicolai Alexandrovitch was reported to have gathered diverse knowledge about the 'proficiency of the Europeans, who are commanding Asia'.

Using mostly Russian and French sources, T.W. Zagorodnikova tries to assess the activities of Ramchandra Balaji, nephew of Nana Sahib, the hero of 1857 mutiny. She narrates his life, mostly in exile, and particularly in Russia. Though his stepmother was wife of a British officer, slowly he became a nationalist and organised activities against the British. Zagorodnikova evaluates him as aristocratic, though nationalistic.

Z.U. Malik analyses briefly the social life and economic situation in Eastern Turkestan (Kashgar and Yarqand) and the diplomatic relations between British India and the ruler of Kashgar, Yaqub Beg, during 1871-72. The essay is based on the eyewitness account of Robert Berkley Shaw, a political agent of the British government.

Bir Good Gill studies the British Indian and Persian trade with Afghanistan during the reign of Amir Abdur Rahman Khan. Both Russia and Britain were vying with each other in their Great Game of finding markets and areas of political influence and, in the progress, Afghanistan became a buffer state. The Amir's ban of silver and gold export out of Afghanistan, monopolising of certain items into state sector for finding increased revenues since 1891, increased demand for Indian tea (*kokchi*) in Central Asia, Chinese tea more or less replacing Indian tea with the Chinese re-occupation of Eastern Turkestan, and Russia's improved position of trade with the expansion of railway network constitute the major aspects of this chapter.

Devendra Kaushik talks on the role of Central Asia in Indo-Russian relations. Like Indo-Central Asian relations, Indo-Russian relations also go back to the remote past. In a way, they are even much older as far as indirect relations are concerned. However, Central Asia has been continuously a vital link in the relations between India and Russia. For being the core of the Eurasian landmass, it is but natural for Russia to put up with itself as part of both Europe and Asia. Because of the absence of a physical barrier on the space between the Urals and the Black Sea resulting in the extension of the Russian steppes to Central Asia, the latter has ideally served as a bridge between Russia and South Asia. Nevertheless, it will be improper to exaggerate the significance of the geo-cultural ties among India, Central Asia and Russia, which though imparting a tenacity to demand types of traditional goods, could not completely counteract the political barriers created by British and Tsarist colonialism. The near monopoly of the British over Indian trade and destruction of Indian handicrafts and manufacturing inhibited the development of trade among India, Central Asia and Russia. The restrictions imposed by the Tsarist administration on Indian trade through Bukhara also adversely affected the growth of economic ties between them. The construction of Indo-Volga Railway Line, joining Orenburg with Samarkand and Peshwar as an extension of a line from Lisbon to Orenburg, was continuously turned down by the Tsarist authorities fearing penetration of British and West European goods into Central Asia.

Devendra Kaushik argues that New Delhi could explore the possibility of reaching an agreement with Beijing for use of its road to Kyrgyzstan through Xinjiang province. India can use this road by constructing a small link road in Ladakh joining the Tibet-Xinjiang road, passing through the disputed Aksai Chin territory. Ladakh is already linked with the Indian state of Himachal Pradesh. The Central Asian Republics can gain access to the Indian seaport of Kandla in Gujarat through this overland route through Xinjiang and Ladakh.

Iqtidar Husain Siddiqui discusses the emergence of the Mangit dynasty under Shah Murad and the socio-economic conditions in the Emirate of Bukhara as well as its relations with India and Russia during nineteenth century, in the backdrop of break-up and decline of the Mughal Empire by the second half of the eighteenth century. The author uses mainly the travel accounts of Alexander Burnes and Mohan Lal Kashmiri.

Warikoo discusses the political overtones along with the trade relations between Kashmir and Russian Turkestan during the nineteenth century in the context of Russo-British imperialist rivalry. The presence of Russian and Central Asian merchants in Kashmir during the eighteenth and nineteenth centuries for purpose of shawl trade is testified by such eye-witness accounts as that of Bernier, Yefremov, Abdul Karim, Forster, Moorcroft and other sources. The shawl goods of Kashmir and the *pashm* (fine wool) yielding goats of Ladakh stimulated the Russian interest in developing trade with adjacent countries in Asia. This trade intensified in the wake of enforcement of the continental blockade by Napoleon in Europe. Tsarist Russia sent several missions to the *Khanates* of Bukhara and Kokand to secure their consent in the free movement of Russo-Chinese trading caravans from Russia to Kashgar via Bukhara and Kokand and vice versa. Once this was achieved, Russia could and did think of extending her commercial relations with Ladakh, Kashmir, and Punjab.

In a bid to meet the growing Russian threat to the Central Asian *Khanate* of Kokand, the Khan of Kokand despatched his emissaries to India for securing British support. Since the Kashgar-Yarkand-Leh route was practically free from robbers, the Central Asians preferred it to the troublesome Kabul route for entering India. It was in 1837 that an envoy from Kokand arrived at Ladakh who had been deputed by the Khan of Kokand to present a pair of rubies and horses to the Governor General of India with a view to establishing friendly relations with the British government.

While measuring the Russian response to the overtures made by Maharaja Ranbir Singh of Kashmir, we need to bear in mind that the Russian policy was not to get involved in the internal affairs of British India. Kashmir's overtures to the Russians in Central Asia need to be viewed in the context of Anglo-Russian rivalry. Though Russia was not strong enough to move beyond the Oxus in the south and Pamirs in the east, yet its military successes in Central Asia had earned it a definite advantage in respect of the psychological influence created on Asian peoples. The disgruntled Indian princely rulers who were already annoyed with the increasing British interference in their domains, derived a sort of moral encouragement from the appearance of Russia close to the British Indian frontiers, which stimulated their anti-British aspirations. On their part, the Russians reciprocated Ranbir Singh's friendly sentiments but they steered clear of any active involvement in internal affairs of British India, which could have led them to a direct conflict with the British.

Sneh Mahajan discusses the political exigencies behind Anglo-Russian bargain on the Wakhan corridor, part of Afghanistan. In Durand and the Pamirs agreements in the 1890s (in 1893 and 1895, respectively) deciding the northern, eastern and north-western boundaries of Afghanistan, which had no ethnic basis, are understood as part of the Great Game played between these two empires on the Pamirs in Central Asia.

T. Shaumian analyses the Tibetan dimension of British India's perceived threat of Russia. Lord Curzon, Viceroy of India, saw a Russian conspiracy of getting involved in Tibet through the Russian Buryat, Dorjieff, attached to the then Dalai Lama, in the first decade of twentieth century. Shaumian briefs the communications and diplomatic efforts that took place preceding the British army expedition under Younghusband deployed by Lord Curzon.

Historical records show continuous exchange of visits by Indians and Central Asians to each other's territories at least for the last six centuries.

Indians travelling to Central Asia were adherents of different faiths, such as Hinduism, Buddhism, Jainism Islam, Sikhism and Zoroastrianism. Surendra Gopal discusses on the Indians in Central Asia in the early decades of twentieth century. While doing so, he finds that, from the second half of the nineteenth century, the nature of Indo-Central Asian contacts have undergone qualitative changes. European colonial powers became entrenched in both these areas: Great Britain in India and Tsarist Russia in Central Asia. Eventually, it affected the nature of contacts between Central Asians and Indians. Along with scholars, travellers, traders and soldiers from India who went to Central Asia, groups of Indians belonging to the lowest rung of the social order also entered Central Asia. The Soviet Indologist Oranskii discovered a group of Pariah in Tajikistan who spoke in a language akin to Punjab and who with great zeal had preserved their language. Of course, they had forgotten from where their ancestors had originally arrived.

The last section deals with the contemporary period (largely covering the second half of twentieth century onwards), of contacts among India, Russia and Central Asia. This section begins with Tabasum Firdaus's article 'India and Central Asia: An Overview of Relationship'. She overviews India's relationship with the Central Asian Republics, which were earlier part of the Soviet Union. After analyzing the Pan-Turkish Programme and export of religious fundamentalism by Saudi Arabia, Pakistan and Iran, the author presents India's secular approach of promoting cultural exchanges and trade, and above all Russia's leading role through CIS and support of anti-Taliban forces in Afghanistan.

Kirill Vasilyevich Novikov, the first Soviet Ambassador to India, presented a report to the Foreign Policy Commission of the CC of CPSU on 5 July 1949, classified as 'top secret'. V.P. Kashin analyses this document, which deals with the political situation in India, affairs of CPI, British-Indian relations and the spread of Soviet publications. He says that the Ambassador could not discover a revolutionary situation in India, to the 'great disappointment of the Commission members'. It should be remembered that Soviet-Indian relationship greatly improved after Nehru's unsuccessful 1949 visit to USA and the subsequent Soviet offer of food help to India following the latter's request.

V. Chernovskaya analyses the Rupee-Rouble trade in the Soviet period, the decline in Indian business with the collapse of Soviet Union, and the prospects of Indian trade now in the Russian regions. Over 80 per cent of Indian exports were to the Soviet Union and the trade turnover between the two countries was 8,000 crores in 1990-91. The major actors were public sector units and state trading corporations. With the break-up of planned Rupee-Rouble trade, the trade turnover declined drastically. In late nineties and the beginning of the twenty-first century, the trade is slowly picking up, despite some Indian brands becoming suspect. As the author reports, the political and business leaders of the regions in Russia such as Sverdlovsk oblast, Voronezh, Ryazan, Vladivostok, etc. and republics such as Bashkhortostan, Tatarstan, etc. have shown interest in Indian business. Indian goods are facing stiff competition from Western goods and cheap Southeast Asian goods.

S.P. Singh looks into the regional and strategic dimensions of political Islam in Central and Southwest Asia. The Islamisation of society and politics, which was undoubtedly intensified in the inordinately vast Muslim region of Central Asia and Southwest Asia during the West-sponsored and Pak-supported 'Jihad' against the Soviets in Afghanistan, has now enveloped several parts of Central Asia. The US administration pumped in eight billion dollars into the 'Afghan pipeline' and allowed the CIA-ISI combine to manage this arsenal. Conscriptions were allowed from the various Muslim countries in the world to take part in this 'Holy War'. The professed aim of this game plan was to defeat the so-called 'evil empire'.

After the withdrawal of the Soviets, the military hawks of Pakistan and the warlords of Afghanistan seized these lethal arms and made use of the opportunity to suppress their adversaries and become paramount political power. Subsequently, the Islamists have caused the virtual destabilisation of the buffer state regions into one 'arc of crisis' and exported Islamic fundamentalism. With the help of drug-money and cross-border terrorists, they have seriously menaced several well-established secular regimes in the sprawling Central Asiatic region and threatened the territorial integrity of Russia in the adjoining areas. These very elements have also fought the decade-long proxy war in the Indian state of Kashmir in order to seize it by forceful means. By many available accounts, it may even escalate into an all-out nuclear confrontation.

While objectively analysing the highly complex issues of conflict and the mercurial role of the various regional actors, which have turned this enormously vast region into a murky battleground, it is important to further discuss how these forces, with the prime purpose of completely Islamising this area, are impinging upon the security scenarios of the vast areas from Central Asia to Southwest Asia, from the Caucasus to Kashmir, Xinjiang to Afghanistan and Iran to Pakistan.

The last article in this volume is on Russo-Indian strategic partnership. Doubting the emergence of unipolar world, as the 9/11 developments have demonstrated the hegemony of the so-called 'core' as unrealistic, Andrei Volodin argues for Russo-Indian strategic partnership and considers its emergence as a historical necessity. He considers the role of the 'superlarge' states, namely, Brazil, China, India and Russia as significant in a newly emerging international community of horizontal ties. Pointing out the long-term trends in the common geopolitical perspective of India and Russia, Volodin proposes cooperation between them on the four basic areas, viz. food security, energy security, economic security, and military security.

Overall, this collection will definitely provide an intellectual feast to the scholars of politics and international relations in general, and the students of the area studies, geopolitics and defence and strategic studies in particular. Moreover, the collection gives hints to the working of the international forces of terrorism and the hidden forces of stakes and global domination behind them operating in Central Asia, Southwest Asia, Eurasia, and the Caspian and the border regions of Xinjiang and Kashmir.

Introductory Note

A.K. Damodaran

The idea of three millennia of contacts among India, Central Asia and Russia is a bit daunting. Our genuine interest is in the twentieth century and the second half of the century after India's independence. The millennium before the modern era begins is full of nostalgia and memories, details to which are, however, lacking. The first millennium of the new era sees more direct contacts between the Russian, Central Asian and Indian civilisations. In the second millennium, with technological changes, the contacts between the two regions became more intimate and continuous. However, there is an unavoidable separation due to India being a colony of a distant Western country. When India became independent, the relationship became rich in political and economic terms.

In the period from 1000 BC to the beginning of the Christian Era, the contacts between these two regions were due to the movement of the peoples across the vast continent. Living evidence of this prehistoric phenomenon can be found in the links between the Indo-Aryan, Turkic, Iranian and most of all Slavic languages. More concrete historical evidence can be found in the archaeological remnants of the Kushana period in Central Asia. The movement of ideas is also important. Buddhism entered China through Central Asia. The sad memories of Bamiyan in Afghanistan remind us of this continuous movement of mind and matter in the distant past.

During the first millennium of our era, the most important single new element was Christianity. The convergence of the various examples of eastern Orthodox Christianity with the Syrian Church on the Malabar Coast from the beginning of this period and the churches in Armenia and Russia and the Slavic cultures is an important historical reality. At the middle of this millennium comes the spread of Islam, which connects from the very beginning Central Asia and the Caucasus with western India, both in the north-west and in the south-west. A minor but important common tradition is that of Parsi religion, which came to India during this period and which had spread outwards from Iran to Azerbaijan as evidenced today in the Fire Temple in Baku. It was during this time that the gypsy exodus to Europe began. It is important to note that Russia was the country most hospitable to these strangers from distant India.

In the first 900 years of the previous millennium there are brief flashes of light like Afinasy Nikitin. Compared to the links with Western Europe, the Russian connections are few and far between, but the continuity is kept throughout the Mughal period with Central Asia—cultural, architectural, and civilisational. Sufism is also an important ingredient. Guru Nanak is central to this discourse, a 'pilgrim soul' connecting Central and South-West Asia to northern India. In the eighteenth century began modern contacts between the Russian scholars and India. This is also the period when the Great Game was played between the British and the Tzarist Empires in Afghanistan, the 'Eastern Approaches' of Europe and Tibet.

At the beginning of the twentieth century, Mackinder saw Central Asia as the heart of the World Island with India, China and Russia and three countries bordering the oceans abutting on this vital centre of human history. Among them developed over the years great civilisations in Central Asia and the Caucasia, Iran, and Western China.

The dominant reality of this epoch is the Soviet Revolution—three generations and seven decades of remarkable success and some conspicuous failures. This was also the period when India under Gandhi succeeded in achieving independence.

During the last 50 years, there has been a great progress in economic co-operation between the two countries. Russia played an important role in the new Nation's heavy industry agenda. Its contribution to the country's defence preparedness was vital. At the global level, India's refusal to be drawn into the anti-Soviet alliance had its roots in the National Movement. This is also the period when there was great increase in people-to-people contact between the Soviet Union and India encouraged by the governments. At that time it also represented a continuing mutual understanding, as demonstrated over the years in Gandhi's emulation of Tolstoy and admiration for Gorky, of the Communist movement in India and its links with Moscow, which spread to ordinary people outside the Party and the contribution of a non-Communist liberal statesman like Jawaharlal Nehru.

Two events are specially important in Indo-Russian relations during the Soviet period. The 'Tashkent Agreement' which represented a successful attempt by an isolated great nation to intervene in a global problem, and the 'Indo-Soviet Treaty', which respected socialism and non-alignment and at the same time provided a crucial element of support to India during the Bangladesh crisis.

In the decade after the division of the Soviet Union into several sovereign states, the relations continue in a rich manner. With Russia, we have a common agenda of peace and creative economic co-operation along with the Central Asian countries, and hopefully Iran and China. The prospects at alliances and confrontational postures between Great Powers were familiar to us in the past.

Finally, India, Central Asia and Russia represent a certain harmony of originally distant and distinct cultures and civilisations slowly finding a certain post-ideological affinity based on geography, recent history and common technological and economic challenges. The core of this conceptual agreement and its policy consequences is in pluralism, secularism, multi-ethnicity, and cultural synthesis. These countries and China should be able in the new millennium to give a definitive answer to the thesis of the clash of civilisations.

List of Contributors

A.K. Bag

Dr. A.K. Bag, MSc, Ph.D. was former Member Secretary, Indian Commission for History of Science, New Delhi. Now he is Member, International Academy for History of Science, Paris.

Address: A-5 B, 217 SFS, Paschim Vihar, New Delhi-221 005.

A.K. Damodaran

Shri A.K. Damodaran was formerly Member Secretary, Policy Planning Committee, Ministry of External Affairs, Government of India. He was posted as a Diplomat in China during 1963-65. In 1971, he was Minister in the Indian Embassy in Moscow.

Address: Editor, *Collected Works of Jawaharlal Nehru*, Teen Murti House, New Delhi-110 011.

A.K. Narain

Professor A.K. Narain is Emeritus Professor of History and of Languages and Cultures of Asia, University of Wisconsin, Madison, USA. He is now editor-in-chief of the *Indian International Journal of Buddhist Studies* (*IIJBS*).

Address: K-76 Nandnagar, Karaundi, Varanasi-221 005.

Aloka Parasher-Sen

Dr. (Mrs.) Aloka Parasher-Sen, Ph.D. (London), is an expert in Ancient and Early Medieval History. She is now a faculty member in the Department of History, University of Hyderabad.

Address: Department of History, University of Hyderabad, Hyderabad, AP.

Andrei G. Volodin

Dr. Andrei G. Volodin is Head of the Department of Comparative Politics, Moscow State University for International Relations.

Bir Good Gill

Dr. (Ms.) Bir Good Gill is a Faculty Member in the Department of History, Guru Nanak Dev University, Amritsar.

Address: Department of History, GNDU, Amritsar, Punjab.

D.N. Tripathi

Professor Dayanath Tripathi took Doctorate on Bronze Work of Greece from Southampton University, UK in 1976. He retired as Head, Department of Ancient History, Archaeology and Culture. He was fellow of Indian Institute of Advanced Study (IIAS), Shimla (2003) and was Chairman of Indian Council of Historical Research (ICHR) during 2004-07. He was Visiting Professor, British Academy, London (2004).

Address: Leela Nilayam, 99-A, Indira Nagar, P.O. Sheopuri, New Colony, Gorakhpur, UP-273 016.

D.P. Chattopadhyaya

Professor Chattopadhyaya took Ph.D. from Calcutta University and London School of Economics, and taught Philosophy at Jadavpur University, Calcutta. He is Founder Chairman of the Indian Council of Philosophical Research (ICPR), New Delhi. Now, he is the General Editor of the *Project on the History of Science, Philosophy and Culture in Indian Civilization*, which is bringing out voluminous series on it.

Address: Chairman, Centre for Studies in Civilization, 25 Park Mansion, 57-A, Park Street, Kolkata-700 016.

Devendra Kaushik

Professor Devendra Kaushik is Russian and Central Asian expert, now retired from School of International Studies, JNU. Presently, he is UGC Emeritus Fellow at JNU and Editor-in-Chief of *Contemporary Central Asia*. Formerly, he was Chairman, Maulana Abul Kalam Azad Institute of Asian Studies, Kolkata. A Sovietland Nehru Award winner, he was awarded the 'Order of Friendship', the highest Russian Government has given for a foreigner.

Address: E-2302 Ansals, Palam Vihar, Gurgaon, Haryana.

G.D. Gulati

Professor G.D. Gulati is from University of Delhi, Delhi. He was Visiting Scholar at Indian Institute of Advanced Study, Shimla (2003).

Iqtidar Husain Siddiqui

Professor Iqtidar Husain Siddiqui is an expert in Medieval and Early Modern History. He retired from Aligarh Muslim University (AMU), Aligarh.

Address: 61, Ahmadnagar, Civil Lines, Aligarh, UP-202 002.

K. Warikoo

Professor Warikoo is Director, Central Asian Studies Programme, Centre for South, Central, Southeast Asian and South-West Pacific Studies, School of International Studies, Jawaharlal Nehru University, New Delhi. He is also Secretary-General (Hon'y), of the Himalayan Research and Cultural Foundation. He is the founder Editor of quarterly journal, *Himalayan and Central Asian Studies*, being published since 1997.

Address: 20, Dakshinapuram, Jawaharlal Nehru University, New Delhi-110 067.

K.N. Pandita

Professor Kashi Nath Pandita, a Sovietland Nehru Award winner, retired from the position of Director, Centre for Central Asian Studies, Kashmir University. Now, he is General Secretary of the Jammu based body, Friends of Kashmir International.

Address: B-320, Fotedar House, Jawaharnagar, Talab Tiloo, Jammu-180 002.

M.R. Ryjenkov

Dr. Ryjenkov is from the State Archives, Moscow.

Mansura Haidar

Professor Mansura Haidar is an expert on Indo-Central Asian History, who retired from the Centre of Advanced Study in History, AMU, Aligarh.

P.K. Shukla

Dr. Prabhat Kumar Shukla took Doctorate in History from the University of Bihar, Muzaffarpur, and worked as Fellow in A.N. Sinha Institute of Social Studies, Patna. Presently he is Deputy Director in ICHR and working as its Member Secretary.

Address: 16, Uttaranchal Apartments, 5, Patparganj, Delhi-110 092.

R.C. Agrawal

Dr. R.C. Agrawal joined Archaeological Survey of India (ASI) in 1972, and participated in and conducted many excavations in India including Buddhist sites. He worked as Director, Monuments, and Director, Projects and Museums in the ASI and as Member Secretary in ICHR. He became Professor of Museology in National Museum Institute, New Delhi. Professor Agrawal is now Joint Director General, ASI, c/o Institute of Archaeology, Red Fort Complex, Delhi.

Address: P-I, Pinjara Pole Apartments, Andrews Ganj Extension, New Delhi-110 049.

R.L. Hangloo

Professor Ratan Lal Hangloo took Ph.D. from JNU. He is specialist in Kashmir history, and in Medieval Indian History. He is now a Faculty Member in the Department of History, University of Hyderabad.

Address: Professor of History, School of Social Sciences, University of Hyderabad, Hyderabad, AP.

S.M. Haldhar

Address: Dr. Siyaram Mishra Haldhar, E-115, MCD Colony, Azadpur, Delhi-110 035.

S.P. Singh

Professor S.P. Singh took Ph.D. from Moscow; Formerly Senior Fellow (JNU, Oxford, London & Hull); Research Visitor (Royal Institute of International Affairs, London); Member ICSSR, Indo-Russian Joint Commission; Awardee of the Leading Professional of the World (2011), IBC, Cambridge, UK.

Address: Principal Investigator of the UGC MRP, School of International Studies, Centre for Russian and Central Asian Studies, Jawaharlal Nehru University, New Delhi-110 067.

Sheikh Saleem Ahmed

Address: D-131 B, Sector 26, Noida, UP-201 301.

Sneh Mahajan

Dr. Sneh Mahajan is from IP College, Delhi.

Address: S-41, Greater Kailash Part-II, New Delhi-110 048.

Surendra Gopal

Address: Professor Surendra Gopal, Gopal Nursing Home, East Boring Canal Road, Patna, Bihar.

T. Shaumian

Dr. (Mrs.) Tatyana Shaumian is the Acting Head, Centre for Indian Studies, Institute for Oriental Studies, Moscow.

T.N. Zagorodnikova

Dr. T.N. Zagorodnikova is from Institute for Oriental Studies, Moscow.

Tabasum Firdaus

Address: c/o Hafizullah Mahajan, Provisional Store, Lane No. 4, 4, Butshah Mohalla, Lal Bazar, Srinagar, Kashmir.

V.V. Chernovskaya

Dr. V.V. Chernovskaya is from University of Yaroslavl.

V.P. Kashin

Dr. V.P. Kashin is from Institute for Oriental Studies, Moscow.

Z.U. Malik

Address: 4/1084, S.S. Nagar, Aligarh, UP.

SECTION I

ANCIENT PERIOD

I

Convergence and Cross-Currents of Civilisation in and Around Central Asia

D.P. Chattopadhyaya

Ideas owe their origin to individual human beings but spread far beyond them. In the geography of culture there is no boundary in the received sense. The territory between China in the east, the Fertile Crescent (around the Euphrates and the Tigris) in the west and beyond (comprising the extended Hellenic world), Russia and Ukraine in the north, and India together with Pakistan in the south, forms a Eurasian cultural continuum. Since time immemorial, the peoples of these countries have been moving to and from different directions. From the archaeological relics of such prehistoric settlements as Mehrgarh (Baluchistan, *c.* 8000–2500 BC), Catel Huyuk (Central Anatolia, *c.* 7200–6100 BC), Dnieper-Donets (Black Sea region, *c.* 5000–4000 BC), Kelteminar (southeast of the Caspian, *c.* 4000–2500 BC), Namazga (southern Turkmenistan, *c.* 4000–3500 BC), Afanasevo (southern Siberia, *c.* 3500–2500 BC) Kuo-Araxes (southern Caucasus, *c.* 3500–2200 BC), Harappa (Indus Valley, *c.* 2700–1900 BC), and Bactria-Margiana Archaeological Complex (BMAC) or Oxus area in southern Turkmenistan, (*c.* 2200–1700 BC), one feels persuaded that from the east of the Mediterranean and the west of the Black Sea to the southeast of the Caspian Sea and beyond, up to the major river system of China, there had been a number of vast and long-lasting human cultures. Geographical formations—mountain ranges (Altai, Kunlun, Caucasus, Himalayas, Karakorum, Hindukush, Ural, etc.); deserts (Gobi, Taklamakan, Arabian, etc.); river basins (Hwang Ho, Yangtze Kiang, Syr Darya, Amu Darya, Indus, Ganges, Volga, Don, Dniester, Dnieper, Danube, Tigris, Euphrates, Nile, etc.); and the Eurasian steppes—have influenced these movements but could never stop the same.

The Caucasus region, the northwestern part of Central Asia, is the narrow neck between the Black Sea and the Sea of Azov in the west and the Caspian

Sea in the east. The Transcaucasia comprises Georgia, Azerbaijan, and Armenia. These countries taken together are often regarded as one of the earliest cradles of human civilisation. To the north of the Caucasus stretches the temperate zone of the Russian plains and to the south lies the sub-tropical fertile regions producing wheat, maize, paddy, sunflower, sugar beets, grapes and a variety of fruits like citrus. In the heart of the Eurasian continent, spreading from the Caspian, Afghanistan and China, lies the region known as Central Asia. This area is extremely hot and dry, full of contrasts—high mountains, vast plains, desert and semi-desert depressions. Central Asia, after the break-up of the Soviet Union, comprises five independent countries—Uzbekistan, Turkmenistan, Kazakhstan, Tajikistan, and Kyrghystan. The populations of these countries are mixed, consisting of Russians, Ukranians, Tatars, Kazakhs, Uighurs and many other stocks who settled there at various points of time. This area is one of the centres of the most ancient cultures of the world. Various examples of the architectural monuments of past centuries and the ruins of temples and fortresses are silent signs of the vanished past. Despite the ethnic diversity of the population, the landscape and the deep-rooted ways of life have imparted a distinct regional personality to the countries of the area.

The population in the Central Asian countries is understandably concentrated where irrigation facilities are high, in the valley of the major rivers and in a narrow area between the desert plains and the mountains. The myths of the river gods/goddesses are inferred from a linguistically cognate set of proto-Indo-European names like *deh(a)nu,* viz. Indian *Dānu,* mother of Vṛtra, the withholder of the heavenly waters, Irish *Danu,* mother of the Tūatha Dē Danann, Greek (gender-switched) god, *Danaus,* father of the Danaids, who for the crime of killing their husbands on their wedding nights were cursed to carry water in a sieve for ever. Deh(a)nu-linked Euro-Slavic rivers are Danube, Don, Dunavas (Latvian), Tanais (Scythian), etc. Ethnic intermixture, mythological and linguistic loaning and borrowing, business contact, and exchange of religious, philosophical and scientific ideas are among the main characteristics of these cultural continuities. The agriculture of the oases consists mainly of cotton, silk, fruits, vegetables, rice, and fibre crops. The synonyms of some agricultural products available in Indian, Arabic, Central Asian and Greek languages suggest the cultural affinity of the concerned peoples. For example, cotton is *kārpasā* in Sanskrit, both *kerpās* and *qutn* in Arabic, *karpados* in Greek and *carbasus* in Latin. Also instructive are the synonyms of silk, viz. Manchurian *sirghe,* Mongolian *sirkek,* Russian silk, Greek *derikos* (der-silk-worm), and Sanskrit *kanceya* (from *koca*—cask, vessel, then applied to 'cocoon' of the silkworm). Wheat in Sanskrit is *godhūma* (*go+dhūma*—'cow-smoke'), in Avesta/Persia it is *gantuma/gandum,* in Khotani, *ganama,* in Tocharian *kanti* (bread), and in Russian *psenica* ([grain] for threshing/grinding). The synonyms of rice are *vrihi* (Sanskrit), *vrize* (Afghan) and *orusa* (Greek).

It is not easy to ascertain definitely the region or regions of the origin of cultivated plants. Even the experts, ancient and modern, are of the view that China, India as well as countries that are Central Asian, Near Eastern, Mediterranean, Abyssinean, South Mexican, Central American and South American are the authors of the domesticated plants. Wheat and barley are believed to have been first domesticated during the Neolithic age. For barley, the Sanskrit word is *yava* and its Lithuanian synonym, *javai*. In the Slavic language, the generic word is *jačam*. It reminds one of the generic Sanskrit words *śaṣya* (grain) and *avestan* (*hahya*).

On the basis of their findings, botanists and archaeologists maintain that the needs for food are so basic that in exploring the origin of agriculture we must not resort to a reductionist or diffusionist single-origin theory. Both China and Southeast Asia cultivated enormous numbers of botanical varieties and their hereditary forms. It seems that the soya bean was first cultivated in China and then taken to Southeast Asia and from there to America and Europe. Fruits like apricot and peach, initially domesticated in the Far East, found their way to Persia, Armenia, Greece, and Rome in the first century BC. It appears that cotton was domesticated first either in India or in Arabia and Syria. During the period of the Indus Valley Civilisation (2500 BC), both in Mohenjo-Daro and Harappa, cotton cultivation and weaving technology were evidently known. The same found its way to Southeast Asia and, through the inter-mediation of Persia, to West Asia. The most well-known Chinese contribution to world crops is, of course, tea. It seems that it was domesticated in the early Han times. It became a popular beverage later on. Tea plantations were adopted in north-east India only in the second-half of the nineteenth century. Even the Indian word for the tea *cā* or *cāe* is of Chinese origin.

In the iconography of Central Asia, India and Iran, certain images related to the fertility cult, water, monster, *Makara* and *Yakṣiṇī* or *Yakṣi* for example, occupy a special place. Life-giving water is worshipped both in the *Rigveda* and *Avestā*. The theme of water cult is evident from the Shumer relief and the Sassanian costumes. The images of demon-destroying goddesses are also found to be common to India and the Central Asian countries.

Kazakhstan is situated between Siberia, the Urals and the southern neighbours. The topography of the country is somewhat like the other Central Asian countries while it is also rich in mineral resources. The use of metals both for making coins, ornaments, utensils and military equipment was widespread. Metallurgical techniques in Central Asia had been influenced by periodic infusions from China, India, and the West Asia. It seems that the Chinese soldiers taught the Central Asian artisans techniques for casting iron weapons and fabricating copper-nickel alloys. Al-Biruni praises the white metal utensils of China and prefers the same to those of Central Asia, criticising the latter as crude. The availability of antimonial copper and lead ores enabled the Central Asian countries and their neighbours to specialise in small and fine ornamental castings and arrowheads.

Uzbekistan, a land of vast desert landscape and fertile oases clustering around the hills of high mountain ranges, is the heart of Central Asia. It is washed by the Amu Darya in the southwest and Syr Darya on the northeast. 'Darya' means 'river' both in Central Asia and north India. Its main cities—Samarkand, Bukhara and (capital) Tashkent—are very old. They attest to a deep-rooted cultural heritage and history in the millennia, not merely in centuries. Traces of human habitation in the area date as far back as the old Stone Age, some 60,000 to 70,000 years ago. Some of these have already been mentioned. The states of Bactria, Khwarizm, and Sogdiana held their power in the first millennium BC. Many invaders/immigrants lived in, arrived and crossed the country—the Persian troops of King Darius in the sixth century BC, the Greek troops of Alexander the Great of Macedonia in the fourth century BC, the Hun forces of Attila (434–453 AD) from North Central Asia, and the Arab forces in the eighth century AD. After the Mongol invasion in the thirteenth century, the area became a part of the empire of Timur and his successors until early sixteenth century. Islamisation of the Uzbeks, which started from the middle of the thirteenth century, infused strong West Asian elements. In Uzbekistan, one finds a unique mixture of many ethnic stocks of Sogdiana, Shash, Fergana, Khwarizm, Iranian, and Turkic origin. Under the rule of the *Khanates* of Khiva and Bukhara, the diverse ethnic groups formed a disinct nationality in the sixteenth century. In the middle of the nineteenth century, it was annexed by Russia.

Peoples from China and Mongolia, particularly traders and political fortune-seekers and religious missionaries, had been moving at irregular (but recurring) intervals to the West, to West Asia, Russia, the Caucasus and to South Asia. The massive invasions of Attila and Genghis, though primarily military, should not be understood purely as episodic events of short duration consequences. The reverse movement from the areas of Southeast Europe, Anatolia and the Pontic, not necessarily military in nature, had also been taking place. There are reasons to believe that they reached the lands of Tocharian-speaking peoples, the regions of Qarashar ('Agni' in Indian and 'Yenqi' in Chinese) and Turfan (in Xinjiang). Natural calamities, pestilence, drought and famine and political turmoil played up and enlarged, from time to time, the scope of these emigrations and immigrations. It is evident that in the prehistoric past, the West Asians, the old Persians and the Indian peoples had moved to the north and the east. The main two eastwest routes or highways of the movements passed through Persia on the one hand and Ukraine on the other. Of course, all peoples had to travel through Central Asia. Hence the importance of the area from the scientific, technological and other cultural standpoints. From the records, both anthropological and philological, it is also clear that the peoples of the Slavonic countries in the north had been moving towards Central Asia and South Asia. These race movements, roughly speaking, took place in the areas between 20° and 135° longitudes and between 20° and 60° latitudes. In brief, one could easily decipher that Central Asia had been the most frequented geographical area of intersection between the East and the West, between the North and the South.

There had been maritime connections between the East and the West right from the early (pre-Christian) period. Different types of boats used to ply between the African coast, the Red Sea and the Gulf area, on the one hand, and Korea, China and Japan, on the other. Naturally, the sailors had to negotiate the coast of India and the Malaccan Strait. During the periods of political upheaval and military action in Central Asia, the importance of the sea routes increased. Besides, the sea routes enabled the traders and merchants to call the ports of different countries. They were importers and exporters not only of commercial cargoes but also of cultural items and of differnt kinds of technology.

Ideas and techniques are never in the nature of jetsam and flotsam. These are invariably rooted in the human ways of living, in the different modes of experience and encounter with nature and fellow human beings, familiar or stranger. Both natural forces and cultural conditions oblige us to face similar or comparable problems of living and surviving. Given the environmental and social constraints, it is not possible for us to tackle problems in an absolutely free manner or in infinitely varied ways. Both our ideas and techniques, oriented to specific needs, have their functional ancestry in the past. Therefore, it is not surprising to come across prehistoric and historic parallelisms between and convergence of diverse cultures. The ship building technology of India, China, the Mediterranean, Persian-Arabic, and Oceanic countries is of the same generic type—the ships are carvel-built. But it has been pointed out that certain boats on the Ganges, *patela melni* and *ulakh* like those of northern Europe are clinker-built. From the history of nautical technology it appears that the Arabic, Indian and Chinese navigators had been mutually influenced. The Indian sailors used to follow their routes looking at the star called 'Polaus Arcticus'. Generally, the sailors of the northern hemisphere were guided by the lodemans-stone. But since most of the sailors in the long course of their navigation had to sail through both the hemispheres and at times under cloudy skies, both the methods were followed.

The 'gunpowder epic', to use the expression of Needham, illustrates how one and the same technique evolved simultaneously in different cultural regions—Chinese, Indian and Arabic. Its history is dealt with extensively in the literature of these nations. The ideas and uses of the projectiles preceded and contributed to the operational concretisation in the military application of gunpowder. Conceptually speaking, gunpowder means action at a distance. It is an improvement upon the Greek (Aristotelian) notion of motion-by-impetus. The use of projectiles in naval warfare is ancient. 'Fire chemical' means the mixture of saltpetre, sulphur and charcoal (ordinarily called gunpowder). The concept was known as early as the ninth century but its military use in Europe was only around the early sixteenth century, presumably directly through Central Asia or through the Portuguese connections with Japan and Malay. The story of gunpowder is incomplete without a reference to fireworks, the ground-rat and the space-rocket. Indians are said to have excelled in the use of rocket missiles. The rocket-arrow attained the greatest prominence in India during the reign of the Mughal emperors from the early part of the sixteenth to the seventeenth century. It is not clear when exactly saltpetre was first recognised and analysed among the people of India. It is estimated that around the late thirteenth and the early fourteenth century, the Arabs and the Indians acquired this knowledge either independently or through their proximity to China. Climatic conditions in which high temperature and suitable humidity cause organic matters to decompose were obtainable in all the three areas—Arabia, India and China. Before the discovery of the nitric source in Chile, the Gangetic Valley of India was the most important source of supply of saltpetre to England in the eighteenth century. During the fourteenth and fifteenth centuries, the Europeans working in the courts of the Central Asian rulers, the Tartar slaves of Northeast Asia, had taken this knowledge to Europe. Further, the maritime connections between the far eastern countries, Indonesia, south India, the Arabic countries must have contributed to the spread of the theory and practice of gunpowder.

The people who live in the desert areas or cold climatic conditions, in the steppe lands or fertile river basins are bound to perceive nature in different ways. Their conflicts and co-operation with nature are found to be diverse. Their means of livelihood, pastoral or agricultural, modes of transport, cart or boat, military techniques of attack and self-defence are also bound to differ. But in certain respects their modes of experience, religious, scientific and practical, turn out to be similar. For example, the causes of different types of disease and their possible cures, even after making due allowance for the variation in the climatic conditions, are perceived to be comparable. So, the medical sciences and curative techniques of different peoples exhibit instructive parallelisms. For example, the Ionian and the Semitic medical systems, rather their synthetic outcome, as represented by the greats like Galen and Isocrates are, on scrutiny, found to be comparable in some respects with the systems of Caraka and Suśruta as developed in India. The availability or otherwise of the climate-related medical plants and the indigenous healing systems account for the unity and diversity of such different therapeutic and prophylactic systems as Unani, Āyurveda and (Chinese) *Nei Ching*.

The reasons for sartorial and residential peculiarities and burial forms are, to a large extent, culture-specific. The same may be said of the sciences concerning flora and fauna, plant pathology and animal husbandry. With the passage of time, given the influence of increasing and composite cultural contacts, the role of both borrowing and innovation saw many ups and downs. But to attain absolute cultural insularity or imperviousness in the name of race, religion or political ideology is just not possible.

The origin and development of mathematics shows, among other things, the close relation between what is perceptual-and-concrete and what is conceptual-and-abstract. The primitive concepts of number, magnitude and form can be traced back not only to primitive man in all parts of the world but also, according to Darwin, to the higher animals possessing such abilities as memory and imagination and the capacities to distinguish number, size, order and form, indicating their mathematical sense. Our early ancestors in every part of the world had to tackle persistent practical problems such as could only be solved by accurate surveying, weighing, measuring and counting. In all such basic operations as house construction, buying and selling, boat-making and road-building, the people had to use some rudimentary number language. Number *signs* perhaps preceded number *words*.

It is difficult to say anything very definitely about the origin of mathematics as these beginnings predate the art of writing. The earliest geometric results found in India in the *Sulba Sūtras* (Rules of the Cord) left behind by Baudhāyana, Āpastamba, Kātyāyana and their followers were being applied in the construction of altars. The authors of the works, it seems, lived between 500 BC and 300 BC. It must be said here that the geometric motivation of the 'rope-stretchers' in Egypt (or of their counterparts in India), was very practical, namely to survey and measure the size of the land-holdings on the inundated banks of the Nile. Similar problems had to be addressed in the river valleys of Mesopotamia, India, and China. Not only for surveying and mapping but also for measuring and weighing, the use of some intuitive concepts of quantity, i.e. number, was essential even to the Palaeolithic man. In the early periods of pre-monetary economy, people did require these concepts for buying and selling, rather for the purpose of barter or exchange of goods and services. Use of metals and alloys and preparation of medicine, intimately related to the life-world, also required the people to apply such mathematical concepts as weight, measure, fraction and ratio.

Some of the important points of mathematical parallelism may be recalled in this context. A numeral notation of only nine figures together with place-value components is found in China during the Shang period (fourteenth century BC). Special symbols for multiples of 10 had been current in India well before the sixth century AD. The Hindu numerals are found in Spain, apparently through the Arab connections, during the late tenth century. The use of the 'zero' was not noticed in Europe before the eleventh century. Secondly, the Rule of Three is found at about the same time in India and the Han *Chiu Chang*. It is to be noted that the technical term for the numerator is the same in Sanskrit and Chinese, *phala* and *shih*, both standing for 'fruit'. For the denominator also the terms used in both the languages, *fa* and *pramāṇa,* are identical in meaning, designating standard unit measures of length. Thirdly, the proof of the Pythagorean theorem was known, according to B.B. Datta, to the Śulbakāras. It is affirmed by Needham that this proof is available in the fourth century commentary by Caho Chun Chhing on the *Chou Pei Suan Ching,* which is said to have been borrowed by Bhāskara (thirteenth century). Fourthly, the idea of fundamental identity of algebraic and geometrical relations seems to have been borrowed by Persian mathematicians like al-Khwārizmi (tenth century) from China. Fifthly, indeterminate analysis, a branch of algebra, was initiated in China in the fifth century, developed in India by Āryabhaṭa (sixth century) and Brahmagupta (seventh century). Through Arabic and Indian intermediaries it reached eastern Europe in the fifteenth century. Sixthly, during the seventh, eighth and ninth centuries a considerable amount of Indian (Brahminical) knowledge—astronomy, trigonometry, and calendrical science—reached China through the Buddhist channels. Seventhly, only in the late thirteenth century, it appears, Euclid's geometry could reach China, thanks to Arab intermediation. Around the same time Chinese mathematicians started using trigonometrical methods due to the Arabic and Indian influence. Eighthly, the concept of negative numbers referred to by Brahmagupta (seventh century) in India was apparently known to the Chinese earlier. Whether such Indian mathematicians as Mahāvīra and Bhāskara were aware of the problem of the square roots of negative number, their Chinese counterparts did not mention it anywhere in their works. Ninthly, the Pascal Triangle of binomial reformed (named after Blaise Pascal, 1665), anticipated by others like Apianus earlier, was known in the Chinese mathematical tradition from the thirteenth century onwards. Omar Khayyam (1050–1123) of Persia, better known as a poet, prepared improved astronomical tables and reformed the Muslim calendar; his methods of finding the fourth, fifth, sixth and higher roots of number, on his own admission, had been derived from the Indian mathematicians (like Brahmagupta). Finally, the old story of zero again brings China and India close.

In spite of their notable mathematical contribution, the Babylonians (2nd millennium BC) had no clear method in the sexagesimal (60-based) system to indicate an 'empty' position, i.e. they did not have a zero symbol. The sign they had was meant only for intermediate, not terminal, position. There was ambiguity in the Chinese place-value principle from the Shang (2nd millennium BC) to the Han (3rd century BC onwards) despite its commitment to the decimal (10-based) system. For, a specific symbol for zero was not available. It seems that the Taoist 'emptiness' was connected in the Chinese mind with mathematical operations. To the Indian mathematicians, emptiness, *sūnya,* i.e. the zero, was a written symbol for the nil value. In the works like *Pauliśa Siddhānta* and the *Pañcha Siddhāntikā,* zero has been used as a specific place-value. Authors like Āryabhaṭa and Varahamihira (sixth and seventh centuries) had been obviously familiar with the importance of the zero as the decimal place-value. On the subject of whether Indians were influenced by the Chinese or the other way round cannot be said very definitely. But it seems that on this issue the mathematicians of West Asia, China and India were in touch with each other. What is more important is the face that during the eighth, ninth and tenth centuries, when the simultaneous presence of Indian culture and Chinese culture in Indo-China was being increasingly felt, historians of mathematics point out that some inscriptions have been found there, which attest the existence of the zero symbol both in its dot and place-value forms. In the known context of the spread of Buddhism and other forms of cultural contact, the role of Southeast Asia, together with that of West Asia, China and India, needs a closer look. When the subject of astronomy is brought into the picture, the facts of cultural transmission between the said civilisational zones becomes even more concrete.

It is almost idle to try to trace the historical origin of mathematics. In their characteristic Eurocentric way, many Western writers on the subject maintained that the Graeco-Roman world was the cradle of mathematical learning. However, they admit that the Greeks did borrow some elementary mathematics from Egypt. Herodotus believed that geometry was a gift of the Nile. A promising line of enquiry into the subject lies in the recognition of the fact, already stated, that the needs of life and living, which give rise to numeration and quantification, are universal in their scope. The hieroglyphic (Egyptian) and the cuneiform (Sumerian) patterns of writing are among the earliest known kinds of communication. After the decipherment of the ancient pictorial (significative) types of writing, it has been established that the sexagesimal (Mesopotamian) system of numeration (additive, subtractive and multiplicative) was superior to the Egyptian one. More light will be thrown on the subject when the Indus Valley script is deciphered. The Mesopotamian mathematics is rated high not only for the system of numeration but also for developing algorithmic procedures.

The mathematical cultures of India and China are of far greater antiquity than those of Greece and Rome. Among the oldest mathematical documents of China are *Chou Pei Ching* (c. 300 BC) and *Chuichang suan-shu* (c. 200 BC) *(Nine Chapters on the Mathematical Art)*. While the former is concerned with astronomical and calendrical calculations, properties of the right angle, the use of fractions, etc., the latter deals with surveying, agriculture, partnerships, engineering, taxation, calculations, the solution of equations, etc. Basically fond of patterns, the Chinese formulated many types of magic squares.

The contact between India and China, on the one hand, and between China and the West, on the other, seems to be very old. But it is difficult to be definite about the extent or direction of borrowing/loaning. It may be mentioned here that the Chinese, unlike the Babylonians and the Greeks, did not make use of sexagesimal fractions. Their system of numeration of all sorts remained essentially decimal.

The similarity between the astronomical views of the ancient Babylonians, Indians and Chinese also display interesting parallelisms. This has to be understood in terms of the universal and natural sense of wonder and awe at the regularity in the movement of heavenly bodies, their power and influence on human life and its basic concerns. In all civilisations of antiquity—Indian, Babylonian, Greek, and Chinese—the reference to and reverence for the heavenly bodies, prayer to propitiate them for human benefit and cognitive curiosity about them are clearly evident. While the ancient Babylonian and Indian records of astronomical observations are nearly lost, the Arabic and, particularly, Chinese ones (fifth century BC to tenth century AD) have survived to a great extent. That explains why the controversy between Indologists, Sinologists and Arabists regarding the first authorship of a so-called Lunar Zodiac (chain of constellations found on or near the equator) could not be settled to mutual satisfaction. Chhuthan Hsi-Ta (Gautama), the author of the most comprehensive collection of Chinese astronomical views (AD 718), is said to be an Indian Buddhist astronomer who, among other scholars, had been resident in Peking during the Thang period. Several Indian astronomers are calender specialists like Chiayeh (Kāśyapa), Chümolo (Kumāra) and Pu-Khung (Amoghavajra) who are mentioned in the Chinese works of the sixth to eighth centuries. Through academic ambassadors of this kind, the works of Āryabhaṭa and Varāhamihira, through translation, reached China.

The Chinese astronomers had close connections not only with Indians but also with Arabs, mainly Persian and Central Asian astronomers. During the Yuan (Mongol) period, astronomers, mathematicians and engineers like Kuo Shou-Ching (AD 1231–1316) in the service of Kublai Khan and his successors were benefited by their interaction with the Persian astronomers like Jamal al-Din (Cha-Ma-Lu-Ting) and Muslim gunners and mathematicians like A-Lao-Wa-Ting and I-Ssu-Ma-Yin. The Muslim influences on the Chinese academia developed to such an extent that, Needham writes, even after the end of the Yuan dynasty (AD 1368), when the Ming dynasty came to power, a separate Muslim Astronomical Bureau was set up.

In yet another context, the relation between China, India and West Asia becomes very clear. All these three civilisations had their own astronomical systems, the Indian *nakṣatara(s)*, Arabic *manāzil* (moon stations) and the Chinese *hsiu*, indicating the star-groupings in the skies following which the concerned peoples used to determine their new year, seasons and months. Nine of the 28 *hsiu-determinatives* are the same as the *yogatārā* (junction-stars) of the Indian system, while a further 11 share the same constellation. The Indian and Chinese calendrical sciences are of the same civilisational age group (*c.* 1400–1000 BC). Some experts, particularly Needham, are of the view that the Indian and

Chinese systems developed independently but later on had their mutual interaction. But some Assyriologists, relying on a number of cuneiform tablets from the library of King Assurbanipal (seventh century BC), try to show that both the systems may be traced back to the Babylonian astronomy *(c.* 1400 BC) through the Persian intermediation. These findings, though intriguing, unless critically examined, often give rise to fanciful, anthropocentric or chauvinistic fancies. Not frequently it has been said that Europe is the cradle of all civilisations or that the Nile Valley is to be regarded as the mother of all other civilisations of Africa, Europe and Asia, if not of the whole world. Similar claims have at times emanated from Anatolia, China, India, Nordic, Teutonic and Celtic countries and Southern Russia as well. Ethnographically speaking, some of these areas like the cultures of Central Asia are evidently overlapping.

Due to well-known political reasons, Euro-centrism has been on the ascent during the last four centuries or so. The technological and maritime domination of Europe over the world was destined to have its political, economic and intellectual consequences. While there is nothing wrong in articulating a particular world-view from a particular cultural standpoint, it can hardly be denied that the basic principles of rational inquiry require the truth-seeker to try honestly bring about maximum possible harmony between the numerous and, particularly, conflicting points of view. The pursuit of harmony must not be pressed at the cost of truth itself or disregarding the uniqueness of different civilisations, especially their creative cultural aspects.

REFERENCES

Chattopadhyaya, D.P., *Science, Technology, Philosophy and Culture*, Delhi, 1996.

Clark, W.E., *The Aryabhatiya of Aryabhata*, Chicago, 1930.

Datta, B. Bibhuti, *The Science of the Śulba: A Study in Early Hindu Geometry*, Calcutta, 1932.

Needham, Joseph, *Science and Civilization in China*, Cambridge University Press, 1954.

Thibant, G. and Sudhakar Dwivedi (ed. and tr.), *Panchasiddhantika*, 1930, reprint 1989, Delhi.

2
Central Asia and Indo-Aryans

D.N. Tripathi

Broadly speaking, Central Asia is the land stretching from the eastern shores of the Caspian Sea to the Great Wall of China bounded by China, Afghanistan, Iran, Asiatic Russia and the Caspian Sea. The cultural dynamics of Central Asia involved in its orbit a large number of countries. Bordering the southern limits of Turkmenistan, Uzbekistan, and Tajikistan are located the homeland of some of the oriental civilisations in Iraq, Iran, Afghanistan and the Indian subcontinent. Similarly, bordering the Chinese province of Sinkiang is the Indian state of Jammu and Kashmir, the homeland of a culture as old as the Chinese Neolithic. Obviously, each of these cultures played some part or the other in the process of cultural interaction throughout the prehistoric and protohistoric times.

The region beyond the Himalayas was never so isolated from India as we often think. The people of northern India, specially of Punjab, possessed some knowledge of this region and were in contact with the nomads in every age. They did not consider them foreigners as we do now, simply because the distinctions between them, both physical and cultural, were not so great as to create a sharp difference between them. Conflict arose only in cases when the newcomers tried to unsettle the established political conditions; but peaceful infiltration was generally welcome as it contributed to the prosperity of the country and proved an added military strength to the local rulers. The Brahmanical social code always provided them with an independent place in the society. Although it meant the formation of new castes, it did not hurt their *amour-propre* but made them willing parties of an ever-growing civilisation (Kaushik, 1985: 11).

As early as the Vedic period, the Indian writers showed an acquaintance with the people beyond the northern and northwestern frontiers. We know that in the *Nadi-stuti* hymn of the *Rigveda* (X.75.5-6) many of the rivers beyond Indus (*Sindhu*) are mentioned. The western tributaries of the Sindhu are thus mentioned in the *Rigveda* (X.75.6):

> *First thou goest united with Tristama on this journey, with the Susartu, the Rasa, and the Sveti, O Sindhu, with the Kubha (Kophen, Kabul river) to the Gomati (Gomal), with the Mehatnu to the Krumu (Kurram)—with whom thou proceeded together.*

Some of these rivers have been identified with modern rivers in Afghanistan, namely *Sveti* (Swat), *Kubha* (Kabul), the *Gomati* (Gomal), the *Krumu* (Kurram) and the Mehatnu. Besides these rivers, mention of the following rivers is found in the *Rigveda*, viz. the Svetayavari River (VIII.26,18), the Shiksha (1.104.3), the Sarayu (X.64.9), which was not the well-known river of Kosal of the post-Vedic times, and the Adinina (VII.18.8). Das is of the opinion (1980: 72) that "it is very difficult to identify most of these rivers with any present rivers ... they may be the names of some of the rivers in Bactria." Who knows some other rivers not yet identified may have been flowing beyond Afghanistan in Central Asia. In this case, the mention of river Sarayu is of special interest, as we know a river named Harayu is there in Afghanistan and is mentioned in *Avesta*.

In the *Atharvaveda* (V.22, 5-9), the fever *takman* is wished away not only to the country of the Gandharis but also further beyond, to that of the Bahlikas. In the Brahmana literature we again come across these people (*SB*, 1, 7, 3-5). Two new people are also spoken of — Uttarakurus and the Uttaramadras — as distinguished from the Kurus and the Madras settled in the Punjab (*AB*, VIII. 14.23). The next writer Yaska, who comes immediately after, speaks of another new people — the Kambojas — probably for the first time *(Nirukta, II.2).*

The Bahlikas are well known. It appears that the Uttarakurus, Uttaramadras as well as the Kambojas too belonged to the still undefined region of Central Asia beyond the Himalayas. The existence of an Uttarakuru in the region is noted by the Greek writers till the fifth century AD. Ptolemy is the first to speak of a town named Ottorokorrha and of a river and a mountain bearing the same name in the Serique (Chinese Turkestan) near the mountain Emodos (Himalaya). Later writers speak of the same place under the name Oporrocorra *(apara* and *uttara* here having the same meaning). The tradition survived till the fifth century as Orosius still speaks of the Ottorogorras. The name Uttaramadra might suggest a connection with the Median tribes (the Mada) and an attempt was made a few years ago to prove that the Maddas or the Madras of the Punjab were Median immigrants to India. Among the reasons adduced in favour of this hypothesis, stress has been laid on the unorthodox customs prevalent among them and mentioned by the *Mahabharata.* The epic distinctly speaks of the king of Madras as Bahlika-pun-gava and thus suggests his connection with the Iranian world.

The Kambojas also point out to the same direction. Although they are constantly associated with Gandhara, it is still impossible to find out their trace on the frontiers of India. The name of Gandharas survived for long centuries but that of the Kambojas were soon forgotten. This makes it probable that they belonged to the nomad hordes of Central Asia, which were moving from place to place. One of their branches seems to have entered India in very early times, but they must have soon lost their identity as a distinct people. Other branches of the same people seem to have entered Eastern Tibet and the valley of Mekong from another direction. But with this assumption only, we can explain why the name Kambuja was given to the kingdom founded in the middle valley of Mekong. In Eastern Tibet also, their name can be traced in the name of the province of Khams and it is probably from that region that the Kamboja invasion of Assam and Bengal took place in later times.

In the early Buddhist texts, the epics as well as the Puranas, we get a more elaborate scheme to systematise the geographical knowledge possessed by the Indians not only of India but also of other Asiatic regions. The principles, which guided the compilers of these texts, are not always evident, but as some of their notions correspond to actuality, it is not fair to reject the cosmology presented by them as fanciful.

The Buddhist texts mention four continents spread around the central mount Meru in the following order: in the South Jambudvipa, in the North Uttarakuru, in the West Apara-Godana and in the East Purva-Videha. Jambudvipa was, generally speaking, India, according to the Buddhists. Uttarakuru, as we know, was the name given to the Chinese Turkestan. Godana was the name by which Khotan was known in ancient times. The oldest form of the name Khotan is preserved in the Chinese transcription of the Han period as Yu-t'ien. The Chinese words were pronounced in the Han period as (g) *iu-den*, i.e. Godana. The name Apara-Godana thus seems to have been used with reference to the region of Khotan. Purva-Videha was the eastern limit of the north Indian world at the time when this geographical notion was formed.

The Brahmanical cosmology, which is sensibly of a later period, gives us a more elaborate scheme. Jambudvipa according to it is no longer India alone but the entire central belt of the continent as known to the compilers of that age. It is divided into seven *varṣas* (regions) of which the first is Bharatvarsa or India. Another known *varṣa* is Uttarakuru. The six other *varṣas* are Kimpurusa, Hari, Bhadrasva, Ketumala, Ilavrita, and Ramayaka. As the central mountain of Kimpurusvarsa is mentioned as Hemakuta, it is possible that this was the name given to the Himalayan zone. Ilavrita might suggest a connection with the region watered by the Ili River further to the north. Jambudvipa is again only one of the seven continents. Among the other continents, two, the Sakadvipa and the Kraunchdvipa, have been described in detail in the *Mahabharata.* Of the two at least the former corresponded to reality.

Although we cannot do full justice to the cosmological notions contained in the Buddhist and Brahmanical texts, there is ample evidence to show that the Indian compilers were acquainted with most of the people of the Central Asiatic regions in the age when these cosmological notions were systematised.

For example, one of the early Sanskrit Buddhist texts mentions Cina Kaushika, Khasa, Bahli, Tukhara, Pahlava, Parta, Saka and Vokkana Ramatha. The *Ramayana* locates to the north of Gandhara and Madraka, the Yavanas, Sak, Parada, Bahlika, Rsika, Paurava, Kimkara, Cina, Apara-Cina Tukhara, Barbara, Kamboja, Darada, Kirata, Tankana, and Pasupala. The *Mahabharata* speaks of the Yavanas, Cina, Kasmira, Pasu (Pala), Khasira (Khasa?), Panhava (Pahlava), Girigahvara, etc. among the people living in the north. The Puranas locate in the same region Bahlika, Vatadhana, Abhira, Kalatoyaka, Pallava, Carmakhandika, Parada, Harbhusika, Dasamalika, Kamboja, Darada, Barbara, Harsavardhana, Cina, Tukhara, Culika, Sulika, etc. The *Bṛhatsamhita* attempts at a more precise classification: in the west—Haihaya, Vokkana, Ramatha, Parata, Saka; in the northwest—Tusara, Madra, Kuluta, Carmaranga, Ekavilicana (Ekanetra), Sulika; in the north—Kuru, Uttarakuru, Vatadhana, Huna; and in the northeast—Pasupala, Cina, Khasa, Ghosa, Kucika.

Many of these tribes are well known. The Tusaras or Tukharas were the people of Tokharestan. The Carmakhandikas are supposed to have belonged to Samartoand. The Sulikas, also known as Culikas, were the Sogdians. The Kucikas or Kusikas may be identified with the ancient people of Kuci or Kucha. Vokkana is identified with Wakhan. The Ekvilocanas remind us of the one-eyed people whom Herodotus locates in the extreme north of Central Asia above the Issedones. Although we cannot identify other tribes in the lists referred above, the identities already noted are quite sufficient to prove that from about the second century BC to about AD 500, Indian writers possessed a fairly accurate knowledge of the nomadic hordes that were moving about in Central Asia.

In the dynastic lists of the Puranas, it is said that the Tusara kings succeeded the Yavanas in India. Their number is given as 14. According to the *Matsya*, the world belonged to them for seven thousand years (*sapta-varsa-sahasrani*) whereas according to *Vayu* and *Brahmanda*, they ruled for *Pancha-varsa-satani*, which may be interpreted either as five hundred years or as 105 years. Five hundred years would be too long a period for 14 kings and so it is just probable that they ruled only for 105 years. The *Matsya* account may be accordingly corrected as *sapta-varsa-satan-iha* and interpreted as 107 years. Some of the early Puranas give Tukhara as a variant of Tusara. It is certain that the cerebral consonant was pronounced as *kha* when the name was adopted by the Puranic chroniclers. The *Ramayana* gives the name as Tukhara. The name is given in the same form by the *Mahabharata* as well as by two old Buddhist texts as *Saddharma-smṛtyupastan* and the *Mahamayuri*. The Chinese pilgrims tell us that the Tukhara Buddhists like the Ceylonese had a special monastery built for them at the Mahabodhi in the seventh century. In the same century, Bāṇa writes in his *Harṣacarita* that Harṣa used to get taxes from the mountainous and inacessible region of the Tusaras *(atra paramesvarena tsarasailabhuvo durgayah grhitah karah)*. This only shows that Tukhara as a distinct people and the land of Tukharas (Tokharestan) as a distinct country in the mountainous region beyond the frontiers of India were known to the Indians as late as the middle of the seventh century AD.

We know this from about the second century BC to about the middle of the seventh century AD. All sources of information, Sanskrit, Greek, Latin and Chinese, concur in recognising a people called Tukhara living in the country, which came to be known in later times as Tokharestan. The original seat of the people was the Upper valley of the Oxus in the region of Badakshan. The Puranic sources would have us believe that kings of this Tukhara origin conquered India from the Greeks and set up their rule. Fourteen of their rulers reigned in India for over a little one hundred years. These are precisely the rulers who are designated Kushana by the historians of India (Bagchi, 1955: 117-27). Between India and Central Asia, close socio-economic and cultural ties have existed all through the ages. Recent excavations by Russian archaeologists have highlighted the intimate contacts between the people in the northwest region of the Indian subcontinent and the southwest part of the former Soviet Central Asia going as far back as the second millennium BC. At Djeitun-Depe in south Turkmenistan (which might have originated in around 4000 BC), aspects of both Jericho and Jarmo are reflected. Masson thinks that in the make-up of Djeitun culture there is the work of the people coming from that direction, around 6000 BC. The cultural similarity that exists among these early cultures is quite important, as we would see that the spread of the IE languages also covers this area.

During the Neolithic period, however, Chinese Central Asia maintained some contacts with the Kashmir and Swat valleys. At Burzhom in the Kashmir Valley and at *Aligrama in Swat valley*, pit dwellings characterised the Neolithic complex, a feature which is also present in the Ordos. Rectangular perforated harvesters of stone and bone from Burzhom and jade beads from Aligrama establish further links with China (Tripathi, 1988).

During the Chalcolithic period, Central Asia, particularly in the region of South Turkmenia, rich cultural sites have come to light. We find at Namazga II and III, painted designs on pottery from Seistan (Shahar-I Sokhta), Kandahar (Mundigak), Quetta, Damb Sadaat and other places, such as Gumla (Gomal Valley) and Jalilpur (Ravi basin). It seems that the 'culture-interaction area' during this period included several regions between Southern Turkmenia and the Indus plains.

The Bronze Age ushers in urbanisation in South Turkmenia and the Russian scholars (V.M. Masson and Y.A. Shchetenko) are of the view that there was a 'cultural-contact situation' between India and Central Asia. We know that Harappan features have been reported from Altyn-Tepe. This definitely proves that the economic interaction area in the later part of the 3rd millennium BC appears to have comprised South Turkmenia, South Afghanistan and the Indus Valley. Some of the findings from Altyn-Tepe, like metal and ivory articles, pottery and beads bear close resemblance to articles discovered at Harappan sites, and many Turkmen terracottas have their counterparts in the Indus Valley terracottas (Masson, 1967: 174-76; Shchetenko, 1968: 35-66). Lyonnet (1977) has brought to light the discovery of Harappan pot-sherds at Shturgai, site of seven stations near Ai Khanum, on the Afghanistan side of the Oxus. While scholars are still faced with the task of determining the specific features of the culture discovered in South Turkmenistan, it is obvious that there were reciprocal influences working between India and Central Asia. It can be assumed that northern India, Afghanistan and the southern parts of Central Asia constituted a zone where painted ceramic pottery of similar rural cultures was fairly common and where proto-urban civilisations developed through similar processes. In the post-Harappan epoch too, strong cultural and historical ties existed between the two peoples.

The Late Bronze Age and the Early Iron Age is associated with the early Indo-Europeans, which include the Aryans. Some scholars view Central Asia as the starting point of Indo-Aryan migration while others believe that the Indo-Aryans reached India from the West through the Caucasus. Notwithstanding this controversy about the route of the Indo-Aryan settlers, scholars are unanimous on the continuation of close contacts between India and Central Asia in the post-Harappan period. As discussed earlier, the Indian tradition (Vedic, Buddhist, Brahmanical, and Puranic literature) always considered this region as a single zone in their cosmological descriptions.

Clearly enough, there are evidences of definite process of the movement of cultures and ideas between Central Asia and India through the Indian borderlands, but they cannot be fully utilised at the moment for a connected history of the third millennium BC. For the second and first millennium we have an entirely different picture. The Oxus now becomes the centre of intense activities. It is now colonised. We have large cemeteries and fortified citadels belonging to the Late Bronze Age and Early Iron Age, such as Spalli Tepe, Dashli Tepe, Yaz-Depe and Tukhar Cemetery. Many of them have yielded grey wares along with red wares. Now we know that there are several groups of grey ware between Asia Minor and the Indo-Gangetic plains and they cover the entire period of proto-history. Even those belonging to the second millennium are at least half a dozen, if not more. Each one is, however, characterised by a definite set of pot-forms and decorative designs as also by a number of associated red wares and movable antiques and definite kinds of structural remains. It means, each of these groups of grey ware represents a totality and, therefore, a culture. As a social scientist, an archaeologist looks at this totally as a unit. Obviously, for him neither the greyness of pottery nor a few common pot-forms alone have any worthwhile meaning in terms of social and cultural mobility. At present, each one of them shows a separate entity. This is, of course, besides individual trait-infiltrations, borrowals and influences. Therefore, the hypothesis regarding the Vedic Aryans and the grey wares have only local and regional applicability, which in itself, is a complete negation of the theory of Aryan migration in India seen through the grey wares. By the middle of the first millennium BC, we reach a stage, which has yielded various kinds of documentary evidence about various peoples and cultures, not only in Central Asia but also within the Indian mainland and the Indian borderlands (Gupta, 1979: 295-96).

The archaeological discoveries discussed above clearly shows that contacts between India and Central Asia — two major cradles of World civilisation — rose at an early period and acquired a durable character. These contacts played a significant role in the development of culture in both the regions. Yet, notwithstanding the considerable mutual interaction and cultural impact on the cultures of the two peoples, they have preserved their distinctive character (Kaushik, 1985: 11-15).

THE HISTORY OF INDO-ARYAN PROBLEM

Since the 'Ninth Anniversary Discourse' in 1792, knowledge of the problem addressed by Sir William Jones has expanded greatly while confidence in its resolution has retracted almost as much in the eyes of at least the Western scholars. The hypothesis that the,

> Indo-European homeland lay somewhere between the south Caspian and the Hindukush plays little if any part in the current debate over Indo-European origins. On the other hand, it is also obvious that those lands lying east of Urals, including Kazakhstan and Central Asia, are still pivotal in any thorough discussion of Indo-European origins or their solution (Mallory, 1994-95: 249).

A fairyland has been conceived in the Central Asian plains. To the question, whence came the Aryans in about 2000 to 1800 BC, the answer is Central Asia. To the question whence came the Medes in about 1000 BC, the answer is Central Asia, and to a similar question whence came the Sakas in 700 BC, the answer is Central Asia. Could Central Asia sustain such a vast population as to send waves after waves of men out of it, to populate entire Asia and Europe, is a point of serious concern. And this hypothesis does not touch the impending questions of migrations of ancient Egypt and Sumer which loom large over us for solution. All this necessitates a new look into the past in the light of the historical data available with us.

Prof. Renfrew suggests that the Indo-European (IE) languages originated with the beginning of agriculture. According to him, the first evidence of regular agricultural activities is to be seen in Anatolia around the seventh-sixth millennium BC, and therefore, the Indo-European languages too may have originated there.

Before discussing the case of Indian subcontinent being the homeland of IE languages, I intend to clearly assert that Jone's acceptance of an Asian homeland for mankind and, in particular, what would later be regarded as the Indo-Europeans, was easily accepted in the early nineteenth century, when the Mosaic chronology still prompted Western scholarship to accept his thesis. Many scholars argued for a 'homeland' between India and the Caspian Sea, usually Kashmir or Bactria, e.g. Young (1813: 255), Picket (1877), etc.

However, as time passed the European scholars started proposing the hypothesis of the European homeland. Nevertheless, Max Müller still held an *Urheimat* 'somewhere in Asia' since it best accorded with the centre of the area of Indo-European expansion, the earliest civilisations were located there, it was the historic home of other migrating peoples such as Mongols and Turks, and since a putative homeland set in Northwest Europe failed to accord with the paucity of sea and fish terms in Proto-Indo-European (Muller, 1888: 116). The noted Celticist, Henri D' Arbois de Jubainville (1889) also supported a homeland between the Jaxartes (Syr Darya) and Oxus (Amu Darya) as the only way to explain the high degree of 'Aryan' civilisation when it first emerges in history. For the most of the twentieth century, solutions to the problem of Indo-European origins centred on putative homelands in Northern Europe, Central Europe or the East European Steppe, particularly at north of the Black and Caspian seas. But some scholars still argued the case of Asian homeland of IE languages (e.g., Wilhelm Koppers, 1934 and Wilhelm Schmidt, 1949) as they considered that the earliest Indo-Europeans emerged out of a pastoral nomadic 'cultural cycle'. The linguists also supported them (Wilhelm Bradenstein, 1936; Alfons Nehring, 1936). Today, a new Asiatic homeland has arisen where the homeland is ascribed to the spread of the earliest agriculturists from Anatolia to Europe (Gamkrelidze and Ivanov, 1984; Renfrew, 1987; Dolgopolsky, 1964; etc.)

CENTRAL ASIAN HOMELAND

Let me first of all consider the case of Central Asia being the homeland of IE languages. Until sometime past, it was the almost universally accepted theory that the original cradle-home of the primeval Aryans was located somewhere in Central Asia, towards the high but fertile tableland of the Pamir region (Ragozin, 1961: 75). Masson and Sarianidi (1972) have also argued the case of Central Asia being the original homeland of Indo-Europeans as the urban sites in the area separating northern populations appear to mirror the cultural behaviour expected of the early Indo-Iranians and various cultural groups to the south, which occupied the earliest historical seats of the Indo-Aryans, as opposed to the ancestors of the (Steppe) Iranians, encounters many solutions that have little to do with the Andronovo culture. This points at one obvious trend in the search of Indo-Iranian origins. Often those viewing the problem from the north, i.e.

the Steppe, find no difficulty in ascribing this region, be it west or east of Urals, to the ancestors of the Indo-Iranians. On the other hand, when one discusses the problem of more immediate origins of the Iranians within Iran itself, the Indo-Aryans of the Mitanni kingdom or, most especially, the Indo-Aryans of India, this southern perspective points at best to some form of contacts, albeit variously disputed, with the cultures of Central Asia and the Southeast Caspian (Gupta, 1979). R. Ghirshman (1977) sought the regions of the Indo-Aryan component along the Mitanni in the Gorgan region in the third millennium BC, long before the Andronovons, while B.B. Lal (1981) intimates that the closest connections for the Indo-Aryans of the *Rigveda,* reflected in the sites of the Painted Grey Ware culture (also Gaur, 1981), are to be found among the Grey Ware sites of the urban centres of Iran and Afghanistan as well as the Gandhara/Grave/Swat Valley culture, which has also been tied to Iran and Central Asia. While there is great room for dispute over the putative relationships between the earliest postulated Indo-Aryans (or Dardic cultures) in the northwest India and Iran or Central Asia, the absence of any firm evidence that might directly link these cultures with those of north of Central Asian urban centres, i.e. the Steppe Andronovo tribes, or even the presumably acculturated Tazabagyab culture of the south Aral region, can hardly pass without notice. If one wishes to press some form of historical relationship between the Steppe and the territories of Iran or India, this generally assumes the form of semi-invisible nomadic peoples (e.g., B and R. Allchin, 1982). Or the presumption that originally nomadic tribes passing through the urban settlements of Central Asia adopted so much of the local material culture as to be almost impossible to get detected as an archaeologically distinct population. What is not an issue is the absorption of Steppe peoples into the cultural sphere of Central Asia. Rather, it is demonstrating that the historically attested Iranians or Indo-Aryans, south of Central Asia can somehow be traced back to migrations either directly from Steppe or even from acculturated populations in Central Asia. All of this suggests the existence of a third faultline running from the Southeast Caspian across Central Asia, separating the presumed staging area of Indo-Iranian migrations from the historically attested Indo-Iranians to the south (Mallory, 1994-95).

THE INDO-IRANIAN LINE

There is a dichotomy between the reconstructed vocabulary of the ancestors of the Indo-Iranians (and presumably Tocharians) and the European stocks. This model has long been discussed in literature (e.g., Brandenstein, 1936) to account for why the voluminous ancient literatures of India and Iran provide such a paucity of linguistic cognates for arboreal and agricultural terminology that is widely shared among the European languages while there is no difficulty in finding cognates for the names of domestic livestock. This apparent dichotomy between what was seen as a primarily pastoral Indo-Iranian society and more mixed agricultural European economy was traditionally resolved in one of three different ways:

1. The Indo-European homeland might be set in Europe among settled agriculturists and the loss of terms for trees and many of the domestic plants in Indo-Iranian was seen as the result of the latter's movement on to the Steppe and a shift to a highly mobile pastoral economy where elements of the inherited vocabulary were no longer needed and subsequently discarded.
2. The Indo-European homeland was set somewhere either on the European or Asiatic steppe, north of Central Asia. A homeland on the steppe would account for the shared pastoral vocabulary of Indo-Iranians and the European stocks while the ancestors of the European languages were believed to have innovated as they moved westwards and encountered indigenous farming populations and new, more forested environments.
3. The homeland was broad enough that it snapped two ecological and economic zones: a western one of more of agriculture and another western one that was more pastoral. This was accomplished by including territories on both sides of the Dnieser/Dnieper line within the Indo-European homeland.

Mallory (1996: 239) has always found some sort of deficiency in the Asian homeland theory of the Indo-Europeans and has listed four faultlines or borders that notionally divide the Europeans and Asians of the Indo-European language family. However, he is of the opinion that "those lands lying east of the Urals, including Kazakhstan and Central Asia, are still pivotal in any thorough discussion of Indo-European origins or their solution" (Mallory, 1996: 249).

Gupta (1979, Vol. II, Appendix II) has given the summary of the views of Russian scholars on this problem presented at Dushanbe conference in 1977 and has concluded that the analysis of the Soviet scholars shows that archaeologically it cannot be proved that the Vedic Aryans came either from Dahistan-Kopet Dag region of Western Turkmenistan and Northern Iran, or from Tedjen-Murgab deltas of Southeast Turkmenistan or from the Oxus basin in southern parts of Uzbekistan and Tajikistan and northern parts of Afghanistan. He is further of the view that the

> distributional analysis of artefacts shows sporadic occurrence of Central Asian objects on the Indian borderlands and in the Indus basin but this phenomenon can at best be interpreted in terms of exchanges — in totality, none of the Central Asian protohistoric cultures could ever travel up to the Indo-Gangetic divide, the original home of the Vedic Aryans.

The search for homeland of the Indo-European languages in Central Asia began with the presumption that the Aryans entered India from the West via Iran and Afghanistan and that the hypothetical ancestors of the Iranians (Proto-Indo-Iranian) must have been living close to Iran, somewhere in Central Asia. Thus, some very clear Indo-Aryan forms were being interpreted as of Indo-Iranian origin. For instance, V.A. Livshitz in the Dushanbe (October, 1977) argued that Sanskrit is such an example. Even a Pahlavi version of Sanskrit *Panchatantra* was available by that time. Even J. Harmata, the great Indo-European scholar of Hungary, is also of the opinion that Indo-Aryan loanwords are to be found not only in Indo-Iranian texts but also in the Anatolian documents. Harmata has clearly mentioned the presence of Indo-Aryans in Mesopotamia in the third millennium BC. It is clear that the original home of the Indo-Iranians was India from where they moved to Western Asia via Iran and Central Asia.

The analysis of archaeological data merely shows presence of Indo-Aryans in the South Russian Steppes in 4000 BC and subsequently Igrar Aliyev and M.N. Pogrebova in their article have also accepted the existence of Indo-Aryans in the Steppes, having a similar theory of horse-breeding and chariots but they could not trace the route of migration. We find borrowed elements of Indo-Aryan outside India in various parts of Asia and Europe, viz. in Uralic languages, in Anatolian records, and in various Syrian and Palestinian documents. There are various Indo-Aryan personal names in the Tell-el-Amarna archives. Gypsies, who left India a few centuries before the Christian era, in third or fourth century BC, settled in different parts of Europe and Asia as is clear from the variations of gypsy languages found there. Oranskaja (1996: 185-96) has analysed at least 20 Indo-Aryan words in the secret languages of Central Asia. It will not be out of place to think that such a migration from India might have taken place in the Vedic period. Similarly, it may be assumed that in the Indo-Iranian stage also the Aryans had India as their original home, *airyanem vaejo*, i.e. India.

Since the Iranians present evidence of their migration from India to Iran, the Hittites present evidence that the Indo-Aryans were going to that area from India, and since the Finno-Ugarian contact with Indo-Aryans speaks of the movement of Vedic Aryans, it seems that the Indo-Aryans migrated from India to Western Asia through Iran and Central Asia.

It seems that the Aryans were autochthonous to the Sapta-Sindhu region, as it used to be called in the Vedic times, or at any rate, had been living in the country from time immemorial and had advanced to a high state of culture from the stage of nomadic hunters living by the chase, before the Rigvedic hymns were composed. Sapta-Sindhu included the beautiful valley of Kashmir in the north, and Gandhara and Bactria in the west. Reference to tools made of *asman* (stone) and *ayas* (copper) in the *Rigveda* (28 and 34 times, respectively) prove that Rigvedic culture has to be placed at least in Chalcolithic phase, if not earlier. The existence of Asiatic Mediterranean at the time when Rigvedic hymns were composed in the Sapta-Sindhu region precludes the possibility of "Central Asia having been the cradle of the Aryans before their alleged immigrations to the south and the west". Their immigration, therefore, from Central Asia, Northern Europe or Anatolia becomes very improbable (Das, 1980: xiii).

In conclusion, I would wish to say that:"the task of reconstructing the history of the ancient Aryans on the basis of researches made in Vedic Literature" is far easier as it reflects the

> real history of these people right from their initial struggles with nature for existence until they were able to speculate on and attempt satisfactory solutions of the highest problems of human life' (Das, 1980: x-xi).

REFERENCES

Adrados, F.R., 'The Archaic Structure of Hittite: The Crux of the Problem', *Journal of Indo-European Studies*, 10, 1990, pp. 1-35.

Allchin, B. and R. Allchin, *The Rise of Civilisation in India and Pakistan*, London, Cambridge University Press, 1982.

Anthony, D.W. and B. Wales, 'Review of C. Renfrew', *Archaeology and Language, Current Anthropology*, Vol. 29, 1988, pp. 441-4.

Arbois de Jubainville and Henri, D., *Les premiers habitants de I "Europe d'aprese ecrivains de l'antiquite et les travaux des linguists*, Paris, Thorin, 1889.

Asthana, Shashi, *History and Archaeology of India's Contacts with Other Countries from Earliest Times to 300 BC*, Delhi, B.R. Publishing Corporation, 1976.

Bagchi, P.C., *India and Central Asia*, Calcutta, Indian Council of Education, Bengal, 1955.

Banerjee, G.N., *Indian as Known to the Ancient World*, New Delhi, AES Reprint (First Published in 1921), 1990.

Bongard-Levin, *The Origin of Aryans*, Arnold-Heinemann, New Delhi, 1980.

Bopp, F., *Uber das Conjugations System der Sanskrit Sprache in Vergleichung mit jenem der griechischen lateinischen Sprache*, Frankfurt am Main, Andrea, 1816.

——, *Die Celtischen Sprachen in ihrem Verhaltnisse zum Sanskrit, Zend, Griechischen, Lateinschen, Germanischen*, Litanischen and Siawischen, Berlin, 1839.

Bosch-Gimpera, *El Problema Indoeuropeo*, Mexico, Direction General de Publications, 1960.

——, *Les Indo-Europeans*, Paris, Payot, 1961.

Brandenstein, W., *Die erste "Indogermanische"* Wanderung, Vienna, Gerold, 1936.

Buddha Prakash, *India and the World*, Hoshiarpur, Vishveshvaranand Vedic Research Institute, 1964.

Bynon, Theodra, *Historical Linguistics*, Cambridge, 1997.

Cardona, G. *et al.* (eds.), *Indo-European and Indo-Europeans*, University of Pennsylvania, Philadelphia, 1970.

Cavalli-Sforza, L.L., Alberto Piazza, Paolo Minozzi, and Joanna Mountain, 'Reconstruction of Human Evolution: Bringing Together Genetic, Archaeological and Linguistic Data', In *Proceedings of the National Academy of Sciences,* Vol. 85, 1988, pp. 6002-6.

Childe, V.G., 'On the Date and Origin of Minyan Ware', *Journal of Hellenic Studies,* Vol. 35, 1915, p. 196-207.

——, *The Aryans: A Study of Indo-European Origins,* London, Kegan Paul, Trench & Trubner, 1926.

——, *Prehistoric Migrations in Europe,* Oslo, Aschehoug, 1950.

——, *The Dawn of European Civilisation* (6th edition), London Routledge & Kegan Paul, 1957.

——, 'Retrospect', *Antiquity,* Vol. 32, 1958, pp. 69-74.

Crossland, R.A., 'Immigrants from the North', in Edwards, I.E.S., C.J. Gadd and N.G.L Hammond (eds.), *Cambridge Ancient History,* 1920, 1971, pp. 824-73, 989-93, Cambridge, Cambridge University Press, 3rd edition.

——, 'When Specialists Collide: Archaeology and Indo-European Linguistics, A Review Article', *Antiquity,* Vol. 66, No. 1992, 1992, pp. 251-54.

Das, A.C., *Rigvedic India,* Vol. I, New Delhi, Cosmo Publications, 1980.

Devoto, G., *Origin indeuropeo,* Florence, Institute Italiano di Preistoria e Protoistoria Italiana, 1962.

Dixon, R.M.W., *The Rise and Fall of Languages,* Cambridge University Press, Cambridge, 1997.

Dolgopolsky, Aron B., 'Gipoteza, drevenejsego rodstva jazykovyx semi severnoj Eutrasil s verojatnostnoj tochi zrenija', *Voprosy Jazykoznanija 2:53-63.* [English translation in Vitalij V. Shevoroshkin and Thomas L. Markey (eds.), *Typology Relationship and Time,* 1986; Ann Arbor Mich, 1964, pp. 27-50]

Feurestein, George *et al., The Search of the Cradle of Civilization,* Delhi, Motilal Banarsidass, 1999.

Finkelberge, M. 'Anatolian Languages and Indo-European Migrations to Greece', *Classical World,* Vol. 9, 1996, pp. 3-20.

Frawley, David, *Vedic Aryans and the Origins of Civilization: A Literary and Scientific Perspective,* St. Hyachinthe, Canada, 1994.

Freidrich, P., *Proto-Indo-European Trees,* Chicago, Chicago University Press, 1970.

Gaur, R.C., 'The Painted Grey Ware and the Aryan Problem', in *Ethnic Problem of the History of Central Asia in the Early Period,* ed, M.S. Asimov *et al.,* Moscow, Nouka, 1981, pp. 326-35.

Ghirshman, R., *L'Iran et la migration des Indo-Aryan et des Iranian,* Leiden, Brill, 1977.

Ghosh, A., *Encyclopedia of Indian Archaeology,* New Delhi, Munshiram Manoharlal, 1989.

Gimbutas, M., 'The Indo-Europeans, Archaeological Problems', *American Anthropologist* Vol. 65, 1963, pp. 815-36.

——, 'Proto-Indo-European Culture: The Kurgan Culture during the 5th to the 3rd Millenia BC', in G. Cardona *et al.* (eds.), *Indo-European and Indo Europeans,* Philadelphia, University of Pennsylvania Press, 1970, pp. 815-36.

Gimbutas, M., 'Old Europe c. 7000-3500 BC: The Earliest European Civilisation before the Infiltration of the Indo-European Peoples', *Journal of Indo-European Studies,* Vol. 1, 1973, p. 1-21.

Gimbutas, Marija, *The Language of the Goddess,* San Francisco, 1991.

Gonda, J., *Vedic Literature,* Wiesbaden, Germany, 1975.

Gramkrelidze, T.V. and V.V. Ivanov, *Indoevropeiski I Indoevropetisky rekonstruktysiya istorikitipologicheskii analiz protokul tury* (Indo-European and Indo-Europeans: a reconstruction and typological analysis of a proto-language and proto-culture), Tibilisi: Publishing House of the Tibilisi State University, 1984.

——, 'The Ancient Near East and the Indo-European Question: Temporal and Territorial Characteristics of Proto-Indo-European Based on Linguistics and Historic-Cultural Data', *Journal of Indo-European Studies,* Vol. 13, 1985a, pp. 3-48.

——, 'The Migration of Tribes Speaking the Indo-European Homeland in the Near East to their Historical Habitats in Eurasia', *Journal of Indo-European Studies,* Vol. 13, 1985b, pp. 49-91.

Greenberg, Joseph H., *Language in the Americans,* Stanford, Calif, 1987.

Gupta, Mohan (u.d.), *Nine Steps into the Antiquity* of *Vedas* (Unpublished work).

Gupta, S.P. *Archaeology of the Soviet Central Asia and the Indian Borderlands,* Delhi, B.R. Publishing Corporation, 1979.

Harris, A.C., 'Kartvelian Contacts with Indo-European', in T.L. Markey and I.A.C. Greppin (eds.), *When Worlds Collide,* Ann Arbor (MI) Karoma Publishers, 1990, pp. 57-100.

Hencken, H., *Indo-European Languages and Archaeology* (American Anthropologist Memoir 84), New York, American Anthropological Association, 1955.

Hood, S., 'An Aspect of the Slav Invasions of Greece in the Early Byzantine Period', *Acta Musei Nationalis Prague,* Vol. 201, No. 2, 1966, pp. 165-71.

Hrozny, B., 'Lentrainement des chevaux chez les anciensindo-europeans 'd' apres un texte Mitannien-Hittite provenant du 14 me siecle avant J.C.', *Archiv Orientalni,* Vol. 3, 1931, pp. 431-61.

Illich-Svitych, Vlaislav, 'Materily k sravnitel' nomu solvarju nostraticeskix jazykov", *Etimologija,* 1965 (Moscow), pp. 321-73 [English translation in Vitaly Shevoroshkin (ed.), *Reconstructing Languages and Cultures,* Bochum, Germany, 1967, pp. 125-76.

——, *Opyt sravnenija nostraticeskix jazykov,* 3 vols. Moscow, 1971-84.

Jones, Sir William, 'Third Anniversary Discource: On the Hindus', Reprinted in the *Collected Works of Sir William Jones* III, 1807, London, John Stockdale, 1786, pp. 23-46.

Kammenhuber, A., 'Das Hattische', in Spuler (ed.), 1969, pp. 428-546, 584-88.

Koppers, W., 'Die Indogermanenfrange in Licht der Vergleichenden Volkerkunde', Congres International des Science Anthropologiques et Ethnologiques, London, Royal Anthropological Institute, 1934, 185-87.

Krantz, Grover S., *Geographical Development of European Languages,* New York, Peter Lang Publishing, 1988.

Kaushik, D., *India and Central Asia in Modern Times,* New Delhi, Satvahan Prakashan, 1985.

Lal, B.B., *The Sarasvati Flows On: The Continuity of Indian Culture,* New Delhi, Aryan Books International, 2002.

Lal, B.B., 'The Indo-Aryan Hypothesis vis-à-vis Indian Archaeology', in *Ethnic Problem of the History of Central Asia in the Early Period*, ed., M.S. Asimov *et al.*, Moscow, Nauka, 1981, pp. 154-66.

Litvinsky, B.A., 'Problem Ethnicheskoy Istorii Srendney Azii Vol II tysyacheletii do n.e.', in *Ethnic Problem of the History of Central Asia in the Early Period*, ed. M.S. Asimov *et al.*, Moscow, Nauka, 1981, pp. 154-66.

Mallory, J.P. and D.Q. Adams (eds.), *Encyclopedia of Indo-European Culture*, London and Chicago, Fitzroy Dearborn Publishers, 1997.

Mallory, J.P., *In Search of the Indo-Europeans: Language, Archaeology and Myth*, New York, Thames & Hudson, 1991.

Mallory, J.P., 'The Indo-European Homeland: An Asian Perspective', in *Bullettin of the Deccan College Post-Graduate and Research Institute*, Vol. 54-55, 1994-95, pp. 237-54.

Mallory, J.P., 'The Indo-European Homeland: An Asian Perspective ', *Bulletin of the Deccan College Post-Graduate & Research Institute*, Vols. 54-55, 1996, pp. 237-54, Pune.

Markey, T.L. and J.A. Greppin, *When Worlds Collide: Indo-Europeans. The Bellagria Papers* (Linguistica Extranea, Studia 19). Ann Arbor, MI, Karona Publishers, 1990.

Masson, V.M. and V.I. Sarianidi, *Central Asia Turkmenia before the Achaemenids*, London, Thames and Hudson, 1972.

Misra, S.S., *The Aryan Problem: A Linguistic Approach*, Delhi, Munshiram Manoharlal Publishers (P) Ltd, 1992.

Müller, Max, *Collected Works*, Vol. X, *The Home of the Aryas*, 1888.

Nehring, Alfons, 'Student zur Indogermanischen Kulher and Urheimat', *Die Indogermanen-und Germanefrage: nena Wage zu ihrer losung*, W. Koppers (ed.), Saleburg and Leipzig, 1936, pp. 7-229.

Oranskaja, T.I., 'Indo-Aryan Words in Secret Languages of Central Asia', *Bulletin of the Deccan College Post-Graduate & Research Institute*, Vols. 54-55, 1996, pp. 185-196, Pune.

Pictet, A., *Les origines Indo-Europeans*, Paris, Sandoz et Fisch-baker, 1877.

Ragozin, Z.A., *Vedic India*, Delhi, Munshiram Manoharlal, 1961.

Rajaram, N.S. and David Frawley, *Vedic Aryans and the Origins of Civilization: A Literary and Scientific Perspective*, St. Hacinthe, Canada, 1964.

Ratnagar, Shereen, *Encounters: The Westerly Trade of the Harappan Civilization*, Delhi, Oxford University Press, 1981.

Renfrew, Lord Colin, *Archaeology and Language: The Puzzle of Indo-European Origins*, Cambridge University Press, New York, 1987.

Renfrew, C., 'Review of C. Renefrew, 1987, Author's Precis', *Current Anthropology*, Vol. 29, 1988, pp. 437-41.

——, 'Time Depth, Convergence Theory and Innovation in Proto-Indo-European "Old Europe" as a PIE Area', *The Journal of Indo-European Studies*, Vol. 27, Nos. 3-4, 1999, 1999, pp. 258-91.

Ruhlen, Merit, *On the Origin of Languages: Studies in Linguistic Taxonomy*, Stanford University Press, California, 1994.

Sankrityayana, Rahul, *History of Central Asia*, New Delhi, New Age Publishers Private Ltd., 1964.

Sehchetenko, Y.A., 'Yuzhno-Turkmenskiye Paralleli la Harappskoi Kulture', in *Problemy Arkheologii Srednei*, Aziiz, Leningrad, 1968.

Schlegel, F. Von, *The Aesthetic and Miscellaneous Works of Friedrich von Schlegel*, London-Bonn, *Portraits of linguistics-l.Bloomington* (IN): Indiana University Press, 1849.

Schmidt, W., 'Die Herkunft der Indogermanen und ihr erstes Auftreten in Europa', Kosmos 45, 116-18 and 159-60 (reprinted in A. Scherer (ed.), *Die Urheimat der Indogermanen*, Darmstadt Wissenschaftliche Buchgesellschaft, 1949, pp. 312-23).

Sethna, K.D., *The Problem of Aryan Origins*, Delhi, Aditya Prakashan, 1849.

Spuler, B. (ed.), *Handbuch der Orientalistika* ![9 ii01/II(2)], *Altkleinasiatische Sprachen*, Leiden, E.J. Brill, 1969.

Swadesh, Morris, 'Perspectives and Problems of American Comparative Linguistics', *World*, 10, 1954, pp. 306-32.

Tripathi, D.N., 'New Archaeology and Vedic Cosmogony', *Man and Environment*, Vol. XXV, No. 1, 2000, pp. 1-13.

Tripathi, D.N., *Archaeology and Tradition*, Ramanand Prakashan, New Delhi, 1988.

Trombetti, Alfredo, L'unita d Oriegine languggio Bologna, 1905.

Tull, H.W., *The Vedic Origin of Karma: Cosmos as Man in Ancient Myth and Ritual*, Albany, 1989.

Untermann, J., 'Ursprache und historiche Realitat. Der Beitrag der Indogermanistik zu Fragen der Ethnogenese', in *Studien zur Ethnologenese*. (Abhandlung der Rheinisch-Wastfalischen Akademie der Wissenschaften, 72). Opladen: Westdeutscher Verlag, 1985, 133-64.

Verma, Vishnu Kant, *Indo-Aryan Colonisation of Greece and Middle East* (2 vols.), Delhi, Pratibha Prakashan, 2001.

Whitney, W. Dwight, *Language and the Study of Language*, New York, 1867.

Winters, F.A., 'A Historically Derived Model for the Dorian Invasion', in E.N. Davies (ed.), *Symposium on the Dark Ages in Greece*, New York, Archaeological Institute of America and Hunter College, 1977.

Young, Thomas, 'Mithradates, Oder Allgemeine Sprachekunde', *The Qurterly Review*, 10, 1813, pp. 250-92.

Zvelebil, M. and K.V. Zvelebil, 'Agricultural-transition, Indo-European Origins, and the Spread of Infarming, in T.L.Markey and J.A.C. Greppin (eds.), *When Worlds Collide: The Bellagio Papers*, Ann Arbor (MI), Karoma Publishers, 1990, pp. 273-86.

Zvelebil, M., 'Indo-European Origins and Agricultural Transition in Europe', *Journal of Indo-European Archaeology*, Vol. 3, 1995, pp. 33-70.

3

South Asia, Central Asia and South Russia: The Saka Connection

A.K. Narain

For the purpose of this chapter, 'India' means 'South Asia', 'Russia' does not mean 'USSR' and 'Central Asia' does not mean 'USSR'. Central Asia is the loose geographical term inclusive of several states of the former USSR as well as certain parts of the Peoples Republic of China. Once the spatial definition is clear, hopefully we may agree that while the contacts between South Asia and Central Asia go much beyond three millennia, it is difficult to cross this limit if we include Russia. To be more precise, I think we cannot go beyond the seventh-eighth centuries BC and the earliest contacts are related to the movements of the Sakas or the Scythians, the names by which they were known in the Eastern and Western world, respectively. This chapter deals with only the first of the three millennia and takes into account the role of other contiguous regions too, like Iran and China.

THE CIMMERIANS: A SCYTHIAN STOCK

Many scholars in the fields of Indo-European linguistics and antiquities tend now to look at South Russia either as the homeland of the Iranian-speaking peoples, or as the secondary centre of their migrations, and an increasing number of scholars now consider the Cimmerians as one of the Iranian-speaking peoples. In the most extreme form, this opinion is expressed by Diakonow, who considered the Cimmerians not as a distinct non-Scythian population of South Russia which preceded the Scythians there, but only "an individual tribal group within the vast Scythian ethions". Khazanov, who finds this opinion cautious and acceptable, thinks that,

> ... the Scythian invasion from Asia in the eighth century BC was apparently not the first appearance of the Iranian element in Europe, but only one of the movements of Northern Iranian nomadic tribes. Such movements repeatedly also took place later on. However, they did not result in drastic changes of population, but only in permutations, and regrouping of the kindred Iranian tribes on vast territories they had occupied since older times.

But when Khazanov distinguished between 'the Scythian incomers (*sic*)' and 'the indigenous Cimmerian population', he seems to confuse the issue again. It is true that archaeology does not provide a clear solution and it has its own limitations. The same language and material culture can be adopted by diverse ethnic groups. Sometimes silence means affirmation, and not negation. If the circumstantial evidence of the written sources are supported by linguistic analysis, the non-commitment of the archaeological evidence may be ignored and benefit of doubt given to the conclusion arrived at. In the case of the Cimmerians and the Scythians, I do not see any difficulty in taking them as part of same ethos. They only moved, one after another, from the east to the west pattern, quite familiar to the historians of Central Asia. Since both the Cimmerians and the Scythians belonged to the same broad ethno-cultural milieu, it is difficult to distinguish their identities in material culture as known from archaeology.

M.A. Dandamaev refers to a Cimmerian, Sakketta in an Achaemenid inscription. This name itself may possibly be connected with the ethnic name *Saka* with suffix *ita*, known from other old Iranian proper names. It is also known that in the Elamite version of the Achaemenian inscription, the Persian *Saka* is rendered as *Sakka*. Saka as an Iranian proper name is testified by Elamite economic documents of the sixth to fifth centuries BC from Persepolis.

Thus, the ethnonym Saka was no doubt known from the earliest times and it was known to all those who belonged in the Indo-European-speaking peoples. Some, of course, had their own alternative names for these alien people, i.e. Scythian or the earlier Iskuza and its variants. The Chinese are the only exception, for they stuck to these peoples' self-designation alone. The name Scythian was no doubt derived from Iskuza, which emphasises the equestrian, or the character of swift mobility of the people, rather than from the myth of the Scythes, which was perhaps a later creation by Greeks.

It is not wholly correct that in modern scholarly literature the denomination 'Scythian' is, as a rule applied to the ancient inhabitants of the northern coastal region of the Black Sea, and the Scythians of Central Asia are called Sakas. There are examples to show that this rule was followed in neither ancient times nor is being followed in modern times. The Sakas planted a colony named after them in Armenia, another in South Afghanistan, and perhaps the third and fourth in the valleys of the Sita and the Indus rivers. However, because of the continuity of usage, both the autonym and heteronym may be alternatively applied to the whole people from the east to the west, and from the north to the south, in the generic sense. This should include not only the earliest known among them, the Cimmerians, but also the ones like the Sarmatians in the West and the later Sakas in South Asia and Khotan. The temporal and spatial world of the Sakas was indeed vast.

But in terms of their internal geo-cultural distribution, the threefold division of the early Sakas made by the Persians seems reasonable. Roughly, the Paradraya would correspond with the 'Western', the Tigraxauda with the 'Central' and Haumavarga with the 'Eastern' of them. The various individual units, sometimes specifically named, and sometimes not, through the time and space of history, may be assigned to these three categories depending upon the evidence of their nature and area of activities. For example, if the Cimmerians, the 'Scythians' of the Black Sea, and the Sarmatians among others, may belong to the first group; the Massagetai, the Dahae, the Sacaraulei/Sacaraucae, or the 'Cis-Imuas Scythians' (of Ptolemy), may belong to the second; and the Indo-Aryan '*haoma* (*soma*) revering Sakas' of the Vedas, the 'Trans-Imuas Scythians' (of Ptolemy), the Sakas of the Altai, the Sai-Wang of the Ili basin, and the Sakas of Khotan and ancient India would fall in the third group. This list is neither exhaustive nor sequential; some of them were separated from their groups by long gaps of time and cultural change. But the linguistic links survived. At times their mobility, adventures and intersections produced mixed nation like that of the Scytho-Parthians, the Pahlavas of the Indian sources.

It is difficult to separate the question of the primary homeland of the Sakas from the problem of the *urheimat* of the Indo-Europeans, which has remained a will-o'-the-wisp for almost two centuries now. It is outside the scope of our presentation to go into the whole issue. But a summary of my present understanding of it, so far as it bears on the Sakas, may not be out of place here.

I do not believe in one, the so-called Aryan race, or any one 'ancestor' people, who spoke the parent language now known as the Indo-European, having an 'original' homeland. I believe that languages have been, and can be, adopted by people of heterogeneous ethnic origins and therefore it is absolutely unsafe to argue from language to race. But this does not mean that there are no linguistic families, and ethnic groups speaking the same or related languages, inherited or borrowed. Credit is due to the comparative philologists for their significant discovery of language relations, and of linguistic families such as the 'Indo-European'. If the broad, even though dated, classification of the Indo-European languages into Centum and Satem is acceptable, the Sakas belong linguistically to the Satem group, also known as Indo-Iranian or more narrowly for some as Iranian. For this reason, they are often referred to as 'Iranians' in modern scholarship which is as misleading as the term 'Aryan'. The fact that they spoke a language related to the Iranian subgroup of the Satem, does not mean that they were 'Iranians' ethnically or even culturally. On the contrary, the Sakas formed distinctly generic groups by themselves which included, through time and space, bound by related ethno-cultural and linguistic features. These were indeed a great people but unfortunately they did not write their own history.

From the recorded history of the sedentary civilisation of Asia and their relations with the West, it is evident that by the eighth-seventh centuries BC the Sakas were already inhabiting a vast territory of the Eurasian Steppes. In the extreme west, they were north of the Black Sea and the Caucasus. In the extreme east they were around the Issyk-kul lake and in the north the Tien Shan, extending even further northeastward towards the Altai. It is difficult to imagine that this expanded geography constituted the primary homeland of the Sakas from the beginning. But it is obvious that the vast majority of the Saka peoples lived in the Asian Steppes. The question is whether they lived mostly in the easterly parts of Central Asia, closer to the Chinese and Mongolian borders, or in the westerly areas of it. The most westerly Sakas, that is, the Cimmerians, were also the earliest known of them. There is no clear evidence to indicate that they were autochthonous in the areas north of the Black Sea. *If they came there from outside*, certainly they did not come from the west or even from further north of it. In fact, the 'Scythian' connection points that they had moved into the region from the East with 'other Scythians' following them. This is in keeping with the general trend of transhumance in Eurasian antiquity. The persistence of the Chinese sources and the material remains of Pazyryk burials no doubt provide pointers to more easterly contraction of the Central Asian home of the Sakas. It is not easy to fix their precise boundaries but most likely it lay north of the Jaxartes and east of the Aral Sea, and west from a line which may be drawn from the lake Issyk-kul and Western Tien-shan toward the Pamirs in the south and to the Altai in the northeast.

It is from this primary homeland, we surmise, that the various units of the Sakas moved out westward and southward and became known by various names in different times and different regions. Their movements started in the second millennium BC on account of either ecological and economic factors or inter-ethnic polity. The historical scenario of one pushing the other in Central Asia is too well known to be retold.

Perhaps the first to move out were the Cimmerians. They were forced to do so by the movements of 'first' Indo-Europeans, i.e. the speakers of one Centum group of languages. The Cimmerians found their secondary home ultimately north of the Black Sea. The 'Scythians' of Herodotus followed. By the beginning of the first millennium BC they had already spread out westward between the Caspian and Aral Sea and had reached north of the Caucasus. These 'Scythians', the Scoloti clans of them pushed the Cimmerians out of their secondary home where they had by then lived for a couple of centuries and had mixed with the natives, to find new territories in West Asia. But the

'Scythians' followed them there too. By the sixth century BC more Saka tribes were moving to the west and southwest; among them were the Massagetae, Dahae, and other groups noted in the Western as well as Old Persian sources. By this time they were known sufficiently well to identify them into the three major groups, the Paradray, the Tigraxauda and the Haumavarga. Some of the Sakas had stayed not only long enough in America to name a territory there, Sacasene, but some fought the Greeks on behalf of the Persians.

The archaeology and early history of the Sakas are still matters of discovery and discussion. But the outlines of our knowledge so far seem to confirm the indications outlined above. Analysis of the archaeological complex in the Asian Steppes shows that the territories of the Pamirs, the Tien-shan and that of the Altai possess all the features demanded for the first of the Sakas. Most scholars would agree about the continuity of the essential elements of the Scythian culture and their physical types, through the various phases of archaeological periodisation from Afanasievo to Karasuk in Central Asia. The material remains, and the artistic location in an area from where contacts with China and Mongolia on the one hand and Western and Southern Asia on the other could become more feasible, shows that there is actually no evidence for their coming into the area from outside. Attempts to separate the Cimmerians from the 'Scythians' and treat them as indigenous to South Russia, formatting part of the 'Srubnaja culture' or link them with the Thracians, are based more on presuppositions than on facts.

From their secondary home in the north of the Black Sea, the Cimmerians first made their way through the Caucasus into Asia Minor because they were forced to do so by the other Saka groups, the 'Scythians' of Herodotus. About 714 BC the Cimmerians, known also as Gimirrai and Gomer, invaded the Armenian highlands. Perhaps Sargon II of Assyria was the first historical figure of the West to have marched out against them in 705 BC but met a soldier's death in battle. His son and successor Sennacherib stabilised the frontier, and the Cimmerian hordes moved westward to burn and sack the western Phrygian capital of Gordium, which resulted in the death of Midas in 696 BC. During the reign of Esarhaddon (680–669) and Ashurbanipal (665–627), the Cimmerians again posed a great threat to Assyria. They had to be either won over or bought off. Esarhaddon defeated a Cimmerian army but the latter allied with the Medes and the Mannaeans and proved threat to the existence of the expanding Uratu and Assyrians alike. And by the beginning of the seventh century BC the 'Scythians' (known as Iskuza in the Assyrian sources) followed on the heels of the Cimmerians and had entered West Asia. Under the leadership of Ishpaka, they allied with Uratu and Mannai, and were settled in the south of lake Urmia, and were raiding as far as Zamua. By skilful diplomacy they were detached from the Medes to the Assyrian side. Their king Bartatua, the same as Protothyes of Herodotus, was offered Esarhaddon's daughter in marriage and substantial largesses. When Kashtaritu attacked Ninevah in 653, Madyas, the son of Bartatua, led his horde to the rescue of Ashurbanipal who was now his kinsman.

Kashtaritu's army was routed and he was killed. The 'Scythians' then attacked Media itself and established their own state which lasted for twenty-eight years, till 625 BC, and around 630 BC the 'Scythians' had penetrated into Cappadocia and defeated the Cimmerians. It seems the Cimmerian chief Dugdamme (Tugadmme) for a time claimed overlordship over all the Saka tribes, including the one represented by Bartatua and his son Madyas. About 639 BC, after Dugadamme, a new leader, Sandaksatru, had succeeded. After a few decades, the Cimmerians and the 'Scythians', and perhaps other Saka units, participated in the final destruction of the Assyrian empire. According to Herodotus, the 'Scythians' directed a destructive expedition against Syria at the end of the seventh century BC and advanced as far as the borders of Egypt. Pharoah Psammetichus I went to meet the 'Scythians' and with the help of gifts, succeeded in persuading them to abstain from penetrating into his country. After the fall of Assyria and their own domination of Northwestern Iran, these early groups of the Sakas, the Cimmerians, and the 'Scythians' became part of the West Asian body politic, changing alliances and fighting for one or the other of rival powers. It is suggested that since they had left their women behind, it is not surprising that most of them gradually merged with local elements in West Asia and Iran and earned notoriety as soldiers; but perhaps some among the ruling clans continued to hold on in Cappadocia for the domination of which the Lydians and the Medes fought in 585 BC.

THE ACHAEMENID ENCOUNTER WITH SAKA ETHNIC GROUPS

The next noteworthy phase of Saka encounter in history is related to the Achaemenids. After his conquest of Lydia, Cyrus turned his attention to the east to subdue the Sakas. No one disputes the successes of Cyrus in Central Asia but it is difficult to determine which group of the Sakas he fought against. According to Herodotus, they were the Massagetae beyond the river Araxes but Ctesias calls them the Daae. Whoever they may be, they seem to be located east of the Caspian and Aral seas and were obviously controlling territories in Jaxartes Valley. Anyway, one of the engagements of Cyrus against these Sakas proved to be the last one of his life, for he died in the battle in 530 BC. It is interesting to learn from Herodotus that the Sakas were led by a queen named Tomyris. Ctesias' story involves a Saka king Amorges or Homarges, who was allied to Cyrus and who even avenged Cyrus' death by defeating the enemies. No doubt, the Sakas continued to be restive in the decade that followed Cyrus' death. So the first expedition of Darius after his accession wars was against the Sakas again in 519 BC. Of the three groups of the Sakas referred to in the inscriptions, Darius' campaigns were most probably directed against only two of them, the Tigraxauda (the pointed-cap) and the Paradraya (beyond the sea). The third, the Haumavarga (the *soma*-revering) were perhaps friendly, or at least not a source of danger to him. Whether or not Darius marched against the 'Scythians' of South Russia depends upon whether or not the Paradraya Sakas were situated there. No one doubts Darius' victory over the Tigraxauda Sakas so vividly attested by the representation of the Saka chief Skunkha with his high-pointed cap carved at the end of the line of 'false kings' on the relief at Behistun. But the text of the Behistun inscription seems to involve other Sakas also.

The text apparently means that the Tigraxauda (the pointed-cap) group of the Sakas avoided fighting and retreated from him, which is known to have been one of the fighting strategies used by them; and the Sakas who were smitten mightily by him were perhaps the Paradraya ones, who could be from among those who were beyond the Caspian, or even those who were north of the Black Sea. If the evidence of Herodotus about Darius' campaign in 519 BC, of the *Naqsh-I-Rustam* inscription where the 'Saka' who were across the sea are mentioned as subjects, and that of the fragmentary clay tablet from Gherla in Rumania are taken together, the possibility of Darius' expedition in South Russia cannot be ruled out. Retrospectively it would also imply that the 'Scythians' of South Russia had already been part of Achaemenid empire under Cambyses and Cyrus. We may then also think of at least two campaigns by Darius, if not more, against the Sakas. Xerxes added the name of Daha (Daae) also in the list of provinces. The army of Xerxes included the Sacae, who are Scythians, and had on their head tall caps, erect and stiff and tapering to a point; they wore breeches, and carried their native bows and daggers, and axes withal, which they call 'sagaris'. The Persian army at Gaugamela facing Alexander also included one thousand mailed Sakas in cataphracts. But the Sakas were so numerous in the Steppes and ever so vigorous, and more often than not under such pressure that they could never be wholly vanquished, nor contained in their own habitats. If one unit of them was taken care of, either in war or in peace, there were always others to take their place.

When the Achaemenids refer to Saka Paradraya, the Saka Tigraxauda and the Saka Haumavarga, they classify the Sakas into three major groups based on their geographical location and distinctive cultural features or style. These are not the same for all individual tribes of them. Each of these three groups included several ethnic units. The two components of the classification terminology indicate on the one hand their Saka unity and on the other their distinctions. In this straightforward group classification, the first included those who lived beyond, or by, 'sea', 'lake', or 'river' or even 'swamp'. The second included those who were distinguished by their use of pointed headgear, and the third, those who were known for their ritual drinking or revering of *haoma* or *soma*. In my view, the first included the westerly Saka ethnic units extending from the Caspian Sea to the Black Sea regions. These were the 'Scythians' who figure in the context of European or 'Western' antiquity. The second group included the Saka ethnic units located in the north of the Oxus and Jaxartes Rivers, in the central parts of Central Asia. The latter were the ones who mattered in the Western and Persian history. The third were the easterly Saka ethnic units located in their original homeland in the Altai-Tien-shan in the north, in the Semirechye, who moved to the Pamirs in the south. No doubt, the various units of the Sakas, who were known for their mobility, interacted through time and space in their history and underwent changes in their culture and style.

THE SAKA HAUMAVARGA AND THE VEDIC CONNECTION

The third group included the Haumavarga of the Old Persian inscription. In spite of other disagreements, it is generally accepted that they were the most easterly ones. I would also go with Herrmann that they were the 'real' Sakas, 'die richtigun Saka'. For I believe the original nuclear homeland of the Sakas as a whole was in the eastern parts and 'not' in the western parts of Central Asia. But whether or not they were the Amyrgioi surely needs examination. This issue is linked with the whole confusion in the Western sources and their interpretation, which are both linguistic and cultural.

Just as Saka Paradraya and Saka Tigraxauda are not the names of individual ethnic units of the Sakas but of the groups of them, so also the Saka Haumavarga was 'not' the name of an 'individual' tribe but that or a 'group' of them, distinguished by their geographical location and cultural features or styles. Of course, it would be unrealistic to think that the Persian classification into three groups exhausted all the Sakas. These must be major groups they came to know of. So far as the Greeks were concerned, they divided them into two — the 'European' Scythian and the 'Asian' Sacae — but with some ambivalence, which was due to the ever-shifting movements of the Sakas and the fact that they all originally came from Asia. The Egyptians too divided them into two, those of the 'marshes' and those of the 'plains'. The Persian classification may not be complete, or all-inclusive, but the Greek one was incorrect and misleading. In any case, any attempt to identify the Paradraya, Tigraxauda and Haumavarga Sakas, each with one particular Saka tribe known from the Western sources, is bound to be futile. It is also not possible to identify all the individual units, which were included in the three categories mentioned by the Persians. But just as the 'pointed-cap' feature of the Tigraxauda cannot deny their existence, the attribute of the Saka Haumavarga cannot be ignored.

For the identity of the Haumavarga we must return to the Iranian sources, which gave us the name. There is no doubt in respect of the ritual drinking, or revering, of *haoma* or *soma*, by these Sakas. Offering of *hoama* was evidently of great importance in pagan Iran. So was the offering of *soma* of Vedic religion.

Together with animal and human sacrifices, it played an integral role in the development of their ideology and culture. There is ample evidence to indicate a link between the pre-Zoroastrian *Daeva* worship of the pagan Iranians and the Vedic religious beliefs and rituals. It is also well known that the dichotomy of *daiva* and *asura* ended up having different meanings in Indian and Iranian contexts. Detailed studies of related problems have been made by competent scholars of comparative philology and religion. In spite of differences on points, which are not relevant to our discussion, one can notice a general agreement on this vital Indo-Iranian linkage. The comparisons in Indo-Iranian history go further. Just as Zoroaster introduced reforms, the *daeva*-worshippers and *hoama*-drinkers were refused of *sura, meraya,* and *majja*. Without going further into these topics of vast proportion, it is fair to assume that before Zoroaster a considerable period must have elapsed since the coming of these people in the eastern parts of Iran and northwestern parts of India who revered *haoma* or *soma*. The date of Zoroaster is no doubt controversial, but responsibe scholars have begun dating him much before 600 BC, even half a millennium earlier. There is linguistic closeness between the *Rigveda* and the *Gathas*. There is every probability thus to find the *hoama* veneration (and drinking) people in the region about the beginning of the first millennium BC. They can be no other than the Haumavarga Sakas. Just as the use of the word 'Aryan' has given rise to many unnecessary problems and identities of distinct ethnic groups speaking one or the other sub-group of Iranian languages in the 'Satem' category of the Indo-European, I think 'Iranian' as an ethic group, if there was any, must be separated from other ethnic groups even if they spoke related languages. These Haumavarga Sakas were probably one among the proto-Indo-Aryans, whose *devas* were regarded as evil by Zoroaster, and who migrated to India and came to be known as the Indo-Aryans. This migration marked the separation of the *s*-peoples (the Vedic) from the *h*-people (the later Iranians) as postulated by Gray. The Avestan evidence concerning the proto-Indo-Aryans in eastern Indo-Afghan borderlands does not in any way deny the presence of their kindred people in Western Asia. The geographical horizons of the *Avesta* and that of the *Rigveda* are limited but those of the Sakas are not. And then, they were only one of the several interrelated ethnic groups of people who spoke various languages in the 'Satem' (or the 'Iranian') category. There is thus no doubt that already in the first half of the first millennium BC these Sakas in the Indo-Afghan borderlands were extending towards the Pamirs. Certainly, they were neither the Saka Paradraya nor the Saka Tigraxauda. They can only be the Saka Haumavarga.

The presence of these *soma*-drinking Sakas in the areas mentioned above and their infiltration gradually into the Indus River basin is amply vouchsafed by linguistic, literary, and archaeological evidence. But before we examine this corpus of evidence, let us examine the *soma* context of these Sakas further.

THE SOMA CONTEXT

In spite of intensive research, the identification of the plant is still eluding. Wasson thought that it was a variety of mushroom, the fly-agaric, *Amantia muscarita*, and hallucinogenic mushroom, that until recent times has been the centre of the shamanic performance in Central Asia. While some agree with Wasson there are others who identify it with rhubarb. But, be that as it may, even if the particular species of the plant cannot exactly be identified, there are certain indications about it which are relevant for our discussion. One of them is that both the Vedic and Avestic sources state that the *soma* grew in the mountains. Mount Muajavant was specially renowned for this. In the *Rigveda*, *soma* is described as Maujavanta, 'coming from the Mujvant' (X.34.1) or as Yaska takes it, 'from Mount Mujavant'. The Indian commentators agree with Yaska in taking Mujavant as the name of mountain. Zimmer thought that this was one of the lower hills on the south-west of Kashmir. In the post-Rigvedic and later period, the Brahmans of India no longer possessed the *soma*, and because it did not grow in their lands, they used a substitute. Gradually, it became a distant thing, and the mountains and the people who lived there also became distant. In *Atharvaveda*, Mujavant is the name of people who, along with the Mahaviras, the Gandharis and the Balhikas, are mentioned as dwelling far away and to whom fever is to be banished. So also in the *Yajurveda Samhitas*, the Munjavants are chosen as a type of distant folk beyond which Rudra with his bow is entreated to depart. But Munjavant occurs repeatedly as the name of a mountain in the Himalayas as late as in the *Mahabharata* (X.785; XIV.180). The association of the Munjavant people with those of Gandhara and Bactria is significant. So also is the visualisation of Rudra with bow, a distinct Saka feature for the time. It is clear that while some of the Sakas, along with other 'Satem' language-speaking groups, spread further southward and eastward, the hard-core *soma*-drinking Sakas, the Haumavargas, remained behind in their mountain fastnesses. This is why they were mentioned in the post-Vedic literature down to the epics as a distinct and distant ethnic group of people with disdain. When a new wave of Saka movement brought them closer to the heartland of India from the second century BC, the Puranas became alarmed and showered hatred for them as Mlecchas. But it is significant that references in the *Rigveda* to them were more positive. H.W. Bailey has drawn our attention to the Rigvedic expression *su-Sakan* in the sense of 'powerful' of 'skilful' men. Similarly, the word for chart, *Sakata* or *Sakati*, which may mean 'purified by cow dung', is thought to be the name of prince (RV, X.132.5). *Sakadhuma* might refer to their suffimentum practices.

Returning to Mujavanta (Mujavant), whether mountain or people, linguistic researches of Morgenstierne in respect of the Munjan become relevant. This is at present the name of the upper part of the Kokcha Valley, a district which formerly extended towards the northwest, right up to the neighbourhood of Khanabad and Talikan. From some place-names it is also indicated that the Munji was a language once spoken even further north than is the case at present. The inhabitants call the district Munj'iroi. Xaun Zhang perhaps referred to them in the seventh century as Mung-Kein (Mun-gun). Morgenstierne state,

> of greater interest is the name for Munjan used in Yidgha, an Iranian dialect spoken in the Lutkoh Valley of Chitral, and very closely related to Munji. There Munjan is called *Bre ye yogo (Brayeyo, Bra, Yayo)*, a word which has the appearance of being native to Yidgha, and very possible one used by the Munji themselves.

It is interesting to note that *som samd* in Yidgha and Munji mean 'to drink'. Morgenstierne goes on to examine the relationship of various dialects in the region and concludes that "in any case it is probable that *Bre'ye yo*, too, contains an original-t- and the original form would be something like *Margata*". He then states that 'the genuine Kati name of Munjan is Mrugul', and that in several Iranian dialects of the Hindukush and Pamir *r n* results in *n*, and a development *Mrg->Murng->mung* does not seem impossible. Bailey and Grantovsky believe that *Bra yo*, the Yidgha name of Munja is linked with *munj*, one of the species of *soma* (*haoma*). Litvinsky agrees in locating the Haumavarga in the region anyway.

Morgenstierne's researches confirm the location of the mountain, and the people, known as Munjvant in the Vedic and epic sources of India, in the environs of Munjan. The mountains in the area must have been among those where *soma* grew and the people, who lived in its valleys known for its grass or meadow, were of Saka origin. Some scholars connect Haumavarga-Amyrgioi with Murghab River in Southeastern Turkmenistan and they took for the Amyrgian Valley in that region. But Bernshtam pointed out another Murghab River in Eastern Pamir. Its etymology is popularly derived from Margob, which form of word is found in Eastern Pamir, and the people there still call it not only Murghab but also Margob. The word *marg* in the medieval and contemporary Tadjik dictionaries means 'fresh grass' used for fodder for animals and also 'a field', or a 'lawn'. Linguistically, this whole region, which included Wakhan, Chitral, Swat, Dardistan and Baltistan, is known to have been Saka.

The association of the Munjavant with Gandhara reminds of the Hecataeus' references, which placed the Scythians along-side Gandhara in his time. Hecataeus was probably using the term 'Scythian' in the general sense and before it got mixed up leading of the dichotomy of 'Saka' and 'Scythians. One may also recall here the inclusion of Byltai, along the Imaon, in the land of Sacae, by Ptolemy.

Archaeological discoveries appear to confirm our historical analysis. The excavations of graves at Butkara II, Katelai I, Loebanr I, Butkara, Barama, Timargarh and Balambat in Swat and other sites in the Karakorum have brought to light a material culture and other elements relevant to our discussion. Although these graves have been called 'Pre-Buddhist' and the culture as 'Gandhara Grave Culture' (which we prefer to name it as Swat or Uddiyana Grave Culture). This is characterised by (i) three distinct types of burial practices: inflexed articulated inhumation, post-cremation urn burial, and fractional I, II and III, (ii) two classes of pottery, red ware and grey ware, (iii) use of copper-bronze period I and II and iron in period III, (iv) knowledge of horse-breeding and related items, and (v) social, economic and religious features, highlighting a tribal federalism, pastoral mobility and limited agriculture, ritual drinking, etc. On the basis of comparative study, the three periods have been dated as sixteenth-thirteenth century BC, twelfth-tenth century BC, and ninth-sixth century BC, respectively. The skeletal material from these graves indicated the presence of Eurodolichomorph or Proto-Europoid type of people in Period I and the Leptodolichomorph or the Mediterranean type in Period III. Mongolian strain has been traced in two skulls and another element termed as 'Veddoid' has been noted in three skulls.

The evidence represents at least two waves of movements of the plain Grey Ware-using people into the region, the first associated with copper or bronze in about the middle of the second millennium BC and the second with iron in the beginning of the first. They may be identified as Indo-Aryans, authors of the Vedic period, and two waves may be explained by the use of the word *ayas* (= copper) in *Rigveda* and those of the word, distinguishing *tamra-ayas* (= copper) and *Krishna-ayas* (= iron) in the later Vedic literature. It is significant that outside Swat, going southwards at Gumla in the district of Dera Ismail Khan, while the remains of this culture have been recognised in the deposits of Period V, the preceding Period IV represented the Harappan occupation brought to a violent destruction.

Archaeologists have found in this culture "a good candidate for identification with Rigvedic Aryan". There is no doubt that the three periods of this culture represent more than one ethnic group and more than one wave of movement. There is also evidence to suggest that the people of Period III destroyed the earlier populace, whose graves they disturbed by robbing the stones and, as though sacrilegiously, built their own houses atop. B.K. Thapar has observed:

> We have yet to be convinced if a second wave of people of the same stock would behave in the aforesaid manner. The identification of both the groups — the proto-Europoid of Period I and II having massive and rugged bony skull with Aryans, therefore seems to be presumptuous or on the analogy of the Scythian-Sarmatian series, we have to conceive of a nomadising Indo-Aryan people penetrating the region and destroying the settlement of their kinsfolk who had arrived earlier.

Surely I would agree with the latter part of Thapar's statement.

In spite of the limitations of the available material, certain features of the Swat Grave Culture and related information about the region from other sources are sufficient pointers to the Saka presence and their recognised participation in the early phases of Vedic society and rituals. The co-existence of the different types of burials in Swat was not unknown to Vedic literature. The peculiar attachment of the Sakas to horse is not only attested by the survival of the toponymy and tribal names in the area, such as Aspasioi, Assaka, Assakenoi, etc., but also by a list of archaeological discoveries related to horse. They are for example: (i) skeletons of horses near the tombs of Katelai, (ii) horse figurines in Katelai, (iii) handle of the cover of a funerary urn decorated with horse-head from Loebanr, (iv) bronze cauldron with handles and projection representing a horse-head found in Gilgit, and (v) the petroglyphs of Gogdara depiciting horse-drawn carts (The *Sakata* of the *Rigveda*).

Tucci observed that "the people to whom the tombs belong used to drink and perhaps, implicitly, offer libations during the funeral ceremonies". Dani states that "the grey drinking vessels are so dominant in the graves that it is possible to drink of some special drink popular among these people". He describes them as bowl-on-stand type, which is different from the dish-on-stand type of the Indus civilisation. Tucci calls these as 'brandy bowls'. So far no scientific examination of the contents are available. We can only speculate if these were meant for drinking *soma* or any other inebriating liquor. In any case, the very fact that in the inflexed burial graves the hand is near the drinking vessel, suggests some special significance to the drink.

Tucci surmises the possibility from the evidence of Aligrama that juniper was burnt on fire-stands for the *suffimenta*, which is practised even today in Swat. I wonder whether this can be related to the term *sakadhuma* of the Vedas.

The presence of the *soma* drinking-and-revering, *daeva* worshipper, Haumavarga Sakas in the mountainous valleys of the Pamirs and adjoining regions, adds to our growing knowledge of the Vedic Age. From the content of the Vedas as well as from the archaeological findings, it is evident now that we cannot think of one single dominant people or culture in the formation of the civilisation we call Vedic. Not only various ethnic groups, though linguistically related (and perhaps some not so related), but also several waves of movements, or infiltrations, were involved in the process lasting at least for half a millennium. In this story there were always the newcomers versus the old entrants. Such older elements which remained behind, and on the fringes, and did not move forward with the mainstream were by turn regarded in later times as 'outsiders' or 'foreigners' or 'inferior beings' still living with queer customs that were forgotten by their remote descendants in the vanguard movements. The Haumavarga Sakas were one of them. Those who became part of the main movement in course of time found substitute for *soma* when it was not available in their new territories and gradually adapted themselves to the changed environment. In the early phase of their movement, as in *Rigveda*, it was possible to get supplies and keep in touch with their kin but later it became marginal and exotic. They were neither liked by the reformists in Iran or by the people in the later Vedic period.

The archaeological explorations and excavations in the region we are discussing have now increased our horizons tremendously and new probabilities loom large. The Neolithic sites like Burzhom and Saraikhola in the east of the Upper Indus, but more importantly Ghilgai, Aligrama, and Loebanr in the west of it, represent features some of which are comparable with Chinese Neolithic elements and offer evidence of trade and other more profound contacts with the Chinese world. It has been noted that "although this culture must have co-existed with the Early and Mature Harappan developments in the Indus Valley and Punjab, there is almost no indication that the two enjoyed contact whatsoever". So also the Harappan evidence at Shortugai, near the lapis lazuli mines of Badakshan, opens the northern gates for the Indus Valley civilisation's contact with Central Asia. Against this background, the recent findings of the Italian, German and Pakistani teams in Swat, Gilgit, Chilas and other sites on the Karakorum Highway provide new strength to our thinking about the importance and role of these northern regions and routes linking movements and developments in culture and polity with territories and peoples of further north in the Tien-shan and Altai in Central Asia in the Semirechye protohistoric and historic times. Certainly these discoveries indicate a probable alternative to the obsessive attention many scholars pay to the western gates of the Indo-Pakistan sub-continent. Just as we have pointed out earlier in the case of the Saka movements in the second century BC from the Issyk Kul region, north of Tien-shan, directly southwards to Jibin, we visualise similar movements in the northern region in the protohistoric Vedic period. History indeed often repeats itself. Archaeology and linguistics seem to converge in the Swat more than once for the Saka movements in the area. The gap which separated the first movements leading to the occupation of the Karakorum and Swat regions by Maues amounted to almost a millennium, and so it should not surprise us if the descendants of the 'first' Sakas called the 'second' Sakas of the later historical period as 'Mlecchas'.

The impact of the 'first' Sakas of South Asia, that is, the *soma*-drinking Sakas, was short-term and limited to its northwestern territories and peoples as well as very long-term ones. Short-term because their roles were subordinated soon to the succeeding political dominance of the Mauryas followed by the Indo-Greeks, and religious and cultural milieu generated by Buddhism. If on the other hand it is assumed that these eastern Sakas, linguistically a 'Satem', Indo-Iranian language speaking group of people, constituted a significantly visible group among the authors of the Vedic culture and society. One of their groups, i.e. *soma*-drinking ones, remained behind to be influenced by the succeeding political and socio-economic cultures, while the majority of their kin-people moved down southwards into Punjab and thence eastward into the Ganga-Yamuna doab area influencing the political and cultural life there. In simple words, the Vedic milieu may be taken as predominantly 'Saka', in which case their impact may be equated with what is known hitherto as the Vedic. This then will indeed be a 'long-term impact' in South Asia. But I am aware that this hypothesis is debatable and would require a very careful in-depth study.

ALEXANDER AND THE SAKAS

When Alexander defeated the Achaemenids he did not consider his task complete without subduing of Sakas; there were other reasons too. For one thing that some of the Iranian nobles had fled beyond the Oxus and were holding on their own with the support of the Sakas, and for another, Alexander after all, did not want to be a lesser hero than Cyrus the Great. When Alexander crossed the Oxus and reached the bank of the Jaxartes, he found a host of the Sakas gathering on the other side and patrolling and challenging him to cross. He took twenty days to organise and having supposedly founded the farthest of his 'Alexandrias', crossed the river, overcame the encircling tactics of the Sakas and broke the nomads, and pursued them a long way, but had to be carried back to camp owing to his illness. His troops sent to relieve Marcanda failed miserably against the Saka Massagetae who were supporting Spitamenes. In any case, Alexander had tougher times in Central Asia than in the centre of the Persian empire. He did not stay there for long and there is no evidence if the Sakas formed part of his empire or that of his successors in the east.

SAKAS IN SOUTH ASIA

It was before the middle of the third century BC, when the independent states of Bactria and Parthia were founded, that the Sakas were contained in their Soma region. The Graeco-Bactrians and the Parthians proved to be solid buffer states for the empires in the south. But this condition lasted only for little over one hundred years. New pressures and new movements arising out of happenings in further east provided the Sakas for the first time in their history an opportunity to found their own kingdoms in the south, which were not ephemeral and which presented them with an opportunity of playing a more constructive role than before in a wider context of sedentary world history and civilisation. While the history of the eastern Sakas, from the later half of the second century BC, becomes centred in South Asia, the Sarmatians and other western groups of them remain involved in the West. With centres of power established in the Punjab and Sind, Mathura and Ujjain, Gujarat and Maharashtra, the Sakas played a substantial role in the history of South Asia up to the end of the fourth century AD and became an integral part of its life and culture so much so that today we have in India Sakadvipi Brahmans and the Saka era has been accepted formally as national system of reckoning of dates.

REFERENCES

Dani, A.H. and V.M. Masson (eds.), *History of Civilization of Central Asia,* UNESCO, 1992.

Litvinsky, B.A., in M.S. Asimov *et al.*, (eds.), *Ethnic Problem of the History of Central Asia in the Early Period*, Nouka, Moscow, 1981, pp. 154-66.

Narain, A.K., *Later Indo-Scythians*, 1962.

——, *The Indo-Greeks*, Oxford University Press, New Delhi, 1980.

——, *Tokharians — A History without Nation, State, Boundaries*, NEHU Publications, Shillong, 2001.

Prinsep, J., *Essays on Indian Antiquities*, 2 Vols., London, 1958 (edited by E. Thomas).

Thapar, B.K., (ed.), *Indian Archaeology, 1975-76: A Review*, ASI, GOI, New Delhi, 1979.

Tucci, Guiseppe, *To Lhasa and Beyond*, Oxford and IBH, New Delhi, 1984.

Zimmer, H., *Myths and Symbols in Indian Art and Civilization*, New York, 1953.

4

Advent of Buddhism in Central Asia

S.M. Haldhar

A long history of Buddhism and its expansion, however, demands regional study, namely that of the western region comprising Afghanistan, Bactria, and Parthia, the central zone covering the present Turkestan, and the eastern one assimilating both the northern and southern wings of Chinese Turkestan. Central Asia in general played an active role through its savants in the translation of Buddhist sacred texts into Chinese as also in other languages of the countries of its adoption. A long list of such scholars who worked in this direction is available from the catalogue of Chinese Buddhist *Tripitakas* in different periods. A study of the list would bring out the fruitful contribution of Buddhist savants from other parts of Asia including India in different centuries. Thus, according to the list of Nanjio,[1] among 72 translators who worked between AD 67 and 420, there were 15 Indians, 7 Yueh-chi, 5 Parthians, 7 Kubhans, 21 from the Western countries, and 17 Chinese; among them, 22 worked in the south, of whom 5 were Chinese. Among 43 workers who worked between AD 420 and 550, 14 were Indians, 10 from Kubha and other Western countries, 4 Sinhalese and Indo-Chinese, and 4 of uncertain origin. Among them, 27 worked in the south. A close study and scrutiny of the list would reveal the contribution of Parthians and those from Kubha (Kabul) as eminent Buddhist scholars who went to China to propagate Buddhism through translation of sacred texts. The Western countries include Central Asia and comprised both the modern sectors of Russian and Chinese Turkestan. The two areas, however, demand separate treatment because of political consideration as also their separate archaeological investigations.

The history of Buddhism in Central Asia is also related to the political history of different regions and the hold of different political powers in later times, like those of the Chinese, Tibetans, and Uighurs. The languages of those people have also left literary remains in Central Asia, which no doubt call for separate treatment. A brief notice of the languages represented in the manuscripts and inscriptions discovered will reveal many influences at work in Central Asia, and its importance as a receiving and distributing centre. Numerous Sanskrit writings have been found, all dealing with religious or quasi-religious subjects, as medicine and grammar. Relatively modern Mahayanist literature[2] is abundant. Unknown forms of Prakrit are not unknown, while two new languages, written in Central Asian Gupta script, provide translations of Mahayanist literature. Three other Iranian languages, all written in an alphabet of Aramaic origin, have left literary remains in Central Asia. Of the three Iranian languages, Sogdian with a more varied literary content also offers Buddhist texts, besides later Manichaean and Christian ones. It was originally the language of the region around Samarkand, but was used by merchants throughout the Tarim basin and spread even to China.[3]

As the Tibetans were the dominating power in the Tarim basin at least from the middle of the eighth century to the middle of the ninth century, it is not surprising to record finds of Tibetan manuscripts in the regions of Khotan, Miran, and Tun-huang. In Turfan, traces of Tibetan influence are fewer, though not entirely absent. The documents include Buddhist translation[4] besides numerous official and business papers. At that time Buddhism seems to have shared with the Bon religion the allegiance of the Tibetans. Of course, there are no Manichaean or Christian transplantations in Tibetan. A large number of Chinese texts—both religious and secular—from the principal centres of Central Asia, including a series of dated documents ranging from 98 BC to AD 153, point to intercourse between China and Central Asia at this period. Some documents of the Tang dynasty are Manichaean with an admixture of Buddhist and Taoist ideas.[5] Besides these lanuages and dialects used as mediums of Buddhist literature in Central Asia, another dialect Uighur[6] was used for Buddhist literature. It spread considerably when the Uighurs broke the power of Tibet in the Tarim basin about AD 860 and founded a kingdom themselves. It extended into China and lasted long.

BUDDHISM IN AFGHANISTAN, BACTRIA AND PARTHIA

Monumental remains, as also reference to Buddhist savants in Chinese Buddhist literature, point to the flourishing state of Buddhism in this part of Central Asia; and Al-Beruni,[7] too, does not fail to record this fact. In his words, "in former times, Khorasan, Persia, Iraq, Mosul, the country up to the frontier of Syria, was Buddhistic, but then Zarathustra went forth from Adharbayjan and preached Magism in Balkh (Baktre)". His doctrine came into favour with King Gushtasp, and his son Isfendiyad spread the new faith both in the East and West, both by force and by treaties. He founded five temples through his whole empire, from the frontiers of China to those of the Greek Empire. The succeeding kings made their religion (i.e., Zoroastrianism) the obligatory state religion of Persia and Iraq. In consequence, the Buddhists were banished from those countries, and had to emigrate to the countries east of Balkh. He also refers to the finds of Buddhist idols, and their remnants from India, China and among the Toghuzghus. The people of Khorasan call them 'Shamanan' (Sanskrit, *Sramana*); the shrine known as *vihara* could be seen in the border district of Khorasan adjoining India. This is the impression about Buddhism and its monuments, as recorded by the talented Khoresmian Al-Beruni (973–1048), the author of *Tahkik-i-Hind* (Inquiry into India).

The history of Buddhism in this part of Central Asia might be dated from the time of the Indo-Bactrians, although the teachings of Lord Buddha might have found their way even earlier. In this context, the Kandahar bilingual edict[8] of Asoka is rightly considered as an eloquent testimonial to the extension of Buddhism in the direction of Central Asia. The finds of other inscriptions of Afghanistan suggest that this part of Central Asia had come within the range of Mauryan cultural activities, it being a part of the empire of Asoka. Buddhism as such must have had a substantial following in the Kandahar area of what is now southern Afghanistan, by the middle of the third century BC. It is proposed by Bagchi[9] that Buddhism was introduced in Balkh during the time of Asoka who, no doubt, speaks of his efforts to introduce his *dhamma* among the people of Gandhara, Kamboja and Yona. The three peoples were neighbours — Kambojas were probably a branch of the Tukhara people, while the Yonas were no doubt the Bactrian Greeks. In this context, a legend recorded by Huan-tsang[10] refers to the first two lay disciples of Buddha, Trapusa and Bhallika as responsible for introducing Buddhism in that country. Originally, these two were merchants of the kingdom of Balhika, as the name Bhalluka or Bhallika probably suggests the association of one with that country. They had gone to India for trade and happened to be at Bodh Gaya when the Buddha had just attained his enlightenment. Offering him cakes and honey out of their provision, they were also ordained by the Tathagata as his first two disciples. The progress of Buddhism to the north of Afghanistan is also borne out by a Kharoshthi inscription on a clay object recovered from the Begram excavations in the first layer, placed between the third and second centuries BC recording a Buddhist name.[11]

The foundation of the Graeco-Bactrian state no doubt contributed to the expansion of Buddhism in this region in the first two centuries preceding the Christian era. Both Demetrius and Menander were interested in Buddhism.[12] The former is supposed to have attacked India to punish the Brahmin Sunga ruler for his anti-Buddhist activities and persecution of Buddhist monks, while the latter seems to have embraced the religion of the Tathagata after his discourse with the Buddhist philosopher Nagasena. The *Milindapanho* or *Discourses with Menander* is the theme of the great work. This is both in Pali and also in Chinese translation.[13] Its composition might have been of a later date, probably after

Menander's death. It is now generally accepted that this Indo-Greek ruler was a devotee of the Tathagata, and certain symbols like the *stupa* on the coins of Agathocles, as also the legends on the coins of Menander, are in agreement with the theory of infiltration of Buddhism in the realm of the Indo-Greek or Bactrian rulers.[14] It seems fairly evident that the Graeco-Bactrian kingdom unified in one political state the north Indian regions, Afghanistan and several parts of Western Turkestan. The political atmosphere was, thus, congenial for the Buddhist missionaries as also for the local followers in those areas to convey the message of the Lord outside the boundaries of this kingdom.

Further information regarding the association of Indo-Greek rulers as also the Yonas with Buddhism between the second and the first century BC is also available from other sources. Two Kharoshthi inscriptions[15]—one from the ancient country of Udyana (Swat Valley) and the other from Bajaur (southeast of Jalalabad) record dedications by a Greek officer named Meridarkh Theodorus who enshrined the relics of the Lord Buddha, and the pious act of one Viyakamitra – an *apracharaja*. The former was an officer of rank and the latter was a vassal – both probably under Menander or his successor. It is also proposed that the wheel on some coins of Menander is connected with Buddhism.[16]

The spread of Buddhism in Central Asia was no doubt stimulated by the formation of the Kushana empire, which at its zenith seems to have overshadowed the Graeco-Bactrian kingdom. The first ruler, Kujula Kadphises, styles himself on his coins as 'stead-fast true law' *(Sacadhrama-thitasa—Satyadharma sthitasya)* and the figure of Buddha is depicted on his coins. His successor appears to be Shaivite, while Kanishka, the great Kushana ruler, was definitely a Buddhist though publicly he professed Eclecticism. Buddha figures prominently on his coins with the legend 'Cakamano-Boydo-Buddha Sakyamuni'. Kanishka's name is also associated with a *vihara* or monastery set up for the Sarvastivadins in an inscription dated in the year 1 from Shah ji Ki Dheri[17] near Peshawar. The Buddhist theologian Ghosaka, born in Tokharistan, who was one of the leading figures at the Buddhist Council held in Kanishka's time at Purusapura, belonged to the Vaibhasika school, a branch of the Sarvastivadins. The finds of potsherds from Kara Tepe, with inscriptions in Brāhmī point to the spread of the Sarvastivada school of Buddhism in Turkestan in the time of Kanishka.[18] The same site also yielded inscribed potsherds in Kharoshthi reflecting the teachings of the Mahasanghika school. The reference to pioneer Buddhist savants instrumental in translating Buddhist canons into Chinese, hailing from the country of the Yueh-chi, indirectly points to the kingdom of the Kushanas as their homeland. It is suggested that Buddhism also consolidated its position in Margiana in the first century AD and reached Eastern Turkestan through the western part of it, and from there it went to China.

Zurcher enacts[19] this process between the middle of the first century BC and middle of the first century AD. Among the early Buddhist missionaries to China

(Lo-Yang) were two Parthians (An-shib Kao and An Hsuan), three Yueh-chih (Chih-Iou-chia-Chien-Lokasena, Chih-vao and Chih-liang), and two Sogdians (Kang Menghsiang and Kang-Seng-hui).

By the end of the Western Chin dynasty (AD 265-316), translators were engaged, among whom six or seven were of Chinese and six of Indian origin as well as sixteen belonged to various Central Asian nationalities—six Yueh-chi, four Parthians, three Sogdians, two Kucheans, and one Khotanese. These appear to be only approximate figures, pointing to the interest of Central Asian Buddhist scholars in the propagation of Buddhism in China, as also its flourishing state in Central Asia. There are also indications of Central Asian monks engaged in Buddhist activities in northwestern India and in the Taxila region in the Kushana period. The earliest reference is to a certain Bactrian (Bahlikena), a resident of the town of Noacha or Noachea (unidentified) in the Taxila inscription[20] of the year 136 of the unknown era (probably of 57 BC). It is recorded on a silver scroll in a vessel containing a small golden casket in which there were fragments of bones. It invokes wishes for the bestowal of health on the great king, the king of kings, the son of God, the Kusane, who is generally identified with Kujula Kadphises. The contents of the inscription show that the Bactrians acted as zealots of Buddhist religion in India.

The existence of the two important schools of Buddhism, namely that of Sarvastivadins and of the Mahasanghikas is noticed in the Brāhmī and Kharoshthi records of the Kushana period. An earlier record from Mathura—the Lion capital inscription of the time of Sodasa,[21] however, points to rivalry between the two schools, and it also specifies the location of the headquarters of the Sarvastivadins at Nagarahara in Jalalabad (Afghanistan). This record is important from the point of view of history of Buddhism, as also for the conflict between the two schools. It refers to the import of dialectician (*Khalula*). The Sarvastivadin monk Budhila came from Nagara to teach the foremost Mahasanghikas the truth. The Sarvastivadins are also noticed in the Kalwan Copperplate inscription[22] of the year 134, probably of the old era. It records the enshrinement of relics in the *stupa* shrine by Chandrabhi, the female worshipper in acceptance of the Sarvastivada for the attainment of *nirvana.* The inscriptions of the Kushana period connected with this school are the famous Taxila casket of the year 1, Zeda of the year 11, and Kurram of the year 20 of Kanishka's era.[23] The donors are Hipea Dhia (Zeda) and Yola Mira Shahi (undated Tordher-Thai Valley, Loralai Baluchistan) who appear to be foreigners. These records from the Kharoshthi region suggest Sarvastivadin establishments in Afghanistan, West Punjab and Sindh. Mathura, of course, was the important centre of the Sarvastivadins who were facing the stiff opposition of the Mahasanghikas there and had therefore to seek the help of their fellow brother dialecticians at the other end of the Kushana empire.

The Mahasanghikas, too, had their establishment in Afghanistan, as is evident from the Wardhak inscription dated in the year 51 of the time of Huviska. It refers to the deposit of the relics of Lord Sakyamuni in the Vogramarega *vihara*, in possession of the Mahasanghika teachers. There is no other Kharoshthi record of this school, although quite a few from Mathura[24] are associated with it. It appears that Afghanistan had several centres of Buddhism and Buddhist activities in the Kushana period, as is evident from these records in Kharoshthi from that country. This is supported by reference to several monks from the Kabul (Kubha) region who went to China and translated Buddhist canonical works into Chinese later, in the beginning of the fourth century AD. This could not have been possible except for a strong base of Buddhism in the Kabul area, established during the period of the Kushanas. These included Khuthan San-Kie-ti-pho,[25] i.e. Gautama Sanghadeva (AD. 383), Pi-mo-lo-kha, i.e. Vimalaksa,[26] a great teacher of Vinaya, with Kumarajiva as one of his disciples, who arrived in China in AD 406; San-kie-poh-khan,[27] i.e. Sanghabhuti who translated 3 works in AD 381–385; and Fu-zo-tu-lo, i.e., Punyatrata[28] who arrived in China in the Hun-sh period (AD 399–415) and was a collaborator with Kumarajiva; Than-mo-ye-sho, i.e. Dharmayasass[29] who translated 2 or 3 works in AD 407–415.

REFERENCES

Agrawala, R.C., *Some Aspects of Indian Culture in the Kharosthi Documents from Chinese Turkestan*, Vivekanand, 1970, pp. 275-81.

Andrews, F.H., *Descriptive Catalogue of Antiquities Recovered by Sir Aurel Stein during His Explorations in Central Asia, Kansu and Eastern Iran*, London, 1936.

Bagchi, P.C., Indian Culture in Central Asia, *JBORS*, 1946, pp. 9-20.

Eitel, *Handbook of Chinese Buddhism.*

Eliot, Charles, *Hinduism and Buddhism*, Vols. I-III, London, 1921.

Puri, B.N., *India under the Kushanas*, Bombay, 1950.

Stein, A., *Sand Buried Ruins of Khotan*, London, 1904.

——, *Ancient Khotan*, 2 vols., Oxford, 1907.

——, *Ruins of Desert Cathay*, 2 vols., London, 1912.

——, *Serindia*, 5 vols., Oxford, 1921.

——, *Innermost Asia*, 5 vols., Oxford, 1929.

——, *On Ancient Central Asian Tracks*, London, 1920.

Walters, T., *On Yuan-Chwang's Travels in India*, London, 1905.

NOTES

1. See *A Catalogue of the Chinese Buddhist Tripitaka*. Oxford (1882), Appendix II, pp. 379 ff. In his *Handbook of Chinese Buddhism*, Earnest J. Eitel refers to the contributions of different scholars in this context (Reprint — Cosmos Publications, New Delhi, 1981; original edition, 1888). This calculation is recorded by B.A. Litvinsky in his booklet entitled 'Outline History of Buddhism in Central Asia' prepared and circulated at the Diushanobe Session (1968) of the International Conference on the History, Archaeology and Culture of Central Asia in the Kushana Period, p. 13. J. Brough suggests that certain Yueh-chih translators may have come not from the land of the Great Yueh-chih, but from the milieu of the Eastern Turkestan 'Little Yueh-chih' (quoted note 63, *op. cit.*, p. 83).
2. Central Asia, according to Eliot, has astonished the learned world with two new languages, both written in a special variety of the Brāhmī alphabet called Central Asian Gupta. One is called Nordarish, regarded by some as the language of the Sakas, and by others as the language of the Kushanas and of Kanishka's empire. The Mahayanist literature translated into this language include the *Suvarnaprabhasa Vajracchedika* and *Aparimatya-sutras.* It appears to have been spoken principally in the southern part of the Tarim Basin (Hoernle in *JRAS*, 1910, pp. 837 ff and 1383 ff; 1911, pp. 202 ff, 447 ff). The other language spoken principally on its northern edge is called Tokharian, associated with the Tokharas or Indo-Scyths. According to Eliot, it is safer to regard it as the language of Kucha or Kuchanese. It exists in two different dialects known as A and B whose geographical distribution is uncertain. Numerous official documents dated in the first half of the 7th century show that it was the ordinary speech of Kucha and Turfan. It was also a literary language and among the many translations discovered are versions in it of the *Dharmapada* and *Vinaya* (Eliot, *Hinduism and Buddhism, op. cit.* III, pp. 190-91 with reference to many articles including that of Sylvain Levi, 'Tokharian b, Langue de Koutche', *JA*, 1913, 11, p. 311).
3. Eliot, *op. cit.*, pp. 191-92.
4. Aurel Stein, *Ancient Khotan, op. cit.*, Appendix B - entitled Tibetan Manuscripts and Scraffiti discovered by A. Stein at Endere; edited by L.D. Barnett and A.H. France.
5. Eliot, *op. cit.*, p. 193. See also Chavannes, *Les Documents Chinois decouverts par,* Aurel Stein, 1913; also Appendix A entitled 'Chinese Documents from the Dandan Uiliq, Niya and Endere' translated and annotated by Eduvard Chavannes in *Ancient Khotan, op. cit.*, pp. 521 ff.
6. The name Uigur is perhaps more correctly applied to the alphabet than the language which appears to have been the literary form of the various Turkish idioms spoken north and south of Tienshan. The use of Uigur in China is evident from the printing of *Sutras* in Uigur at Peking in 1339, and Uigur manuscripts were copied in the region of Kang His (1662-1773) (Eliot, *op. cit.*, p. 192).
7. *Alberuni's India,* translated by F.C. Sachau, Vol. I, London, 1888, p. 21.
8. J. Harmata, 'Sino-Indica', *Acta Antiqua,* Vol. XII, No. 1-2, Budapest, 1964, p. 4.
9. *India and Central Asia, op. cit.*, p. 32. Foucher, however, holds that Buddhism did not appear in Bactria until the end of the 1st or the 2nd century AD (*La Vielle route de l'Inde*

de Bactres a Taxila, Vol. II, Paris, 1947, pp. 280-84). Litvinsky, however, considers Foucher's view to be erroneous *(Outline History of Buddhism in Central Asia,* Dushanbe, 1968, p. 77, n. 15).

10. T. Walters, *On Yuan-Chwang's Travels in India*, Photoprint edition, New Delhi, 1973, Vol. I, p. 112; II, p.131.
11. J. Harmata, 'Sino-Indica', *Ariana Antigua*, Vol. XII, No. 1-2, Budapest, 1964, pp. 4-5.
12. L. Levi, *Le Bouddhisme et les Grecs: Revue de I 'Histoire de Religions,* XXIII, 1891, pp. 436-49; reprinted in Memorial Sylvain Levi, pp. 204 ff. *The Questions of King Milinda*, SBE, XXXV; P. Denievitte, *Les versions Chinoises de Milindapanho,* BEFCO, XXIV, pp. 168 ff.
13. The Chinese version of the *Milindapanha*, written several centuries later, describes Alasanda as 2,000 *yojana* from Sagala instead of 200 (Demieville, *op. cit.*; cf. Pelliot, JA 1914. Pt. II, pp. 413-19; Levi, IHQ, 1936, p. 126).
14. The Pali texts represent the Greeks as taking part in missionary activities. We are told that after the conversion of Yavana (Greek) country to Buddhism, Moggoliputta Tissa went there and selected an elder Dharmaraksita for missionary work. He was then sent to Aparantaka where he made a large number of converts. The Greeks were also represented by this Elder Mahadharmaraksita at the Great Stupa ceremony in Ceylon, initiated by Dutthagamini in the middle of the second century BC (Levi, *op. cit.*).
15. Sten Konow, *Corpus Inscriptionum Indicarum* (CUD) II (I). These are discussed by K.A. Nilakantha Sastri in *A Comprehensive History of India,* p. 219.
16. J. Marshall, *Taxila,* 3 vols., Cambridge, 1951 , Vol. I, pp. 33-34; Narain, Indo-Greeks, *op. cit.*, p. 98. According to Tarn, the idea that Menander ever became a Buddhist in the sense of entering the order may be dismissed at once (*op. cit.,* p. 268).
17. Sten Konow, *Corpus Inscriptionum Indicarum* (CII) Vol. II (I), pp. 134 ff.
18. B.A. Litvinsky, *Outline History of Buddhism in Central Asia,* Diushanbe, 1968, p. 10.
19. E. Zurcher, *The Buddhist Conquest of China, The Spread and Adaptation of Buddhism in Early Medieval China,* Vol. I (text), Leiden, 1956, pp. 22-23.
20. *Corpus Inscriptionum Indicarum* (CII), II (I), *op. cit*., pp. 70 ff.
21. *Ibid.*, pp. 30 ff.
22. *Journal of the Royal Asiatic Society* (JRAS), 1932, pp. 949 ff.
23. B.N. Puri, *India Under the Kushanas* (IUK), pp. 141 ff. for consolidated references and comments.
24. *Ibid.*, p. 142.
25. Nanjio, *op. cit.*, II, 39, p. 399. He was a Sramana of the country of Ke-pin, i.e. Kubha. In AD 383 he arrived at Khan-an, then the capital of the former Tshin dynasty of the Fu family where he translated two works. Between AD 391and 398 he translated five other works in two different places.
26. *Ibid.*, II, 44, p. 400. He was a Sramana of Kubha (Kabul) and a great teacher of Vinaya in Kwei-tsz, i.e. Kharakas or Kuke, where Kumarajiva was one of his disciple. After the latter's death, which happened between 409 and 415, Vimalaksa went southward and translated two works. He died at the age of seventy-seven.

27. *Ibid.*, II, 54, p. 404. A Sramana of Kubha (Kabul) who translated 3 works in 27 or 37 fascicule during AD 381-85.
28. *Ibid.*, II, 60, p. 408. He was a Sramana of Kubha (Kabul) who arrived in China in the Hun-Sh period (AD 399-415) and in AD 404 he, together with Kumarajiva, translated one work in 58 fascicule (Sarvastivadavinaya).
29. *Ibid.*, II, 62, p. 408. He also belonged to the country of Kubha and translated 2 or 3 works in AD 407-415.

5

Travelling Names to and from Central Asia and Beyond

Aloka Parasher-Sen

> In India we were treated with the utmost courtesy by the government through Lord Curzon, to whom we would express our gratitude. The American traveller expects kindness from his English cousins, and is never disappointed. It is less common to be treated with unfailing courtesy and consideration by Chinese officials. It is therefore with peculiar pleasure that I put on record my thanks to the Chinese government for its genuine and ready help at all stages of my journey in China. In Russia and Siberia, through which lay my hasty homeward way, similar official courtesy was shown. The best was placed at my disposal; and although it was the midst of the revolutionary crisis, my passport was not once asked for until I was about to cross into Germany at Warsaw. [Ellsworth Huntington, written around 1916.][1]

Notwithstanding that this quotation jolts us to think about our present in more nuanced ways, to begin with it is to emphasise the complexity of social and political relations that individual travellers have always had to face in historical time. It is through them that civilisations have been cemented and, despite war and greed, human relations have been fostered within the warmth of tradition.

This paper is about people who travelled more than a thousand years before our times and about whom we only know through the names they inscribed on rock surfaces during the course of their journey. Moving beyond boundaries, these travellers from and to the subcontinent interacted with each other on various planes in locales that were alien to all of them. Hitherto, historians have been too concerned with looking at histories of such people within the confines of so-called 'National Histories' and therefore, with understanding the dynamics of invasions and political conquest. Or, this has been done as part of the histories of trade and commerce in order to define the material concerns of countries. For India in particular, the religious methods of such interactions have been overemphasised. That travelling away from home, for whatever reasons, also entailed interactions at various other levels—of learning different languages, of understanding the terrain, and of communicating across lineage and country—have so far hardly been captured in scholarly writing.

For this chapter, one does not dwell much on the existing historical literature[2] that has quite effectively captured the sub-continental relations, primarily political, with both West Asia and Central Asia prior to the contact of Islam with Al Hind. Many of these works, beginning with the early twentieth century, were concerned also with economic and religious dimensions of these contacts.[3] One important dimension, that is often left out from the more narrow historical accounts of the regional contacts, is that of the travelling accounts of early twentieth century. In the present context, we would like to dwell on them more closely. It is not that travellers only crossed the hardy terrains between India and Central Asia during these recent times but that we have vivid descriptive and detailed accounts left by them on the geography and environment of the area under discussion that graphically tells about the particular difficulties of geography, language and communication faced by these recent travellers. For instance, two points that we would like to highlight in the context of the ancient material in this paper, namely interaction between different linguistic groups and the difficulties faced by travellers due to the terrain, are both the subject-matter of these more recent writings.

It is interesting to note that for the period between roughly the second century BC and the fourth century AD the names of foreigners coming to the subcontinent have been noted in various inscriptions of the country and we are familiar with them. The earliest and most familiar of these are the names of the Greeks going back to as early as the first century BC like Theodorus Datiputra (Swat Valley inscriptions), Theodama (Bajaur inscription), Denipa or Deinippos (from Taxilla) and so on. From other parts of India too, such examples can be cited like Yashvardhanas, Dhammayavana from Karle, Yonaka from Nasik, Culayakas or Kshurayakasha from Dhenukakata and so on. Some of them even acquired Indian names like Yonaka Indragnidattha, the son of the Dharmadeva, who came along with his son Dharmarakshita for the purpose of honouring the Buddha.[4] The subsequent era of foreign contact with the Sakas and Pahlavas was rather massive causing mass migrations, leading many of these communities to settle on the subcontinent; their names are too numerous to cite here.[5] The heart of the Ganges Valley was, however, affected by the inroads and invasions of the Kushanas.[6] The resultant effect of this was witnessed on the social, economic and cultural life of the people that was more deep-rooted than what had been witnessed on the subcontinent before this period.[7]

This is contrary to the general trend in ancient literary accounts to either describe foreign invasions or dwell on the nature of these contacts with different parts of the subcontinent.[8] There are exceptions to the general norm like *Yuga Purāṇa*[9] and in the context of Jainism, the *Kālakācārya Kathanaka*[10] that not only give an account of conquering hordes but also the names of some of the ruling foreign elites. However, it is not so common to find the names of people from the Indian subcontinent travelling out or returning from long journeys. This is why the present material we propose to discuss becomes so significant. It strongly questions the hitherto unsubstantiated, but popular, understanding among scholarly writing on Indian social history that due to the strict injunctions of the *śāstras,* travelling abroad, outside *āryavarta,* was looked down upon and therefore forbidden. We argue below that it was not simply the Buddhists but generally, the practical necessities of life demanded the people, especially merchants of all faiths from the subcontinent, to travel far and wide. This has to be captured in certain, perhaps, fragmentary and minute ways in terms of the evidence available rather than simply in terms of understanding the totality of our ideological and social systems.

In this chapter we explore these kinds of interactions in an important geographical zone—the Karakorum and the upper Indus Valley. This northwestern part of the present-day state of Pakistan is the meeting point of three major mountain ranges—the Western Himalayas, the Karakorum and the Hindukush. This is also the well-marked pathways for the people travelling between the subcontinent and other Central Asian countries to take. Not surprisingly therefore, some of the biggest and most important collection of art and inscriptions that are spread over the upper Indus Valley—Gilgit, Baltistan, Ladakh—have been found here over the years. The most has been the work done by the combined German and Pakistani team of archaeologists who discovered thousands of inscriptions along with a variety of rock art.[11] We are informed that these discoveries were largely concentrated in the area east and west of the village of Chilas, under the shadow of the famous Nagna Parbat, in the Diamir District of northwestern Pakistan. In quantitative terms about 30 sites have been found, which are located on both sides of the upper Indus basin over a stretch of about 1000 km. It is further reported that at these sites a huge number of about 30,000 petroglyphs and 5,000 inscriptions in ten writing systems have been "pecked or chiseled into the dark brown varnished surface of the boulders scattered on the river banks and the terraces of the valley."[12] A substantial part of this material is now available through publications[13] of the Heidelberg Academy that has been systematically documenting these remains. Apart from Chilas, other important places about which documentation is available are Oshibat, Shatial, Hodar, and Thalpan.[14]

The magnitude of the data thus collected provides scope for a great variety of historical research that, as said by the scholars involved in this project, "provides a remarkable source for the study of the cultural history of Central and South Asia".[15] Cultural histories primarily focus on the artistic and religious symbols as they must do since these are most visible symbols inscribed for posterity. At almost all these sites it is impossible not to be struck by this kind of visual form of reverence and dedication. Our concern in the present paper, however, is to dwell on the accompanying inscriptions that are in form of different kinds of names and dedicational phrases, giving an account of the travellers who passed through this area. In doing so we move into a "cultural terrain that is as much concerned about its beliefs as about its identity". Since the rocks on which these names were inscribed were located at an important meeting point of Central Asian and South Asian influences, it naturally means that social groups from a multitude of social backgrounds flocked here.[16]

> Their religious learnings, as also their economic goals, may have coalesced but this did not in any way mean that they lost their respective identities.

It is through a study of these names then that the complexity of this aspect of the cultural and socio-economic history of region can be fully grasped. In order to do so it would be difficult to analyse the data from all the sites for the time being. Therefore, only the small label inscriptions from the site of Oshibat have been taken up for critical scrutiny.

Oshibat is the first site for which the data has been published.[17] Like most of the sites for this project, the archaeological survey and documentation were done with the help of the Government of Pakistan and under the guidance of several scholars led by the German Academy of Humanities and Sciences, Heidelberg. Azam Chaudury[18] is said to have initially discovered Oshibat and then he and Volker Thewalt did the documentation work at this site during 1984–87, whereas R. Kauper prepared the map of this area.[19]

Oshibat is 20 km west of the district headquarters Chilas, situated on the north bank of the river Indus. To its east, at a distance of 8 km south, lies the site of Hodar that has also been documented by the Heidelberg Academy and to its west, at a distance of 8 km towards the south, is a place called Thor. Scholars explain the meaning of the word Oshibat as follows. It is said to be derived from the term *Oshi* meaning 'air' and the suffix *Bat* is said to mean 'stone', denoting thereby, a place with stones or rocks open to the air and skies. Indeed, as will be noted below, this site was famous for the rocks of huge magnitude. To the north of Oshibat lies the vast bank of the river Indus where the water is almost silent. This thus provided a natural junction at which travellers could cross the river. In summer the climate here is dry and extraordinarily hot, as the monsoon does not reach here. There is very little rain in the autumn and winter as well. Though the place is said to be famous for fragrant herbs and plants and a variety of reptiles, the conditions represent a desert-like climate. Due to this a tarnish is accumulated on the rock making them dark brown. Scholars who have worked on the field here suggest that once the rock surface is scratched, one gets to see the light brown of the original rock surface. For this reason they put forth the supposition that it was suitable and very good for inscribing.[20]

The site of Oshibat is spread over an area of 1 sq. km. Rock/Stone no. 18 at this site is particularly striking not owing to its huge size that provides shelter for the people who come to this place as travellers, and also because of some special significance attached to it. Till a few years back it was found covered with small and big round stones. It is different from other places like Shaital in that the inscriptional rocks are not situated in one place alone but are spread over both sides of the road giving a hint of the old trade route. On the whole, it can be said that most of the inscriptions and artwork are on the eastern rocks of Oshibat. Chaudhury has made significant note of the fact that because Rock no. 18 was covered with small and big stones, in all probability, an effort was made to hide the earlier association with it. With the Islamisation of the region at a nearby place, a burial of a Muslim saint (*Pir*) emerged and the faith of the local people interestingly is that if you put beautiful stones on it you get religious merit.

The inscriptions found here, in a majority of cases, are invariably set alongside the engraving of *stūpas*, Buddha images, altars on which phallic symbols were mounted, *swastika* signs, human, animal, and floral forms of all kinds, hunting scenes, demon-like creatures, etc. All these depictions have been broadly classified into broad periods or phases from the prehistoric time to about the fourteenth or fifteenth century AD. The earliest examples of animal and human figurines, hunting scenes and demon-like creatures in different styles have been dated back to the prehistoric times. A clear-cut Buddhist phase has been identified that is said to start from around the first century AD and to last until the ninth-tenth century AD. The chronology is based on the main subject represented in terms of the carvings of *stūpas*, Buddha images and other Buddhist symbols. It is further suggested that "during the ninth-tenth century AD, the Buddhist belief was replaced by a new socio-religious movement"[21] as gleaned from the emergence of aces, sun-symbols and the like in their depiction on the rock surface. Finally, the most recent period is marked by the Islamisation of the region after the fourteenth-fifteenth century AD. We thus take up a description of the names, reflecting different religious affiliations, for the period from the first century AD to the tenth century AD. These engravings and inscriptions show a unique continuity of these interactions over time involving several generations. It also reveals that this continuous stream of travellers who passed through this difficult terrain on their way to different countries was substantial in number.

About 230 Brāhmī fragmentary inscriptions have been found at Oshibat.[22] In comparison with the Brāhmī inscriptions there are only 36 Sogdian and 9 Kharoṣṭhī inscription at Oshibat.[23] With reference to the Kharoṣṭhī inscriptions,

Fussman is of the opinion that the same groups of travellers wrote them. Only in some of these inscriptions we have the writer's names that invariably happen to be the travellers who visited the place. One of them, namely, a Kharoṣṭhī inscription at Oshibat gives the date [Plate no. 47]. It is given as "sam 20+20+20+20 sam +++" that is translated as 'Year 80' (18:20).[24] Fussman deciphers this to suggest that it belongs to AD 158.[25]

A suggested chronology for the inscriptions at Oshibat and the accompanying art is given as follows:

> Scholars admit that this cannot be done through a scientific method. One of the methods therefore adopted to date the inscriptions was their colour and the form and style of the art of engravings accompanying them.[26] Care has been taken to use this method only if the images and the inscriptions are on the same level, close to each other, on the same stone.[27] There are only a few engravings like those of *stūpas* and *chaityas* where something is written and these can be historically dated to between the fourth century AD to the eighth century AD. Thus, it is noted that the Kharoṣṭhī inscriptions are the oldest and can be dated between the first BC to the second AD. After this the Brāhmī inscriptions are, in principle, generally dated to between the fourth century AD and the eighth AD. The few Proto-Sārada that are known are fixed to the last phase of the Brāhmī inscriptions, namely, within the eighth century AD. Finally, the Sogdian inscriptions that have not been studied in detail by us for this presentation have been dated to between the fourth and the eighth century AD.

These inscriptions yield an overwhelming number of personal names. This is not unusual to find at some of the earliest and popular Buddhist sites of the subcontinent like Sānchi, Bārhut, Amarāvati or the Buddhist cave sites along the Western Ghats. The difference, however, is that Oshibat was neither the site of a *vihāra*, or a *chaitya* or a *stūpa* containing the sacred relics of the Buddha. On the contrary, it was located in close proximity to an ancient trade route and thus, apart from the Buddhists, other travellers, merchants and their accompanying support staff or guides visited the place. Some of the latter must have been the local population of the region as a whole. Given this rather cosmopolitan nature of the place, the personal names inscribed on the rock surface here were of considerable variety; people coming from different parts of the subcontinent and also from regions to the north and west of it. Further, related to this point about the diverse population passing through this area, there is the other accompanying self-evident aspect that is revealed in the personal names, namely that most of them indicate the kin or *kula* affiliation of travellers. There are many names that are referred to in the context of them being the sons of a given person whose name is inscribed (11:2; 13:1; 15:6; 17:10; 18:17; 18:75). Typical phrases in this regard are *jambhagavibhaṭṭa dhīra upalavarisaputra, naśuputra* and so on. In the case of the Sogdian inscriptions this relationship is most often and clearly stated in almost all the cases deciphered.[28] *Jāti* or *varṇa* is rarely explicitly stated and is done so only in the case of the *brāhmaṇas*. Pertinently, this is a feature apparent in other inscriptions of the subcontinent as well.

Some examples of the personal names may be cited here. These occur as part of larger phases but in many cases the total writing has not been deciphered or, has simply disappeared through natural processes of erosion. General references to *varṇa* are few except in the case of the *brāhmaṇa* in two instances (4:2; 18:83).[29] The identity was sometimes noted along with the personal name as in the case of an interesting one known as Aśokaḥ Brāhmaṇa (18:15) or, as the Parohita Kīrtibhūṣaṇa (18:45) but the most preferred method was simply to write one's name as Mahāśarma (17:8), Bhaṭapusvāmi (18:33), Rahuśarma[30] (18:89; 91), or, as in one case, as simply Dhīra, the son of Jamhagavibaṭṭa (11:2). Names carrying a particularly Śaivite connotation were as follows: Bhadrasoma (17:1), Bhadarasa (18:14), Dakṣaddhoṭṭaka (18:31), Īśāna (18:60), Śrī Rudra (18:100), Paramamēheśvara, Mamāheśarah[31] (56:1), Soma (19:4), and Mahākara (18:24). Similarly, there are those that are typically Vaiṣṇavite names as Śrī Maghaviṣṇu (17:5), Śrī Viṣṇurakṣita (18:22), Śrī Jayaviṣṇu (18:47), and Śrī Mādhave (27:1; 112:1).

A large number of the clearly identifiable names undoubtedly show the influence of Buddhistic teaching and ethos. It is not clear whether the names of rulers, leaders, heads of guilds should all be taken to mean that they were Buddhists. There are many with the suffixes of *pāla*, *sena* or *sigha* that suggest they were retainers of either political or economic power—the *gahapatis* and *seṭṭis* of early Buddhist texts. In the former category we have such names as Rājaputra Vaṣoṭa (7:1), Kumāradevaputra (11:6), Bharuṇaspāla (11:7), Ratnasenavarma (13:3), Ratnavarma (18:37), Maghaspāla (18:40), Śrī Ajitasena (18:78), Śrī Padmaspāla (21:2), Śrī Jayatṛsingha (21:16), and Kīrttivarmma (18:2). In the latter, indicating their association with the merchant or Vaiśya community, are such names as Māṅgalaguptaḥ (16:1), Śrī Bhavagupto (18:84), Śrī Nānajeṣṭha (18:18), and Śrī Viṣṇugupta. Typical Buddhist names such as Amvaṭabha (11:14), Śrī Yuddhamo (?) [ksha] (18:11), Vajradhīra (18:35), Śrī Buddhadharmika (18:61), Śrī Pāloṭṭaka (18:64), Śrī Jīvoṭṭaka (18:65), Mitradāta (18:77), Bodhisattva (18:94), Hayapriyamitraśrī (18:98), Yaśoṭa (18:263), Vasutara (1:4; 29:1), Dattaśrī (63:1) and so on are not hard to come by as inscribed on these rocks. Needless to say, all these people were travelling for different purposes as is clear from the dedicational phrases that were most probably left behind by the monks travelling on this route.

The above in no way exhausts the variety of names inscribed on the rocks and stones at Oshibat. They are, however, clearly indicative of a part of their identities if not the whole of it. Several examples exist of names that do not reveal any sense of belonging to faith or social station in life. The meanings of these names are to either indicate of a virtue or moral, a quality, servitude or simply an aspect of nature. For instance, Prāṇoṭa (5:7), Siddha (5:14), Vīraputra (15:6), Devarāja (15:8), Naśuputra (17:10), Jīvaraṇa (17:14), Śrī Devīca (44:1), Vimalacitra (55:1), Dāsaka (18:116), Dhīra (18:117), Uttaradāsa (13:3), Jammbavīra (13:2) and so on. What is most interesting in these fragmentary inscriptions is that often the names cannot clearly be read but what they had intended to convey has been deciphered clearly. The shortest of these examples are those giving the honorific *Śrī* (2:5; 18:10; 28:29) or words like *soma* (19:4), *namo* (21:12), *mada* (18:70), *dejapa* (18:19), *satya* (18:93), *ratnaka* (19:92), *vicarati* (15:1; 18:68), *divira* (19:5) and so on. Many of the above words do convey a meaning but without a context. There are certain other longer words and phrases that give a fuller import of what is being intended but again they are without names. Some examples of this type may be cited. *Mahāśradhopāsaka* (4:1); *vikalabhaya* (5:1); *carmavidaka* (11:4); *capalaprakāsā* (10:3); *sugabhūtidevīḥ, mulavandhaka* (16:1); *sagujendra* (18:13); *jivamadapu* (18:49); *Śrī samgrāma* (18:50); *apurvamadabhara* (18:71); *kṣīṇanareptra* (18:82); *Śrīrājahaāaanasa* (18:97); *bhraṣṭika* (18:107); *nāgadharmamaśa* (18:110); *mahabhava* (18:174); *amdhavacā* (21:1); *Śrī śabha* (21:10) are some of the clearly understood phrases. There are some very rare instances, and clearly the most important of the examples, when the name can be read along with the intentions of the inscriber or writer. These are usually meant to define actions that either the traveller came to the place, has left the place and most often, that he has written (18:85) — this example refers specifically to the writer Samanga; 18:112 refers to the writer Candra. Thus, for instance, we have some typical Buddhist ones that read: *namo vuddha vasucandra divīra[s]ya* that means "in honour of the Buddha. The inscriber of writer Vasucandra" (4:5). Other examples of the same type are found on stones 6:1; 18:56; and 18:76. Such salutations were also made in respect of other monks and Bodhisattvas like the one that reads: *namu vajradhīra + yaśreṣṭhendra* (18:34-35). Other instances clearly articulating the Buddhist faith read as: *vicarati dharmavāṇaka śūra* and *vicarati dharmabhāṇaka pāla* (11:4, an identical example in Guṇasena doing the same as found inscribed on stone 15:9), each conveying the meaning that Śūra and Pāla respectively travelled this way to communicate enthusiastically the teaching of *dharma*. In one example there is the explicit mention of the Wheel of the *Dharma* or Law (18:44). Example of the type where the person is indicating the movements as a traveller are also present. In one case it is noted that Śrī Harimi 'came together with' Giriyoṭu (18:3). In another case (18:120), two sons 'have come and gone'. Yet again, in another example Guṇadāsa is said to 'have come here and gone' (21:11) or that Vīghnadeva, son of Indraśira, 'has come here and gone' (39:34). Both firm beliefs as well the notion of the impermanence of life are articulated in two of the clearest inscriptions. In one that reads: ... *devadharmo yamrāhovīrasya* (93:1), it emphasises that 'these are the religious foundations' of a person called Rāhovīra. Ironically, the most clear of all inscriptions is the one that reads: *martavyam smartavyam* (81:2), namely that "Man should remember that the day of death is fixed". Azam Chaudhary tells us that it is even today a popular saying in the northern regions of the Indus.[32] These examples are the most poignant as they convey to us an inner meaning of the uncertainties and tribulations that these people were experiencing while being on these journeys through difficult terrains. Far from referring to the purpose for which they travelled, they simply etched their names, signed in honour of the Buddha or simply said that they had passed through the place.

The above inscriptions are accompanied by an array of rock-engravings, many of them affiliated to the Buddhist faith. This compliments the maximum of Buddhist names and dedicational phrases discussed above. The depiction of the *stūpa* is the most popular. The variety of its form is partly due to it being made by lay persons but also indicates the changing form of it over time. Thewalt in his study of this aspect of these depictions primarily at Chilas, Thalpan, and Thor is of the opinion that,

> the carvings ... display a vast variety of Buddhist iconology and of the development of architectural forms and designs .... The oldest representations of *stūpas* very closely resemble the types in Central India (e.g., in Sānchi and Bhārhut) and some monumental *stūpas* in Gandhara as well.[33]

Interestingly, these evolutionary patterns of the *stūpa* forms at these sites show a number of influence that makes these engravings different from the usual sculptural narrative art of the Buddhists both in India and abroad. In other words, it is difficult to mark out a clear-cut style or authorship that they can be characterised with.

Apart from most popular Buddhist symbols, images, visual forms and symbols of other kinds have also been found. For instance, Plate no. 23 is of a *Lingam* (17:15) that is clearly visible. It is made on a platform of four steps with a part of a Brāhmī inscription on it. Other depictions of what look like *Lingas* with two-step platforms and fragmentary Brāhmī inscriptions are also found illustrated on these Plates. The maximum date to these is given as the eighth century AD as can be gleaned from looking at the colour of the *Lingas*. On the top of one of them a flag has been made at a later stage and it is suggested that it was part of an attempt to convert it into a *stūpa*.[34] Related to the Śaivite affiliation, another interesting non-Buddhist symbol found is the depiction of the *trishula*. The arches and circles on certain Plates (nos. 22 and 23) show a lot of variation in their drawing. Several *swastikas* have also been found [Plate no. 27]. Out of 7 of them at Oshibat, 5 revolve looking towards the left and 2 revolve looking to the right. All these have been found on the eastern part of Oshibat. The scholars who have studied them at the site have pointed out that they have been made rather carelessly. The one at 21:25 is made differently because it has a circular formation at its end like a hook. Chaudhary opines that this variation in making the *swastikas* may have been due to the ignorance of the inscribers, or may be due to some tantric or magical faith of the inscribers, known only to them.[35] Four of the *swastikas* are with human figures, whereas two of them are with *trishulas* alongside (78:4 and 21:25). These are normally dated to the sixth century AD. The one with a hook-like formation (21:25) has been dated to be between the fourth and the sixth century AD due to the existence of a Brāhmī inscription there.

The maximum of non-religious engravings or etchings are found in the form of anthropomorphous figures. Those that dwell on hunting scenes and with images of god in a primitive form have rightly been discussed as part of the prehistoric phase at this site. However, some of these forms continue till as late as the seventh century AD. It is difficult in the present context to discuss in detail the intricate symbolism. Some relevant examples can be noted. There are, for instance, nine items drawn on the rock surface that are symbols of some family or tribe that were most probably used to brand horses, bulls and sheep as just generally can be understood as some mark of identification.[36] For, later in the signs that emerge, there are some that have been interpreted as royal symbols. For instance, for the Kushana period the one depicted at 28:31 [Plate 28] is common. It is a symbol that has been seen on innumerable coins of the Kushana dynasty.[37] Forty-eight plates [Plates nos. 32-36] are those of some sort of scenes. Twelve of these describe hunting, 1 is of war, 3 are of human groups, 1 is depicting *maithuna,* (?), 6 of *stūpas,* 2 show dance, and 10 are of animals. Thirteen are not clear.[38]

Some very general engravings have also been documented but it is difficult to clearly understand their meaning and significance. Two arches are shown with innumerable rays that have been identified probably as the sign of Sun (28:45; 39:97) [Plate no. 27]. The age of these cannot be established. Some boards of games have also been found. It is possible that to keep themselves busy while waiting for their onward or return journey, these were drawn and some such games were played. It is suggested by Chaudhary that these could also simply be decorations.[39] Three spiral drawings were also found again as a form of decoration but their age cannot be established. On Plate no. 24 is depicted a picture of a single star (18:250) which, if looked at along with the one at 18:278, looks like the picture of a flower. It is indeed possible that some of these depictions were done to kill time since often weather conditions or other expediency must have made travellers wait at Oshibat before proceeding further.

For a moment we turn to dwell briefly on the broad historical contours of the region under discussion in order to place the above descriptions in context. It is well known that the area as a whole was under the sway of various political forces since as early as the sixth century BC. The Achaemenians (559–330 BC) controlled parts of the region—Gandhara and Kamboja—as the twentieth satrapy of their empire.[40] The eastern frontiers of these contacts vacillated and it was only when Alexander marched into the area that they extended clearly up to the Indus and Punjab. With the break-up of the Macedonian Empire, the Seleucides (302 BC) and the Mauryas (323 BC) emerged as the dominant powers in the region. Herat and Hindukush became the northern and western frontiers of India during these times.[41] Later, Parthia (250 BC) and Bactria (227 BC) had asserted their autonomy and became independent of the Seleucid Empire; they began to cast their sway over the region. The Graeco-Bactrian culture penetrated much into this area and beyond, both to the northwest and the southwest. These early political conquests and influence had far-reaching impact. Even in Indian texts of the period that usually did not discuss foreign invasions, we have ample reference to the changing social complexion of the region in the emergence of the frequent mention of such names as Yavana, Saka, Pahlava indicating the new significance of their presence on the northwestern borders of the subcontinent.

However, it was not till the late century BC and the early century that the political control of the frontier slackened and the area became the core target of the invasions by the Central Asiatic tribes. The Saka penetration (138 BC) was followed by a set of invasions by the Yueh Chi. Well known as the Kushanas, they conquered first Bactria (140 BC) but soon most of northwestern India and Kashmir were under their control (AD 78).[42] Their inroads into the Ganges are too well known to recount here. Interestingly, contacts with the West, Central Asia, and China, known during the early period, were all consolidated during this period.[43] It was only during the fifth century that the Kushanas were really uprooted from parts of the region by the Ephthalites. After this period independent kingdoms emerged on the western frontiers of India, and the Persians once again reasserted themselves in areas around the Hindukush. Small Kushana principalities continued and, therefore, restricted for some time the penetration of Arabs. The frequent political changes in the region as a whole had a significant impact around the Hindukush and Karakorum areas. They developed gradually but consistently as important strategic frontiers that marked an important division between the Central and South Asian lands. Throughout this period, the region of our present study thus saw a continuous stream of people of diverse origin and languages flock through the high altitude passes and along the banks of the Indus diverting to various destinations. Trade continued unabated and culture and religion thrived. Thus, though historical boundaries kept changing with civilisation frequency and overlaid the region from time to time, the travellers by habit moved the shifting boundaries, motivated both by the economic thrust of their endeavours as well as their religious urges.

The Kushana period in particular reflected a flourishing urban economy[44] that was marked by a flourishing craft production guilds. Guilds or *serṇi* are often mentioned in literature since as early as the sixth century BC. However, during the early centuries of the Christian era their mention becomes clearer and more prolific through both literature and votive inscriptions. Their association with the Buddhist and Jaina faiths is also well known. More than sixty occupations are mentioned in the *Milindapanha* and the *Mahāvastu*.[45] It is significant to note that the leaders of these called *śreṣṭhipramukhonaigamo* and the leaders of the caravan tradesmen called *sarthavāhapramukho vanijagrāmo* had not only acquired a social status but were also holders of political power at the local level. They were powers to reckon with and the law books even made stringent rules about controlling their activities.[46] It is of some significance that even during periods of protracted warfare in Central Asia, material exchanges between various segments of population continued between the oases states of Central Asia, India and China. Writes Liu,

> that the border markets continued to function even during the war suggests that there was regular trade with Central Asians along the border. Even soldiers guarding the watch towers along the frontiers engaged in trade.[47]

She further explains that all concerned shared a common interest—the states as well as the ordinary merchants and their guilds—to protect trade that was so essential for the region on a seasonal, and even on a monthly, basis.[48]

The routes that these travellers took during this entire period from about the late centuries BC to roughly about eighth century AD did not remain unchanging. In fact, the choice of what routes to take was significantly determined by the vagaries of the political, particularly, military activities of different periods. That these happenings posed risks for the traders is self-evident. For the early period, one usually talks about the efficacy and solidity of the Silk Route between the Roman World and China. Everything else in central India and northwest India are seen as offshoots of this. Though the distance between India and Central Asia was short compared to that between Rome and India, there were many physical difficulties and dangers. This trade had to pass through diverse geographical locales as also through various peoples. In one sense the centrality of the Rome-China Silk Route was dependent on these offshoots that really determined how successfully the goods could be transacted. For the early phases of these transactions, Wheeler[49] had suggested that Bactria was the mode for this international trade. From this city it ran through Kapisi and Kabul Valley to the most important cities of the Kushana Empire, namely Pushkaravati and Taxila and thence into the Ganges plains using the well laid-out Mauryan highway. Another route from Kashgar in Central Asia that also led to the core region of the Kushana Empire was the one that passed through Gilgit in Kashmir. The route along the Indus was then used to proceed further south and thence into the heartland of India. It is this route that was used by the travellers we have been discussing in this paper. Whereas the former route was important for the early centuries AD, the latter became increasingly important for the last period. A.K. Narain had pointed out the significance of this short-cut from Central Asia through Kashmir as early as 1957,[50] but it is only after the archaeological discoveries discussed above by us that scholars now fully recognise this as a crucial artery of communication for centuries. Other archaeological studies across Central Asia, China, and Afghanistan have also indicated that many of the earlier flourishing sites were depopulated from the fourth to fifth century AD so that when the Chinese Buddhist monk Fa-hsien travelled to South Asia in the fifth century AD, he took this short route through the Pamir Plateau to the Gandhara region. The change was also probably promoted by the Bactria region having been inflicted due to the pressure of the Sassanians and the subsequent damage caused by Hapthalites or White Huns.[51]

The Kashgar to Gilgit route was shorter and had to be resorted to on occasions when there were severe political disturbances and the like. But it is well known that it was also more treacherous. Ancient travellers in perfunctory statements mention the difficulty of travelling through it (Chinese pilgrims, Stein). However, it is most graphically captured in Huntington's experience of more recent times that are worth quoting here. He writes about his crossing of the Karakorum Pass at 8,300 feet above the sea level thus:

> This was the culminating point of the highest trade route in the world. In twenty-one miles I counted four hundred and seventy-four dead horses, not to mention numerous dismembered skeletons, thirty-two bales of merchandise, and one human corpse ... At the top of the pass our carvan halted, as its predecessors have done for ages.[52]

Interestingly, Huntington too recounts for us the two possible routes that travellers could take if they needed to travel from what he calls Chinese Turkestan to the subcontinent. They were "those of Karakorum and Term Davan. The latter runs westward from Kashgar at the western extremity of the country ... reaching Russian Turkestan." He further notes pertinently that,

> in every way it is an easier route than the other, for it rises to an elevation of only about 12,000 feet, and the part of at higher altitude can be crossed in a day or two. In the past, however, as now, communication with the west by this route, more frequently than by the other, must have been interrupted by wars, during which travellers and merchants were forced to use the harder, cheaper and more peaceful Karakorum route.[53]

This then sums for us why the early travellers also chose this route despite the fact that it was more difficult to journey through. These difficulties affected the very physical existence of the travellers. Writes Huntington:

> Almost without exception, the caravans which cross the 'ridgepole of the earth,' as the Karakorum plateau is sometimes called, suffer disasters from famine, storm, or mountain sickness. It is by no means rare for a caravan to

> lose a quarter or half of its animals. Yet in spite of its difficulties, the same baleful route has been followed century after century by panting, famished caravans. Nothing illustrates more forcibly the strength of the distinctively human passions for novelty and gain, or whatever leads to trade and pursuit of wealth.[54]

As during the time of Huntington, so also in ancient times, the demands of the two very diverse and different physical conditions, namely tropical India (with its vegetable products, tea, spices, and textiles) and temperate Central Asia (the notorious hemp for smoking, fine wool, felt, skins), created the objective condition for commodities to be exchanged and consumed in large quantities on both sides.

Quoting the Chinese source, Xinru Liu writes:

> A culture heavily influenced by West Asia, South Asia, and China came to be formed in Central Asia. In addition to using commodities from surrounding regions the people of Central Asia wrote Kharoṣṭī Brāhmī, and the Chinese scripts.

This is true for the region under study as well. In fact, these well-developed communication and language skills were central to interaction across the regions. There must have been difficulties as well, but these were most certainly overcome, much like the anecdote Huntington tells us about after he crossed over the Karakorum and was at the threshold of small market-towns that heralded his entry into the Central Asian plains at the fertile oasis of Khotan. He informs us that there was a population of about hundred and fifty thousand around 1905. Some of the first people that thronged around him in the market were Indian merchants. However, first the Chinese officials met him and he explains the way he had to communicate with them. There, with two mandarins from the other carts, we drank tea and tried to talk. I spoke in one dialect of Turki or in English to Rasul, he in another dialect of Turki to the official interpreter, and he in Chinese to the governor. The conversation was undeniably diluted, but as Rasul put it: "Your plenty sweet matter telling to governor. I think he liking very much. You making talk to soldier-man very good. Yes, that was very best. All men very pleased."[55]

The extensive trade and urbanisation during this period is reflected in a number of coins found all over India during this period. The early Kushanas used bilingual legends in Greek and Prakrit on their coins. Kanishka only used the Greek script on his coins, but most of these kings used symbols from diverse religious cultures on their coins—those pertaining to Buddhism, Śaivism, Persian gods, etc. This indeed reflected not only the religious diversity of the Kushana Empire but also that the kings made an attempt to have a liberal attitude so that they could foster contact and communication within the confines of the territory they ruled. They were particularly interested in fostering commercial exchange on the basis of which much of the prosperity of their empire rested. This eclectic spirit had definitely seeped into the cultural ethos of the people as is seen in the data presented above. The travellers, in fact, had to inculcate the spirit of accommodation, as they were journeying over different cultural and social landscapes. Once again one can draw on the more recent experiences of Huntington who, having crossed the dreary Karakorum Pass, recounts:

> Our pious Mohammedan servants gathered around the roughly squared head of stone which, though a hundred miles from the nearest habitation, marks the boundary between India and China, the two most populous countries of the globe ... Here they made offering of home-made bread and apricots on the stones. There was fanaticism about it, simply reverent gratitude to Allah for bringing them safely to the top of the dreaded pass. Even the despised Buddhist (the Tibetan who looked after the horses on the journey) and the half tolerated Christian (Huntington himself) were invited to share the offering, and in the short prayer which concluded with reverent stoking of the bread in memory of the Prophet.[56]

Much like the experiences the ancient travellers and merchants with their guides, servants and pony caretakers must have enacted, though espousing other faiths, they offered a thanks-giving for their safe passage. Apart from building people in deep faith, irrespective of their personal religions, there was also another code of ethics that bound the travellers together and that was their spirit of camaraderie and trust. In this regard, Huntington observed:

> We also passed, that day, thirty-six bales of tea, spices, cloth, and Korans, abandoned the previous fall by a caravan which started too late from Leh. Rasul, our headman, had heard all about it: then a snow storm came on, and the men fled for their lives, leaving the remaining loads, ropes and all, in the middle of the floodplain of a stream. The owner expected to send a new caravan in a month or two to get the foods and carry them on to Yakand. He knew that they would be safe, for such incidents are common. Custom, stronger than law, binds all travellers to respect the property thus temporarily left in the road.[57]

Discussing these aspects of the journey on some of the most high altitude trade routes of the world was important to drive home the fact that given these precarious conditions, travellers had to be co-operative and bound together in humanity, despite the fact that in the original homes of their origin they were competitors.

Scholars who have closely studied and documented the material discussed as above had suggested that it is clear from the depictions at Oshibat that they belong to different ages. Further, in contrast to Oshibat, at Chilas and at other places discovered by them, more or less, all the depictions had belonged to one period, namely what they called the Buddhist. We summarise now the major reason cited by them as to why Oshibat existed in this area with its inscriptions, mainly of personal names, for such a long period of time. It is pointed out that at present there is no habitation of any significant kind and perhaps this was also the case in the past. Neither is their a stream that joins the Indus at this place. In the same way, it is neither the starting point of a journey nor the destination. They characterise it as a place that is like a rocky desert since the beginning and nothing is available here but a desolate territory.

Given these conditions the particular significance of Stone/Rock no. 18 is highlighted since during a later period it had developed as a pilgrimage site where the burial of a Muslim Pir or saint was found. The date of this burial cannot be established but that it was a place of pilgrimage is now beyond any doubt. Thus, it is pointed out that according to Jettmar, Rock 18 itself must have been a local prilgimage since beginning of time and this hypothesis gets substantiated from the existence of two very big pictures of the prehistoric period on this stone that are now not clear because of the innumerable Brāhmī writings and inscriptions on them. Citing this as an important indicator that the stone was holy for the local people in some sort of way even before the writers of the Brāhmī inscriptions came along, he goes on to argue that any place that becomes holy then, for the coming generations, it remains an important place of worship without knowing the reason for its earlier true significance and irrespective of the religion they belong to. The general concept articulated is that the souls living in such old pilgrimages and holy places should be kept happy and not be harmed. In turn, in venerating such a place there would be no harm to the people involved. The Brāhmī and Sogdian writers can be thus understood as those people who did not want to affront the local gods or ghosts during their journey that in any case were full of danger. Moreover, it can be added that most of the travellers were Buddhists who respected the relic remains of the past. For them to make picture of the *stūpa* at any holy place was to show respect to relic remains and this was thus a source of permanent *punya.* That is why on Rock no. 18 there are maximum drawings of *stūpas* and the personal names of the visitors to the site are also written near them. These inscriptions found here are up to that period when the local population was attracted towards Buddhism. So, it can be assumed to be a holy place and the proof of this is the large quantity of small round stones found on this rock just before the documentation work began at the site.[58]

Having stressed on the religious significance of Oshibat, Jettmar has also explained the relative importance of Oshibat vis-à-vis Shatial as a centre of economic importance. Shatial, it is pointed out, was an important trade centre during early times. The Sogdians, he opines, who were not Buddhist, did not have the permission to come to Shatial and sell their things as they were not allowed to proceed to Upper Indus. On the other hand, the traders of the Buddhist affilation coming from other parts, especially the subcontinent, had no such restrictions. The evidence to support this supposition is based on the relative number of Sogdian and Brāhmī inscriptions available at Oshibat, Shatial, and Thalpan. In all the above places the Sogdian writings are very less compared to the Brāhmī ones. In Shatial although the Sogdian writings were more, they were still less compared to the Brāhmī ones. It is also to be considered that the majority of Sogdian writings are on the north bank of the river Indus at places like Khanbary, Thora, Helordas, Dadamdas, Thalpan, and Bedas. One route to the east that the Sogdians might have used was temporarily open for traders who went to those trading points under the guidance of local people to sell their products without paying toll or taxes. It is then suggested that Oshibat was a meeting point when travellers were waiting or resting here before they crossed the river. Most of the inscriptions and artistic drawings are all found beside the old pathway on the Indus bank. This can be contrasted with the east bank of the river, which is large and the flow is also very calm and, even today, the gold washers cross the river from this point in their self-made boats. The other side of the river is an open plain of sand and small stones where the fleet can be harboured easily.[59] This is indeed a plausible reason why travellers in such large numbers passed through Oshibat.

Oshibat thus critically fell on the old pathway along the Indus Valley that constituted a branch of the Silk Road system. Travellers like merchants and pilgrims from Central Asia, China, and India undoubtedly executed many of the carvings and inscriptions but some must also be attributed to the inhabitants of the region who must have assisted the travellers in various ways. In fact, while studying the carvings in detail, Thewalt writes:

> Many of these elaborate rock carvings must be attributed to highly skilled craftsmen who received their artistic training in the great monasteries of Gandhara, while others are crude imitations, executed by travelling laymen or the inhabitants of the neighbouring villages, wishing to gather some spiritual merit by reproducing these sacred monuments.[60]

Questions of the identity remained intact. But in the far-flung regions of isolation and uprooted away from familiar connections of village, town and family, it is interesting to note that none of the travellers, but for a few Sogdian ones, particularly emphasised on their caste, guild or family affiliation. It is rather that as individuals they left a stamp of themselves. But in the process of doing so, these rock surfaces had become a meeting point of belonging in that the people of different religions and ethnic affiliations wanted to be known by their individual identities but, at the same time, mingled with each other in the act of their larger endeavours of making a success of their travels. Thus, to get to know each other, learn each other's languages and scripts and share experiences was practical necessity to effectively communicate. Oshibat thus emerged as a critical meeting point as a significant route of communication both in reality and metaphorically. Whatever the reasons for travel, the crossing over the Karakorum mountains into Central Asia was a daunting task and this fear of the difficult and treacherous terrain made people pause a while in mediation and solace before they continued the journey. The same relief must have resulted on their return. Further mundane necessities required as porters, ponies, horses, food and other aids must have been necessary to collect and all these facilities took time to procure that compulsively made the travellers halt on the plains of the Upper Indus Valley before they embarked on their journey of solititude and hope.

The writing of phrases like "Man should remember that the day of death is fixed" undoubtedly transported them to their inner deep feelings of understanding the simple notions of the impermanence of life that had been taught to them by the teachings of the Buddha. Yet they moved on in this difficult terrain to complete their journeys to carry on with the essential practical necessities of life. They did not come to Oshibat for pilgrimage but made it a site for defining their existence in this life that was inextricably linked to their multiple identities intermingling with each other in land alien to all of them—the Brahmins, the Buddhists, the leaders of caravans, merchants and so on. We tend to identify the significance of Oshibat today in only spiritual sense or, merely understand it as a strategic location as meeting or departing points for trade. To those who travelled through Oshibat, it had the relevance as a place where, despite being competitors, they all could effectively interact socially, something that was not possible in their countries of origin.

Despite the difficult terrain, we conclude, the travellers from all directions found their way to this important junction, rested for a while before they moved on and, in the process, left behind for posterity to understand the complexity of social interactions beyond boundaries of nations, communities and faiths. These travellers were located in different historical contexts and, therefore, must have undoubtedly been influenced by the dominant political or economic happenings of their times that would have either accelerated or inhibited these processes of interactions. Nonetheless, they went beyond boundaries in more than one sense: at the ideological level, in terms of linguistic and religious exchanges and at the spatial and material level, in terms of conquering new terrains and establishing economic linkages. These early contacts away from home generated new ideas and further strengthened interactions that we must now remember.

We end with the seventh-century Buddhist traveller's accounts of the region, which he was crossing into India around Kashmir. Hiuen-Tsang wrote:

> The Sramana coming to the western borders of the country, crossed a rapid river, whilst doing so the boat was nearly overwhelmed—. The master of the ship examined (his goods), found the tooth of Buddha—. Many miraculous circumstances occur in this mountain. Sometimes a stone barrier is split across, sometimes on the mountain-top there remain the traces of horse; but all things of this sort are only mistaken traces of Arhats and Sramanas, who in troops frequent this spot and with their fingers trace these figures, as if riding on horses or going to and fro (on foot) and this has led to the difficulty in explaining these marks.[61]

The discoveries along the Karakorum have thus struck travellers from time immemorial. Reading Hiuen-Tsang against the backdrop of the recent discoveries made by the Joint Pakistani-German team, only further endorses how the idea of the permanence of human actions can become reminders.

NOTES AND REFERENCES

1. Ellsworth Huntington, *Across Central Asia: A Journey in Central Asia Illustrating the Geographic Basis of History*, Cosmo Publications (reprint), New Delhi, 1995, p. xxv-vi. It is not clear when this book was first written, but definitely it was between 1916 and 1920.
2. Some of this has been mentioned by me in an earlier article. The tendency to write about political and economic history of northwestern regions of the Indian subcontinent flourished in the first half of the twentieth century. See 'The Foreigner as the "Other" in Early India', *The Indian Historical Review*, Vol. XVI, nos. 1-2, 1989-1990, pp. 109-113.
3. Relatively more recent studies take into account the complex relationship of the political and economic with the larger fabric of social and regious changes that were taking place in the contacts between Central Asia and the subcontinent. For instance, the extremely incisive account of these relations in the context of ancient India and ancient China, bringing in the contacts with the Roman world and most importantly, Central Asia by Xinru Liu, *Ancient India and Ancient China: Trade, Religious Exchanges, AD 1-600*, OUP, Delhi 1988.
4. Cited in Sarojini Chaturvede, *Foreign Influx and Interaction with Indian Culture, 6th century BC-1st century AD*, Agam Kala Prakashan, Delhi, 1985, pp. 214-15.
5. Debala Mitra, 'Foreign Elements in Indian Population', in *The Cultural Heritage of India*, Vol. II, Ramakrishna Mission Institute of Culture, Calcutta, p. 621.
6. G. Sharma and Negi, 'The Saka-Kushanas in the Central Ganges Valley', in B.G. Gafurov *et al.*, *Central Asia in the Kushana Period*, Vol. II, 1975, pp. 22-29, on the archaeological evidence conducted in these parts.
7. B.N.S. Yadava, 'Some Aspects of the Changing Order in India During the Saka Kushana Age', in B.G. Gafurov *et al.*, *ibid.*, pp. 123-36.
8. They were rather generally alluded to in a generalised way as *mlecchas* as being excluded from the society dominated by *brāhamaṇas*. See Aloka Parasher, *Mlecchas in Early India*, New Delhi, 1990, Chapter VII.

9. *Ibid.*
10. Yadava, *op. cit.*, 1975, p. 127.
11. This monumental work was initiated in 1978 under the leadership of Prof. Karl Jettmar from Heidelberg and Prof. A.H. Dani from Islamabad. A joint Pakistani-German research project started its surveys in 1979 and by 1982 enough work had been done to start a documentation cell at the Heidelberg Academy of Humanities and Science. Since 1989 this is headed by Prof. Harald Hauptmann with contributions from scholars of different countries contributing to documenting and analysing these interesting archaeological and historical remains—As reported by Martin Bemmann and Ditte Koenig, 'Rock Art & Petroglyphs: Rock Carvings and Inscriptions along the Karakorum Highway', *Tracce: On Line Rock Art Bulletin*, The Footsteps of Man, May 1997.
12. *Ibid.*
13. *Materialien zur Archaologie de Nordgebiete Pakistans*, Vol. 1, M. Bemmann and D. Koenig (eds.), *Die Felsbildstation Oshibat*, Mainz, 1994; Vol. 2, G. Fussman and D. Koenig (eds.), *Die Felsbildation Shatial*, Mainz, 1997; Vol. 3, D. Bandini-Koenig (ed.), *Die Felsbildation Hodar*, Mainz, 1999.
14. The nature of the documentation done of these sites by various scholars in terms of catalogues on the art work, the editing of inscriptions and generally, on details pertaining to this project, valuable information has been posted on the *Heidelberger Academic Der Wissenschaften* web page. An exhaustive bibliography of books and articles on subject matter relating to these sites has also been posted, which was of tremendous help in the formulation of this paper.
15. Bemmann and Koenig, *op. cit.*, 1997.
16. *Ibid.* We are informed that the majority of the inscriptions are executed in Indian scripts like Brāhmī, Kharoṣṭhī, and Proto-Sārda. However, a large number of Sogdian (c. 700) inscriptions were also found along with Chinese, 13 and Hebrew 1.
17. Martin Bemmann und Ditte Koenig (mit Beitragen von gerad Fussmann. Oskar von Hinuber and Nicholas Sims-Williams), *Materianlin Zur Archaologie Der Nordgebiete Pakistani (Materials for the Archaeology of the Northern Regions of Pakistan) Die Felbildsation Oshibat*, Band I, Mainz, 1994. [Henceforth *MANP*, Vol. I]. This is part of the publication under the directorship of Harlad Hauptmann for the Heidelberger Akademic Der Wissenschaften.
18. Azam Chaudhary, 'Oshibatt Mein Nakashi aur Kundhakari' (Urdu), in *MANP*, Vol. 1, 1994, p. 1.

    (Translation of Martin Bemmann, 'Inscriptions and Rock Carvings at Oshibat').

    Reading and translation of portions of this article into English has been done with the help of Professor Rehamat Ali Yousuf, Head, Department of Urdu, University of Hyderabad. Its initial reading and Hindi translation was done by Professor Noorjehan Begum, Department of Hindi, University of Hyderabad.
19. Robert Kauper of the Munchen University did the geographical surveys for the present project, before the current discoveries, in 1982 and the Kalshruhe University further carried out the work after 1982.

20. Chaudhary, *op. cit.*, 1994, pp. 1-2.
21. Bemann and Koenig, *op. cit.*, 1997.
22. Oskar von Hinuber, 'Zu den Brāhmī Inschriften', in *MANP*, Vol. 1, 1994, p. 20.
23. Gerard Fussman, 'Zu Den Kharosthi-Inschriften', in *MANP*, Vol. 1 and the numbers in square brackets refer to the Plates as given in *MANP*, Vol. 1.
24. Henceforth, these figures in round brackets refer to the stone numbers as documented in *MANP*, Vol. 1.
25. Fussman, *op. cit.*, 1994, p. 19.
26. For all these places, Thewalt has done this by closely analysing the *stūpa* architectural form. See Home Page, Volker Thewalt Verlag.
27. Chaudhary, *op. cit.*, 1994, pp. 3-4.
28. See *MANP*, Vol. 1, pp. 37-144. These have not been discussed in the paper.
29. These numbers refer to the stone on which they were found as cited in *MANP*, Vol. 1, for all the inscriptions and engravings documented. These can be found on pp. 37-141 of this volume.
30. He is as a Vaishnava, see *MANP*, Vol. 1, p. 63.
31. The word *trisula* occurs along with these names. See *MANP*, Vol. 1, p. 121.
32. Chaudhary, *op. cit.*, 1994, p. 3.
33. V. Thewalt, 'Rock Carvings and Inscriptions along the Indus. The Buddhist Tradition', J. Schotsmans and M. Taddei (eds.), *South Asian Archaeology* (Papers from the seventh International Conference of the *ASAAWE* held in Brussels, 1993), Naples, 1985, pp. 779-800. The above quote is from the internet version of the paper, 1997 Home Page, Volker Thewalt Verlag.
34. Chaudhary, *op. cit.*, 1994, p. 10.
35. *Ibid.*, p. 12.
36. *Ibid.*, 13.
37. This symbol is called Soter Megas in the symbol Chart appended in Bhaskar Chattopadhyaya, *The Age of the Kushanas – A Numismatic Study*, Calcutta, 1979, p. 226, line 14.
38. Chaudhary, *op. cit.*, 1994, pp. 13-14.
39. *Ibid.*, II, p. 11.
40. D.C. Sircar, *Select Inscriptions Bearing on Indian History and Civilization*, Vol. 1, Calcutta, 1965, 'Inscriptions of the Akhaemanians', Nos. 1 & 2, 4 & 5 on Achaemenian presence as known by their inscriptions in northwestern India.
41. E. Hultzsch, CII *Inscriptions of Asoka*, Vol. 1, Oxford, 1925, Rock Edicts V, XIII Mansehra and Shabhazgarhi versions for the northern limits of the Mauryan territory.
42. Baldev Kumar, *The Early Kusanas*, Delhi, 1973, pp. 213 ff. for the diverse regions, peoples and tribes under the early Kushana Empire.
43. Bhaskar Chatopadhyaya, *Kushana State and Indian Society*, Calcutta, 1975, pp. 27-60 for a detailed description of the different territories within and outside the Indian subcontinent under Kushana control.

44. Buddha Rashmi Mani, *The Kushana Civilization*, Delhi, 1987, pp. 16-37 on the extent and distribution of the material and socio-economic pattern of the Kushana period, the intensity of which was not uniform throughout the period of their rule for all segments of the empire.
45. Xinru Liu, *op. cit.*, 1988, pp. 36-42.
46. G.L. Adhya, *Early Indian Economic*, Bombay, 1966, p. 86.
47. Xinru Liu, *op. cit.*, 1988, p. 16.
48. *Ibid.*, p. 18.
49. R.E.M. Wheeler, *Rome Beyond the Imperial Frontier*, London, p. 156.
50. A.K. Narain, *The Indo-Greeks*, OUP, London, 1957, p. 135.
51. Xinru Liu, *op. cit.*, 1988, p. 27.
52. Huntington, *op. cit.*, 1975 (rp.), pp. 83.
53. *Ibid.*, p. 87.
54. *Ibid.*
55. *Ibid.*, p. 154.
56. *Ibid.*, p. 84.
57. *Ibid.*, p. 83.
58. Jettmar's views as cited in Chaudhary, *op. cit.*, 1994, p. 15.
59. *Ibid.*
60. V. Thewalt, *op. cit.*, 1985. The above quote is from the first internet version of the paper, 1997-Home Page, Volker Thewalt Verlag.
61. Samuel Beal, *Si-Yu-ki Buddhist Records of the Western World.* Translated from the Chinese of Hiuen Tsang (AD 629), (Reprint edition), Delhi, 2001, Vol. 1, pp. 159-60.

SECTION II

MEDIEVAL PERIOD

6

Indo-Central Asian Contacts: A Turkoman Initiative in the Medieval Period

R.L. Hangloo

Despite the immensity of distances, the history of India's contacts with Central Asia goes back to antiquity. The earliest evidence of contact between the two civilisations is located in Early Bronze Age, when the invention of bronze improved the techniques of production of metal objects, which enabled Iran to increase export supply of copper, lead, tin, etc. to the neighbouring regions, including India.[1] As these transactions grew, the movement of people and materials on routes, which connected India to Central Asia, became more frequent. Among others who worked extensively on these early Central Asian contacts with the outside world, the work of Masson and Sarianidi has served to establish the key role that this trade played in maintenance of these contacts. They say:

> It seems likely that trade was the motivating force behind connections between India and Central Asia, which became much more marked in Middle Bronze Age. We see then that the settled agriculture communities of Southern Turkmenia in the Middle Bronze Age comprised societies with a complex and highly developed economic structure, with craft as a special sphere of production on one hand and agriculture on the other, the very existence of this division suggesting an internal exchange system growing into trade as an essential link in the economic system as a whole.[2]

Contacts like this occurred in every part of the world but they followed different patterns and ended in diverse ways. Unfortunately, history never reveals the basis of such contacts in a pure state because the cultures mingle and interpenetrate. They also display specificities and complexities that result both from the variations of time and place and also from differing mentalities of participants in these contacts.[3]

Initially the course of Indo-Central Asian contacts was crucially determined by the geophysical situation of Central Asia, which led to major migratory movements out of this region.[4] This can be observed from very early times. Around the first millennium BC when the Eastern branch of Iranians came from Transoxiana (Mavara-un Nahar), they were unable to move towards the south of Hindukush, because by that time the entire region of Arachosia and Punjab had already passed into the hands of a sister branch of Aryans.[5] Between the seventh and fourth centuries BC when Achaemenids extended their area of influence, they incorporated a part of India into their dominion and introduced Aramaic as an official language in that part.[6] By the end of the first century BC, a group of Kushanas under their king Kujula Kadphises conducted a series of conquests and after crossing Hindukush they discovered that the wealth of India was much more tempting than the region of Eastern Iran. Subsequently, they established the Kushana kingdom in India.[7] When the Sassanians came to power, they maintained very friendly relations with the Gupta rulers in India for a long time. They also blended the Western influences penetrating into Central Asia, with those from India.[8]

The focus of this evidence is not only the simple assertion of the existence of contacts between Central Asia and India; but we are more concerned with the operational reality of these contacts and the attitude and responses of people from both the regions (Central Asia and India), which contributed to their stability to the extent of allowing them to establish ruling dynasties one after the other. The hypothesis underlying my argument at this stage is that unless there is a correlation between any given society and the forms and the effectiveness of social domination or control that penetrates from outside, the contacts do not grow on a more stable basis and for a longer duration. For example, the Medieval Indian civilisation was preceded by a variety of material cultures within the Indian environment (prehistoric, protohistoric, early historic, ancient, etc.), the nature of which is clearly identifiable.[9] There is little doubt that this pre-medieval culture was essentially a proving ground for civilisation that followed. Like any other material culture, it constitued foundation and anticipated some of the social arrangements. But could they have supplied the necessary impetus that the transformation seems to have required?

While those preceding material cultural formations located within the pre-medieval Indian context were a necessary prerequisite for transformation, they do not constitute sufficient reasons for a transition to take place. Therefore, the real breakthrough always came because of India's contact with the outside world from where also came new ideas, institutions, technology, and values.

The evidence provided by Andre Gunder Frank and Denis Sinor lends credence to this argument here. They state:

> The domestication of horses began in Czechoslovakia, the Ukraine, and Southern Russia about 6000 years ago, but the most important development occurred further east in Central Asia in the second millennium BC. For thousands of years these animals were the main source of human overland transportation, military superiority, animal protein, warm clothing, tenting, etc. Moreover, these developments were complemented by others in transportation, military technology, and metallurgy (especially in Caucasus) much of which also came from Central Asia. The incursions of Central Asia into more civilised outlying areas in the period 1700-1500 BC were victorious largely on account of horse-drawn, spoked war chariots, which were developed or improved in Central Asia. They must have also brought with them a social organisation, which was effective enough to organise their military campaigns and to make them victorious against their 'more' civilised neighbours. As noted earlier, around 1000 BC Central Asian incursions were again victorious. They again made important advances in transportations and military technology, including metallurgy to bring on the Iron Age. This time they rode larger, domesticated horses and came armed with weapons made of iron. The fact that Central Asians were again victorious suggests that they had developed something of a value in a competitive world. Their near sedentary neighbours also developed a technology and social organisation in response to their relations with Central Asians and of course with each other. This organisation includes the formation of states and the organisation of political power.[10]

It is certain that these developments accompanied Central Asians during their Indian occupation. In fact, a rich spectrum of variants can be observed, from the extreme indifference to the overwhelming displays of friendship with which the newcomers from Central Asia would have been welcomed. Sometimes the presence of Central Asians in India can be regarded as a special form of collision in which the subjugated population of India survived liquidation albeit, in circumstances which largely precluded the survival of their political institutions.[11] The establishment of Kushana rule, Turkish Sultanate, Bahmani Sultanate in the Deccan, Shahmir Sultanate in Kashmir, and even Mughal occupation are the best examples to illustrate this point.[12] This advanced Central Asian culture with adequate military equipment, transportation, metallurgical developments, and craft production technology was bound to dominate the societies that came into contact with it.[13]

Many scholars who worked on some or the other aspect of these Indo-Central Asian contacts during medieval times have provided very interesting analysis of the information on the subject, but by and large their work has remained an appendage without linking the discussion to large geographies in which the specific typologies of these two civilisations interacted.[14] Fernand

Braudel very rightly remarks, "All the Social Sciences must make a room for an increasing geographical conception of mankind".[15]

But one of the problems raised by the larger geographical complexity in this context is rooted in the very characterisation of what is termed as Central Asian.[16] Because while studying the structures, institutions and roles as determinants in medieval Indian social life many scholars have tended to clothe the social production of these contacts with generalisations like Indo-Islamic, Islamic, and Indo-Persian.[17] Even the most celebrated historians like K.M. Athar Ali, whose writings played a significant role in establishing and reinforcing the progressive or secular nature of Indian historical writing, do not seem to have (consciously or unconsciously) hesitated while doing so. K.M. Ashraf says:

> As a result of Muslim impact, the ancient Hindu order was almost completely destroyed. Political and social institutions were levelled, caste was modified, religious tendencies took a new direction and force and finally the conception of India as a whole was made possible.[18]

Similarly, Athar Ali also attributes the changes that took place in India between thirteenth to fifteenth centuries, to the 'intrusion of Islam'.[19] We do not intend to undermine the role that Persian or, more particularly, Islamic influences played in structuring Indo-Central Asian contacts during medieval centuries but our problem is to consider how to return attention to more specific problems within that larger geographical complexity in which the people's participation from both the regions was registered.

While evading some of the legacies of these contacts and attributing everything solely to Persian, Indo-Islamic, and Islamic narrows down the very definition of Indo-Central Asian contacts. This results in overtheorisation and also in unsettling the difficulty in perceiving the Central Asian beyond Persian and Islamic.[20] Obviously, something was lost by this unfortunate neglect of larger complexities and conversely there is something of a value to be gained by stretching the discussion and its conceptual links across the abyss that exists in the Indo-Central Asian contacts. Therefore, any effort that intends to provide even cursory glance of such contacts, which are spread over thousands of years or millennia, cannot ignore the fact that the whole social world from both India and Central Asia has entered into these contacts at one or the other point of time. Such contacts have been both temporarily and geographically structured in a number of different ways because the social world always comprised space, time and entities having casual powers, which might or might not have realised depending on the patterns of interdependence between such entities. Hence, we need to understand the nature of these processes, which produced people who constituted social world at different levels in these contacts as occupants and users of particular space within the temporary and geographical system. This can be readily observed in medieval Indian context through an examination of a host of collisions and co-operative efforts from which stemmed the reinforcements of these contacts from time to time at the hands of various Indian and Central Asian elements.[21]

In order to clarify this point, I have specifically chosen the role of Turkomans as one of the representative instance from Central Asia in reinforcing these contacts between India and Central Asia during the Sultanate period (thirteenth-fifteenth centuries). This is done not only because our sources are also fragmentary to permit a generalisation covering all the ethnic groups spread across the entire Central Asia, but also because it becomes historically unintelligible and geographically diffused enactment of the complex variety of ethnic, regional, religious groups inhabiting such a wide world of centrality between the east and the west amid enduring conflicts.[22] Therefore, I have tried to attempt how a particular group associated explicitly with military campaigns through which they gradually built up their influence and then took over a wide variety of elements within Indian society and corresponded to them before and after the establishment of their power.

In post-Gupta period, the contacts between India and Central Asia were promoted by various ethnic groups in wider geography, but the role of Turkomans stands out as the most significant and central to this relationship.[23] From AD eighth century onwards, we get more organised and consistent information on this aspect. *Rajatarangini*, the earliest authentic historical record composed by Kalhana (the Sanskrit chronicler of Kashmir) in AD 1149-50, provides indisputable evidence about the Turkoman presence in India from earlier times, which helps us to structure our argument with a little more clarity. Kalhana says: "It is by his, i.e., King Lalitaditya (AD 725–753), command to display the mark of their bondage that the Turshukas carry their arms at back and shave half their heads".[24]

During AD 883–903, King Lalliya Sahi perceived the Turshuka rulers as a great threat to his authority.[25] In early AD eleventh century, Trilochanapala, the last ruler of Sahi dynasty, sought the military help from Kashmiri king Sangram Raja (AD 1003–1028) against the Turshukas.[26] When King Kalasa (AD 1063–1089) of Kashmir wanted to put a gilt parasol over the temple of Shiva, he sought the help of Turshuka artist from Turshuka country (Central Asia).[27] At another place, Kalhana refers to Turshuka girls being brought to the Seraglio of King Kalsa (AD 1063–1089).[28] King Harsha (AD 1054–1101) of Kashmir employed hundreds of Turshuka captains in his army for their military skill and strength.[29]

Many Indian and Central Asian towns owed their existence to caravan trade on the Silk Route linking various parts of Central Asia to India. The traders from places like Kashgar, Khotan, Yarkand, Herat, Bukhara, Khurasan, Turkestan, Armenia, Azerbaijan, Kazakhstan, Balk, Urumchi, Karashar, Andijan, Kokand, Aksu, Taskent, Merv and many other parts of Central Asia were actively engaged on the Silk Route trade with Indian merchants from Ladakh, Kashmir, Punjab, Himachal Pradesh, Bengal and other Indian regions.[30]

Interestingly, the profession of arms was a supreme aristocratic vocation of Central Asian society in general and the Turkomans in particular from very early times.[31] Discomforting though the thought might seem to some people, the Ghaznavid rulers whose armies invaded India occasionally owe their origin to Turkomans.[32] Even though the contacts between India and Central Asia were irrevocably set on a collision course by some of the invaders including Mahmud Ghazni, this collision never meant the end of contact between the two cultures. Instead it resulted in enlarging the range of Indo-Central Asian contacts and also in increasing the volume of Indian response to it. Since the variety of contacts were there for a long time, Turkoman entrance did not appear as a cultural shock to Indians; instead, they seem to have located the incident within the horizon of their expectation. The only thing that was new this time was that the newcomers had associated themselves with Islam as an important historical experience and tradition.

Here it is interesting to note that even while conducting the conquest in India, Mahmud of Ghazni expressed his displeasure against his superiors when he said, "The creed of Islam was being used as a bulwark for protection of vested interests and time honoured abuses in Islam".[33]

What we need to keep in view is that the unity of religious institutions and the state was a characteristic of pre-Sultanate state formations in India but not of the Turkoman polity in Central Asia. It was because of their agnostic ideas that they were more concerned about the material progress than religion.[34] Perhaps this was also one of the reasons that enabled them to make progress in terms of science and technology and gave them leverage over other societies that they came into contact with.[35] Besides this, the frequent interventions into each other's disputes or other political affairs by supplying soldiers, weapons and other materials to alter the balance of power to their own advantage or to destroy the equilibrium that had existed previously were an age-old practice. This happened on several occasions as illustrated by Kalhana also. During the Second Battle of Tarain in AD 1192, Mahmud of Ghur fought with Prithviraj Chauhan, and Indian ruler Hamir of Kangra assisted his army.[36] The Raja of Jammu, Bijay Dev sent his son Narsing Dev to facilitate the Turkoman army's victory in India.[37] When this was the nature of response it is most likely that people at the popular level were also guided by their rational considerations and economic and political expediency. Hence, such collisions cannot be characterised by their casualness or intermittent nature because they ultimately transformed into a contact, which laid the groundwork for the establishment of the Delhi Sultanate and the subsequent developments in the different regions of India, wherever the Turkomans went.

The main concern of the Turkomans like Kushanas and their other predecessors was to lose no time in establishing peaceful relations with native people on whom they depended upon for their sustenance, trade, geographical knowledge and assistance in many other fields, which created a social basis for their political power. The establishment of the Sultanate saw trust and a relationship based on mutual dependence and adjustments, which led to the growth of distinctive settings in medieval Indian environment. Even though at the political plane we have evidence of some conflict between the Turkomans and some of the Rajput chiefs, the contacts at the popular level between the people of the two cultures do not reflect even the slightest symptom of aggressive behaviour.[38] Everything that the Turkomans did on Indian soil as loyal soldiers of their masters had no theological motivation but was intended to demonstrate that their presence had brought a new and a final authority of monarchical nature as an alternative to the then existing conditions in northern India.[39] Interestingly, it is precious to find an unbiased assessment of such a phenomenon by colonial historians like Eriskine. He says:

> In India the Turks never effected to monopolise all the authority of kingdoms which they obtained. The natives shared in the administration of the country and in the military commands. They found a country already populous and its territories fully occupied by civilised inhabitants as well as by a race of conquerors of their own religion. They had none of the ferocity of Chengiz and were not so insane to have a wish to expel their cultivators from lands, the value of which was solely owing to their labour.[40]

The commencement of the functioning of the Central Asian ideas and institutions in early thirteenth century India can be understood in terms of a Central Asian Turkish warrior aristocracy's efforts towards territorialisation and administrative coherence. The fundamental element in this was the growth of a centralised monarchy revolving round the personality of the Sultan, which was not possible for them in Central Asia.[41] In times of war, the Turkoman Sultan was expected to be braver and fiercer than any warrior he had (this was the Central Asian military ethic), but in time of peace he sought to tamper the violence of his people.[42] The contacts further culminated in application of *iqta* and enforcement tribute paying relations that helped the newly established Sultanate to seek acquiescence of Indians as loyal subjects. *Iqta* was a territorial assignment and was originally evolved by Abbasid ruler Mutawakkil (AD 847–861) when he handed over Armenia, Azerbaijan, and Faras to his younger brother Mutazz.[43] When a branch of Turkomans ruled over Persia as Seljuq rulers (AD 1037-1157), they further organised the *iqta* system on institutional basis as a widespread form of beneficium.[44] As an element of Central Asian administrative heritage, it helped the Turkomans in establishing their administrative institution based on *iqta* (transferable territorial assignment) and linked together various parts of India. According to Athar Ali, "It clearly reinforced the concept of India as a country if not as a nation".[45]

That is how the Indo-Central Asian contacts produced a new administrative pattern and territorial organisation defining carefully the roles and responsibilities of Central and provincial authorities in India. It also helped Turkomans to tackle the fiscal crisis in northern India more effectively and to resolve the problems concerning their lack of legitimacy both by guaranteeing the governability and by resolving the varied contradictions, which were likely to surface in a newly acquired political space.[46]

The Turkoman Sultans worked hard at the task and they bestowed powers on many Turkoman officials at various levels and developed a community with a distinct identity as members of Turkoman royalty and nobility.[47] At the coronation ceremonies, each Sultan made his commitment to protect his subjects from external threat and internal violence. Born in the family of Ilbari Turkoman tribe, Balban was the first Sultan to blend the Turkoman tribal traditions, which were embedded in traditional Central Asian tribal polity, with Indian polity and developed the institution of kinship in medieval India. Sultan Balban made all efforts to restore the etiquette of the court and the prestige of the crown.[48] He believed in enforcement of submission and clothed coercion with ceremonial surrounding.[49] This was to signalise the importance of political discovery for establishing dominance. It also meant to leave lasting impression on the natives to ensure their respect and obedience. Our sources constantly attest the Turkomans' unquestioned mastery of ceremonial. Making his nobles kneel down or prostrate to ensure their loyalty powerfully enhanced Balban's sense of own importance. None of the natives had the faintest notion or idea as to what this ritual meant and hence their ignorance made it more inspiring. While trying to seek increased personal prestige by even claiming descent from the mythical Turkish hero Afrasiab and insisting on practice of *Paibos* (Kissing of monarch's feet) and *Sijda* (Prostration), Balban was also imitating the regalia of Seljuq and Khawarizam kings of Central Asia and tested their legitimacy in the medieval Indian context.[50]

In fact, the process of medieval Indian state formation owes much to Central Asian politics and its origin has to be sought partly in response to developments in Central Asia. What facilitated the legitimation of these contacts in various fields can partly be attributed to the nature of Indian and Turkoman typologies, because India also had to adopt its political organisation according to the exigencies of Central Asian influence. For example, in introducing Persian as the official language, the Delhi Sultanate, the Bahmani Sultanate in Deccan, and the Shahmir Sultanate in Kashmir underlined the enduring importance of Central Asian culture to Indian state as well as highlighted the central position of Indian relationship with Central Asia.

When these developments were taking shape from above, from within the Indian society was building its bridges at social, economic, and cultural planes. From very early times, Indian culture was acting at the popular level as an autonomous entity, expanding, contracting and submitting to outside influences;

and again under the Turkomans it was subjected to a process of reconstruction. Therefore, the Indians also saw the onset of thirteenth century as part of the continuous process that had been going on from Early Bronze Age. But in the process, this time, the Central Asians including Turkomans felt unquestionably superior to the caste-based society at popular level. They blended Central Asian military, administrative, technological and cultural know-how of their heritage and Sufism with principles of peaceful coexistence of Indian religious systems. The establishment of *khanqas* and *madrasas* as centres of mediating the new language, i.e. Persian as a source of information and knowledge developed in almost all parts of India, where disciples from various social and religious layers devoted themselves to music and art forms and placed spirituality at a different level of reality.[51]

In the field of technology also, the Turkomans promoted the importation of varied art forms, the decorative elements, craft production technology, masonry, cloth printing, paper making, calligraphy, new styles and techniques in building technology from Central Asia to gain the confidence and support at the popular level in various regions of India.

Zain-ul-Abidin of Kashmir invited skilled craftsmen from Turkestan, Sijistan, Samarkand, Khurasan, Bukhara, Herat, Gilan and Balkh.[52] The calligraphists from Samarkand were given assignments of land in Pargana, Phag of Kashmir[53] for teaching the art of calligraphy. Mulla Zada, a disciple of Mulla Qadiri of Khurasan was invited to teach lute recitals.[54] These developments were not confined to Kashmir alone. Even in the Deccan the establishment of the Bahmanis and Qutb Shahis (who directly came from the Qara Quyunlu tribe of Central Asia) would not have been possible without the growth of contacts between the two cultures.[55] The Sufis' claim to universal brotherhood, egalitarian society and assertion respecting the new religious fraternity were backed by a new pattern of military organisation, economic activity and their residence in the midst of non-Muslim Indian population. This provided a chance to the Indians' newer identities.[56] As a result, people were obliged to repudiate their allegiances and entered into contacts with Central Asians to organise themselves in new social settings.

The spinning wheel was introduced into India on a wide scale in the thirteenth century.[57] The multiple spindles, which made appearance in China around the last quarter of thirteenth century, were brought into India in early fourteenth century.[58] Among other technological devices, which figure in thirteenth and fourteenth century are the Persian wheel, art of manufacturing of paper, horseshoe and horse stirrup.[59] Athar Ali has appropriately summed up these details. He says:

> It was in these centuries (thirteenth to fifteenth) that India received the spinning wheel, the pedals of loom, cloth printing, paper, magnetic compass, techniques

> of large scale arcuate construction, lime mortar, pin drum gearing (to complete the apparatus of Persian wheel) more effective devices for distillation and sericulture. These undoubtedly led to an expansion of craft technology, possibly even to greater cloth production per capita and certainly to more extensive use of masonry. There is evidence, literary as well as numismatic, that commerce expanded and archaeology attests to the fact that the urban decline postulated from the previous period was over and the urban economy of impressive size rapidly developed.[60]

All these tools helped the growth of contacts between the two civilisations at popular level. The popularisation of these items by Turkoman soldiers, Sufis, artisans, and traders provided them much wider audience particularly in society where other means of vertical and horizontal social and economic mobility were very limited. Technology played crucial role in growing the popular receptivity towards Central Asian ideas and institutions, and facilitated the legitimation of their rule. According to Mohammad Habib,

> they (Turks) could do so because public opinion was with them because to an extent and only to an extent, in pursuit of their careers the selfishness of which no one should deny, they were consciously or subconsciously sub-serving to the public good.[61]

What was novel about these new relations between the two civilisations was that both of them possessed long historical traditions. While Central Asia regarded itself as the centre of inhabited world, India as a cradle of ancient civilisation and centre of all refinement and culture also radiated equally to the outside world. As a result, this Turkoman initiative to everything at popular level got reflected in mutually profitable relationships between Indians and Central Asians.

After loosely weaving together a relatively coherent tapestry from these disparate threads of evidence and briefly touching upon some of the aspects, which added to the distinctively significant dimensions of these contacts, we are able to notice the comparative nature of the two types of Indian and Turkoman social formations. Although some ideas of synonymity are possible, a clear identification cannot be made in many respects. On the eve of Turkoman arrival in the post-Gupta period, the Indian society represented a type in which the regional polities were organised relatively on stable basis, even though social hierarchy of caste and occupational grading divided people both vertically and horizontally. In comparison, the Turkomans were in a disruptive phase during their long history. The internal strife had always brought the societal breakdown.

In Central Asian society where sub-cultures were distinct, discrete, and discordant, the sense of shared values was weakened. The question of legitimate political ends and means was not easily resolved in such tribal political cultures.

The long-term stability of the regime was uncertain. The critical question in Central Asian society was not the mere presence of ethnic pluralism or actual workings of tribal groups and clans but the degree to which they were set apart from each other in separate value systems and priorities. It is an established fact that the plural ethnicity in Central Asia (of which Turkomans were an integral part) implied more intra-group and intra-tribal tribe hostility. The group and the value system were often shaken and violence ruled the streets. One of the classical examples is that the Sultan Sanjar saw the consolidation of Qara Khita power in Turkestan and the Guz Turks carried him in cage and plundered district by district. The solution to such violence was seen in returning to migration, stability, and security by expressing loyalty to join the invaders.

In comparison, the Indian type differed from the Turkomans in the sense that it possessed powerfully persuasive, theocratic ethic (Brahmanism) which was integrally harnessed to the interests of Indian state. In India, it gave greater amount of stability and strength to the state in evolving political ideology and deriving legitimacy to subject the majority classes. But the Turkoman polity in Central Asia was characterised by ethnic disputes and rivalries, which always erupted and re-erupted to challenge each other's boundaries. According to Andre Gunder Frank,

> State power was organised and reorganised by nomadic peoples on the basis of first tribal allegiance then of political alliances, rivalries and conquests and lastly on shifting and temporary territorial basis.[62]

In India, the polity was centrally controlled by the king whose will was mediated by a body of officials mostly including priests who mediated the will of the king as divine. The will of the priest was a law. The bureaucracy constituted the literati in society where position was determined by the amount of land they possessed. The achievement was not possible on the basis of merit but was the prerogative of the dominant class. Among Turkomans, society was democratically governed and diffusedly controlled by a body of elders with rotating political roles. All the subsidiary organisations were responsible to this body of elders whose authority was granted by the tribe. George W. Obnnon rightly remarks:

> The Turkomans had no position in their social structure equivalent to King, Khan, Shah ruler with special powers which would be used politically, militarily in controlling or in directing action of all the Turkoman as a nation.[63]

Among Turkomans, there were a variety of occupational categories but limited functional differentiation status, which tended towards achievement. This was not the case in India, where learning was only confined to literary elite while caste was acting as restrictive mechanism. But among Turkomans, it was open to all. Among them the actual political operation did not necessitate literacy but it could hardly have functioned without informed citizens. In India, the incorporation of tribes into *varna*-oriented society led to social fragmentation.

The Central Asian society was always given to experimentation and innovation. It was brilliant and transient, democratic and violent. It was one of the coalescent states, which could never satisfactorily unite except for occasional hegemonic leagues, which were known for their fragility and dissensions. This state of affairs prolonged itself indefinitely because Central Asia was an actual congeries of conflicting tribal formations each packed with its own weaknesses and contradictions. But outside Central Asia and particularly in India, the Central Asians in general and Turkomans in particular proved themselves a desirable cultural asset representing skill and strength for shaping the Sultanate, which was the ultimate product of the convergence of these contacts. When a relationship lasts for such a long time it is bound to encourage a process of acculturation and comprehend those aspects, which result when groups of people having different cultures come into continuous first-hand contacts for such long periods with subsequent changes in the original cultural patterns of either of both groups. In India this process of acculturation made its appearance in so many forms that one needs to be selective because the different aspects of polity, society, economy, history and culture are so deftly interwoven that it becomes difficult to separate one from the other.

Perhaps the most important basis of these contacts was the exchange of people's ideas epitomised by the millennia of contacts, which produced and reproduced the cultures of India and Central Asia from time to time and are now too strong to be broken.

NOTES AND REFERENCES

1. Even before the beginning of these metal production techniques, references exist on Indo-Iranian treaties on trading of horses, which were introduced to West Asia. R. Ghirshman, *Iran: From the Earliest Times to the Islamic Conquest,* Penguin Books, Great Britain, 1951, pp. 62-72; See also for details, E. Herzfeld, *Archaeological History of Iran,* London, 1935. Also by the same author, *Iran in Ancient East*, London, 1941, pp. 149-209.
2. V.M. Masson and V.I. Sarianidi, *Central Asia: Turkmenistan before the Achaemenids,* London, 1972, pp. 124-28. See also, V.M. Masson, *Turkmenistan in Mirror of World History,* St. Petersburg, 2000, p. 7.
3. Studying mentalities in the pre-modern history is indisputably of great relevance. It helps in examining multiple social realities that motivated people of different regions, ethnicities and religions to contact each other before their rulers patronised or promoted these contacts. This establishes the fact that the history of mentalities grew much before the formal definition of concept came into being. It needs to be emphasised here that French historians of Annals School played a very important

role not only in studying the history of mentalities but also validating the applicability of this concept as an important methodological tool. M. Vovelle, *Ideologies and Mentalities* (Originally in French). First English edition, Polity Press, Cambridge, 1990, pp. 4-12. See also Elsepth Davies, *The Years of Barbarians*, Edinburgh, 1988, pp. 7-13, 183-91.

4. From very early times there were frequent migrations from Central Asia to other parts of the world. Marija Gimbutas recorded three major migratory movements: (1) Between 4300 and 4200 BC, (2) Between 3400 and 3200 BC, and (3) Between 300 and 280 BC from Central Asia to Western World. For details see Marija Gimbutas, *The Early Civilisation of Europe*, Los Angeles, Indo-European Studies Centre, 1980. But the migrations of Central Asians to India are continuously spread over the entire pre-modern period. Apart from the Persian chronicles of Sultanate and Mughal periods in Indian history see also: E.D. Philips, *The Royal Hordes, Nomadic People of Steppes*, London, 1965; Gravin Hambly, *Central Asia*, Wedenfeld and Nicholson, London, 1969; and also William McNeill, *Rise of West: A History of Human Community*, Chicago University Press, Chicago, 1963.
5. R. Ghirshman, *op. cit.*, p. 74. See also Andre Gunder Frank, *The Centrality of Central Asia* (Comparative Asian Studies, 8), VU University Press, Amsterdam, 1992, p. 9; Y.Y. Kuzmina and K.F. Smirnov, 'The origin of Indo-Iranians in the light of recent archaeological data', *Journal of Central Asia*, Vol. I, No. 1, 1978, pp. 68-70. For details of early migrations of Aryans to India, see R.S. Sharma, *Advent of Aryans*, Delhi, 1999, pp. 74-96.
6. Apart from Indian portion, the territories which constituted their dominion included Mesopotamia, Syria, Egypt, Greek cities and Asia Minor. About their Indian contacts Ghirshman says: "Abandoning narrow nationalism, the Achaemenians as a concession to imperial interest introduced it (Aramaic language) to India when under its influence Kharosthi, the oldest known alphabet, was developed". Ghirshman, *op. cit.*, pp. 126-47. When Achaemenians lost Egypt, Palestine, Southern Syria and some parts of Coasts of Asia Minor, the King Selecus ceded the territory of Arachosia and Gedrousia to King Chandragupta of India in exchange for elephants, which he needed for protecting his Western Frontiers, *ibid.*, pp. 163, 204, 220-22.
7. The Kushana Empire extended to Russian Turkestan, Port of Chinese Turkestan and a large portion of India, *ibid.*, pp. 223 and 355. Romila Thapar also attributes a Central Asian origin to Kushanas; Romila Thapar, *A History of India*, Vol. I, Penguin Books, London, 1966, p. 97. However, Kalhana is more specific and traces the origin of Kushanas to Turshukas. Kalhana, *Rajatarangini* (Sanskrit). English translation by M.A. Stein, 2 Vols., London, 1900, Vol. II, Verse 3412, p. 268.
8. Earlier also, Selucid king Antiochus crossed Hindukush to renew his friendship with Mauryan king. Selucids also imported gold from northwest of India, Armenia, Bactria and Caucasus and in return exported iron, copper and lead. Ghirshman, *op. cit.*, pp. 126-47 and 223.
9. See Romila Thapar, *op. cit*; Also see, A.L. Basham, *Cultural History of India*, OUP, Delhi.

10. Andre Gunder Frank, *op. cit.*, pp. 12, 13. See also Denis Sinor, *Inner Asia, History – Civilisation – Languages – A Syllabus*, Bloomington, Indiana University and The Hague, Mouton, 1969, p. 171.
11. No doubt, the reasons for the transformation of Indo-Central Asian contact into the collision at times must have been complex. Their nature can be reconstructed from the sources, which are scattered in various regions. The early days of the settlement of Central Asians in India (even on the periphery of India) would have been hard and it could not have survived without the local support in many respects. But at the same time there must have been many reasons for the conflict also.
12. G. Watson, 'Interpretations of Central Asian influence of Mughal India: The Historical Debate', *South Asia*, Vol. XVIII, No. 2, 1995, pp. 1-22.
13. William McNeill, *op. cit.*, pp. 316-91; See also Thomas Barfield, *The Perilous Frontier, Nomadic Empires and China*, Cambridge, 1989, pp. 6-7.
14. Aziz Ahmad, *Studies in Islamic Culture in Indian Environment*, Clarendon Press, Oxford, 1969, pp. 23-52. See also Yusuf Hussain, *Indo-Muslim Polity (Turko–Afghan Period)*, Indian Institute of Advanced Study, Simla, 1971.
15. Fernand Braudel, *On History*, London, 1980, p. 52.
16. Central Asia is a huge landmass bounded to the west by Caspian Sea, to the south by Kopet Dagh mountainous regions of Iran and Parapamisus and Hindukush mountain ranges in Afghanistan, to the east by Pamirs and Tien Shan mountains and to the north by Kazak Steppe roughly from Lake Balkash on the east to the northern edges of Aral and Caspian seas. The topographical specificity is located in its Kizlkum and Karakum deserts and the two main rivers of Central Asia—the Amu Darya (Oxus) and the Sir Darya (Jazretes). Central Asia's unique attributes result from her geographical position, which allows her to harmoniously integrate the varied influences of the Western and Eastern world. G.W. Obnnon, *The Turkmen Carpets*, London, 1974, pp. 13-33.
17. Aziz Ahmad, *op. cit.*
18. K.M. Ashraf, *Life and Times of People of Hindustan*, Delhi, 1969, p. 5.
19. M. Athar Ali, 'Encounter and Efflorescence, Genesis of Medieval Civilisation' (Presidential Address), *Indian History Congress Proceedings*, Golden Jubilee Session, Gorakhpur, Delhi, 1989, p. 14.
20. Marc Gaborieu, Muzaffar Alam, Francoise 'Nalini' Delvoye, (eds.), *Making of the Indo-Persian Culture*, Manohar Publishers, New Delhi, 2000.
21. In general it can be firmly stated that in course of medieval Indian history, the Central Asian culture was never adopted as a seamless whole. Its individual components always met with very different degrees of receptivity in different regions of India, but the nature of response does not reflect the outright rejection or opposition to it but a synthesisation.
22. See for details, Lawrence Krader, *Peoples of Central Asia*, Bloomington, Indiana University Press, Hague Monton, 1966. Also E.D. Phillips, *The Royal Hordes, Nomadic People of the Steppes*, London, 1965. The other ethnic groups referred to by our sources

are *Uzbeks, Kazakhs, Tajjoks, Iranians, Mongols,* etc. The Arab historians and geographers in the history of Central Asia first introduced the terms Turks and Turkoman. The term 'Turkoman' appears for the first time in the works of Arab geographer al-Maqdisi in the second half of tenth century AD. At that time, the Turkomans were located on the eastern frontiers of Arab Empire in the vicinity of present day Chemkent and Tashkent. The Arabs referred to them as Oghuz. They mention that there were 22 to 24 tribes of Turkomans always sold their services as warriors to the Persian *Khans* of Khiva or *Amirs* of Bukhara and at times even to Indian rulers. This is how they came into contact with the outer world. G.W. Obnnon, *The Turkoman Carpets,* London, 1974, pp. 13-33. For details see also, V.V. Barthold, *Four Studies on History of Central Asia*, Vol. 3, p. 90; and F.H. Skrine and Edward D. Ros, *The Heart of Asia*, pp. 267-75; also Kalhana, *op. cit.*, p. 311; R.L. Hangloo, 'Sufism in Medieval Deccan: Politics and Worship', Presidential Address (Medieval Section), *Proceedings of Andhra Pradesh History Congress,* XXIV Annual Session, Rajahmundry, January 2000, 4 fn. 13.

23. It is generally believed that Turkomans extended their influence all over the world. Many of their tribes served the *Khalifa* of Baghdad and many of them attained distinction for being the best soldiers in Asiatic armies. Many of them rose to very important positions. Subaktagin was also a Turkish slave whose son Mahmud not only extended his domain upto Oxus and Caspian but carried his victorious armies into the Central India. Eriskine, *History of India,* Qutoed in S. Lane Poole, *Medieval India under Mohammedan Rule,* London, 1903 (Indian reprint), 1994, pp. 14-18; H.G. Knee rightly remarks, "Few races of men at any period of world, have acted a more distinguished part than the Turks, who in one form or the other for centuries ruled a great part of the old world and who, even at present day influence, directly or indirectly, the government, manners, and the limits of Hungary and Poland to the farthest bounds of the empire of Hindustan"; H.G. Knee, *The Turks in India,* Delhi, p. 9.
24. Kalhana, *op. cit.*, Vol. I, Verse 179, p. 138.
25. *Ibid.,* Vol. I, Verses 152-155, p. 206.
26. *Ibid.*, p. 272.
27. *Ibid.*, p. 311.
28. *Ibid.*
29. *Ibid.*, Verse 1149, p. 357.
30. For details see William Moorcraft, *Tour Diary,* Ms. EURD-265 available in Jammu University Library, Jammu; T.D. Forsyth, *A Report on Mission to Yarkand,* Calcutta, 1875; Robert Shaw, *Visit to High Tartary Yakand and Kashar: Mir Izzullah Safar-Nama* (AD 1812-13) Research Department Library, Kashmir University, Srinagar, Kashmir. Besides these, there is bulk of evidence on Indo-Central Asian relations and Silk Route trade between these two regions in English, Persian and Urdu in various archives and repositories in India and abroad.
31. A. Azzaroli, *An Early History of Horsemanship,* Leiden-Brill, 1985, p. 66.

32. Hassan Nizami, *Taj-ul-Masir* (Persian), English translation by Elliot Dowson, *History of India as Told by its Own Historians*, Vol. II, pp. 204-43. For details see also S.D. Dwivedi, *Relation of Rajputs with Delhi Sultans, AD 1206-1526*, Delhi, 1978, pp. 22-57.
33. Mohammad Habib, *Sultan Mahmud of Gaznin*, Delhi (reprint), 1967, p. 2.
34. Andre Gunder Frank, *op. cit.*, pp. 9-20.
35. *Ibid.*, pp. 12-13.
36. Minhaj-uddin Siraj, *Rabqat-i-Nasiri*, (Persian) text edited by W.N. Lees, Hussain and A. Hayy. English translation by Major H.G. Raverty, *Bib. Indica*, 2 vols., Calcutta, 1881, Vol. I, pp. 466-67.
37. Minhaj-uddin Siraj, *op. cit.*
38. A.B.M. Habibullah, *Foundations of Muslim Rule in India*, Allahabad, 1961, pp. 1-72.
39. Mohammad Habib, *op. cit.*
40. William Eriskine, *History of India*, cited in H.G. Knee, *Turks in India*, Delhi, p. 9.
41. K.M. Ashraf, *op. cit;* pp. 52-65.
42. *Ibid.*
43. A.K.S. Lambton, 'Reflections in Iqta', in George Makdisi (ed.), *Arabic and Islamic Studies in Honour of Hamilton*, A.R. Gibb, London, 1965, pp. 358-76.
44. Bert G. Fragner, 'Social and Internal Economic Affairs', in Peter Jackson and L.L. Kockhard, *The Cambridge History of Iran*, Vol. 6, London, 1986, pp. 501-02. See also, *The Cambridge History of Iran*, Vol. 6, London, 1986, pp. 501-02; 'The Origins of Iqta' in M.A. Shaban, *Islamic History of New Interpretation (AD 750-1055)*, Cambridge, 1976, pp. 71-88.
45. Athar Ali, *op. cit.*, p. 14.
46. Irfan Habib, 'Agrarian Economy', Tapan Raychoudhri and Irfan Habib, *The Cambridge History of India*, 2 vols., Vol. I (1200-1750), pp. 68-75.
47. Some of these Turkoman officials were Malik Tja-uddin Sanjar, Kazlakh Khan, Kabir Khan Ayaz, Malik Nasir al-din al Tamar-al-Bahai, Malik-Saif-uddin, Aibeg Uchch, Yughantat Khaitai Turk, Malik Nusrat Al-din, Tayisi-ul-Maizzi, Malik Izz-al-din, Tughan Khan Tughril, Malik Tamar Khan, Malik Hindu Khan, Muayyid Aldin, Karkash Khan, Iktiyar al-din Ai Tegin, Malik Babar al-din, Sungar-al-Rumi, Malik Saif-ud-din, Arkali Dad Beg, Malik Babar-ud-din Nausrat Khan, Malik Nusrat-al-din Shakan, Malik Kesli Khan, Saif-al-din, Ai Beg al Sultani, Malik-al-Hajjab, Alkhanal-Muazzam al Khaqan, Azim Ulag Khan (Ie Balban), Baha al-Haqq, Wal-al-din and many others who held very important positions under Turkoman Sultans of Delhi, Minhaj-uddin Siraj, *Rabqat-I-Nasiri*, *op. cit.*, Vol. 2, pp. 1-89.
48. Yusuf Hussain, *Indo-Muslim Polity (Turko-Afghan Period)*, *op. cit.*, pp. 61-65.
49. *Ibid.* See also Ziauddin Barani, *Tarikh-I-Firuzshahi* (Persian), text edited by W.N. Less, S. Ahmad Khan and Kabiruddin, *Bibliothica Indica*, Calcutta, 1860-62, pp. 34-37.
50. *Ibid.*
51. R.L. Hangloo, *op. cit.*

52. Mirza Haider Dughlat, *Tarikh-I-Rashidi* (Persian), English translation by N. Elias and E. Denison Ross, London, 1895, p. 434.
53. Sayyid Ali, *Tarikh-I-Kashmir*, Persian manuscript, Research Department Library, Srinagar, folio 16a.
54. Pandit Srivara, *Jain Rajatarangini*, (Sanskrit), English translation by J.C. Dutt, Calcutta, 1898, Vol. I, pp. 31-32. See also R.L. Hangloo, 'Kashmir under Sultan Zain-ul-Abidin', *NEHU, Journal of Humanities and Social Sciences*, Vol. I, Shillong, 1998, pp. 21-30.
55. R.L. Hangloo, Presidential Address, *op. cit.*, pp. 4-7.
56. S.A.A. Rizvi, *History of Sufism in India*, 2 vols., Delhi, 1978, Vol. I, pp. 131, 135, 136, 151, 169 and 191. For details see also K.A. Nizami, *Some Aspects of Religion and Politics in India during Thirteenth Century*, Delhi, 1961.
57. Irfan Habib (Technology and Social Change), *Presidential Address, Indian History Congress*, Varanasi, 1969, pp. 139-61. See also *American Historical Review*, Vol. LXV, No. 3, April 1960, p. 517.
58. Isami, *Futuh-us-Salatin*, p. 134.
59. Amir Hassan, *Fawaid-al Fawad*, edited by Latil Malik, Lahore, 1966, pp. 334-35. Also, Irfan Habib, *op. cit.* pp. 139-61.
60. Athar Ali, *op. cit.*, p. 16.
61. Mohammad Habib, *op. cit.*, p . 94.
62. Andre Gunder Frank, *op. cit.* p. 14.
63. G.W. Obnnon, *op. cit.* pp. 15-16.

7

Hospices and Hospitality En Route Khwarizm to Sind: Evidence of Ibn Battuta

G.D. Gulati

Of all the Arab geographers and historians, Ibn Battuta occupies a distinguished place as a medieval traveller and chronicler. He had a versatile talent as a scholar, theologian, adventurer and explorer. His travel account is acclaimed as an encyclopaedic work on political, social, economic and religious life during fourteenth century. It stands as an eyewitness report of the contemporary events and attributes the author as the 'Marco Polo of the Muslim World'.[1] More than seventy articles and few monographs on his travel and personality have been contributed by scholars in European languages. Recently an Indian scholar[2] has dealt with the economic activities in the region of Sind and Punjab based on Ibn Battuta's account. In this paper we are informed of his long tour into more than forty-four countries covering about 1,70,000 kilometres in Asian regions through rapid streams, burning deserts, treacherous ravines, dusty roads, rough and even dreadful and unknown seas.

The fame of the Sultan of India, Muhammad bin Tughluq, and of his apparently limitless generosity to foreign scholars, was an irresistible lure to a man of Ibn Battuta's character, and hence his journey to Delhi. His journey through the length and breadth of Asia, welcomed and befriended by the numerous dignitaries including kings, nobles, scholars and merchants, is one of the most valuable sources for studying relations between India and Central Asia. He covered the journey between the two regions through Khwarizm, Bukhara, Samarkand, and Balkh and thence by a route difficult to follow through Khurasan and Afghanistan until at last he reached the frontiers of India on the Indus River on 12 September, 1333, with an imposing train of attendants.[3]

As we know, seeing the hazards of travel, the medieval rulers ordered strong measures to maintain peace and security on the routes. Internal security and safe movement of the travelling caravans were facilitated by building caravan-serais or *ribatat*. These were situated on the outskirts of the towns or in the *bazaars* and were the centres of commercial activities. Ibn Battuta during his journey through Iraq, Persia, Turkestan, and Khurasan noticed a large number of caravan-serais and hospices in every town. The hospices were of small structure with lodging facilities for the travellers not as big as the caravan-serais, though there are references of few hospices run and governed by the state with large endowment. The caravans used to be self-sufficient and having their own security with animated *bazaars* and other facilities. But the role of hospices cannot be minimised as it played equally a significant role in the medieval trade and commerce. Hospices were generally owned by individuals who were pious and devotee persons like Shaikhs and Sufis. However, there are references of certain ladies who also held hospices and extended hospitality to the travellers.

The first city of Central Asia visited by Ibn Battuta, was Khwarizm (modern Khiva), which was at that time the largest, greatest, most beautiful and most important city of the Turks having fine *bazaars* and broad streets, a great number of buildings and abundance of commodities. Ibn Battuta was highly impressed by the people of Khwarizm who were excellent in conduct, generous in soul, and more friendly to strangers. Outside Khwarizm was a hospice built over the tomb of the Shaikh Najm al-Din-Kubra, who was one of the great saints.[4] Food was supplied to all wayfarers and its Shaikh was the teacher at the college, Saif al-Din ibn Asabra, and one of the principal citizens of Khwarizm.[5] In the town also, there was a hospice, run by the pious Jalaluddin al-Samarkandi, one of the most saintly men. He received Ibn Battuta and his party hospitably in it.[6]

Ibn Battuta also refers to a hospice in the city built by one Turabak, wife of the governor of the city of Khwarizm. She gave a banquet in honour of the Moroccan traveller, Ibn Battuta, for which she assembled the doctors of the laws and the principal citizens in this hospice. The food was supplied to all wayfarers in the hospice, as observed by Ibn Battuta.[7]

The next reference of a hospice by Ibn Battuta is in the suburbs of Bukhara called Path Abad, which had the tomb of the learned Shaikh and the pious ascetic Saif al-Din al-Bakharzi.[8] According to Ata Malik Jauvaini, the author of *Traikh-i-Jahan-i-Gusha..*, this hospice was founded by the mother of great Khans Mongke and Qubilai, although she herself was a Christian,[9] still in existence. This hospice was a large institution with vast endowments from which food was supplied to all and its superior was a descendant of the Shaikhs, namely, the much-travelled pilgrim Yahya al-Bakharzi who entertained Ibn Battuta at his residence. He invited all the leading men of the city on this occasion. The *Quran* readers recited with beautiful modulations and sang melodiously in Turkish and Persian.[10]

From Bukhara, Ibn Battuta reached a place called Nakhshab (Nasaf) about 100 miles southeast of Bukhara. It was a main station on the old route through the iron gate to Tirmiz and Balkh. It was a small town surrounded by gardens and streams. Ibn Battuta with one of his slave-girl lodged outside it in a house that belonged to its governor.[11]

In the outskirts of Samarkand we are told about a tomb of Qutham which had a hospice. It had chambers for lodging of travellers. The tomb was visited by the people of Samarkand on the eve of every Tuesday and Friday to seek blessings of the saint. According to Ibn Battuta, the Tatars too visited it and made large votive offerings to it, bringing cattle, sheep, dirhams and dinars, which was spent for the maintenance of travellers and survivors at the hospice. Being a large endowment, it was looked after by a superitendent appointed by Sultan Taramashirin.[12]

The old city of Tirmiz was built on the bank of the Jaihum (Amu River) and when it was ruined by the Mongols, the new city was built two miles away from the river. The lodging of Ibn Battuta and his party was in the hospice of the pious Shaikh Azizan, one of the great and most generous Shaikhs. He possessed great wealth, houses and orchards and spent his wealth to supply the needs of travellers.[13]

After crossing the river Jaihum, Ibn Battuta entered the land of Khurasan and reached Balkh, which was completely dilapidated and uninhabited. At Balkh he noticed a beautiful mosque, hospice and a convert (for Sufi devotees), which were built by a woman whose husband was the governor of the city for the Abbasid Caliphs named Daud B. Ali. Here Ibn Battuta recounts how that woman got the hospice built by selling one of her garments embroidered with jewels and of great value because the robe was shown to the Caliph. Since the Caliph had lighted the eye on it, she ordered the robe to be sold and built with its price the above structures. After the buildings were completed there remained of the (price of the) robe as much as one-third and the story goes that she ordered it to be buried under one of the columns of the mosque, so that it might be available when needed. The tradition was related to Chengiz who gave orders in consequence to pull down the columns in the mosque. After about a third had been pulled down without finding anything he left the rest as they were.[14] On the way from Balkh to Herat, Ibn Battuta refers many hospices in the villages inhabited by pious devotees,[15] but does not mention whether he stayed there.

From Herat our Moroccan friend reached al-Jam, a place of midding size, pretty, with orchards and trees, abundance of springs and flowing streams. Ibn

Battuta relates a story of Abu Said, the Sultan of al-Iraq, who came to Khurasan on one occasion and camped in this city, in which was the hospice of Shaikh Ahmad. This Shaikh entertained the Sultan with immense display of hospitality. He gave one sheep to every tent in the Sultan's *muhalla,* one sheep to every four men, and to every riding beast in the *muhalla*, whether horse, mule, or ass, one night's forage, so that not a single animal was left in the *muhalla* without receiving the share of his hospitality.[16]

From al-Jam the party reached Tus where he mentions a hospice with a college and a mosque adjoining it. All these buildings were of elegant construction, their walls being colourfully decorated with Qashani tiles.[17] From Tus, Ibn Battuta reached Naisabur via Sarakhs and Zawa. Naisabur was one of the four metropolitan cities of Khuras, which was called sometimes 'Little Damascus' because of its quantities of fruits, orchards and streams and owing to its beauty. The city had a hospice where Ibn Battuta lodged himself. It belonged to one Qutub al Din-al-Naisaburi who gave our traveller excellent and most generous hospitality and also showed some miracles.[18]

From Naisabur they went to the city of Bistan where Ibn Battuta's lodging was a hospice of the Shaikh Abu Yazid-al-Bistami.[19] He continued his journey from this city by way of Hindukhir (stands for Andakhudh, 100 miles west of Balkh) to Qunduz and Baghlan, which were regions of villages where there were to be found Shaikhs and pious men, fruit-gardens, and streams. Ibn Battuta and his party encamped at Qunduz by a flowing river where there was a hospice belonging to one of the Shaikhs of the poor brethren, an Egyptian who was called *Shir Siyah*, which means 'The Black Lion'. Here they were entertained by the governor of that land who was living in a large garden there. Ibn Battuta and his party remained on the outskirts of this village for about forty days, in order to pasture the camels and horse. The other reason for their halt was the fear of snow. "For upon this road there is a mountain", writes Ibn Battuta, 'called Hindukush, which means 'slayer of the Indians' , because the slave-boys and girls who are brought from the land of India die there in large numbers as a result of the extreme cold and the great quantity of snow'.[20]

On setting out from Baghlan they journeyed to a place called Andar (Andarab on the headwaters of Suirkhab River). The valley of Andarab leads to the Khawak Pass (13000 feet). The party alighted in a large village in which there was a hospice belonging to an excellent man named Muhammad al-Mahrawi. They lodged with him who treated them with consideration. He would drink the water in which the traveller had washed their hands after eating, because of his strong belief and his benevolence. He travelled with Ibn Battuta until they scaled the mountain of Hindukush.[21]

They next reached Parwan (45 miles north of Kabul), and from thence to village of al-Charkh where they were offered hospitality of the governor, Muhammad al-Charkhis whom Ibn Battuta met again in India.[22]

Reaching Ghazni, which was in ruins at that time, Ibn Battuta camped outside it in a village and was received honourably by its governor, Mardak Agha, meaning little man of great family. He mentions the tomb of Mahmud with a hospice, but does not mention the facilities available there.[23]

The party next travelled to Kabul where a hospice of one Shaikh Ismail al-Afghani, the disciple of Shaikh Abbas, was located.[24] From there they rode to Karmash and thence to Shashnagar (Hashtnagar), which was the last inhabited place on the confines of the land of the Turks as described by Ibn Battuta. From there they entered the great desert, which extended for a space of fifteen nights' march. The Indus River at Attack is only 40 miles from Shashnagar.[25]

On reaching Indus, Ibn Battuta found a well-recognised intelligence services, which took care of each and every person entering India. The travellers were treated as state guests till they reached the court of Muhammad bin Tughluq where they were well received and enjoyed the Sultan's generosity and Ibn Battuta is one, who served the Sultan in various capacities as Qazi and Ambassador to China.[26]

Thus, the hospices played an important role in the medieval town and travelling, enabling the travellers to perform their functions to meet their goal and mission in those odd days. Ibn Battuta's account in this direction is invaluable and source of inspiration for the scholars working on the various aspects of medieval society.

NOTES AND REFERENCES

1. Ross, E. Dunn, *The Adventures of Ibn Battuta,* London, 1986, p. 5.
2. Joginder K. Chawla, 'Ibn Battuta at Multan', in *Proceedings of Punjab History Conference,* 28th Session, Patiala, 1996.
3. H.A.R. Gibb, *The Travels of Ibn Battuta: AD 1325-1354,* Vol. I, First Indian edition, Delhi 1993, p. xii.
4. G.D. Gulati, 'Ibn Battuta in Transoxiana', *Proceedings of Indian History Congress,* Banglore, pp. 772-78.
5. *The Travels of Ibn Battuta, op. cit.*, p. 542. He was one of the major saints of the Suhrawardi order, killed in the Mongol capture of Gurganj in AD 1221. See *ibid.*, p. 542, note 16.
6. *Ibid.*, p. 542
7. *Ibid.*, pp. 542-43.
8. *Ibid.*, pp. 546-47.
9. *Ibid.*, p. 554.
10. Ata Malik Juvaini, *Tarikh-I-Jahan-I-Gasha,* English translation by J.A. Boyle under the title *History of the World Conqueror*, in 2 vols., Manchester, 1958, p. 552.
11. *The Travels of Ibn Battuta, op. cit.*, p. 554.
12. *Ibid.*, pp. 568-69 and note 107.

13. *Ibid.*, p. 570.
14. *Ibid.*, pp. 572-73. Marco Polo mentions it as a splendid city of great size. *Travels of Marco Polo*, Tr. by Ronald Latham, Penguin Books, 1959, p. 43.
15. *Ibid.*, p. 574.
16. *Ibid.*, p. 584.
17. *Ibid.*, p. 583.
18. *Ibid.*, p. 584 and note 181.
19. *Ibid.*, p. 585.
20. *Ibid.*, p. 586 and note 190. According to H.A.R. Gibb, the reference of Hindukush seems to be the earliest or one of the earliest.
21. *Ibid.*, p. 587 and note 192.
22. *Ibid.*, p. 589 and note 199.
23. *Ibid.*, p. 590.
24. *Ibid.*, p. 590-91.
25. *Ibid.*, p. 591.
26. For details, see G.D. Gulati, *India's North-West Frontier in Pre-Mughal Times*, Delhi, 1985, Chapters on Trade and Commerce. Also Joginder K. Chawla's Ph.D. thesis entitled *India's Overland Trade with Central Asia and Persia during Thirteenth and Fourteenth Centuries* awarded by Jamia Milia Islamia, New Delhi, 1999.

8

Status of Sine Tables in India and Central Asia during Medieval Times

A.K. Bag

India and Central Asia had close contacts in various fields of human activities since time immemorial. I will take here only few examples from ancient Indian astronomy and will show that Central Asia received some basic trigonometry and astronomical knowledge from India. It was nurtured and nourished by the Central Asian scholars so well that it became the part of the world heritage. Three Indian astronomical works, *Āryabhaṭīya*[1] (Ar. Arjabadh), *Brāhmasphuṭasiddhānta*[2] (Ar. Sindhind) and *Khaṇḍakhādyaka*[3] (Ar. Arkand) are known to have been introduced at the court of Abbasid Caliphs. The first one was composed by Āryabhaṭa I in AD 499 and the latter two by Brahmagupta in AD 628 and 665, respectively. These works were studied and translated into Arabic with the help of Indian scholars under the patronisation of the Abbasid Caliphs from Abu Jafar al-Mansur (AD 754–75) onwards.[4] Many scholars have interpreted these three texts as three different schools, though actually it is not so. Among the Arabic astronomers, al-Fazari (AD 796), Abu'l-Hasan al-Ahwazi (AD 771), Umar ibn al-Farrukhan al-Tabari (died in AD 815), al-Khwarizmi (AD 825), Abu Ma'shar al-Balkhi (AD 886), Al-Bīrunī (d. AD 1050), al-Zarkali (Toledan tables, *c.* AD 1080) and many others, became more or less acquainted with the *sine cosine* concepts, sine table, and astronomical theories of the Indians. The Greek work, *Almagest* of Ptolemy was also translated into Arabic during the reign of Caliph Harun ar-Rashid (AD 786-808) and became well known during the reign of Caliph al-Mamum (AD 813–833).[5]

The Greeks used chord in a half circle taking 180 degree arc as the basis, whereas Indians used half-chord (known *jyā)* in a quarter circle taking 90 degree arc as the basis. Indian process was much simpler and of course had a natural advantage. Nallino,[6] the great historian of Arabic history, states that the Arabs learnt from the Indian works the calculation of the movement of the stars and other matters of astronomical importance. Michio Yano,[7] who has studied both Indian and Greek sine tables, remarks, "Anyone who uses both Greek and Indian tables in his geometrical calculation will immediately realise the far greater convenience of the latter." Al-Bīrūnī gives the explanation how the name of Āryabhaṭa became *Arjabhar.* He says,[8]

> The Hindus pronounce the word the 'ḍ' of this word something between a 'd' and an 'r'. So the consonant became changed to an 'r', and the people wrote *Arjabhar.* Afterwards it was still more mutilated, the first 'r' to a 'z', so people wrote *Azjabhar.*

The word *jyā* or *jīvā* (which means 'bow-string') likewise was read as *jaib* in Arabic literature, literally meaning 'a hollow' or 'a pocket'. It was translated into *Sine* in Latin, which has given us the modern *Sine.*

SINE (*JYĀ*) AND COSINE (*KOJYĀ*) CONCEPTS

The circle was conceived as the representative of celestial sphere. The names, Sine and Cosine, are derived from two Sanskrit technical words, *jyā* and *kojyā* (complementary to *jyā)* respectively. Another Sanskrit technical term, *utkramajyā* is known as versed Sine. To explain these terms, it will be better if we take help of a figure (Fig. 1). Let us consider the quarter circle ZA and let P be any position of a planet on the circumference. Then when arc AP = θ, arc PZ = compliment of $\theta = 90° - \theta$, since arc AZ = 90°. If from P, a perpendicular PC is drawn to OA, then a right-angled triangle POC is formed, of which,

$\angle$ POC = θ, $\angle$OPC = $\angle$ZOP = $90° - \theta$, $\angle$PCO = 90°, and OZ = chord of the arc 90° = radius = OP = OA. Obviously,

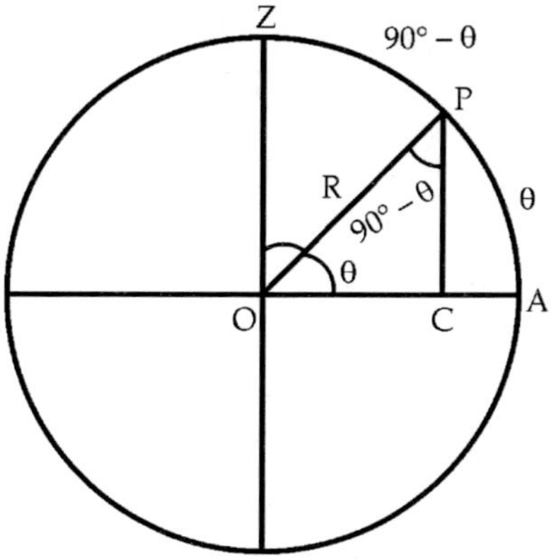

Fig. 1

PC = jyā of the arc θ = jyā θ,

OC = jyā of the arc $(90° - \theta)$ = jyā $(90° - \theta)$ = kojyā θ

and CA - utkramajyā θ = OA – OC = R – Jyā $(90° - \theta)$

In modern symbols, PC = R Sine θ, OC = R Sin $(90 - \theta)$ = R Cosine θ, and CA = R Versine θ. Comparing, we get,

PC = jyā θ = R Sine θ,

OC = kojyā θ = R Sine $(90 - \theta)$ = R Cosine θ,

And CA = utkramajyā θ = R – R Sine $(90 - \theta)$ = R – R Cosine θ = R. Versine θ.

A series of important trigonometrical results are also arrived from these relations by Āryabhaṭa, Varāha Mihira, Brahmagupta and other *Siddhantic* authors. The details of rational may be seen from my work on Mathematics[9]:

1. jyā$^2\,\theta$ = kojyā$^2\,\theta$ = R^2
   Or, $\{R \text{ Sine } \theta\}^2 + \{R \text{ Sine } (90° - \theta\}^2 + R^2$
   Or, R Sine $(90° - \theta) = \sqrt{\ } \{R^2 - R^2 \text{ Sine}^2\ \theta\}$
2. (jyā $\theta/2$) = $\sqrt{\ }$ {jyā$^2\,\theta$ + utkramajyā θ)/4}
   or, R Sine $\theta/2 = \sqrt{\ } [R^2 \text{Sin}^2\,\theta + R^2 \text{ Versine}^2\ \theta)/4\}$
3. kramjyā $\theta/2 = \sqrt{\ }$ [R^2 – {jyā^2 θ + utkramjyā^2 θ)/4}]
   or, R Sine $(90° - \theta/2) = \sqrt{\ } [R^2 - \text{Sine } \theta + R^2 \text{Versine}^2\ \theta)/4\}]$
4. jyā $\theta/2 = \sqrt{\ }$ [R/2. utkramajyā θ),
   or, R Sin $\theta/2 = \sqrt{\ }$ (R/2 R Versine θ)
5. Jyā $(90° - \theta)$ = R – utkramajyā θ, and jyā θ = R – utkramajyā $(90° - \theta)$, which in modern symbol: R Sine $(90° - \theta)$ = R Cosine θ, R Sine θ = R Cosine $(90° - \theta)$.
6. In a right triangle, sides and sines of the opposite angles are proportional to each other.
7. The four basic values, jyā 90° = R, jyā 60° = $\sqrt{\ }$ 3/2 R, jyā 45° = $\sqrt{\ }$ 2/2 R, jya 30° = R/2 are obtained respectively from the radius, and from equilateral triangle, square, equilateral hexagon inscribed in a circle.

SINE TABLE

Indian works usually divided the circumference of a quarter circle into 24 divisions, each being 3° 45', and calculated the values of chord lengths, known as *jyā* table or sine table with the help of the above formulae. The intermediate values from arc to *jyā* lengths and vice versa were calculated by the method of ratio proportion. The *Siddhantic* texts also divided the quarter circle into 6 (Brahmagutpa, AD 665; Vatesvara, AD 904) equal divisions at an interval of 15° and 56' 15" respectively. Different authors have also used circles of different radii. For instance, R was taken as 3438' by Āryabhaṭa I and his followers and Bhāskara II, as 120' by Varāhamihira in his *Pañcasiddhāntikā*, as 3270' and 150' by Brahmagupta. The south Indian medieval astronomer Mādhava (*c.* AD 1400) used R = 3437' 44" 43'" and obtained better sine table with the application of sine and cosine series.

In this connection, it will not be out of place to mention that the Greek scholars, Hipparchus (*c.* 150 BC) possibly had sine table for R = 6875 units and so had Ptolemy (*c.* AD 150) for 60 units. Both have taken 180 degrees as the basis for geometrical construction of sine table, which is quite cumbersome in comparison to the Hindu method. However, Pingree and his students believe that the Indian *jyā* tables were obtained from the Greek tables by halving the Greek tables though they do not follow the same logic, since 3438 is approximately the half of 6865; but 120 is the double of 60 units of Ptolemy. P.C. Sengupta has shown that Indian astronomy might have some linkages with that of Hipparchus but not with Ptolemaic astronomy. That Hindu astronomy shows no influence from the *Almagest* of Ptolemy is also confirmed by Al-Bīrūnī, for he himself intended to translate the *Almagest* in *slokas* for the Hindus.[10] Ptolemy's work is first known to have been translated by Jagannath Pandit under the patronage of Jai Singh in the beginning of eighteenth century. Bina Chatterjee,[11] however, has calculated the values of *jyā* tables for the same radius from three sources of Āryabhaṭa I, Varāhamihira and Brahmagupta, and opined that the methods of computing the *jyā* tables are the same and possibly all have borrowed from Āryabhaṭa I. Let us now see how Brahmagupta gives his sine table along with the values of declination in his *Khaṇḍakhādyaka* for R = 150 at an interval of 15°.

Arcs	Khandakhadyaka		Umar and Al-Zarkali table	
	R Sine	Declination	R Sine	Declination
15°	39	6° 2'	38, 49, 22	5, 56, 15
30°	75	11°43'	75, 0, 0	11, 31, 39
45°	106	16°42'	106, 3, 2	16, 25, 17
60°	130	20°38'	129, 54, 54	20, 15, 0
75°	145	23°8'	144, 53, 23	22, 42, 36
90°	150	24°	150, 0, 0	23, 33, 30

This also shows that Brahmagupta used maximum declination as 24 degree whereas both Umar and al-Zarkali used this as 23 degree 33 minute 30 seconds.

LATITUDE OF PLACES AND ALTITUDE OF SUN BY MIDDAY NOON SHADOW

The astronomical calculation is characterised by the equinoctial noon shadow measurement, the standard procedure of the *Siddhantic* period. This has made use of Hindu sine function widely, which Brahmagupta and other *Siddhantic* astronomers[12] have given (See Fig. 2).

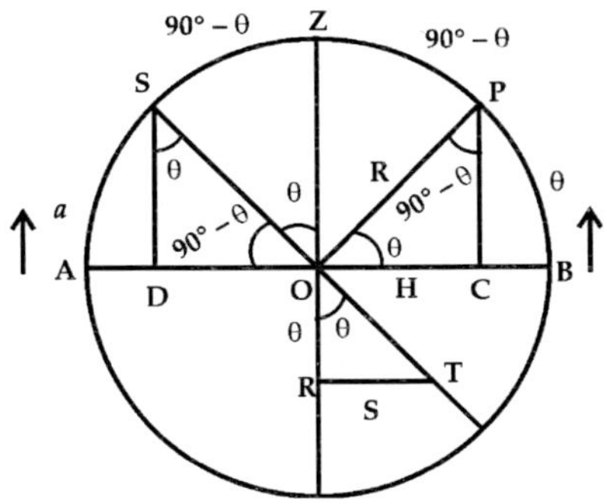

Fig. 2

(*i*) In a latitude triangle OPC, and shadow triangle ORT on an equinoctial day,
Akṣajyā = R Sine of the latitude = R Sine Φ = (S × R) /H,
Lambajyā = R Sine of the colatitude = R Sine (90 – Φ) = (g × R)/H, and
Then, S = g × R Sine Φ/R Sine (90° – Φ) = 12 Tan Φ,

where, g = 12 *angulas*, S = equinoctial midday shadow, and H = shadow hypotenuse on equinoctial day.

(*ii*) In an altitude triangle OSD, and shadow triangle on any other day,
Unnata = R Sine of altitude = R Sine a = (g × R)/h,
Nata = zenith distance = R Sine (90° – a) = (s × R)/h, and
s = {g × R Sine (90° – a)} / R Sine a = 12 Cot a,

where, g = 12 *angulas*, s = midday shadow of any other day, a = altitude of the sun, 90° - a = zenith distance of sun.

It may be noted that the latitude and altitude triangles are inversely related.

INTEREST IN CENTRAL ASIA AND LATIN EUROPE

Al-Khwārizmī prepared an abridgement of the *Sindhind* and astronomical tables of *Arkand*, which discussed the midnight astronomy of Brahmagupta. Neugebauer,[13] the teacher of David Pingree, has made studies of al-Khwārizmī's *Astronomical Tables* with the help of a commentary and has shown with modern symbols that al-Khwārizmī practically used the following results:

(*i*) $d = \sqrt{(s^2 + 12^2)}$,
(*ii*) s = 12 R Sin (90° – h)/R Sin h,
(*iii*) s = 12 R Sin h/R Sin (90° – h),

where height of the gnomon = 12 *angulas*, altitude of the sun = h degrees, length of the shadow angulas, the inverse shadow or equinoctial shadow = s.

Al-Khwārizmi's formulae show that he used sine function exactly similar to that of Brahmagupta. Only al-Majriti's edition (thirteenth century) of the al-Khwārizmī's *zīj* contains cotangent and tangent function along with sine function which has been suspected as interpolation by al-Majriti. Some scholars have believed that al-Khwārizmī used R = 60 following Ptolemy, which has been contradicted by Neugebauer. He further writes in his studies of al-Khwārizmī's tables: "It seems doubtful, however, the extent table of sines is of al-Khwārizmī's original tables, since we know from al-Bīrūnī's *Rasail* that this table used R = 150 and not R = 60". The table with R = 150 are also presented in Toledan tables of al-Zarkali.

Al-Bīrūnī (AD 973–1048) who stayed in India for 13 years (from AD 1017 to AD 1030*)* studied many *Siddhantic* texts. He gives 57 references to Brahmagupta's works of which 16 references are adduced to *Khaṇḍakhādyaka*. In his *Al Qanun al-Maśūdī*, he gives sine table at an interval of 15° from Brahmagupta's work, and constructed tangent {R Sin θ/R Sin (90 – θ)} and co-tangent {R Sin (90 – θ)/ R Sin θ} tables. His *al-Maśūdī*[14] has used the word *zill* for shadow for both tangent and co-tangent. The argument with which the table is entered, the co-tangent appears as the compliment of the given arc. Both Abu al-Wafa (940–997) and Al-Bīrūnī realised that putting R = 1 would save time in computing since R (not 1) implies frequent multiplication or division by R.

It will be interesting to note how Indian results became popular through Arab intermediaries. Umar ibn al-Farrukhān (died about AD 815) belonged to the early period of the development of Islamic science. A Latin manuscript,[15] *Ashmole 191.* II is now discovered which is based on Umar's work, which in turn has relation to *Siddhantic* sources. This manuscript has used Feb. 16, 3102 years as an epochal era, a date which is identical with the beginning of *Kaliyuga* era, commonly used in Indian *Siddhantic* astronomy. In Greek works the geographical latitude is characterised by the length of daylight unlike *Siddhantic* works in which length of equinoctial shadow is used. The Latin manuscript has also quoted many formulae involving equinoctial noon shadow lengths of a gnomon of 12 *angulas*, which shows the Greek and Indian linkages through Central Asian intermediaries. The formulae also contains R = 150 and further application of the Brahmagupta's formulae in the preparation of shadow table for finding the altitudes of the sun. The shadow tables of different places on equinoctial day for gnomon of 12 *angulas* are given by many Indian astronomers. Five such tables have been traced by David Pingree[16] in the Sanskrit collections of America and Europe, which according to him, were mainly used for finding latitude of places, preparation of local *pañcāṅgas*, etc. The shadow tables for gnomon are also found in many medieval Central-Asian astrolabes of fifteenth and sixteenth century AD. As an example, the backside of the Muhammad Muqim's astrolabe[17] contain shadow lengths for 7 feet (Greek tradition) and also 12 *angula* gnomon (Indian tradition), and the shadow lengths were determined by the formula s = g cot h, where g = height of the gnomon, and h = altitude. This shows a clear indication that the Central Asian scholars have not only preserved and simplified but also enriched both Greek and Indian astronomical traditions with the use of Cot and Tan functions and tables, and contributed greatly to the scientific heritage of the world.

ACKNOWLEDGEMENTS

The author is grateful to the Indian National Science Academy and the Mathematical Sciences Trust Society, Delhi, for sponsorship. Thanks are also due to Prof. J.N. Kapur for his academic interest in this paper.

NOTES AND REFERENCES

1. *Āryabhaṭīya* of Āryabhaṭa, critically edited with Introduction, English Translation, Notes, Comments and Indexes by Kripa Shankar Shukla in collaboration with K.V. Sharma, Indian National Science Academy, New Delhi, 1976.
2. *Brāhmasphuṭasiddhānta* of Brahmagupta, edited with his own commentary by Sudhakara Dvivedi, Benares, 1902.
3. *Khaṇḍakhādyaka* of Brahmagupta, ed. with *Vāsanābhaṣya* of Āmarāja, ed. by Babuaji Misra, Calcutta University, 1925, tr. into English by P.C. Sengupta, Calcutta University, 1934.
4. *Brāhmasphuṭasiddhānta* was translated into Arabic by Muhammad bin Ibrahim al-Fazari (d. AD 796) and Ya'qub bin Tariq (second half of the eighth century); *Khaṇḍakhādyaka* translated at Sind shortly after AD 735 (vide *Dictionary of Scientific Biography*, Vol. II, pp. 416-418; *Encyclopaedia of Islam*, old edn., ed. by K.V. Zettersteen, 1936, Vol. IV, pp. 248-249, Vol. III, 1136, M. Plessner, *Encyclopaedia of Islam*, new ed., Vol. I, pp. 1101-1102, 1960.
5. Ibn an-Nadim, *Kitāb al-Fihrist*, ed. by Gustav Flugel, Vol. I, p. 276, 1872; K.V. Zettersteen, *Encyclopaedia of Islam*, old series, Vol. IV, pp. 221-23, 1936.
6. Carlo Nallino, *IIm al-alak* (Arabian Astronomy, Its History in Medieval Times), p. 370, Rome, 1911.
7. Michio Yano, 'Three Types of Hindu Sine Tables', *Indian Journal of History of Science*, Vol. 12, No. 2, p. 88, 1977.
8. Al-Bīrūnī, *Kitab al-Hind*, Hyderabad, Dairat al-M' arif (ed)., 1958, p. 356; English tr. by Edward C. Sachau as *Alberuni's India*, New Delhi, repr. 1992, Vol. II, p. 19.
9. A.K. Bag, *Mathematics in Ancient and Medieval India*, pp. 235-46, Chaukhamba Orientalia, Varanasi, 1979.
10. *Alberuni's India*, English tr. by Edward C. Sachau, repr. ed., 1992, Vol. I, p. 137.
11. The *Khaṇḍakhādyaka* of Brahmagupta with the commentary of Bhaṭṭotpala, ed. and tr. by Bina Chatterjee, pp. 211-12, World Press, Calcutta, 1970.
12. *Brāhmasphuṭasiddhānta* of Brahmagupta (ed. by Sudhakara Dvivedi with his own commentary, Benares, 1902), iii 10; *Pancasiddhāntikā* of Varāhamihira (ed. K.V. Sharma and tr. into English by T.S. Kuppanna Sastry, Adyar, Madras, 1993), iv., pp. 20-21; *Mahābhāskarīya* of Bhāskara I (ed. and tr. by Kripa Shankar Shukla, Lucknow University, 1960), iii. 5; *Laghubhāskarīya* of Bhāskara I (ed. and tr. by Kripa Shankar Shukla, Luknow University, 1963), iii. pp. 2-3; *Sūryasiddhānta* (ed. by Kripa Shankar Shukla, Lucknow University, 1957).

13. O. Neugebauer, *Studies on the Astronomical Tables of Al-Khwarizmi* (with tr. and comm. of Latin version), ed. by H. Suter, supplemented by Corpus Christi College MS. 283, Kobenhavn, 1962, chap. 28, 28 a and 28 b, pp. 55-7, see also p. 104.

14. *Al-Qanun al-Maśūdī* (Canon Masudicus), 3 vols., Hyderabad, 1954-56, vide Vol. I, p. 338.

15. O. Neugebauer and Olaf Schmidt, 'Hindu Astronomy at Newminister in 1428', *Annals of Science*, Vol. 8, No. 3, pp. 8, Sept. 1952.

16. David Pingree, 'Sanskrit Astronomical Tables', *Indian Journal of History of Science*, Vol. 31, No. 2, 1996, pp. 173-220.

17. Archaeological Museum, Red Fort, Delhi, Regd., No. 40-420.

9

Indo-Central Asian Trade Relations

Mansura Haidar

Central Asia which had earlier been one of the important regions on the old 'Silk Road' is said to have become commercially a 'subdued phenomenon'[1] during sixteenth century. The period is characterised by the feeble overtures of the Ottomans for an alliance with Central Asia against the increasing challenge of the Portuguese and Russians. This was countered by the Russo-Persian co-ordination against the allies and subsequent disturbances and conflicts created by Qazaqs and the Persians in the region alternately. European travellers observed with dismay that in sixteenth century there was no hope of good trade in any part of the country and that the trade in Persia and Tartaria alike was 'little utterance and small profit'.[2] To the early medieval Persian chronicler, however, the brisk commercial transactions at various entrepots of Central Asia seemed to show no decline. In Ibni Hauqal's estimation, the wealth of the people of Khwarizm (in the absence of mines of gold, silver and precious stones) depended mainly upon two things—cattle-breeding and trade with Turks in slaves from Saqlab, Caspian and its vicinity and in that of ermine furs and skins.[3] Writing in 1405 Clavijo comments, 'every year to Samarkand much merchandise of all kinds came from Cathay, India Tartarj and from many other quarters for in the countries round Samarkand territory commerce is very flourishing'.[4] Ibn Battuta refers to the nice Khwarizm melons, which were sweet and syrupy and dried under the sun, were carried to India and China and nothing among the dried fruits seemed better than these. The merchants brought it to Delhi. Similarly, he refers to the *Alu* dried and carried to India and China. Later, in fifteenth century, the trade to China was hampered.[5] Clavijo also found each corner of Samarkand thronging with crowds of people from diverse sect, creed, race and language—Mongols of Central Asia, turban-clad Iranians and Indians, Russians, and Chinese. The caravans on camels with the loud noises of ringing bells and loads of merchandise (*Kala*) passed through the city. They disembarked and placed their luggage in the vestibule or inner yard of the caravan-serais. The shops were full of Chinese goods (*parandi chini*), as it was just six months' journey; the leather and cotton goods from Russia and Central Asia; and medicines, swords, armour cuirasses and precious stones from India, which were in abundance.[6] Babur refers to the dried plums of Bukhara, Samarkand paper, excellent wood *tabulghu* and cramoisy velvet being taken from one place to another and claims that the best paper in the world was manufactured in Samarkand.[7]

Isfahani noted appreciatively that Andijan was 'perhaps developed exclusively for trade purpose'. Uruganj and Arquq were the two famous entrepots in Khwarizm region. At Sighnaq, rarities were brought from different places and it happened to be a 'junction of traders' (Mahall I Tujjar)[8] from Transoxiana, Kashghar, Khotan, and Turkestan. In sixteenth century, Yasi was also said to be a centre of brisk trade where novelties from Uzbek countries (in Dasht) in the north and from Andijan up to Khitai (China) in the east were brought by traders.[9]

From Dasht and Haji Tarkhan, traders used to carry away sheep, horses, camels and other rarities like fur and skins (*samur* and *sanjab*), strong arrows and bows, and fine silken cloth.[10] Several articles like shoes, cotton cloth, saddles, arms and a number of consumer goods were supplied by the Central Asian traders to the Steppes. In return, they received wool, skin, slaves, and cotton.[11]

In the presence of a great variety of handicrafts, internal trade flourished. Several trade routes were established connecting Samarkand and other towns and villages of the Shaibanid empire. Caravan-serais were built on these routes. In certain areas, bridges were built over the rivers, and reservoirs and wells were also provided on the routes. Internal trade was being carried on between quite distant towns and villages. For example, wheat and barley were brought from Tirmiz to Khwarizm since Ibn Battuta's time, as during summer, the river Amu was navigable for ships and boats as far as Tirmiz, the journey downstream taking ten days between Khwarizm and Tirmiz.[12] When there was a shortage of grain during Herat campaign, Abdullah Khan requested Khwaja Juibari to send 1,000 camels laden with 10,000 *mans* of barley from the stocks of Andkhui. If, however, the grains were not available in Andkhui, it was to be brought from the *sarkar* of Merv.[13]

There was always some relationship subsisting between the city and the village markets. Fruits, corn and other rural products were brought to the city for sale; certain manufactures were taken from towns to the village. The sources refer to the sale of melons and grapes at the city gates.[14] Metal vessels, clothes, saddle and cheap jewellery were most in demand from the village consumer. The cloth imported to another town carried the name of its place of manufacture. The caravans with a number of camels transported the goods from one city to another. Each magnate, therefore, used to have several hundreds of camels. The Juibari Sheikhs had more than 60 *qatars* (row) of camels, each row consisting of 10 camels.[15]

During the fifteenth-sixteenth centuries, monetisation appears to have developed to some extent in the countryside. During the first three quarters of the sixteenth century, small-scale retail trade was carried on by copper coins. The opening of temporary mints in big and small towns, suburbs and even villages for exchange of coins shows the expansion of money use.

Apart from generating commerce from its own products, the role of Central Asia in international commerce as an intermediary state was also important. India's commercial relations with Novgorod and the Baltic during eighth to eleventh centuries 'carried down the Oxus and up the Volga'[16] by the Russians of the Steppes had been confirmed by Le Conte d' Alveilla on the basis of his numismatic researches. Under the Abbasids, Sogdians were famous for commercial enterprise and were highly interested in Chinese silk trade. Dobson says that Bukhara had always served as the depot and agency for distributing Indian tea as well as Russian wares throughout the surrounding countries. The Sogdian centres of Chinese silk trade were at Samarkand, Kash and Paykand, which worked as intermediaries between the East and West. Suq as Soghd (the market of Sughdians) was one of the most ancient quarters of the city of Merv. According to Bento de Goes, "even in the very earliest periods of history, it was through Turkestan that China and the west were in touch with each other".[17] It seems that no direct contact between India and Russia had been established. It is reported that the Bukhara ambassadors to India in 1671 were asked about the products of Russia, which could be acquired direct from Central Asia being available there. The envoy narrated the entire list enumerating such things as fishbones, sables, shelves, vixen and so on which could be supplied from Russia through Central Asia to India.[18] Similarly, an Indian merchant Mail Baqqal who was in Moscow in 1675 along with his companions, is said to have reported that several Russian things like sables, vixen of varied colours, fishbones, mirrors of different sizes, velvet, gerfalcons and greyhounds are much required in India.[19] It can be inferred that trade relations between Russia and India could be pursued indirectly through Central Asia. Although a Russian envoy is said to have come to Aurangzeb in 1696, the Russian traders did not have a free and consistent direct access to Indian commerce.[20]

Clavijo found the markets of Samarkand "amply stored with merchandise imported from distant and foreign countries".[21] Indigo brought from India and sold in the markets of Samarkand and Bukhara by the *neelfarushan* (indigo sellers) was also exported from Central Asia to Moscow. *Ruyan* (madder) was one of the export items to Russia brought by Khivan traders along with cotton cloth since the Russians sold madder to the Kazan manufacturers of red calico.[22] The traders from various countries including Arabia and Persia assembled in the two large stone caravan-serais built by Khwaja Juibari in Charasui and Sarrafan areas in and outside Bukhara.[23] Another serai was built by Khwaja Qutubul Abrar. Samarkand served as a trans-shipment centre for *baqam*

(Brazilian wood) brought here from other countries.[24] Samarkand was very rich in producing azure, golden dye and other paints, though Jenkinson mentions that colours were imported from India.[25]

The role of Bukhara traders in Russo-Persian trade is evident from the document of 'secret deals' containing the lists of items traded between the two lands.[26] To Astarakhan came caravans from Central Asia, Iran, Caucasus, Armenia, and India. The Ottomans are also said to have played an intermediary role in the caravan trade between countries of Far East and Near East through Central Asia.[27] The traders from Persia, Arabia, Turkey, and Kazan lived in Samarkand and Bukhara and carried on trade in Central Asian handicrafts through Bukhara. The Tartar merchants from Kazan were called 'Bukhara Yurtchi'.[28]

The cotton growing areas of Turkestan exported fabrics to Iraq.[29] From Merv *abresham* (silk thread) was exported to other countries.[30] Bukhara woollen carpets were especially in demand. Although exports from Central Asia to Egypt have been mentioned in earlier centuries, there is little evidence of trade relations between the areas in the sixteenth century. Stray references to Egyptian Katan (*katani misri*) and Egyptian sword (*teghi misri)* however occur.[31] Zendani cloth was much in demand in Iraq, Fara, Farmina and India from seventh to nineteenth century.[32]

The arrival of Central Asian merchants in Asia Minor is mentioned by Ibn Battuta.[33] The role of the Ottoman Empire in Central Asian commerce needs to be discussed separately. Throughout the sixteenth century, the Ottomans tried to find an ally against Russia and Persia in the Shaibanid rulers by establishing direct relations with the *Khanates*. Trade was revived along the route, stretching from Khwarizm through Astarakhan to Crimea, a route that was then under Ottoman control. Ibn Battuta found the coastal town of Azaq (Azov) as a 'well-built' town visited by the Genoese and, other merchants. Bayazid Bayat refers to a place 'Tokhta', the 'bajgah of Balkh'.[34] In Ibn Battuta's time, Hormuz was a 'well-provisioned' market from where the products of India were exported to the two Iraqs, Fars and Khurasan. Abbe Raynal found it 'an agreeable city in the east' where "persons from all parts of the globe exchanged their commodities and transacted their business with an air of politeness and attention seldom seen in other places of trade."[35] A number of letters were exchanged between the Ottoman rulers and various Uzbek sultans, the latter pleading for an Ottoman intervention against Persian 'high-handedness'.[36] Almost simultaneously, the rulers of Shervan and Gilan also asked for intervention of Sultan of Turkey against the Persians. The Ottoman wazir Sokollu Muhammad Pasha was thus "planning to solve the Persian and Muscovite problem in one stroke and Czar and Persia hastened to draw together".[37] The conquest of the *Khanate* of Siberia (1598) by Russia also had long-lasting effects. Apart from facilitating the penetration of Russia into Central Asia later, it caused traffic between eastern Europe and eastern Asia to move over to Siberia in the following centuries, thus bypassing Central Asia. Consequently, the importance of Turkestan declined considerably.[38]

TRADE WITH INDIA

In Babur's time, there were two trade marts on the land routes between India and Khurasan, namely Kabul and Kandahar. The caravans to Kabul came from Kashgar, Farghana, Turkestan, Bukhara, Samarkand, Balkh, Hesar and Badakshan, and the merchants made higher profits in Kabul as it was an excellent trading centre.[39] Clavijo says that from India were brought to Samarkand the lesser spiceries, which are most costly of the kind such as nutmeg, cloves, mace and cinnamon.[40] Every year the caravans of ten, fifteen or twenty thousand heads of houses bringing slaves, white cloth, sugar candy, refined and common sugars and aromatic roots came to Kabul from Hindustan and many traders were not content with a profit of 30 or 40 on 10 (i.e., 300 to 400%).[41] Over three hundred years later, Burnes (1837) tells us of Luhani merchants carrying precisely the same articles of trade.[42] Hafiz Tanish refers to a serai situated on a transit route (Peshawar) where a large crowd of people was always engaged in the commerce (*sud-o-sauda*). The same chronicler refers to a multitude of traders from Khurasan, Turkestan and Transoxiana who had spent quite a long time in the countries of 'India, Deccan and Gujarat'.[43] While returning to their country, they brought with them the rarities of various places in India and stayed in Peshawar, then a dependency of Kabul, for obtaining local supplies.[44]

According to Babur, Abul Fazl, Hafiz Tanish and Jenkinson, the chief commodities of export from Central Asia to India in sixteenth century were almonds (also of *kandi badam*), apples, pears, raisins, Khwarizm melons, Russian furs, hunting birds, red hides, wrought silks, slaves and horses.[45] Abul Fazl gives a long list of the Central Asian fruits (both fresh and dried) along with the season and prevalent rates.[46] Bernier[47] found Central Asian fruits in Indian markets and observed that India consumed an immense quantity of fresh fruits from Samarkand, Bukhara, Balkh and Persia such as melons, grapes, pears eaten at Delhi and purchased at a very high price nearly the whole winter and likewise dried fruits such as Bukhara prunes (*alu Bukhara*), almonds, pistachio, plums, apricots, various other small nuts, white and black raisins, which were available the whole year round.[48] The Indian merchants 'brought less goods' to Central Asia, exporting fine whites for turban and other whites made of cotton for the apparel, tea, spices, pearls and colours.[49]

One of the most important and profitable trade of Central Asia to India seems to have been the export of horses.[50] Babur, Manucci, Bernier and others refer to the continuous import of horses from the Uzbek regions of Balkh, Bukhara, and Kabul to India. The number of horses coming down to Kabul annually is said to have been 7 to 10 thousand by Babur.[51] Even in Yuan Chwang's times, Samarkand was 'yielding many fine horses'.[52]

Abul Fazl reports that "droves after droves of horses arrived from Turan and Iran" and in his times there were 12,000 in the stables of Akbar. The horses were usually brought from Iraq, Turkey, Turkestan, Badakshan, Qirghiz, Sherwan, Tibet, Kashmir and other combines. Ibn Battuta found the horses in the Uzbek empire of Dashti Qipehaq. According to the classification given by Abul Fazl, the horses "imported from Turan, though strong and well-formed" belonged to the fourth class as 'they do not come up to the preceding classes'. The first class were Arab bred (720 p.m.) second Persian (680 D p.m.), third class Mujannas–Turkish or Persian (560 D p.m.) and Uzbeks received 480 D p.m.[53] Manucci says that,

> most of the horses used by the Mughals came from the regions of Balkh, Bukhara and Kabul and thence came every year more than 10,00,000 horses and on them the king maketh a great profit by the duty he imposes, the usual number taken being 12,000. The horses called Turki are courageous in war, can stand much fatigue and never forsake their masters unto death.[54]

Manucci probably exaggerated in his estimate of the number of horses.[55] Bernier says that India received 25,000 horses from Uzbeks.[56]

Indian traders were seen in Astarakhan and Haji Tarkhan by Barbara Contarin in fifteenth century and by Jenkinson in 1558.[57] Indian merchants and usurers lived in one of the quarters of Bukhara.

During Timur's time, the two prominent and profitable points of trade routes were said to be the two iron gates (*darband-I-ahinin)*.[58] Babur says that there were seven roads existing in the Hindukush mountains.[59] Abul Fazl also mentions seven routes employed by the people of Turan from Balkh and Badakshan to reach Kabul and five practicable roads to Turan from India, namely Karapati, Khyber, Bangash, Naghar and Farmul. While Karapati was not used in Babur's time the travellers from Turan and India took the Khyber route in Akbar's time.[60] The fact is corroborated by the accounts in *Abdullahnama* as Hafiz Tanish refers to the caravans of Indian traders from Deccan, Gujarat, Multan and other regions of India who were carrying goods in 1584 through Peshawar for Khurasan, Transoxiana, and Turkestan.[61] The same routes were being used at least till eighteenth century. Chandra Bhan Brahmin (AH 1230) also mentions the same number of routes between Kabul, Badakshan, Balkh, and Hindukush through which the Turanians travelled to and from India.[62]

TRADE WITH RUSSIA

The trade of Central Asia with Russia had considerably developed after the conquest of Astarakhan and Kazan. The Russian sources speak of 'friends' (merchants) from Urganj who came to Astarakhan in July 1557 from Hajim Khan as envoy and reached Moscow in October 1558 along with the Bukhara envoy.[63] Jenkinson's mission was also an attempt to promote commercial relations between Central Asia and Russia.[64] In Moscow itself there was a Tajik colony engaged in trade.[65] Abul Ghazi refers to the exchange of a number of embassies and trade missions between Russia and Central Asia.[66]

Soviet scholars describe a special pattern of trade existing between Russia and Central Asia. According to Baikova and Yuldasheva, individual trade did not receive much encouragement. Individual traders who could manage to send or take their goods by any route did so at their own risk. All sorts of taxes (sale, custom, etc.) were imposed on them in addition to *zakat*. Generally, the Russo-Central Asian trade was of three categories, i.e. (1) the usual trade in cheaper wares for common use such as cotton fabrics; (2) the sale of goods of the Khan or Czar through their own personal representatives, merchants coming with the envoys. No custom duty was imposed upon these. They comprised an assortment of cheap as well as expensive objects; and (3) custom-free trade between the first merchants of the states called 'amateurish feast' or 'disguised trade', consisting of exchange of rare goods of both countries (in which gifts exchanged between the rulers were valued by the experts and gifts of the same value returned).[67]

An important feature of the sixteenth century Russo-Central Asian trade seems to be that state trading had started, though in a rudimentary form. In view of Abdullah's efforts to combine diplomatic assignments with commercial responsibilities for his ambassadors to Moscow, trade relations with Russia had further progressed.[68]

Khwaja Qutubul Abrar is said to have sent a certain Maulana Jan Muhammad to Moscow for a year, from Bukhara. He returned after enjoying the hospitality of the Czar and conducting commercial transactions[69] and favourable agreements were concluded.[70] Hafiz Tanish refers to the return of an envoy whom Abdullah Khan sent to Moscow to bring falcons *(shunqar)*, armours and coats of mail *(zirah, joshan)*.[71]

In 1557, the Uzbek Khan sent an embassy to Czar Ivan IV (1530-1584), congratulating him on his victory in Astarakhan and requesting him to widen the route of south-eastern Europe with a grant of freedom of trade to Central Asian merchants in Moscow. The 'free trade' in this context meant "the freedom to carry on trade in any place, commodity; to sell your goods at your own price and buy whatever you want". The Caspian became especially advantageous for Central Asian traders as the Khivan Khans in their documents often requested for increasing the trade between Astarakhan and Karaghan haven (on eastern bank of Caspian Sea) where twice a year in spring and autumn, merchants clustered and even the Czar's pearl (boat) came with eastern and Russian merchants. Astarakhan *voivode* (governor in ancient Russian) supervised the trade, gave *strelets* (soldiers) for safety, verified documents, checked merchandise and sent information through *Khabarshik* (messenger) to Khiva and Bukhara. The commercial transactions continued for a month at the shore of Caspian.

At the end of the period, officials came to write down the details for imposing taxes.[72] The distance between Karaghan and Astarakhan was traversed from 2 to 8 days depending upon the weather. In Astarakhan, Kazan and Samarra, envoys and merchants stayed and waited till the Czar received the kings' *yirligh* and allowed them audience. Nevertheless, Jenkinson found 'this island of merchants' near Kazan completely 'forsaken'. Although, "earlier merchants from Russia, Kazan, Crimea, Nogailands and from other countries did resort to keep mart for buying and selling here, the place was now (1558) without any such resort thither or at any place about it from Moscow until mare Caspium".[73] The same traveller even noted that there was no trade worth the writing, neither any hope of trade in all those parts worth the following. Ibni Arabashah writing in mid-fifteenth century refers to the 'convoys of travellers' from Khwarizm to Crimea earlier which had stopped during his own time, "none moves or rests and nothing ranges there but antelopes and camels".[74] Similarly, Jenkinson found that Astarakhan had 'beggarly and small trade though Russian, Persian and Tartar traders come there".[75]

The main items of export from Russia were red hides, sheep-skins, woolen garments of various kinds, falcons, armlets, vests, sugar, hardware, tin, mercury, candles, kerosene, paraffin, armaments, wooden vessels, metal goods, bridles, and saddles. In exchange Russia imported cotton wool, varied type of silks, craska, dye stuff and other things.[76] Narshakhi says that many villages near Bukhara, particularly Zandan, prepared nice cotton fabrics called *Zandanchi*, which was not only used by the local population but also was sent to Iran, Fars, Kirman, India and other regions.[77] Writing in 1552, Rhode reports that the Russians, particularly common people, could not do without *Alacha* and *shai*. These were light, inexpensive but durable and good for *caftans*.[78] The Bukhara to Moscow trade had no competitors due to its cost and quality. Thus, the main items of export from Bukhara to Moscow were textiles, raw cotton, Karakul skins (Astarakhan or Persian lamb), wool hides, carpets and silks like *atlas*, which in the words of the Bukhara envoy, Mulla Farrukh, "was not available at all in Bukhara or when available was of coarse quality".[79] Even in nineteenth century, Shergul Afghan says that the cotton and dry fruits were quite profitable for the *dihqans* in their trade with Russia and Siberia, for these fetched them cent per cent profit (*yaki bar sad faeda midihand*).[80] The same traveller refers to the commerce in cotton, fresh and dry fruits, dried grapes, apricots and apples especially sent to Russia and Siberia from Tashkent.[81] In 1585 alone there were 4200 *zendani* pieces among 5000 pieces of material set for sale in Russia.[82] After the fall of Kazan and late Astarakhan to the Russians, Russia had its own float ships in Caspian Sea in sixteenth century. These ships (called the Czar's Bussi-pearls) were sent at least twice a year mainly to obtain animals, horses and other such merchandize for the Czar. Owing to the extortionist demands of feeders and rowers (on the Czar's boats) from Central Asian merchants, there often arose serious troubles between them, whenever Central Asian merchants boarded the Bussi. In one of the petitions to Czar Ivanovich in May 1589, a certain Muhammad Ali complained that rowmen and feeders had taken away 5 *caftans*, 6 *zedani* silk pieces and 60 sash all of which even in the lowest estimate cost 22 roubles 20 kopeks. The merchandise was always opened for Czar's 'first pick', by his trusted servants who usually thought themselves to be entitled for a 'second pick'. When the tax collector came to see the merchants at the latter's first halting place wanting them to declare their goods sold to the Khan, they charged a fee before declaration on each *pood* (around 35 pound) or by weighing the merchandise. Over and above were the Czar's taxes. These merchants again paid a number of other taxes like *tamgha*, fee and charges of tax collectors, 'main', 'ordinary' and 'fives'.[83]

There were two main trade routes between Central Asia and Russia in the southeast and Siberia, the former called 'Karaghan haven', being the Caspian route via Astarakhan, and the other was the land route along the Volga from Astarakhan to the interior of Moscow. The voyage from Karaghan to Astarakhan was from two to eight days depending upon the weather. The Siberian land route ran from Tobol via Irtish, Ishim to Turkestan and then to Bukhara by a nice road; from Bukhara to Siberia a trade route also ran through Qazaqstan.[84]

Official documents of tax collectors in Siberia and *aul* orders (issued to nomadic regions) show a number of petitions submitted by Siberian and Bukhara merchants, e.g. Alim Sulaiman's petition with his companions demanding from Russian officials the restoration of their right to carry on trade. In such documents, we can see the reflection of competition between merchants settled in Siberia and local merchants. It appears from Bukhara petitions that, for Bukharians, Khans and Czars made continuous reassurances for respecting the protection of free trade 'as existing earlier'. There is, however, no mention of the agreed terms in clear words. One thing is ceratin that with whomsoever trade went on, the chief beneficiaries were only Czar and the Khan's own exchequers. The regulations were tilted consistently from one side to another to serve the Czar's interests. The permission for free trade (excluding furs, forbidden things) was given among others to Jenkinson's Moscow company of Englishmen for 20 years on the Volga Caspian route.[85]

The privileges granted to English merchants in 1569 by Czar authorised them "to be and abide freely, to barter and bargain freely all wares of sale without custom of people" not only in Russia but also "to pass through our land to Boghar, Persia, Caspian and other countries".[86] They were also asked to bring "fine wares out of England or from Bukhara, Persia, etc". The first pick was done by the Czar whose 'Chancellor' had a look over them and selected those 'needful' for him. The remaining articles would then be bartered or sold. Similarly, these 'Russian adventures' were to serve these merchants in trade. They were not to be checked at Astarakhan and Kashan and "our authorised people were to quietly let them pass, not viewing their wares nor taking any toll or custom of their wares".[87] These privileges were exclusively for English merchants. There are two more documents issued in August 1596 and December 1609 by Feodore Ivanovich (1584–1598) and Ivan. From February 10, 1596, from Moscow ordered the opening of trade between local inhabitants and coming Bukhara and Nogai traders who could also go forward without hindrance to Tobol and other Siberian towns. Another order of August 31, 1596[88] allows Bukhara and Nogai traders not only permitting free trade of 'forbidden things' like Siberian fur, saddles, axe, etc. but free of custom duty as well.[89] Bukhara traders could move with their merchandise in north, as a result of Moscow document of 1600.[90]

During the years 1620–1630, the Kalmuk invasions from the east disrupted the trade and the indifferent attitude of the Czar towards high-handedness of their officers, harassment of Central Asian merchants and complaints of the Khans further aggravated the situation. Things came to such a pass that Isfandyar Khan (1623–1642) of Khiva wrote a letter to the Czar lamenting that while Russian merchants were travelling and trading comfortably in his territory, the Khivan merchants were harassed by Russian captains and compelled to sell their goods at less than cost prices or be denied passage and that officials in Astarakhan levied heavy illegal duties upon them. Notwithstanding the Czar's reassurances, the harassment of Central Asian merchants continued and the Khiva and Bukhara ambassador merchants in 1623 received a very impolite reception at the Czar's court.[91]

The kings often had a share in the commercial enterprises. It is said that Ulugh Beg gave money to the merchants to engage in trade and in return received a share of the profit. A merchant of Turkestan named Fazil had been coming to Shaibani, received the status of Tarkhan and was even assigned the task of supervising the defence of the gate of Samarkand.[92] Hussain Alauddin, who was one of the traders of Bukhara, used to have many transactions with Sultans. The Uzbek Khan Ubaidullah is reported to have been in his debt.[93]

Sometimes the kings sent their representatives to buy luxury goods for their personal use as these were not produced indigenously. One of Imam Quli's *souzomiz* (order) dated early June 1633, orders the *hukkam, ummal, alighdaran, Qarawuls, rahdars* of the *wilayat* of Russia not to demand any *rahdari* or *garawuli, kharj, baj*; allow the merchant to travel from whichever route he wishes without any interference; and to let him buy the goods, grains, spices and rarities (*asbab, ajnas, masaleh, aqmasha* and *ajnasi-nafisa)* by way of trading (*ba tariq I saudagari*) to purchase for the imperial needs (*ba'aze az zaruriyat I sarkar I khassa*) from India, Iraq, Kazan, and Moscow.[94]

The merchants themselves were entirely dependent upon the ruling class and only a few privileged persons could carry on trade on favourable terms. Alkashifi refers to a number of Khwajas like Khwaja Kalan, Khwaja Maulana

Sa'aduddin, Shamsuddin Muhammad Ruhi, Khwaja Juibari, Khwaja Qutubul Islam who travelled far and wide for commercial transactions and sent their representatives to Moscow and other places for profitable trade (*sud-o-sauda*).[95] The Tarkhan traders continued their commercial activities in indigenous and imported goods. In their own vested interests, the elite supported this privileged merchant class, shifting the share of collections from them to the shoulders of those who were expected "to pay *zakat* at proper time and avoid appropriation of others' property".[96] Unlike the *Tarkhani* granted to landlords and other such magnates, the trading *Tarkhan* was completely exempt from all forms of taxes, state dues, customs, *padnashini* and even voluntary formalities to the local and central ruler. One such trader, though not himself of Samarkand, received *Tarkhani* privileges in lieu of his services from Shibani Khan.[97] The Tarkhani privileges could be given to the foreign traders as well and exemption from some taxes were granted to them. One such person Haji Ilyas Chelebi was given the *Tarkhani* or exemption from *tamgha*, *Kharaj* as well as an exemption from the fulfilment of *ulagh* on the territory of Transoxiana.[98] Certain *nishans* exempting the grantee from all taxes and obligations refer to 14 such taxes. Another *nishan*—a specimen of *Tarkhan* grants, refers to the order of the ruler exempting the holder from *darughaghi, rahdari, khidmatana, kishtibani* and unforeseen demands; still another such *nishan* issued to a merchant refer to exemption from *baj*, *kharaj*, *tamgha*, *zakat*, and *ulagh*.[99]

Apparently, the internal market suffered from a shortage of supplies of various commodities. Wasifi drafted two such letters, one on behalf of Sultan Ali Muhtasib and addressed to Khwaja Sheikh Muhammad Diwan requesting him to release some peas and pulses (*mashi gurini*) from his store as the petitioner was unable to acquire them from the market. Another letter of Maulana Fathullah Haravi addressed to a candle-stick maker (*shamma'a*). In it Khwaja Husain asks him to provide some candles as they were not available in Samarkand market for the past several days.[100]

The trading communities in Central Asia were Sarts, Tajiks and Jews.[101] In later centuries the wholesale trade in silkworms in the *khanates* was held by the Bukhara Jews.[102] Although the existence of credit operations, letters of credit (*suftah* or *suftaja*), pay order within a time and *khatti sarraf* (cheques for local transactions) in the form of 'dumb bartering' are mentioned in the sources, no detailed information about the working of these is available. Muqminova says that wholesale trade was carried on not only in ready money but also by promissory notes (*tamassuk*). One such legal document signifying the receipt of goods was prepared at a *qazikhana* in Samarkand. The document refers to the delayed payment for textiles. In the list of goods received, there are mentioned 14 names of textile articles, most of them being of Indian origin.[103]

REASONS FOR DECLINE IN TRADE

The Central Asian trade followed an erratic pattern throughout the sixteenth century. This was undoubtedly due in part to lawlessness and civil wars which threatened peaceful commerce in and around Central Asia. The strained relations of Central Asian rulers with certain neighbouring countries also caused commercial blockade; e.g., Shaibani had issued a *farman* that the people of Turkestan should not have any contact with the merchants from the Qazaq lands that the Qazaq traders should be harassed, deprived of their belongings and even killed, if they were found in Turkestan and Khwarizm.[104] During the period 1586–1598 the import of Central Asian goods to Siberia declined considerably owing to wars between Abdullah Khan and Qazaq ruler Tawwakkul. Consequently, Moscow merchants replaced Bukhara traders in Siberia. The death of Tawwakkul and the conquest of the *khanate* of Siberia (1598) by the Russians further restricted Siberian trade with Central Asia.[105]

The commercial relations with Persia and China had also fallen on bad days due to recurring hostilities in the case of the former and disorders in the intervening zones in the case of the latter. During the wars in Qandahar a mass of Hindustani traders in Kalat "fell prey to Babur's followers who wanted to plunder them as they were coming to an enemy's country". Babur, however, persuaded his men to accept *peshkash*.[106]

While recounting the twenty years of 'most perfect peace and security' under Mansur Khan, Haider Dughlat says that anyone could travel alone from Kamul in Khitai to Andijan without having any duties levied upon him and would be taken every night as a guest into some house on the road at that time.[107] Similarly, Clavijo described the peaceful atmosphere and opportunities provided for trade under Timur.[108] But the accounts of Sidi Ali Rais (1553–1556) and Jenkinson (1558) present a very different picture of Central Asia. Sidi Ali Rais speaks of Nogai tribe 'committing violence' upon travellers and the roads being 'swarmed with robbers and highwaymen'.[109] Jenkinson was harassed by thieves on his return journey and even his hundred well-armed escorts supplied by Abdullah Khan could barely protect him.[110] The same traveller mentions, "certain field people as well as Gentiles and Muhammadans living between Bukhara and China on borders of the cities of Tashkent and Kashghar who had made it almost impossible for any caravans to pass unspoiled".[111] The tribal population (Manghits, Turkomans, Hazaras, Baluchis) inhabiting the area between Central Asia and India on the one hand and Central Asia and Persia on the other also caused much trouble. Babur calls the Afghans of Kabul and Lamghan (Ning Nahar) 'thieves and abettors of thieves even in quiet times'.[112] Hafiz Tanish refers to perpetual danger from the Raushanais.[113] In his letter to Abdullah Khan and Shah Abbas of Persia, Akbar repeatedly refers to the numerous Afghans entrenched in the hills of Bajaur Swad, Tirah and Bangash who 'intercepted the caravans proceeding to Turan' and were a 'stumbling stone to travellers to Turan'. Similarly, Abul Fazl refers to the 100,000 Yusuf Zai tribals who 'caused much injury to traffic and intercourse'.[114] Bento De Goes (1603–1607) also found the area 'infested with robbers who lie in wait for caravans and commit many atrocities ==.[115] He speaks of the 'perils' and 'encounters', which overtook the travellers necessitating 'eight months compulsory rest' besides 'loss of companions'. He recounts how they had to take shelter for a 'full weary month' in Taliqan due to Calcian revolt against the Khan of Bukhara and their 'ravaging and plundering'. When they departed, they were 'attacked' near Taliqan then under Abdullah Khan and 'escaped complete ruin' only by paying a tribute on their merchandise. He was harassed by the rebels also. In Badakshan even the escort of Goes 'made common cause with the populace' and fell upon the traders.[116] Such experiences often deterred a 'number of travellers from continuing the journey'.[117] The caravans from India and Persia were once looted and the travellers massacred by robbers while on their way to Bukhara. Not only that the trade with Astarakhan, Mongolia and Persia suffered due to unsafe routes, but also the caravans could not travel safely even through Kashghar and Tashkent.[118] Even Ibn Battuta records how the armed and well-built Turks near Herat used to invade over environs of India almost continuously — plundering and capturing slaves.[119] Shergul Afghan says that after the accession of Yunus Khan as Khan of Tashkent, Qirghiz and Qazaqs who were busy in 'plundering (*Yaghmagari*) feasts' were taken to task and severely dealt with resulting in complete suppression of such troubles.[120] Nevertheless, the routes remained unsafe even when Burnes travelled in these areas.[121]

Civil wars too were a continuous feature of Central Asian political life in sixteenth century. Both Sidi Ali Rais and Jenkinson describe the horrors and the evil effects of these wars on commerce. While in Central Asia, both of them were asked to leave as the civil war was imminent and they would be in danger of losing their lives and goods.[122] Such wars, whether long or short range, must have diverted capital and manpower from trade investments to mutual non-productive military enterprises internally. Inter-state trade also received a setback. In a letter to one of the Naqshbandi saints, Khudai Piradi, a brother of Sultan Said, urges him to ensure that those who bring in grain to the province or export whatever they deem proper (for sale elsewhere) should not be obstructed.[123] Jenkinson describes how the civil wars led to highway robbery in Urganj:

> When there are wars between these brethren (as they are seldom without) he that is overcome if, he be not slain fleeth to the field with such companies of men as will follow him and there liveth in the wilderness resorting to watering places and so robbeth and spoyleth as many caravans of merchants and others as they be able to overcome continuing in this sort his wicked life until such time as he may get, power and aid to invade some of his brethren again.[124]

This evidence cannot be brushed aside as the exaggerations of a prejudiced traveller. Haider Dughlat himself refers to such 'desperadoes'.[125] According to him, Vais Khan, the Mongol ruler took to the life of a robber because he found the 'science of his uncle (rulership?) irksome'. Many youths[126] volunteered to follow him including Haider Dughlat's grandfather Mir Ali. Even the reigning kings of Khwarizm are alleged to have indulged in such activities.[127] Abdullah had once received a petition from his special envoy returning from Russia, asking for protection against the high-handedness of the Khwarizm Sultans to ensure a safe conveyance of goods brought from Moscow. Abdullah had accordingly appointed Tinash Haji to escort the envoy and warned the Khwarizm rulers through a *farman*. Again on the arrival of another envoy from India, special measures were taken to thwart the attempt of the plundering tribes and rulers to harass them.

But such imperial protection was not always effective. Jenkinson and his party had to face the danger from robbers at every step, notwithstanding the 'letters of safe conduct' issued to him by the various kings and the detachments appointed as escorts.[128] Jenkinson wails that though one of these groups 'consumed much of victuals' they escorted them to a certain point only, after which they demanded a fabulous amount for the journey ahead and on being refused, returned to their Sultan of Urganj who was 'privie to the conspiracie'. Jenkinson and party fought bravely against the robbers for two hours. These robbers were again 'banished princes' and their followers. Ultimately Jenkinson and his companions had to buy their safety by giving them 'twenty times nine several things and a camel for carrying it'.[129] Some of the companions were even kidnapped in the journey later on.[130] Jenkinson says that peaceable travellers usually 'go in a caravan with camels' whereas all those 'horsefeeting travellers without camels to be doubted'.[131] Bento De Goes who happened to be in Central Asia in 1602–1607 also says 'the country between Cialis and Chinese wall' is notorious for Tartar raids so that,

> the traders always crossed it in the greatest fear, sometimes even in the strictest silence and under the covers of the night.[132] One often came across the dead bodies of Muhammadans who have attempted the journey, unaccompanied though on the other hand, the Tartars were not wont to kill the native population considering them as their servants and herdsmen who they occasionally rob of their flock.

Goes himself travelled at night. Similarly, near Astarakhan Thomas Banister and Geofrey Ducket, the agents for the Moscovie company, met Nogai Tartar in 1568 who were "thievish and cruel and attacked them with 18 boats of theirs each of them being armed, some with swords, some with spears and some others with bows and arrows".[133] It seems that the trade between Russia and Central Asia was frequently disturbed by Turcoman Khivans' inroads on western routes, by Kalmuks, Qazaqs and Qara Qalpaqs in the east and Afghan and Turcomans on the south. In seventeenth century, Uzbek Khan even looked for support from the Czars in their struggle against the Kalmuks.

Apart from the highway robbery there were other difficulties as well. Jenkinson had to cope with 'bad and brutish' people whose fighting, stealing, begging, raising the prices of horses and camels and victuals, forcing them (Jenkinson and party) to buy even the drinking water, selling provisions according to their own demands "so that for every camel load 1400 weight of our three hides of Russia and four wooden dishes", forcing to pay tribute to princes of governors (one-ninth and two-seventh, namely nine several things and twice seven several things). Jenkinson's caravan was detained at another place in the name of Menguslav Prince Timur Sultan. The Tartars took the choice things again from him as *tuquz* (gift for the king in ninette) without paying any money. Even Timur Sultan himself did not give Jenkinson any money. Jenkinson complains against Abdullah Khan who 'showed himself a very Tartar', as he went on an expedition without paying the money for the purchases he made from Jenkinson and the latter had to come back to recover the debt. Jenkinson was, however, very 'ill satisfied', when he was paid in kind and forced 'to rebated part' which compelled him to say that he could expect no 'better payment from a beggar'.[134] At the gulf of Caspian Sea, the 'customers of the king of Turcomans took a custom of every 25 one and 7 ninths for the said king'.[135] The system of *Silao* (offering presents before being allowed to cross the frontier without let or hindrance) had also continued up to nineteenth century and those found recalcitrant 'were beaten up'. The repeated experiences of this kind were naturally great irritants for traders.[136]

Then there were the taxes. Jenkinson gave a long list of custom duties: "a custom of every five and twenty-one and seven-ninth for the king and his brethren"[137] at Urganj; a custom 'as well for our own heads as for our camels and horses'; and 'petty custom' at river Ardock and later at Kait. He also paid custom of every camel one red hide of Russia besides petty gifts to his officers. At Bukhara a 40th part of merchandise was to be paid on goods as toll.[138] The Central Asian merchants had to pay *baj*, *kharaj*, and *tamgha* at Peshawar.[139] Bento de Goes records as a strange fact that while passing through Jilalabad and Aliabad on the Qunduz River, "the Brahmins had the right of exacting tribute given to them by the king of Bucarate (Bukhara)".[140] The caravan of Burnes had to pay at Sighan "a Nakeen Pelisse with eight or nine rupees (the usual tax on a caravan) to its chief Ali Muhammad Uzbek. At Khulm also the ruler Rahmatu'llh Khan claimed a tax on the traveller though he is but a tributary of Qunduz".[141] The imposition of heavy duties by the Central Asian Sultans at their provincial borders[142] restricted the free movement of traders with a resultant increase in the price of commodities.

The custom officers could detain merchants and artisans not holding immunity grants and could even inflict physical punishment. The documents given to the privileged few specifically enjoin officials 'to allow the merchants to go safe and healthy' and 'to give him co-operation and assistance in all dangerous spots'. Such merchants must have been closely associated with the Khan and presumably might be carrying even the kings' own goods. The attempts of the Khans and rulers to subjugate trade (particularly international) and to exploit the traders is borne out by the order contained in *Maktubat wa asnad*[143] directing traders 'from wherever they may be' to bring their valuable goods and precious things for an inspection by the king's nominee who could acquire the goods at set rates for the Khan. The traders were asked 'not to conceal anything' and 'no one could buy anything from the merchants till the inspection was over'. Generally speaking, in sixteenth century, there was no guarantee of immunity and safety in respect of personal property of artisans and traders. Berthold rightly concludes that absence of all guarantee from new and unforeseen taxation was partly responsible for the stagnation of the economy. Decline in general prosperity also restructured the market for commodities. Enumerating the cause of the poor trade, Jenkinson says "the few ships upon the Caspian Sea, the want of mart and part towns, the poverty of the people and the ice maketh the trade nought".[144]

NOTES AND REFERENCES

1. Cf. Spuler; *The Muslim World,* part III, Leigen, 1969, p. 243; for silk route cf. the map 16, in *The Art of Central Asia,* p. 9; for details about early trade, M. Boulnois, *The Silk Road,* London, 1963, pp. 149-63; C.G.F. Simkin, *The Traditional Trade of Asia,* London, 1968, p. 58; Khuda Baksh, *The Renaissance of Islam,* pp. 468-79; Barthold, *Sochinenija* VI, pp. 368-72, iii 54-8; Bretschneider I 269; Shaban, *The Abbasid Revolution,* Cambridge, 1970, p. 15.
2. Jenkinson, 15, 30; also see Hakluyt Ser. II 108-9.
3. Ibni Hauqal, *Surat ul Arz,* Tehran ed., pp. 209-10; also see Alijahiz, p. 35.
4. Clavijo, p. 278.
5. Ibn Batuta, Persian tr. 406, 411-14, English tr., 168.
6. Clavijo, p. 278. Also see *Nuzhathai Iranian,* Vol. III, part II, p. 275; Haider Dughlat English tr., 406.
7. *B.N.* 4, pp. 48-49; *The Renaissance of Islam,* pp. 468-69.
8. Ruzbehan Isfahani, *Mehman Namai Bukhara,* Tehran ed., 85, 200; Fsi 50.
9. *Ibid.,* p. 256. Ibn Batuta describes the fine port of Karsh in Dasht "which was a magnificent harbour with about 200 vessels in it, ships of war and trading vessels, small and large for it is one of the most notable harbours in the world" (Ibn Batuta, pp. 142-43).
10. Ibni Hauqal, p. 195. The same geographer notes that cotton and silken clothes were prepared in Khwarizm and were sent to various places. Ibni Hauqal, 209; Mehn, 85, pp. 199-200.
11. Ahmedov, Bori Gasudarsstova Kochivikh Uzbekov, p. 151.
12. For a detailed and interesting description of *Serais* cf. *Abdullahnama* of Hafiz Tanish; Obruchev's *Travelogue* and Fazil Samarkandi's *Tarikh;* Manazili Bukhara.

13. *Rauzat-ur Rizwan*, pp. 260-61.
14. Wasifi, z Badain' l Waqai, Tehran ed., p. 278.
15. Examples Rashhat, p. 221.
16. Sourin Roy, 'From the Ganga to the Volga—The History of an Ancient Trade Route', *Studies in Asian History*, New Delhi, 1969, pp. 171-72.
17. Shaban, *The Abbasid Revolution*, Cambridge, 1970, p. 15; *Russian Railway Advance*, p. 374; also see Bento De Goes, 30. Not only the 'horrifying tales of bitter experience narrated by Nikitin discouraged the direct future commercial relations between India and Russia' (E.P. Magudovitch, *Ocherki Pa istori geograficheskikh atkriti*, Moscow, 1957, pp. 81-84).
18. *Russko Injiski atnashenija*, Vol. V, XVII 48, Collection of Documents, Oriental Institute, Moscow, 1958, p. 171.
19. *Russko Injiski atnashenija*, XVIII, B.M., 1956, p. 5.
20. Spuler, 243. The Mughal chroniclers however do not seem to have recorded this event.
21. Clavijo, 288.
22. Cf. Muqminova 88. The other items brought to Bukhara were copper, steel, iron, blue paper, mercury, painted stone, pens, cloth (*parchai* undraping, *fulful*, write), coral, gold threads, etc. For details see *Manazil I Bukhara*, pp. 13-15.
23. Rauzat, 295.
24. *Ibid.*, 157.
25. Jenkinson, p. 22; Istorija Samarkand, 277.
26. Baujiya, pp.108-15, Ziaev Kh. Urta Azia va Siberia, Tashkent, AN UZSSR, 1962, pp. 68-70, M.V. Plickner, Targovliya Russkovo Casudarstova sa Stranami Vastoka va XVI vekov, trud, State Historical Museum, issue 31, M. 1956; also see Obruchev, p. 37.
27. Obruchev Travelogue, p. 37.
28. Robert Mantran: L. Empire Ottoman et Le Commerce Asiatique, *Islam and Trade of Asia*, pp. 169-79.
29. Ibni Hauqal, p. 362.
30. *Ibid.*, pp. 246, 362.
31. Ibni Hauqal, pp. 246, 316. *Islam from the Prophet Muhammad to the Capture of Constantinople*, ed. and tr. by Bernard Lewis, Vol. II, 1974, USA, p. 155; even the cotton growing area of Turkestan exported fabrics to Babylonia. For details; cf. Ibni Hauqal 362. al Jahiz (p. 35) says that paper from Samarkand, sweet grapes and Ghawshana, triffles from Balkh, zither and zither player, carpets and fur suits from Merv, musk ermine, marten, foxfurs, sweet sugar from Khwarizm were exported to Iraq.
32. Narshakhi Russ. Tr., p. 18; Clavijo.
33. *Ibn Battuta*, Vol. I, Pers. Tr., 365; English tr., p. 144.
34. Nars Tazkira I Humayun wa.
35. *Ibn Battuta*, Vol. II, 314; also see V.A. Gardlevski, *Izbraniyi Sochinenija*, Moscow, 1960, p. 145; also see, Nicola A. Ziadesh, 'Change of Trade Centres in the Persian Gulf in the Middle Ages', *Studies in Asian History*, New Delhi, 1969, pp. 296-301.

36. See *Faridun Bey Munshaat us salatin.*
37. *Cambridge History of Islam,* I a 335.
38. *Cambridge History of Islam,* I a 469.
39. *B.N.* 129-130, English tr., 2002-06; also see, Spuler, *Islam and the Trade of Asia,* pp. 16-19.
40. Clavijo, 289.
41. *B.N.* 129, 149 English tr., 202, 235.
42. *B.N.* text 129, 149, English tr., 202, 235; for Indian merchants in medieval Azerbaijan and Shirwan. Cf. S.B. Ashurbeh; Injishki kuptsi va sredni vekovikh goradakh Azerbaijan e Shriwan, pp. 92-6; Narod Azi e Afriki, 4, 1964.
43. Abdn f. 456.
44. Abdn 456 for interesting details on Armenian traders in India; cf. Surendra Gopal, *Central Asia,* New Delhi, 1970, pp. 200-14.
45. *B.N.* text 129; Jenkinson, 24-5; Tuzuk I Jahangiri I, 350.
46. Abul Fazl, *Ain I Akbari* I, English tr., Blockmann; see list of fruits, pp. 65-9.
47. F. Bernier, *Travels in the Mughal Empire,* Delhi, 1968, pp. 118-19, 203-4.
48. Bernier, 118-9, 203-04. Even Marco Polo saw the export of white salt and fruits from Central Asia to foreign lands. The almonds and pistachio nuts from the southern hills of Taliqan were carried to distant lands (Marco Polo, pp. 57-59); also see Maqdisi, 234; Adam Mez, *The Renaissance of Islam,* English tr. by Margliouth and Khuda Baksh, Delhi, 1979, pp. 438, 442.
49. Jenkinson, 24-25. *Ajaibul gharaib* MS, 47 Ouseley, Badleian Library, ff. 55. If Soviet accounts are to be believed, gold was also an important object of export from Central Asia to India in exchange for cheaper silk and cotton material. For details, cf. Davidovich, Monetnovo dela, pp. 194-96.
50. In Marco Polo's time, this trade was in the hands of the Persians. Marco Polo found in Turkomania an excellent breed of horse called Turki and also fine mules sold at high prices (Maco Polo, *Travels* pp. 24, 40, 61, 194, 288, 322). Ibn Battuta (167) refers to the cheapness of the horses in Saraichik as he sold his exhausted horses there at the rate of 4 silver dinars per head or even less.
51. *B.N.* 129, English tr., 202.
52. Watters, p. 94.
53. *Ain* 49, *Ain I Akbari,* English tr. by Blochmann, Vol. I, New Delhi, 1977, p. 140.
54. *Ibid., Ain* I, II *Ain* 1, Part 2, *Ain* 2, p. 243-44.
55. Manucci, pp. 390-91.
56. Bernier, pp. 203-4.
57. For details, cf. Baikova, 102-10.
58. Cavijo says that the first was where the eastern spur of the Caucasus range comes down to the Caspian a narrow pass between mountain and sea in the kingdom of Shirwan, which was a gateway between Persia and Golden Horde. The other was situated in the mountain range between Samarkand and Balkh called 'the guard house of the imperial city' through which all who travel up to Samarkand from India, Leh

can come, nor can those who go down from imperial city voyaging to India travel by another route (Clavijo, 204-205). For interesting details about Darband, cf. Bretschneider II, 115-19; Hilda Hookham, 165-67.

59. *B.N.* 129-30, English tr., 202-6. Babur says that these seven roads separate Kabul from Balkh, Qunduz, and Badakshan (namely, three leading to Panjshir Khwak, Tul and Bazarak) and four other roads leading to Kabul from India.
60. *Ain* II, 405-06; *B.N.* 206.
61. *Abdn*, 451.
62. Chandra Bhan Brahmin, *Chahar Gulshan*, Abdussalam Collection, Maulana Azad Library, MS NO 292/62 ff 93.
63. Soch III, 90.
64. Allworth, *Central Asia: A Century of Russian Rule*, pp. 23, 31, 38, 40.
65. Ghaffurov, *Tajiki*, pp. 538-42.
66. Abul Ghazi II, 293-94; Soch III, p. 90; Abul Ghazi III, 293-98, 338-43.
67. Baikova, *Role Sredni Azi va Russko*, Injiskish targoirkh svyazi, Tashkent, 1964, pp. 51-2; Yuldasheva, *Kistori targovikh e pasolskikh svyazi sredni Azi c Russie*, Tashkent, 1964, pp. 1-70.
68. *Abdn*, 378.
69. MS Oriental Institute 77, No. 2094 f. 90.
70. Rauzat, f. 18.
71. *Abdn*, 378.
72. Yuldasheva, 60-2.
73. Jenkinson, Hakluyt I, 440; Purchas XII, 3-4.
74. Ibni Arab, English tr., 77.
75. Jenkinson, Hakluyt I, 44.
76. Jenkinson, 24-25, Ghaffurov 538-42; Wheeler, 44.
77. Muhammad Narshakhi, *Istorija Bukhara*, Russian Tr. by Likoshima, Tashkent, 1897, Frye Bukhara, the medieval achievement Norman, 1965, p. 31.
78. Baikova, 100-08.
79. *Ibid.*
80. Shergul, 137. The value of exports to Russia between 1827 and 1837 is said to have exceeded that of imports by 20,00,000 roubles, Wheeler 44; Lyashchenko, 54-60, 605-18; Becker, 170-76.
81. *Turkestan*, 136-38. Spuler includes satins, bludgeons, metal goods, axes and firearms, silver needles, nails, and dishes among the exports from Russia to Central Asia, though he does not cite his source. Central Asian exports to Russia comprised Krakul pelts, carpets and even precious stones and ornamented weapons (Spuler, *The Muslim World*, 243. Also see *Cambridge History of Islam*, I A 483). Both Krader and Allworth believe the slave trade being remunerative and as one of the prime source of Russia's wealth, Allworth, 30-37; Krader, *Peoples*, 98; also see Belk, 'Turkestan: Russian Mennonite Promised Land, Studies in Islam', *Journal of Indian Institute of Islamic Studies*, New Delhi, Jan-April 1973, pp. 58-62, 95.

82. M.V. Fahner, *Targovlya Russkovo Gasudarstova*, p. 75.
83. Baikova, 75-98.
84. There exists a controversy regarding the location of Kabakal; for details, cf. Chuloshnikov, *Targovlya Moskovski gasudarstova kistori targovikh pasoskikh svyazi sredni Azie Russia va XVI-XVII vekov*, Tashkent, 1964, pp. 56-64; Baikova 98.
85. Baikova 108-115.
86. Hakluyt Soc. Ser II, 85-7.
87. Hakluyt II, 88-93, 324; Baikova, pp. 108-15.
88. G. Miller, *Istoria Siberi*, Moscow, 1937, p. 207; also see *Puteshestivya Ispafaria Zapiski Russkovo Geographicheskova Obsnestva pa otdel ethnografi*, Vol. X, SP, 1182, p. 43.
89. *Ibid.*
90. Yuldasheva.
91. *Material pa istori uzbekskoj, Tajikskoj SSR*, Leningrad part I, 1923, pp. 428-31; also f.n. 178; Allworth, pp. 23-4.
92. T. sh., 8-9.
93. *Muzzakira*, pp. 166-67.
94. For similar example of exchange and purchasing missions, see Riazul Islam, *A Calendar*, pp. 159-60, 164, 165-66, 178-79, 184, 186.
95. For original document see Yuldasheva, p. 75; *Rashhat*, ff. 130, 221; also *Rauzat*, f. 9; *Muzzakira*, 164, 484-485; *Vazliublemnni Sirdsa*, 31; *Ocherki pa remesla*, pp. 189-90.
96. *Ibid.*
97. *B.N.*, English tr., p. 132.
98. *Makwasnad*, 171; *Ocherki pa remesla*, p. 190.
99. *Makwasnad*, 77, 170; *Ocherki pa remesla*, p. 190.
100. *Badaiulwaqai*, p. 114-19.
101. Bruchev, 63; *Cambridge History of Islam*, I, 483; *Islam and the Trade of Asia*, pp. 13-17.
102. Imamuddin, Baitu mal, *Islamic Culture*, 1960; Spuler, 'Trade in the Eastern Islamic Countries', *Islam and the Trade of Asia*, 13-17.
103. Muqminova, pp. 190-91.
104. Mehnama, p. 156.
105. For details, *Cambridge History of Islam*, I, 469.
106. *B.N.* text 207, English tr. 331.
107. T.R., English tr., 126-27.
108. Clavijo, 75; Sidi Ali Rais, 72-73.
109. Sidi Ali Rais, 25, 72-73; T.R., English tr., 126-27; Jenkinson, 2-24.
110. *Ibid.*
111. Sidi Ali Rais, p. 25.
112. *B.N.*, 213, English tr., 341.
113. *B.N.*, 159, 213, English tr., 341, 251; *Abdn*, 456, 475, 489; also see *Akbarnama*.
114. *Insha*, 7, 20; AN iii, English tr., 1010, *Rauzat*, p. 156.

115. *Jahangir and the Jesuits*, p. 146.
116. C. Wessels, *Early Jesuit Travelers in Central Asia*, pp. 16, 19, 20.
117. *Ibid.*
118. Jenkinson, 20-21, 23-6; Sidi Ali Rais, 66-67, 72.
119. Cf. Ibn Battuta, Persian tr., 437.
120. Shergul Afghan, *Turkestan*, State University Library, Tashkent, pp. 238-58.
121. Jenkinson, pp. 14-15, 18-26; Sidi Ali Rais, pp. 66-72.
122. Jenkinson, 14-15, 18-26; Sidi Ali Rais, 66-72.
123. Rauzat, pp. 157-58.
124. Jenkinson, pp. 15.
125. T.R. English tr., pp. 60, 63-64.
126. T.R. English tr., pp. 60-64.
127. Jenkinson, pp. 10-14.
128. *Abdn*, p. 378.
129. Jenkinson, pp. 10-14.
130. Jenkinson, 18-20; Hakluyt I, pp. 445 -6, 451-5.
131. *Ibid.*
132. *Ibid.*, pp. 18-20.
133. Bento De Goes, pp. 37-38.
134. Haklyt's *Voyages* II, pp. 27, 119; also see Boies Penrose, *Travel and Discovery in the Renaissance* (1420-1620), Cambridge (Mass.), 1955, p. 193.
135. Jenkinson, *Purchas*, pp. 11-12, 22-23; Hakluyt, pp. 446-8. The non-payment for the purchases made by the king seems to be common way with the medieval Asian Sovereigns. Thomas Alcock and Richard Cheini both have the same complaints against Abdullah Khan, a provincial ruler in Persia. It was after a long stay and with much trouble that Cheini 'recovered' some of it. Arthur Edwards also did not receive certain debts while Thomas Alcock's debts were 'past hope of recoveries' (Hakluyt II, 31-32, 35-36).
136. Jenkinson, *Purchas*, 11-12; Hakluyt I, 446-8; Marco Polo, pp. 57-87.
137. Jenkinson, pp. 13-14; Hakluyt I, pp. 448-52.
138. Jenkinson, Hakluyt I, p. 464.
139. Hafiz Tanish, p. 456.
140. *Early Jesuit Travelers*, pp. 19-20.
141. Burnes, p. 194.
142. Sochinenija V, p. 208.
143. *Maktubat wa asnad*, p. 30.
144. Jenkinson, pp. 15, 30. The same situation prevailed elsewhere also. Hakluyt, p. 108.

10

Naqshbandiyya Sufi Order: A Link between India and Central Asia

Sheikh Saleem Ahmed

Naqshbandiyya has more socio-political overtones rather than mere anthropological interests. It constitutes one of the leading Sufi order in the Muslim world. Its history dates back to the fourteenth century Bukhara in Khurasan. Kh. Mohammed Bahauddin Naqshandi (1318–1389) was considered its founder. His father was an embroider (Kamkhab Baf) by profession, hence the Order came to be known Naqshbandi. But Trimingham says that the Order begins from Abu-Yusuf-al-Hamdani (d. AD 1140) as per *Rashate-e-Ainul Hayat*, a history of the Order written by Fakharuddin Ali Husain Kashafi. Earlier, Naqshbandiyya was known as Tariqate Khwajagan. Khwajagan is plural of Khwaja. Perhaps it is distorted form of Khoja, a title for Syed in Turan or Mwaraunehar Khoja who hailed from the Holy Tribes of which other names are Ata, Sheikh, Mehtun, etc. and provided spiritual leadership to the Sufi Order from Central Asia. Naqshbandiyyas seek their spiritual descent from second Caliph of Islam, Hzt. Abu Bakr.

By the sixteenth century, Naqshbandiyya became a worldwide organisation spreading over major areas of Sunni Muslim world like West and Central Asia, Ottoman society and Indian subcontinent, including China.

Bahauddin Naqshbandi and Abdul Khaliq Gujdwani were the early leading figures who formulated rules for the Order and made efforts to establish its centres in whole of the Central Asia, Herat, Balkh, Badakshan, and India. The practice of *Zikr* (repetition of the name of Allah) is found almost in all Sufi Orders. But in Naqshbandiyya, *Zikr* is a fundamental principle. There are two types of *Zikr-Zikre Khafi* (silent–*Zikr*) and *Zikre-Jali* (loud–*Zikr*). Most of the Naqshbandis believe in *Zikre Khafi*. Abu Yusuf has traced the practice of *Zikr* to Hzt. Abu Bakr in his very early treatise, *Risala-e-Sahabiya* (1204). *Jap* in Hindu religion is equivalent to *Zikr* on the condition that the Sultan would strengthen adherence to the Sharia and promote the welfare of his subjects.

The Khwaja accompanied the Sultan on his campaign offering both military and spiritual assistance against his enemy Mirza Abdullah of Samarkand. The Khwaja moved there too from Tashkent. The encouragement given by the Khwaja enabled Sultan Abu Said to repulse the invasion of Samarkand by another Timurid prince Babur.

Throughout the rule of Abu Said, the Khwaja remained a tower of strength to him. He urged the Sultan to introduce reforms beneficial to the peasants and the merchants. It seems that the Sultan and his successors gave Khwaja a large farming property as gift. He owned thousands of helmets and crores of dinars. Khwaja gave several lakhs of dinars to Umar Shaikh Mirza, the father of Babur and a son of Abu Said to relieve the Muslims of Tashkent from the burden of excessive taxes. Abur Rahman Jami, a well-known Naqshbandi poet, who was instrumental in bringing Alisher Navai into the Naqshbandi fold, gave a description of Khwaja's property, which extended the whole way from Tashkent to Samarkand. Besides agricultural and grazing land, his assets included orchards, houses, shops, mills, etc. A couplet from Jami's *Masnawi* is quoted here:

"The splendour of Faqr (derveshi) of Ubaidullah
Beat the monarchical drum."

In spite of this affluence, Khwaja led an ascetic life and lived in his Khanqah like other dervishes. All revenues from his holding were put into *auqaf* (religious endowment) for benefits of Madrasas, Khanqahas and mosques, Sufis and others.

The conquest of India by Babur in 1526 gave considerable impetus to the development of the Naqshbandi Order in India. Many Sufis form the part of the itinery of the new king including a large number of chieftains, nobles, etc. Many of them like Aziz Koka, harem's ladies like Gulrukh Begum, Salima Sultan, and Babur also sought allegiance to Mohammad Naqshband or Khwaja Ahrar, because they too belonged to their ancestral homeland.

Vernon James informs how Khoja Ahrar was portrayed in Soviet literature in different light contrary to what has been stated about him earlier. In the Soviet period the Naqshbandiyya and Sufism in general were presented as the tools of the state used to control the lives of working class. For example, fifteenth-century Naqshbandi saint Ahrar was commonly portrayed as:

(a) A large feudal landowner who used his religious status to oppress the peasantry;
(b) A rival and enemy of poet Navai; and
(c) A signatory to the unjust death warrant against Ulug Beg Mirza.

Khwaja Baqi Billah (1564–1603) who was a disciple of Khwaja Ahrar came to India during the time of Akbar. He established Naqshbandi Order in India. He was born in Kabul around 1564. His father Abdus Salam Khalji Samarkandi was an *alim* and Sufi as well. His mother was a descendant of the family of

Khwaja Ahrar. Shaikh Ahmed Sirhindi met him in Delhi enroute to Makka and immediately was initiated in the fold of Naqshbandiyya by the hand of Khwaja Baqi Billah.

Shaikh Ahmed Sirhindi (1564–1624) entitled Mujaddid Alfsani, was an original thinker, known for his wisdom and learning. He was also involved in social and political affairs of his times. He belonged to a highly respectable family. His father Abdul Ahad was also a Sufi. Sirhindi traced his lineage to the family of Umar Farooq, first Caliph of Islam. He was proud of it. The contents of his thought are mainly found in his letters which he addressed to his sons, devoted followers and to the leading *amirs* of the Royal Court. These letters were compiled in three volumes entitled *Maktubate Iman Rabbani* and published in 1873 after two hundred and fifty years of his death.

In India Sirhindi confronted with a different situation quite dissimilar from Central Asia, though India was ruled by the Mughals, and there was peace and prosperity abound. But Sheikh Ahmed Sirhindi was not a happy man and felt uncomfortable to see increasing alien, non-Muslim and Shia influence in the Muslim society of India. Due to his upbringing and education, he had a very orthodox frame of mind. His concern was the supremacy of pure and pristine Islam and wanted to revive the period of Khulfae Rashidin (first four Califs). He believed that *ahle sunnat-wal-jamat* was the only right sect which should have supremacy over the Muslim society. Sirhindi founded the doctrine of Wahdatul Shahud to counter the influence of Wahdatul Wajud, which he considered the main evil.

Vernon James Schubel viewed the Indian scene in right perspective. He says:

> There was a time when Sufism seemed to treat the border between the Ummah (community of Muslim believers) and potential converts in the non-Muslim world as fluidly as possible in order to facilitate conversion to Islam. To this end many *tariqas* emphasised vernacular poetry and the Islamisation of indigenous practice. The Mujaddid, born in India where the Ummah was surrounded by Hindus and where Shias minorities were playing a major role within Islamic culture, attempted to draw the boundaries of Sunni Islam more rigidly, treating the border between the Ummah and the non-Muslim world as a wall to protect the 'True Islam' from external and internal pollution. The Mujaddiyya presented a form of Sufism which can easily exclude Shia Muslims by emphasising Bahauddin Naqshbandi Silsila through Abu Bakr rather than through Ali. Its primary goal was not the spread of Islam to non-Muslims but the protection of Islam from 'heretical influence' (cited in *Rizvi* 1978).

Prof. Ishtiaq Quraishi explained this point in another way:

> The rejection of monism was the great need of the age and provided the basic diagnosis of the disease from which Islam was suffering at that time. When seen in the perspective of history, whether accepted by the Sufis or not it is on

the rejection of monism that Shaikh Ahmed Sirhindi's claim for being the Mujaddid of the age is based.

Quraishi further observed, "The common ground between Vedanta and Sufism was provided by monism alone, take out monism from Sufism and the resemblance with Vedanta ceases to exist". It would be pertinent to quote from Mujaddid's letters, he addressed to Khwaja Fared Bukhari, which throws more light on this aspect. He writes: 'The whole world is lost in the darkness of *bida* and who has the courage to oppose and speak out for Ahlae Sunna' (54/II).

He further laments,

> You know what passed on Muslims in the past time. Prior to that in spite of their weakness they had not undergone such a misery. In those days matters did not go beyond the limits as indicated in the sacred verse that you have your religion and I have mine (Lakum Dinakum Walia Deen). But during these days infidels authoritatively issued the decrees of infidelity in the country of Islam (India) and the Muslims were unable to express the dictates of their religion and if they did they were killed. Alas! What a pity! What grief!

One of the tenets of Sirhindi's policy was based on the assumption that the reforms should proceed from top to the bottom, i.e. from the king to the people as the popular maxim goes, 'Annas ala deena muklukehim' (like king like subjects); in addition, he also used to say that 'Sharia can flourish beneath the shadow of the sword' (Ash Shara Tahat us saif, 65/II). He was of the opinion that the 'King is the soul and the rest of the people are just like the body. If the soul is pure, the body is also healthy. If any ill attacks the soul the body too falls ill' (57/II).

Shaikh Ahmed was successful to put a check on the influence of Wahadatul Wajud by advocating Wahadatul Shahud, namely the theory of dualism. The Mujaddid stressed that man cannot know God through intuition or mystic experience (Kashfo Shahud); one should revert to the revelation and to the teachings of Ulema because the Ulema derived the knowledge of God direct from the revelation. The concept of Tawhid as advanced by the Mujaddid was:

> The Holy existence of God is self-existent. Every other things are his own creation. God is alone in the *Zat* (existence) and *sifat* (attributes) and actually there is no participant in these attributes; it may be *wajud* or non-*wajud* neither in name nor in resemblance. It was purely a theologian concept of official Islam. God was divorced from his creation. Consequently, seeds of hatred and division were sown by him. Tendency was developed to divide the world into *'them'* and *'us'*.

Mujaddid preached hatred against non-Muslims and Shias. He wrote *Risale Radde Rawafiz*, refuting Shiism. In his several letters addressed to Shaikh Farid Bukhari we found bitterness against Hindus. As a result Hindu-Muslim and

Sunni-Shia riots broke out with the tightening grip of exclusivism and intolerance preached by the Mujaddid. In one of his letters to Sheikh Farid Bukhari, he writes:

> Every person has some wish in his heart. But the only wish of this faqir is that the enemies of God and their prophets be oppressed and those damned be insulted and their false-gods be humiliated. This faqir knows for certain that for God there is no other act more desired than this one.

What reveals most the bigoted aspect of Sirhindi thought is his rejoicing of Guru Arjun's execution in 1605 at the order of Jahangir. He did not bother to see whether the order was correct or not. In this act of the king he found the degradation of the infidels and the thriving of Islam. He showed similar narrow outlook in response to the letters written by one Harday Ram, who asked a question as why Ram and Rahim could not be one. He replied in very harsh words stating as far as Krishna and Ram are concerned they are among the base creatures of God. When Ram could not keep an eye on his wife what help he could offer to others. It is greatest folly to call Ram and Rahim one. On another occasion, Mujaddid became furious when he came to know one Muslim poet had adopted his pen-name *Kufri*.

In *Rude Kausar*, Ikram has drawn attention to the point that Sirhindi never uses the word Zimmi for Hindus; instead, he always prefers to call them *ahlekufr*.

Change is the law of nature and it is the only permanent law. Foreign elements always creep in whether it is language, creed or culture. Absorbing them in their fold is strength and not weakness. If so-called alien or innovatory elements are given place and made parts of Islamic fabric, it would have enhanced the strength of the Islam. Sirhindi, denying to accept change, closed the doors for any progress among the Muslims. It can be illustrated by narrating another interesting event of his life. He was invited to Fatehpur Sikri to help Abul Fazl and Faizi in their literary works. In these meetings there was open discussion on philosophers and their achievements, which were being appreciated by them. Sirhindi did not like this atmosphere. In his excessive zeal he could not remain silent on the praise of philosophers. He said that Imam Ghazal has written in his book that useful sciences, which these philosophers claimed as their inventions like astronomy and medicine, were plagiarised from the books and wisdom of the former prophets. Other sciences such as mathematics were of no use to the religion or in the life after death. Upon this, Abul Fazl retaliated and said that Imam Ghazal was unreasonable (*Na Maqool*). On this Mujaddid walked out of the assembly in anger. Similar reaction was shown in *Ibne Khaldun* when he came to know about the new invention in the field of physics being carried out in the West, and remarked that physics was not helpful in religious affairs. Sirhindi expressed his dislike about modern sciences in his letters as well and one of his friends also ridiculed algebra.

About his various claims of spiritual supremacy Sirhindi faced severe criticism not from Ulema alone but from his disciples also. He always remained surrounded by controversies. He claimed that he acted upon his intuition. He was against Wahdatul Wajud. Many other Ulema of the time were also against the doctrine. But their opposition was based on arguments. When Sirhindi was asked about the basis of this opposition, he said, "I consider it wrong because my intuition (*Kashfo shahud*) say so". Similarly, he claimed that the title of Mujaddid Alfani had been mystically bestowed upon him by God, though he was making ground since long to assume this title writing letters to his sons and disciples and mustering support from the Ulemas. Though Sheikh Ahmed Sirhindi committed mistakes, which proved harmful to his community, but they were mistakes of assessment. He failed to understand the ground reality. The Mughals' roots in Islam were not very deep since they professed it recently. Besides, they were more enamoured by their own ethnicity and culture. They were more concerned with governance rather than Islam. Mughals were basically secular.

It was an irony that in spite of his closeness to royalty and his desireness, Ahmed Sirhindi could not get a position in the court. Sheikh Farid Bukhari asked him to give four names to consititute a religious council who could advise the government in matters of religion. The list of names could not be provided to Sheikh Farid, because it was his own name which was in his mind to be appointed as sole advisor. Hence, the proposal could not go ahead and Sheikh Farid also lost interest in it.

The fallout of Mujaddid's teaching proved fatal to the Muslim Ummah as borne out by the following.

All the orthodox revivalist movements of eighteenth and nineteenth centuries, whether it is declaration of India as *darul harb* by Shah Abdul Aziz or Wahabi Movement of Syed Ahmed Shaheed and Shah Ishmael, author of *Taqwiatul Iman* or *Jamate Islami*, *Tabilighi jamat* or *Deoband Seminary* — all owe their origin to Mujaddid thoughts. Allama Iqbal and Maulana Maududi too were products of Sirhindi School who in twentieth century laid the foundation of pan-Islamism, which led to two-nation theory and ultimately resulted in partition of the country. As Spear has observed, "We Muslims are harvesting the crop of their deeds. Mujaddid no doubt placed the Sharia on the highest pedestal but he did it at the cost of the ruins of the Muslim community at large." Mujaddid Movement was the biggest one, which almost influenced the entire Muslim world except the areas where Wajudi thought prevailed.

However, one cannot but acknowledge that the sincerity of Sheikh Ahmed Sirhindi in his beliefs could not be questioned. To the last breath of his life he remained true to himself. Even when he was on the death bed he advised his sons, 'Hold the Sharia by your teeth.'

I may conclude narrating an interesting Sufi story variously told:

One day a court official came upon a dervish sitting in the middle of the road. The dervish refused to get up or even acknowledge the presence of the courtier. The courtier asked him, "Who are you and why haven't you stood up upon seeing me?" The dervish asked the courtier who he was and he replied proudly that he was a person of high stature. The dervish asked him if there was anyone higher than he and the courtier replied that certainly the king was higher. The dervish then asked if there was anyone higher than the king and the courtier replied that of course God was higher than the king. The dervish then asked if anyone was higher than God and the courtier replied that no one was higher than God. At this point the dervish replied, "That 'No one' that you say—that's me! Leave and don't remain on this road". Arif Usman uses this story to demonstrate the meaning of *wahdat ul-wujud*, which he sees as a source of the humanism in the Sufi traditions.

With due respect to Sirhindi, I may say that he could not see the contemporary situation in right perspective. Wajudi thought which represented the logical corollary of historical forces deserved to have been seen more sympathetically and rationally.

REFERENCES

Saiyed Athar Abbas Rizwi, *A History of Sufism in India*, I & II, Munshiram Manoharlal, Delhi, 1978.

Spencer Trimingham, *Sufi Orders in Islam*, Oxford Clarendon Press, 1971.

Alexander Bennigsen, S. Endors Wimbush, *Mystics and Commissars, Sufism in the Soviet Union*, C. Hurst & Company, London, 1985.

Gavin Hambly, *Central Asia*, Weigdenfeld and Nicolson, London.

Mohamed Yasin, *A Social History of Islamic India*, 1605-1748, Munshiram Manoharlal, Delhi, 1974.

Sheikh Mohammed Ikram, *Rude Kausar, A Religious History of the Sub-continent, During Mughal Times*, Idar Ishate Adabiyate, Delhi, 1991 (Urdu).

Shah Wali-Ullah, *Anfasul Arifin*, (autobiography), Alfalah, Deoband (Urdu Tr.).

Fakharuddin Ali B. Husain, *Rashhate Ainul Hayat*, (Persian).

Naqshbandis—In Western and Central Asia, Edited by Elizabeth Ozdadge, Papers read at conference held at the Swedish Research Institute in Istanbul, June 9-11, 1997.

Markash Akber Abadi, *Masaile Tessawuf*, Anjuman Tarraq Hind, New Delhi, 2000.

A Foregotten Vision: A Study of Human Spirituality by Shuja Alhaq in the light of Islamic Tradition, Vikas Publishing House Pvt. Ltd., 1997.

M. Said Ahmed Naqshbandi (trans.), *Maktubate Imam Rabbani*, Faisal Publishing House, Deoband, 1988.

Mohd. Hanif Nadvi, *Ibne Khaldun*, Idare Saqafate Islamia, Lahore, 1995.

II

Indo-Tajik Relations: A Curtain Raiser

K.N. Pandita

Russian and Tajik scholars have tried to trace the root of the word Tajik. Arab and Persian scholars have written it variously. Tajik, Tazhik, and Tazik are some of the variants we know. Many researchers are of opinion that the Tajiks did not descend, either from the Turko-Mongoloid or from the Semitic stock. Opinions converge on their Aryan origin. In that case, of all the Aryans who descended from the Central Asian plateau to the Indo-Gangetic plains in the hoary past, the Tajiks have the right to claim to be the forefathers of the Aryans who settled down in northern India including the desert plains of Rajasthan.

The first task in tracing Indo-Tajik relations is to establish the Aryan identity of the Tajiks. After the Arab conquest of Central Asia, Qutaiba ibn Muslim built the Jamia Mosque in Bukhara in 94 AH/AD 746. But the Bukharans who were the local Tajiks refused to read the *Qur'an* in Arabic. Qutaiba allowed them to read its Persian/Tajik version.[1] This proves that the Tajiks did not descend either from the Semitic or the Turkic stock. In Turkish dictionaries, Tajik is defined as *ahl-e Furs*, meaning the people of Fars.[2] The same source says at another place that the Tajiks were not migratory as the Turks, Uzbeks, Tatars, and Avaghanis were.[3]

But before we proceed with the history of Tajiks, what appears important to deal with is the geography of the land called Tajikistan. This geographical connotation was not known until the establishment of the Soviet Union in 1917. Persian and Arab historians continued with their tradition of mentioning an area or region by attributing it to the people of specific ethnic or linguistic group. Thus, we find the mention of only Tajiks in Firdausi's *Shahnameh* whereas he repeatedly speaks of Iran or Iranzamin or *Iranshehr*.[4] Firdausi tells us that King Feridun distributed his empire among his three sons. Iraj got Iran, Tur got Turan (present-day Turkestan) and Salam got 'Eastern and Upper' region or *Khavar*. The lord of this region was also called Khavar Khudai. In Tajik, *bala* is used for upper and hence we have the compound word *velayat-e-bala*. Mughal historians like Abu 'l-Fazl in *Ain-i-Akbari* and *Akbarnamah* called it *velayat-e-bala*, meaning the Upper Lands.[5]

The Badakshan and Hindukush mountains determined the upper and lower lands. Generally, Persian historians speaking of people coming to India from Iran or Central Asia used the Persian phrase *Sarazir shudand*, literally meaning 'flowed down' just as water flows downwards. Thus, the lands beyond these two mountains were called Upper Lands and the Indo-Gangetic plains as Lower Lands. Kalhana also uses the term Upper Lands in *Rajatarangini*.

The most important landmark in the *velayat-e-bala* has been and is the Oxus of the Greeks, Jayhun of the Arabs and Amu Darya of the Persians/Tajiks. This river stands out as the most significant demarcating line around which the fabulous stories of the rise of the Aryans in the hoary past down to the days of Khans and Satrapies are woven. In Firdausi's *Shahnameh*, the lands lying across the Oxus were known as Turan or the land of the people of Turkish stock. The lands on this side of the Oxus or cis-Oxus, as we may call it, constituted Aeran/Iran. Firdausi makes a clear distinction between the people of two stocks, namely *Aer* (plural *Aeran=Iran*) and *Anaer*. It means the Aryans and the non-Aryans. From this we find that the precise geographical region of the rise of the ancient Aryans and their movement outward, towards south in particular in the Indian context, is the region in which the Oxus rises and flows northwest or the present Tajikistan and Khurasan, the eastern province of Iran.

Therefore, when we speak of Tajikistan, we must forget the present geographical boundaries between Tajikistan, Afghanistan and Khurasan and should revert to the ancient names found in Indian mythological fund as well as in Persian and Arab annals. Before I proceed, let me concentrate on the word Khurasan, the name of the present eastern province of Iran. This has been a very important and rather crucial region in pre- and post-Islamic history of the region. In etymological terms, Khurasan is constituted of three parts: khur+as+an. Khur is the Farsi version of Avestic khvar and Pahlavi (Parthavi) *hur*. In Sanskrit we have *surya* for the Sun and we know that *s* and *h* sounds in Sanskrit and Avestic/Pahlavi are interchangeable. As such *surya* becomes *hurhya/hur* in Pahlavi meaning the Sun just as we have *haoma* becoming *soma*. The second part is drawn from the verbal noun *asdan*, meaning to come. And the third part *an*, common in Farsi language, is a suffix. Thus, Khurasan literally means the land wherefrom the Sun rises. Sun worship has been an important tradition of the ancient Aryans and *Mithra*, the Sun God, is common to Irano-Aryans and Indo-Aryans (*Mehr*).

It will be reminded that the ancient Iranian national flag bore the picture of the rising sun and the lion. Even the Pahlavi ruling dynasty, whose last ruler assigned the sobriquet of *Aryamehr* to himself had the sun and lion emblem as the national flag. Of the three medieval *Madrasahs* in Samarkand, one is called

Madraseh Sher Dar. On its frontispiece, we find the picture of the rising sun and the lion. More evidences of sun worship are to be found in the artefacts at Penjikent museum in Zarafshan Valley in Central Asia.

Two geographical names recur in ancient histories of the region. These are Tukharistan or Tukhar and Soghdiana or Soghd. We are of the opinion that these two regions definitely lay on the southern and western course of the Oxus. The Badakshan and Hindukush[6] mountains formed the main determinants of the Tukhar region. In this region, Balkh remained the most important town. In Avestic literature it is called Bahli and in Vedic it is recorded as Bhakri. The Greeks raised the first civilised township here. Later, Balkh became an important site of Zoroastrians, the fire-worshippers who raised a fire-worshipping temple (*atashkadeh*) and set up a religious institution. Kalhana tells us recurrently about the interaction of Kashmiris and Tukhars.[7] When Buddhism spread in the regions of Kapisa (modern Kabul/Afghanistan) and beyond the Oxus, its missionaries converted the *atashkadeh* into a *vihara* called *Inava I'ihara,* which came to be known to the Muslim historians as Navbahar. Close to Balkh at a place called Bamiyan, the tallest statue of the Buddha was carved from a rock. Before the outbreak of Afghan war, Indian Archaeological Department contributed its expertise in repairing this historical statue.

When during the early Abbasid caliphate (AD 749–1258) Tukharistan came under Islamic sway, the keepers of the temple at Balkh converted to Islam and were taken as captives to the court of Caliph Mansur in Baghdad. They were known in Balkh by the title of Pramukh, a Sanskrit word meaning a leading person. Pramukh was the caste of Brahmans of high status in the ancient Trigarta (Kangra) and Kashmir kingdoms. The Arabic corrupted form of Pramukh is Barmak from which we have the Barmecides of the Western historians. The Islamised Barmaks became a distinguished house in the Islamic history and the history of the Abbasides of Baghdad. They rose to be the viziers of the Abbasides, and, according to some historians, became more powerful than the Caliphs. In his very meticulous research work titled *Barmakiyan*, the astute Iranian scholar, Professor Zabihullah Safa, who died last year in exile in Germany, believes that the Barmaks are traceable to a high class Hindu house of northern India.[8]

A little digression at this point would not be out of place. Under the patronage of Caliphs Harun-ar-Rashid and Mamun-ar-Rashid, the House of Barmaks (Barmecides) instituted at Baghdad the famous translation bureau called *Baitu 'l-Hikmat* where the celebrated scholars and polyglots of different faiths were invited to translate precious books of Greek philosophy. The entire world owes a debt of gratitude to this celebrated house through whose instrumentality Greek sciences passed on to the Arabs and from them to the Romans and the European communities. The Renaissance of mid-sixteenth century in Europe owes much to the impact of these scientific works.

Returning to the expansion of Buddhist philosophy in Central Asia, it has to be remembered that a number of Kashmiri scholars made a valuable contribution in bringing the message of Buddha to the regions around Badakshan and beyond to the west of Kashmir and to Tibet to her east. The very name of Hindukush indicates that the mountain very much made part of ancient India.

A few years ago, near Penjikent, the archaeological team of Tajikistan excavated a mud and lime statue of Buddha in lying posture (*nidra-mudra*). It has been preserved in the State Museum in Dushanbe.

Turning to the other region, the lands lying along the Oxus right up to the point where the river emptied itself in Aral Sea were given the name of Soghdiana. It must be noted that the Oxus changed its course many times in the past as a result of geographical changes. The last one before its present course was that which carried it to the Aral Sea. At the confluence of the waters of Aral and those of the Oxus, stood the kingdom of Khwarizm or Khiva, which though linguistically different from the Turkic, was yet considered outside the pale of the Aryan stock.

Two towns in ancient Soghdiana have always attracted the attention of historians. These are Samarkand and Bukhara. Samarkand is made up of two parts, Samar and Kand. While it is not possible for this writer to explain the etymology of the first part, viz. *samar,* the second part *kand* is a very common suffix for place names in Central Asia. Indologists are of the opinion that in all probability this suffix is the corrupted form of Sanskrit *khanda,* meaning region/part. Thus we have Tashkent, Penjikent, Kokand, Yarkand, etc. all within the territorial jurisdictions of Turkestan. In Kashmir, the word *khanda* of Sanskrit origin corrupted into *gund* and we have numerous place names carrying the suffix *gund* such as Kazigund (Sanskrit, *Kanchankhanda*), Hangalgund (Shanghalakhanda), etc. I believe that *khanda* word of ancient Aryans corrupted into Avestic *kat.* In many Avestic and Pahlavi texts, *kat* is to be found suffixed to place names like Muscat. In some Persian histories, particularly of Fars, a town is sometimes called just *kat.*

In the case of Bukhara, in etymological terms it is the corrupted form of *vihara* as *b* and *v* are interchangeable. The Russians and the Turkic people generally pronounce *h* as *kh.* Din Muhammad is pronounced as Din Mukhammad (under Soviet regime it became Dimukhamadov). Thus the explanation of *vihara* becoming Bukhara is clear.

Though we lack dependable historical evidence, yet one has a hunch that there existed a monumental *vihara* on the basis of which the town got its name Bukhara. The presence of the famous Mir Arab mosque in Bukhara and the adjoining *madrasah* should lead us to think about the existence of a Buddhist monument around the site if not at the precise site.

Today in the old part of Bukhara, there is a dilapidated site called by the locals as *Sara-e-Hunluan* or the caravan-serai of the Indians. The Central Asians never used Hindu in a religious sense but as those who came from the land of India. This writer had the opportunity of visiting this dilapidated market-place in 1982. True that caravans laden with Indian goods and traversing the famous Silk Route must have been unloading the merchandise here and reloading local goods for transporting these to Indian lands. This was not a very big caravan-serai. Nevertheless, it still retains its name and is situated close to the market-place. Bukhara was an important entrepot from where merchandise was dispatched and received to the Western countries beyond the Black Sea.

For us in India, Bukhara has conspicuous significance. After the conquest of the Arabs, Bukhara became a very important centre of Islamic learning and its diffusion. The greatest work on tradition, namely *Imam Bukharai* was compiled here. Such was the reputation of Bukhara in Islamic learning that it came to be called *Madineh-e-thani* or the second Medina. Numerous Islamic theologians of repute and eminence brought the Islamic sciences to India in medieval times. Very often, and also even during Mughal rule, theological matters causing serious variations in interpretation were referred to the Ulema in Bukhara for a final decree. Travellers from Bukhara coming to India in medieval times often carried with them excellent copies of important treatises on theology, medicine, veterinary science, astronomy, exegesis, which were copied and distributed among local scholars. India, therefore, owes much to Bukhara in the proliferation of Islamic sciences. Apart from that, the contribution of Bukharans in the fields of music, particularly Sufiana music, architecture, laying of gardens and other aspects is commendable. The construction of dome, a speciality of the Mughal architecture, was adopted from the Bukhara dome architecture. The double dome model of Taj Mahal is precisely the one we find in the dome of the Samanid king, Nasr bin Ahmad in Bukhara. At Mazar-e-Salatin graveyard in Zena Kadal, Srinagar, we find the double dome model in the tomb of Zainu'l-Abidin's mother built around AD 1480. The layout of Shalimar Bagh in Kashmir attributed to Emperor Jehangir reminds one of the Juy-e-Muliyan garden in Bukhara though when I visited it in 1982, it had deteriorated owing to weather conditions and neglect.

Perhaps it may be said that Samarkand and Bukhara are now in Uzbek republic and not in Tajik republic and as such would not concern us. The fact is that both of these towns have ever since the dawn of history been the cradle of Irano-Aryan civilisation. They passed on to Uzbek republic as a result of cartographic engineering of the Soviets. The Mughals were more interested in Mawara-an-Nehr (Transoxiana) than in Iran. It should be remembered that at the Mughal court, there were more nobles and grandees of Central Asian (meaning Tajik) extraction than of Iranian extraction. The word 'velayat' for the Mughals meant Central Asia and not Iran. They did not use Tajikistan as a geographical entity though they did use Tajiks as a people. Therefore, when we speak of Indo-Tajik relations, we have to take into account all those people in Central Asia who have affinity to Indo-Aryan stock.

NOTES AND REFERENCES

1. See *Tarikh-e-Narshakhi*, the chapter Bukhara.
2. Fars/Pars is the late form of Partha or Pahlava, the name of the tribe in northern Iran around the Azerbaijan Lake or the southwest region of the Caspian Sea. It had conquered Southern Iran and settled down there giving it the name of Parsi which continues to be the name for the Southern province with capital at Persopolis (*Takht-I-Jamshid*). Herodotus borrowed Persis (the son of Jupitor in Greek mythology) from Par/Parsa giving the country its name as Persia. See also *Qamusu'l-Elam* compiled by Shamsu'd-Din Sami in the nineteenth century.
3. *Qamusu'l-Elam*, Vol. III, p. 1608.
4. Shahri is the corrupted form of Avestic *shathro* and *shathrustana* in Tajik became Sharistan, meaning a town. Sometimes Shahr was prefixed to the country like Shehr-I-Iran, meaning the land of the Irano-Aryans as Firdausi used as suffix to the country as Iranshahr, meaning the country of Iran.
5. *Ain-I-Akbari* and *Akbarnamah* by Abul Fazl.
6. Kush is the Avestic form of Pahlavi *huj* (Urdu *koh*), meaning mountain.
7. *Rajatarangini*, tr. Aurel Stein.
8. See also *Tarikh-e-Adabiyyat dar Iran* by Zabihulla Safa, 3 vols., Tehran, 1965.

SECTION III

MODERN PERIOD

12

Indian Image in the Military and Political Circles of Russia till the End of the Nineteenth Century

M.R. Ryjenkov

The problem of image of India and Indians in Russian mentality and of Russia and Russians in Indian mentality is one of the most important issues in the study of history of Russo-Indian relations.

War and trade formed the basis of the first international contacts, but from the very first steps, knowledge of cultural aspects of neighbour's life was added to them. This knowledge of everyday life and mentality of another nation influenced political and economic ties either making them stronger or, under some circumstances, produce hostility. It depended mostly on quantity and quality of information about the country. Lack of true information produces rumours and myths. Combination of truth and myth creates the image of another country and people, more or less adequate to the real existing one.

The formation of the image of another country is a very complicated process, influenced by many factors such as frequency of contacts between the nations, profession or social strata of those who are participating in these contacts, means of communication, etc. The image of a country, which exists in the military and political circles of its neighbouring country, influences and produces the official image about the country.

Russians knew about the existence of India since eleventh century, either from European travellers or the Asian neighbours. The image of India of that period was of a country full of treasures, miracles, and natural fertility. Seventeenth century was the time of the first direct contacts with Indians (travel of Afanasy

Nikitin who died on his way back, had no influence on Russian society). Indian merchants came to Astrakhan trade fairs and lived there. The end of the seventeenth century was marked by the first Russian embassy to India. Russian merchant Semen Malenky reached Aurangzeb's court, delivered Tsar's message but he died on his way and did not add anything to the existing image of India. Gerasim Lebedev could have added real facts to it, but he was not heard by the society.

The military aspect of our relations came into being in the very beginning of the nineteenth century when Napoleon suggested an alliance to Paul in order to fight with Britain in India. Russian Tsar did not wait for his ally and began this campaign alone. It was soon finished with the murder of Tsar Paul, but we must underline two features of that campaign. First, inadequate image of real political situation and living conditions in India existed because of lack of information. The army was to reach India in three months without any maps and all the treasures of India were to be the reward to the Cossacks. Secondly, during the whole of the nineteenth century, Russo-Indian relations were strictly tied to Russo-British confrontation in Europe, Asia or Far East. This fact stimulated military circles to gather information to create the true image of India.

During the nineteenth century Russia did not have either diplomatic or military representatives in India. Diplomats used merchants (Mehti Rafailov, for example) to gather information. In the 1830s, Caucasian war and growing unrest in Central Asia aroused the interest to India in military circles. Captain Mochulsky was ordered to compile a survey of northwest India. He based his work on interrogations of Armenian merchants and of a German who served in Ranjit Singh's army and also on well-known book of Burnes, *Travels in Bukhara.* Captain Mochulsky drew the first Russian map of India. In his work, Captain Mochulsky tried to prove that English influence and supremacy were not total. High military officials refused to believe his conclusions and the results of the first Afghan war proved that he was wrong.

Russo-Turkish war of 1853–56 showed that Britain was our bitter enemy, and Commander in Chief and the Governor General of the Caucasian region Baryatinsky wrote a letter to Defence Minister Sukhozanet regarding the possibility of a conflict with Britain in Asia and the necessity to prepare for military expedition to India. This plan was shown to the Tsar. Being a prudent person, Alexander-I asked the opinion of Ministry of Foreign Affairs and Defence Ministry. For the first time, India was discussed at the highest military and political levels. The conclusion of this discussion was as follows:

> Of course all over Asia hatred for the English is apparent, but in India what is more apparent is deep conviction in the powers of the British in the invincibility of her fleet ...

The Tsar's resolution was: "I totally agree with this." Let us underline that it was 1857, just some months before the Mutiny. News about the Mutiny came from London from Russian military agent Colonel Ignatyev. All reports of military agents, legal representatives of Russian Empire abroad, were considered to be highly reliable and sent straight to Defence Minister or to the Tsar himself. Colonel Ignatyev gathered his information in London from official papers and rumours only. That is why his main idea—the existence of widely spread Muslim conspiracy—was not true to life. The names of the leaders of the Mutiny were also false. Still the report of Colonel Ignatyev gave a real picture of the situation in India and depicted the sequence of events. Russian government did not depart from adopted decision and abstained from any step in that direction.

Russo-Turkish war of 1877-78 and new confrontation with Britain inspired once more interest of military officials towards India. This time they sought co-operation from famous Sanskritologist Minaev. Ivan Pavlovitch Minaev visited India three times, saw a lot and made friends with many persons from different strata of the society. So his image of India was neither mythological nor idealistic and he did his best to introduce it and to warn military from imprudent steps.

> In the most critical moments, in the moments of its greatest antagonism with Great Britain, Russian valour think it possible to organise crusades to India or Russian patriotism places its hopes on military marches towards India and dreams that due recovery of the wounded pride of the national will come from there, from India ... This idealistic theoretical view of India did not materialise just yesterday—it has existed for a long time.

Notes on his visits to India were sent to Ministry of Defence and personally to General Obruchev, the Head of the Main Headquarters, one of those who pulled ropes of the empire at that time. The goal of Professor Minaev had nothing to do with espionage. He wanted to introduce the true image of India to Russia.

The journey of Russian Crown Nicolai had the same aim—to show to the future Tsar eastern countries, to help him to make his own image of them, but in vain. Prince Ukhtomsky, who chronicled that journey wrote that Nicolai Alexandrovitch "is daily gathering most diverse knowledge about the proficiency of the Europeans, who are commanding Asia ..." Such an attitude towards the East was reflected during the reign of Nicolai II, especially during Japanese war of 1904-05.

Travels of Professor Minaev and journey of Crown Prince Nicolai reflected two tendencies in Indo-Russian relations. Minaev's and further travels, the foundation of the first courses of Hindustani in Tashkent, and the establishment of Russian Consulate in Bombay, helped the Russian society to accumulate information to steer clear of the image of India from myths. The second tendency was characteristic of the conservative snob part of high aristocracy. It lay in the field of colonial solidarity with Europeans. The development of Indo-Russian relations in the twentieth century reflected both these tendencies.

REFERENCES

Burnes, Alexander, *Travels in Bukhara*, 3 vols., London, 1836.

Bongard-Levin, G. and A. Vigasin, *The Images of India, The Study of Ancient Indian Civilisation in the USSR*, Progress Publishers, Moscow, 1984.

Kemp, P.M., *Bharat-Rus: Introduction to Indo-Russian Contacts and Travels from Medieval Times to October Revolution*, Indo-Soviet Cultural Society, Delhi, 1958.

13

Nana Sahib's Nephew in Russia

T.N. Zagorodnikova

In 1878–80, inhabitants of Saint-Petersburg, Russian capital, used to meet a strange dark-skinned person with a scar on his cheek walking along the streets. His shabby clothes and deep dark eyes full of pain, sometimes even hungry looks were somehow in disharmony with his proud way of behaviour. He was earning his living by small loans here and there and by tutoring in rich families, that was a typical way of earning one's living by poor students, but he was not a student. He had powerful friends and sponsors among different strata of Russian society: famous orientologist, specialist on Central Asian problems Professor V.V. Grigoriev, top officials of Ministry of Foreign Affairs Baron Jominy and Fon der Osten-Saken, Grand Duke Nicolai Konstantinovitch Romanov, famous traveller Semenov-Tyan-Shansky, editor of the newspaper, *Moscow Vedomosty*, M.N. Katkov and others. He had friends among diplomats of Japanese and Persian embassies. All of them tried to get work for him or to help him in any other possible way. Who was that strange fellow?

He came from India. His name was Ramchandra Balaji from Bithoor. "I am the nephew of Nana Sahib, leader of Mutiny", he used to add.

There are many documents left about that person and his activities in the archives of former USSR, most of them either in Moscow or in Tashkent. The majority of these documents are in Russian or in French.[1]

He claimed to be born in 1850 and brought up in harem of Nana Sahib. In 1857 when the Mutiny was almost suppressed by British army during the siege of Peshwa's palace in Bithoor by English soldiers he fell out of the window and broke his cheek-bone. An English officer, Captain Brandon or Brandan, captured him and afterwards took the boy first to Calcutta and then to London. Childless wife of the English officer conceived affection for the little orphan. Unfortunately, the climate of Great Britain did not suit him and he had to live mainly in Italy, visiting his stepmother from time to time. In 1859 he was sent to Lausanne in Switzerland where his studies began. Ramchandra lived there in a boarding house till 1868. Every summer he used to come to Great Britain to visit the family of Captain Brandon and his compatriots, who lived in England. There he learnt the language and faith of his motherland from a Brahmin, who came to Great Britain with Dulip Singh, another captive, the last Maharaja of Punjab. All expenses were paid from India Office funds. Ramchandra was given 10 francs as pocket money. During his last years in Lausanne he earned some money by tutoring English and music. So, when he heard that a relative of his, Raja of Kolhapur, came to Italy, Ramchandra was able to pay the fare and visited him. When in Florence, Raja of Kolhapur died and left everything he had to Ramchandra. That was enough to buy a ticket of India and in 1869 he found himself once again on his native land. After several months' stay in his motherland, Englishmen found him and under false pretext of finishing his education he was escorted back to Switzerland.

In 1870 Ramchandra entered Berlin University. There he made the acquaintance of Professor Veber, specialist on Sanskrit, who later recommended him to K.A. Kossovitch, one of the first Russian Sanskritologists. One of Japanese princes was among his friends. All these people played certain role in his future life. He continued spending his vacations in Britain where he made friends with Iskandar Khan of Afghanistan.[2] The latter annoyed by the attitude of English authorities towards him made his mind to go to Persia and invited Ramchandra to follow him. Ramchandra was not yet ready to quit and returned to Berlin.

Suddenly he received an official invitation or even an order to go to London. Simultaneously, one of his friends warned him that in Britain he would be seized and sent to West India, to Jamaica. The only possible explanation was that the English were aware of Iskandar Khan's proposal and were afraid that from Persia he would again try to come to India. So Ramchandra left his studies and started to Tehran. He really tried to reach India via Herat. There he found out that he was under strict surveillance of British agents. On his way to Kashmir he was robbed by Afghan rebel tribes and was forced to return. In Tehran he agitated in favour of Persian-Japanese commercial treaty to import to Persia green tea from Japan instead of Bombay and thus to damage British commercial interest in that part of the world.

In 1878 the Russo-Turkish war was finished and peace treaty was to be signed in San-Stephano. Ramchandra, who turned out to be in Turkey by that time, came across a Japanese officer, whom he used to meet in Berlin. It was this officer, who introduced him to Russians. His new friends invited him to visit Russia. Same year he appeared in Saint-Petersburg.

That was the story, which he narrated to Russian authorities when he was asked about the circumstances of his birth. The information about the life of

Ramchandra before 1878 differs in some details if we compare the report of Colonel Korolkov with the article of S.B. Petrov-Baturich and other documents.

We tried to compile it from different sources so that it seemed quite logical and contained minimum lacunas. His activities in Russia can be easily reconstructed from the documents of military archives.

Before analysing the life of Ramchandra in Russia it is necessary to describe the situation in world politics between peace treaty of San-Stephano and Berlin Congress, that is, between 3rd of March and 13th of July 1878. Russo-Turkish war of 1877-1878, though victorious one for the Russian army, was real strain for its economy and human resources. That is why the peace treaty of San-Stephano was welcomed not only in Istanbul, but in Saint-Petersburg as well. The attitude of Great Britain towards this treaty, which was an ally of Turkey in this war, was a polar one. The British did not recognise the treaty, which was signed by both exhausted belligerent powers, Russia and Turkey. So Russia was facing another war in Europe. One of the possible ways to prevent this war was to begin a military expedition to India, the most valuable British colony.[3] Ramchandra, who understood the situation, decided to make use of the moment and to initiate an expedition in order to liberate his motherland. Unfortunately for him, he came too late. We do not know the exact date of his arrival to Saint-Petersburg, perhaps somewhere in summer; but even if the Berlin treaty had not been signed by that time, he still would not have had enough time to make the acquaintance of proper influential persons for initiating such a plan.

First year of Ramchandra in Russia was full of hard work. He hardly made two ends meet. Professor V.V. Grigoriev showed great kindness to him and recommended him to Grant Duke Nicolai Konstantinovitch Romanov and to governor-general of Russian Turkestan M.P. fon Kaufmann as an expert on the Orient. Military authorities gave a measure of hope but did not offer anything concrete. During the period June-November 1879, upon recommendation of Professor V.V. Grigoriev, Ramchandra took part in the third expedition of Grant Duke Nicolai Konstantinovitch Ramanov to Central Asia. While in Tashkent Ramchandra visited Abdurrahman Khan of Afghanistan, who showed him several letters from Afghan leaders of Balkh, Maimane and Kounduz, inviting him to join them. "More than half of the Afghans remain faithful to me", he said. Grant Duke also visited Abdurrahman Khan.[4] According to Grant Duke he turned out to be very industrious, helpful, and competent member of the team.

> To my mind, this person may be very useful for Russia in the East. That is why I invited him to take part in my travels along Turkestan next year also. Next spring he is going to explore the course of Amu River unknown to the world.[5]

Ramchandra also wanted to continue his co-operation with Grant Duke Nicolai Konstantinovitch, to take part in his expedition next year. His main aim was to explore the route to India from Russian Central Asia, but by that time his friends in the capital succeeded in kindling the interest of Russian nobility and authorities in him, especially in military and diplomatic circles.

Russian nobility was always interested in every stranger, especially in those who suffered. In the eyes of ladies, dark-haired Indian with romantic looks and glamour of martyr turned out to be hero. He received a lot of invitations to parties. Once he was told that an opera was being written about his life.[6] An article about his hardships appeared in one of the periodicals.[7] So he became a celebrity.

The attitude of official circle was a bit of another type. First of all it turned out that from the very beginning of Ramchandra's stay in Russia in 1878, they knew about him and tried to collect maximum information about him and his previous activities. Colonel L.N. Sobolev, Head of the Asiatic Department of Main Headquarters, handed in a report about Ramchandra to the Head of Main Headquarters as far back as in autumn of 1878.[8]

The second-half of the nineteenth century was the time when two great empires, Russia and Great Britain, were bitter enemies. In Russo-Turkish war of 1877-78 Great Britain was on the side of Turkey. Confrontation in Middle Asia was about to turn out into the second Anglo-Afghan war. That was why every Indian in Russia was regarded at that time as a potential British spy. Besides, Ramchandra had several letters of introduction from Iskandar Khan,[9] who after his departure for Great Britain, was considered to be highly suspicious and not at all a reliable person.

Russian ambassador in Persia, I.A. Zinoviev wrote that while in Tehran Ramchandra and his friend were selling medicine and did not claim to be the relative of Nana Sahib at that time, Russian diplomats supposed that this Indian should not be trusted so far.[10] The rest of the references collected by the military were perfect. There was no doubt that this Indian was of a noble origin, well educated (he knew several European languages, spoke a little Russian and understood everything, knew history well), his judgements and comments were very interesting and unusual. By no means he was a British spy, but an arch-enemy of Britain. His aim was to return to India and liberate it. Colonel Korolkov, Assistant to the Head of Zaravchan district, who knew Ramchandra personally, wrote about him:

> The supposition that Ramchandra is a British spy to my mind is not proved by any fact. The English themselves must invent it. The attitude of Hindus in Samarkhand and his desire to go to India by an extremely dangerous route from Samarkhand to Kashmir contradict to that supposition. All Indians of Samarkhand, including famous envoy of tribe of Sikhs Guru Charan Singh and Brahman from Central India (Gwalior) treated Ramchandra with deep

> respect. If Ramchandra had been an English spy, then by all means Englishmen would have given him an opportunity to travel to India by more comfortable way than it is the route from Samarkhand to Kashmir. And at last, by my personal acquaintance with Ramchandra I am convinced that he is the last person to be suspected in liking for English and in intention to support their rule in India. To my mind Ramchandra is able to accept any risky affair in order to do harm to the British.

In 1880s no modern Indian language was taught in Russia, and as a result there were no interpreters of Indian languages in Russian Empire. If any need occurred they had to translate from Hindustani or any other Indian language into Persian and then from Persian into Russian. So Ramchandra might have been of great help to Russian authorities, both diplomatic and military, but mainly in Turkestan. On 13 March 1880, Tsar's order (*ukase*) was delivered that he was acceded to the Asiatic Department of Main Headquarters and sent at command of adjutant general M.D. Skobelev.[11] Mikhail Dmitrievitch Skobelev, famous hero of Russo-Turkish war of 1877-78, military governor of Ferghana district, was then preparing his second campaign to Trans-Caspian region.

Financial problems of Ramchandra at last were also settled: he was given generous allowance both from the Main Headquarters budget and Ferghana district incomings.[12]

Military authorities in Petersburg and Tashkent were planning that Ramchandra would fill in some unknown problems of Indian and Central Asian geography and ethnology. Adjutant general M.D. Skobelev thought that this Indian might become useful in his relations with Iskandar Khan of Afghanistan and some nobles of Trans-Caspian region. Collective opinion was that "he would be very useful in talks with the envoys of Indian native rulers, who from time to time came to seek support from the Tsar. In order to be ready in case of war with Great Britain in Asia it was necessary to arrange intercommunication with our possible allies in India, especially with Maharaja of Kashmir." They were planning even Ramchandra's trip to India or to Herat. They thought that with his help they would be able to facilitate Indian youngsters coming to Russian Turkestan to make them interpreters or agents or to join Russian army. If there were enough to form a special unit it had to be used during any confrontation, either military or diplomatic, in Russian Turkestan, Afghanistan or even in India.

Pieces of useful information had already been dipped out from conversations with Ramchandra by the time of Tsar Ukase. Some of them were true to life; for example, in 1876 Chitral ruler Aman-ul-Mulk really declared himself a vassal of Maharaja of Kashmir; others were mere rumours: Badakshan did not secede from Afghanistan and become part of Bukhara state.[13] According to Ramchandra, the events of the second Anglo-Afghan war inspired Burma ruler to withdraw Englishmen from his state and to declare himself independent from Britain,[14] which was not true. Ramchandra's data about the routes in Turkestan and Afghanistan were especially valuable because he himself travelled there and estimated them from military point of view, their suitability for any march.[15]

Ramchandra had peculiar thoughts about the situation in India and perspectives of British Raj there. According to him Indian people lived in extreme poverty because of scarcity of tillable land as compared to the size of population. The best fields cultivated were in the hands of the British who had vast plantations of indigo, opium and other herbs, for export. So, according to Ramchandra, Hindus would be somehow content if Great Britain conquer Afghanistan because their two enemies, Muslims and the British, were beating each other and as a result some Indians would be able to move to Afghanistan and settle there.[16] Another way out was to move to wastelands of Russian Turkestan and there were many Indians eager to do so. Such emigration might lessen the stress of poverty and oppression by the British Raj in India.[17] The British did their best to propagate negative image of Russians. Nevertheless, many Indians looked upon Russians as their liberators from British Raj. Maharajas of Kashmir, Patiala and Gwalior were eager to co-operate. They were, according to Ramchandra, "representatives of 150-million population, truly devoted to Russia."[18]

Before beginning his work in Turkestan, Ramchandra asked for permission to leave for Persia as he had some urgent problems to solve there. He was given necessary orders, money and papers. While in Persia he was to act as an interpreter to the Japanese Commission. They were travelling along Persia with a view to establishing commercial relations and negotiating a treaty between the Japanese and Persian governments.[19]

On 6 June, he wrote his first letter from Baghdad, addressed to Colonel L.N. Sobolev. There he rejected his service in Turkestan because of some misfortunes, which he faced while in Russia. He wanted to go to Abdurrahman Khan, emir of Afghanistan.[20] The second letter of 12 August came from Shiraz. There he was not so resolute about his resignation. He wrote that Japanese mission, in favour of which he agitated, was welcomed in Persia and now he wanted to establish relations between Afghanistan and Japan.[21] Simultaneously, Ramchandra wrote to adjutant general M.D. Skobelev that he was ready to start working under his command. On receiving this letter adjutant general M.D. Skobelev sent a telegram to Major-General[22] L.N. Sobolev: "Are you wont of Ramchandra's service?... I don't know what he was doing during 4 months. I don't foresee any use of his work. He is mentally ill."[23] Major-General L.N. Sobolev proposed not to answer him officially but privately.

In autumn of 1880 Ramchandra once again appeared in adjutant general M.D. Skobelev's camp in Trans-Caspian region. The instructions, which were adopted by the Tsar himself, were very resolute: "Let Ramchandra be attached to Trans-Caspian troops, but under strict surveillance. Do not let him interfere in our policy".[24]

In February 1881 another telegram from Trans-Caspian region was sent to the capital to Major-General L.N. Sobolev... "His stay here is quite useless, the best way out is to call him off".[25] Ramchandra did not want to wait for the answer from the Main Headquarters and escaped. He was caught in Ashkhabad en route to Herat. This time adjutant general M.D. Skobelev used more violent language in his telegram: he called the Indian 'an evil person'.[26] The order was delivered to send Ramchandra to Saint-Petersburg at the command of the Main Headquarters under police escort.[27]

In March 1881 Ramchandra found himself in Moscow. His escort was removed and he was allowed to go anywhere he wanted. He was free again but without work and without money. He was down on his luck. So he went to the capital and tried once again to seek his fortune in the Main Headquarters. Military authorities did not want to deal with him any more. Then he decided to go abroad, but where to get money?[28]

A petition was handed to the Tsar for giving Ramchandra an allowance of 1000 rubles, and was replied: "I think this is too much. Send him to our border for account of the government, he does not deserve any allowance."

That was the decision of the Tsar, written by his own hand on the margins of the petition.[29]

This is the end of Ramchandra's story, his almost three years' stay in Russian empire.

The documents from Russian archives did not give us answers to three main questions: Who was Ramchandra? Did he want to gain any benefit for himself? What was the continuation of his life and activities?

To our mind, he hardly was the relative of Nana Sahib. Nana Sahib was the eldest adopted son of the last Peshwa. His only nephew from Peshwa's side was Panduranga Rao, son of Peshwa's second adopted child. His own kinsmen were rather poor; they belonged to the same *gotra* with the last Peshwa. As far as we know, there also were no nephews from that side.

British authorities and intelligence described him as the nephew of Nana Sahib. He was addressed as Indian Prince or simply Prince Ramchandra or Ramchandra Pradhan. Only once the name of Nana Rao was mentioned in this connection: a letter was published in a newspaper full of invectives against British administration in India and the author described himself as being the nephew of Nana Sahib. The British were sure that it was Ramchandra.[30]

Moreover, on 17 July 1857 during his retreat from Bithoor, Nana Sahib took his harem, women and children of the palace and escorted them to Nepal. On 19 July, when British troops walked into the practically deserted palace, there was hardly any Big siege or battle.[31]

To our mind, Ramchandra was a nationalist who wanted to strike the right chord in that situation, trying to explore the attitude that Russian people had towards Nana Sahib, leader of the Mutiny and Indian national hero. His desire was to take advantage of the Anglo-Russian confrontation in Europe and Middle Asia just after Russo-Turkish war of 1877-78, to liberate his motherland with the help of Russian troops. That was perhaps the only right moment for initiating such an expedition, but he had only several months from March till July 1878 to do it and he missed that opportunity and failed. I doubt if even more influential person, than Ramchandra was, could manage such an affair.

His failure as civil official of Turkestan military administration was inevitable because of his own character. He was an ill-tempered person, always quarrelled with count N.Y. Roctovtzev,[32] who was the Tsar's special agent attached to Grant Duke. In one of his letters, mentioned above, he accused adjutant general M.D. Skobelev for being unfair to him. Another letter of his about his way back from Central Asia depicted its author as an absent-minded person leaving behind piece of luggage, his pet animal, etc. He did not blame himself for these misfortunes but a person, accompanying him.[33] Besides, Ramchandra, in spite of his life in Europe and European education, had a strong feeling of high caste and contempt for common people.[34] One can imagine the attitude of Russian battle-tried general M.D. Skobelev towards such a person, who simply failed in duties entrusted to him.

The attitude of Russians, who dealt with him, changed from blind admiration first to incomprehension and even kind of pity and then negativism, distrust and suspicion. But in any case nobody held the view that he wanted to gain anything for himself from planning military campaign and liberation of his country.

Ramchandra happened to visit Russia during one of the moments of Russo-British confrontation in 1878. That is why he was under strict surveillance of British intelligence, especially because of his visits to Abdurrahman Khan of Afghanistan. In 1885 the question of Ramchandra was visited once more. Russian authorities answered that he was dismissed from Russian employment years ago and was not in Russia. 'Punjab Akhbar', *Zehar*, dated 24th of June, stated that a Hindustani, who gives himself out to be the son (?) of Nana Rao, was that time serving in Russian army.[35] But the most reliable, to our mind, information came from Tehran. A Nicolson, Her majesty's charge' d' affaires, wrote in his telegram of 11 November 1885 that two or three years ago Ramchandra was living in quiet manner in Tehran and gaining a livelihood 'by instructing in oriental languages.' Then he moved to Constantinople and lived there for some time in strained circumstances.[36]

Documents from Russian Archives narrated the story of Ramchandra, gave us some information to answer the first and the second questions, the third question was answered by the documents in National Archives of India.

NOTES AND REFERENCES

1. The information about Ramchandra was specially collected by military authorities from different sources, including Ramchandra himself and the whole story was related by Colonel Korolkov in his report submitted to the Head of Military Scientific Committee of the Main Headquarters in January 1880. Rossiyskiy Gosudarstvenniy Voenno-istorocheskiey Arhiv (RGVIA) (Russian State Military-Historic Archives), f. 400, op. l, f. 657, pp. 14-27.
2. NAI, Foreign Department, Secret, May 1880, N. 203.
3. RGVIA, f. 400 , op. 1, f. 657, p. 88.
4. RGVIA, f. 400, op. 1, file 657, p. 88-9.
5. Gosudarstvenniy Arhiv Rossiyskoy Federatzii (GARF) (Russian State Archives), f. 1155, op. 1, f. 2830, pp. 1-2 and op.
6. S.V. Petrov-Baturich, Vstrecha s plemyannikom Nana Sahib v Petersburg (Meeting with a nephew of Nana Sahib in Petersburg).
7. 'Russky Vestnic', 1879, N. 6.
8. *Ibid.*, p. 25.
9. Arhiv Vneshney Politiki Rossiyskoy Imperii (AVPRI) (Russian Empire Foreign Affairs Archives), f. SPb. Glavny Arhiv, II-8, op. 45, 1878, file 2, p. 2.
10. RGVIA, f. 400, op. 1, f. 657, p. 16 and op.
11. *Ibid.*, p. 32 op.
12. *Ibid.*
13. *Ibid.*, p. 32 op.
14. *Ibid.*, pp. 3-4 and op.
15. *Ibid.*, pp. 45-8 and op.
16. *Ibid.*
17. *Ibid.*, p. 4, op.
18. *Ibid.*, p. 45.
19. *Ibid.*, p. 48 and op.
20. NAI, Foreign Department, Pol. B., December 1880, N. 33; July 1880, N. 128.
21. *Ibid.*, p. 52.
22. *Ibid.*, pp. 52-3.
23. *Ibid.*, p. 51.
24. *Ibid.*, p. 65.
25. *Ibid.*, p. 69.
26. *Ibid.*, p. 73.
27. *Ibid.*, p. 86.
28. *Ibid.*, pp. 113-14 and op.
29. *Ibid.*, p. 36 op.
30. NAI, Foreign Department, Pol. B., July 1880, N. 128.

31. A.S. Mishra, *Nana Saheb Peshwa and The Fight for Freedom*, Lucknow, 1961, p. 297.
32. *Ibid.*, p. 36 op.
33. GARF, f. 1155, op. 1, f. 2830, p. 1-2 and op.
34. Rossiyskiy Gosudarstvenniy Arhiv Literaturi i Iskusstva (RGALI) (Russian State Archives of Literature and Arts), f. 472, op. 1, f. 84.
35. NAI, Foreign Department, Secret, F, February 1886, N. 16.
36. *Ibid.*, N. 19.

14
Muslims in Eastern Turkestan 1871: Diplomatic and Trade Relations with British India

Z.U. Malik

This chapter seeks to briefly analyse a few aspects of social life and economic conditions in Eastern Turkestan (Kashgar-Yarqand) and diplomatic relations between the ruler of Kashgar, Yaqub Beg, and British India during the years 1871-72. It is based on an eye-witness account given by Robert Berkley Shaw, a political agent of British government who visited its main towns, cities and villages and held negotiations with the ruler to establish trade and political relations with the Kashgar government. Berkley Shaw was a fellow of Royal Geographical Society, and a linguist, having command on both Persian and Turkish languages, as he seldom took the help of interpreters in conversation with Yaqub Beg or his officers. This may be illustrated by the fact that he compiled a dictionary of Turkish-English words under the title, *A Sketch of Turkish Language as Spoken in Eastern Turkestan* (Kashgar and Yarqand) published in 1880 (Baptist Mission Press, Calcutta). After his return from Yarqand in 1870 he submitted the Report of his Mission to the Government of India and separately published a brief sketch of his observations, findings and experiences he had made in the course of his journey and his long stay at Yarqand. His narrative was so interesting, vivid and candid that it attracted the attention of Syed Ahmad Khan (1817–1898), and he translated the book in Urdu under the title *Muslimanan-i Yarqand* and published it in his journal, *Tehzib-ul-Akhlaq*, part-II (pp. 536-556).[1] His purpose of translating this travelogue was to acquaint the Muslims of India with the manners and ways of life, hospitability and treatment of strangers prevalent among the Muslims of Yarqand. Their friendly feelings for the Englishmen, and their keen desire to continue trade relations with them were brought into focus in his preface to the translation. He emphasised that customs and traditions practised in India by Muslims were generally based on legends and traditions, and clearly differed from what their co-religionists followed outside this country. Secondly, Muslims of India were absolutely ignorant about the historical developments and social changes, currently taking place in other Muslim lands.

R.B. Shaw set out from Kangra and reached Leh through Ladakh in 1868, adopting the same usual route the Kashmiri and other Indian merchants had since long used for journey to Yarqand, Kashgar, and Khotan where they had set up their business houses. For the growth of trade and commerce, Robert Montgomerie, lieutenant governor of Punjab had repaired the road through Kangra to Ladakh, and constructed bridges over Sutlej and Chandrabhagra rivers. In Tibet, Robert Shaw saw a group of persons coming and going into a Turki market, while others were sitting in a row silently, and all of them looked quite different from the local people of Tibet. They wore big turbans on their heads, heavy big black shoes on foot, wore a long coat *(qba),* open in the front and under it a waist-coat *(sadri).* In colour and complexion they appeared like Europeans, having red lips and rosy cheeks. Their physical features, manners and dignified behaviour gave an impression that they were civilised, self-confident people, free from the evils of flattery, imitation and prejudices. Some of them came to his camp, greeted him, talked freely and drank tea offered to them, and though they enjoyed humour, they never transgressed limits of patterned behaviour. At that moment came a person from Yarqand and joined them: he resembled an Englishman, but did not know English, and, therefore, sat with his Muslim Indian servants. Being a Haji, he talked on matters relating to religion.[2]

Robert Shaw writes that he became so enraptured with their attitudes and norms of behaviour that he gave up the idea of staying any longer in Tibet to investigate political and economic conditions prevalent there and decided to proceed towards Yarqand and see the country to which these Turks belonged. Yarqand had been for ages the large and principal emporium where merchants and traders from the surrounding countries—China, India, Bukhara and Badkhshan—and other towns of Central Asia came with their merchandise and carried lucrative business. The Kashmiri merchants travelled from Leh to Yarqand and Kashgar, and from there to Farghana Valley and to Kokand. Apart from being a chief trading centre, Yarqand occupied strategic position of immense significance, and every neighbouring country entertained the ambition of gaining monopoly of trade, commerce and foothold through political manoeuvre in this golden land. In the past, there existed economic, political and cultural links between Kashgar and India, and people of both the countries were mutually benefited by the close and continuing relationship. The Mughal Emperor Akbar

(1556–1605) had sent an ambassador to Kashgar after his conquest of Kashmir in 1586 to cultivate friendly relations with its ruler with a view to isolating Abdullah Khan Uzbeg, and promised to help him if invaded by the latter. Akbar requested the Sultan of Kashgar to send him detailed information regarding Khata (Northern China), its elites, philosophers, artisans, craftsmen, and religion of people.[3]

Under the Mughal, exchange of envoys between the two countries continued till the mid-eighteenth century, and during this long span, trade and commerce increased, tourist traffic expanded, and migration of armymen, scholars, poets and craftsmen from Kashgar remained unceasing.[4]

However, in the late sixties of the nineteenth century, the political scenario in Eastern Turkestan changed as 'the huge civilising machine of Russian imperialism rolled forward at a high speed,' bringing several lands of Central Asia within the orbit of its political domination. Russian expansion into Central Asia was characterised by similar motives—territorial and commercial gains—which lay at the root of British imperialism in India. In 1865, Russian armed forces captured Tashkent, Samarkand in 1868, and Bukhara in 1869. In 1873, the *Khanate* of Khiva was subjugated, and they established their undisputed authority on the banks of Oxus (Amu Darya). The Russians occupied Ili Valley in North Sinkiang, 1871, which was agriculturally, minerally and strategically very important, its Muzrat Pass, twelve thousand feet, facilitated control of all Sinkiang, and thus possessed great military and commercial potential. The Ili trade grew rapidly in the mid-nineteenth century, reaching a million pound sterling a year. By the treaty of 1851, the Chinese government had allowed the Russians to establish consulates and duty-free trade mart at Ili and Tarbagatai on the Mongolian border. Taking advantage of the disturbed state of affairs in China, the Russian governor-general, K.P. Von Kaufmann, brought it under his control.[5]

At the beginning of 1860, the Muslim Turks in Sinkiang rose into rebellion against the corrupt and cruel local Ching administration. The Central Government in Peking was occupied with Taiping Rebellion (1850–1864), Nier and other uprisings, and was unable to despatch any punitive expedition, while the local administration was too weak and ill-organised to put down the revolt. The Manchu officers treated the subject Muslims with contempt, imposed heavy taxes, and forced them to pay illegal contribution. The widespread discontent caused by repression and injustice gave rise to rebellion. Then, the former occupants of the land, expelled by the Ch'ings to Kokand in 1759, also appeared on the scene in full force to restore their rule over the strife-stricken land. In the midst of these convulsions a Kokandian military officer, Yaqub Beg (1820–77), ambitious and astute politician, launched attack on Eastern Turkestan in 1865, and through a series of exhilarating military victories and political tactics he consequently succeeded in establishing supreme authority independent of

China or Russia over Kashgar and part of Northern Sinkiang. To protect their commercial interests in Ili Valley the Russians signed a commercial treaty without according recognition to his authority in 1872. The British government of India, by contrast, granted recognition in return of trade and commercial privileges to the new ruler of Kashgar who now assumed the title of Ataliq Ghazi. For more than five years Yaqub Beg (Ataliq Ghazi) resisted the spread of political influence by relying on the friendly alliance with the British government.

While the menace of Russian invasion loomed large on the frontiers of Afghanistan, the seizure of Ili Valley opened the path for steady advance of her armed forces from Syr Darya through Ladakh towards Kashmir and into the Punjab. These aggressive designs of Russia, intensely pursued under Alexander-II (1858–1881), constituted direct threat to the security and peace of British north-western provinces and their commercial interests in Kashgar-Yarqand region. In order to stem the growing tide of Russian expansion Lord Mayo, the British Governor-General (1869–1872), invited Sher Ali, the Afghan ruler, to Ambala (March 1869) and entered into friendly pact with him, assured him support, good will and amity to strengthen his government against his rivals, but gave no definite undertaking of military and financial assistance in the event of war with Russia. On the suggestion of Douglas Forsyth, the commissioner of Jullundur, the British government decided to send an able and experienced envoy to the court of Yaqub Beg to bring Yarqand within British sphere of influence and take other necessary steps to eliminate the threat of any possible Russian attack. In his note, Douglas Forsyth wrote:

> From this fact and the general Russian interest in opening the country of Yarqand, he concluded that there was danger to the integrity of that state and that the establishment of Russian power in Kashgar and Yarqand would adversely affect British interests in India and their security.[6]

Douglas Forsyth pointed out that prospects of trade and commerce in this region and beyond it seemed bright, and as this potential included cultivation of tea in the Himalayas, control of safe transit route through it for export of tea, cotton and other British goods to lands of Central Asia and even to Russia was indispensible. He further argued that apprehensions of Ghazi Ataliq from both Russia and China were genuine, and to ward off the threat to the safety and stability of his newly constituted independent state of Kashgar he relied on the British material and moral support. The growing ambitions of Russia were reflected in the construction of a fort at Naryn and extension of railways towards Yarqand. Thus, British policy towards the ruler of Kashgar should be determined principally by commercial interests as well as strategic concerns. Ataliq Ghazi sent at the end of 1869 Mirza Shadi, as his envoy to India and he met Lord Mayo on 28 March 1870. He had come with specific purpose to purchase arms and ammunition in India, to secure artisans and expertise for the manufacture of arms in Kashgar, and invite a British envoy to visit his capital. Lord Mayo, the Viceroy, advised Ataliq Ghazi to strengthen his internal administration and the defence of the kingdom, arm well and train his army, and avoid interference in the affairs of his neighbours so as not to furnish a pretext to invade his country. But he expressed his inability to render any active military assistance in case he was involved in fighting with an external power. He was allowed to purchase arms and obtain the services of experts in the manufacture of arms on private basis. It was also agreed that British envoy will accompany him to Kashgar.[7]

The envoy appointed by the Government of India was Douglas Forsyth who went along with Mirza Shadi to Kashgar. The main object of his mission was to establish trade relations with this strategically important country and cultivate friendship and amity of its ruler on the basis of mutual co-operation and understanding. He was forbidden to take any interest in political disputes and matters which did not concern the British. Douglas Forsyth could not meet Ataliq Ghazi who was at that time far away from Yarqand, engaged in some warfare, and he returned without achieving the objective of his assignment. However, Ataliq Ghazi, soon after his return to Yarqand, deputed Ahrai Khan Turra at the end of 1871 with letters to the Viceroy and the Queen of England. In these despatches he stressed the need of continuing the practice of sending envoys to his country. Accordingly, Douglas Forsyth was again directed to visit Kashgar, which he did in the winter of 1873-74. This time Forsyth found opportunity to negotiate a treaty of commerce and friendly alliance with Kashgar. It was signed on 2 February 1874 and ratified by the governor-general Lord Northbrook (1872–1876), on 18 April 1874. In 1874 Disraeli had succeeded Gladstone as Prime Minister of England, and Lord Salisbury became the Secretary of State.[8]

The treaty of 1874 was a landmark in British relations with Kashgar which affected the attitude of Russia towards lands of Central Asia. Promotion of commercial interests, free entry of traders and merchants into each other's country and exchange of envoy between British India and Kashgar on regular basis were the main provisions of the treaty. In January 1875 Ataliq Ghazi sent his envoy, Syed Yaqub Khan to India, and insisted on the appointment of a British envoy to represent it at the court of Kashgar. In view of the imminent threat of invasion of Yarqand by China to recover the lost territory, the Government of India was reluctant to implement article VI of the recent treaty lest they became entangled in any future fierce warfare between a small state and formidable power of China. Nevertheless, fear of breach of faith that could be prejudicial to their good name and interests, the Government of India nominated R.B. Shaw as their next envoy to Kashgar, which he had already visited in 1868. But his departure was delayed on account of bad climatic conditions.

MEMORIES OF ROBERT BERKLEY SHAW

It is against this historical background that the significance of R.B. Shaw's travels to Kashgar-Yarqand and its neighbouring lands in 1868-69 may be assessed and on the basis of information gleaned from his memories a portrayal of the general character of socio-political structure, institutions and patterned behaviour, material conditions prevailng in Eastern Turkestan, and attitudes and values held by people may be formed and evaluated.

R.B. Shaw records that from Tibet he proceeded to a place called Chang Chamun where it was reported to him that rice was very costly, as the price of full one load of rice that a male goat could carry was worth eight *tola* of gold, equivalent to 12 pounds sterling or nearly Rs. 120. Then Mr. Shaw and his party consisting of Hindu and Muslim Indians and no other Englishman, reached Shaheedullah where a small fort stood and there a few soldiers sent by the ruler of Yarqand came to welcome them. They arranged dinner for them, talked in friendly manner, and gave information regarding geography, topography, and economic condition of the area. These soldiers frequently visited his camp to ask his welfare, and requirements for his comfortable stay, and were also entertained at his camp.[9] After some days, Shaw resumed his journey to Yarqand, and when he reached nearer to the city, a government officer, designated *Mahmandar* (keeper of guests) responsible to look after the guests, came with his associates riding on horses to take Shaw and his party to a house reserved for their stay. Yuzbashi, brother of the Wazir of Yarqand also came to meet Shaw. After introduction they all moved on horses to his camp. Yuzbashi had spread costly and beautiful carpets for him in the camp and Mr. Shaw was entertained with tea and food, and he presented to his host a turban of Kashmiri silk of safron colour.[10]

The ruler of Yarqand had repaired bridges and roads in the villages and settlements adjacent to the city for the reception of Shaw. The principal administrator of every village came to pay a visit to him, and the *Beg* or officer of Karghalik, 3 miles from Yarqand, came and met him, and talked in a frank and friendly manner. A long tablecloth *(dast-khwan)* was spread under the shadow of trees for lunch and several kinds of dishes including soup, fried rice mixed with meat *(biryani)*, bread of big size, dry and fresh fruits were served. He had invited one Haji of Bukhara to lunch who had travelled to Arabia, Turkey and India, and conversed with Shaw in Persian and spent two hours in his company. Then, they took him to a house well-decorated with carpets, furnished with chairs, table and fireplace *(atash-dan)* reserved for his residence, and lunch was served. Next day, Shaghawal, brother of the *wazir* took him to the house of the *wazir* who came to the gate to receive him. They sat in a room near the fireplace; the *wazir* expressed his feelings of satisfaction on his safe arrival after such a long and arduous journey.[11]

In a conversation that followed, the *wazir* dilated on the cordial relations between the British government and the ruler of Kashgar. He said:

> We know how a friendly alliance existed between Turkey and England (referring to the military exertions England made to save the position of Turkey in the Crimean war, 1854-1856) and we also consider that English people are our friends. Peace and friendship bring progress and prosperity, while enmity is the cause of destruction, to both the parties.

Shaw reciprocated these sentiments of concord and conciliation by explaining the same attitude and emotions of friendship the British government displayed towards the people of Yarqand. He stated that his arrival in this place will initiate the process of forging bonds of co-operation and association between the two countries to promote common interests in the spheres of commerce, and exchange of tourists and envoys. He wanted that people should come and go freely in each other's country. He also informed that Englishmen held high opinion for Turks and even Queen Victoria will feel delighted when reports of his warm welcome and the way he was treated and honoured would be conveyed to her. He deliberately avoided to talk about any military assistance to the Amir of Kashgar in the event of hostilities started by his foes, Russia, or China. When Shaw got up to leave, a servant of Shaghawal entered the room and placed a fine silken long coat on his shoulders.[12]

One day the *Munshi* of Shaw brought a letter from Shaghawal in which the *wazir* complained that Shaw's servants had sold some commodity in the local market to procure money in exchange. If he needed money he should have asked him without any inhibitions because he was the guest of government and according to traditions of hospitality it was the responsibility of the host country to arrange whatever was required by him. Shaw replied that he needed money to purchase cloth for his servants. One day in the month of Ramzan he went to the house of the *wazir*, and found no servants or guards around. Though the *wazir* kept fast, he himself prepared tea for his guest. In another meeting Shaw presented gifts to Shaghawal consisting of one gun, one rifle, one revolver, one silken turban, some cloth, 120 pounds of tea which he accepted willingly. For the Christmas day the *wazir* sent cooked food in a large quantity, two silken long coats, one cap, besides arranging all necessary things for the festival. During the month of Ramzan, Shaw arranged a dinner to which were invited Yeuzbashi, four Panjabashi, his own *Munshi*, and Diwan Baksh. They broke their fast with a piece of bread and salt, and then prayed, and began to eat food only after having been assured that pork had not been served. During his stay in Yarqand the glass of Shaw's wrist watch broke, and he sent it for repair to the market. A reporter informed the *wazir* who sent a new watch to Shaw. When the watch was repaired Shaw returned the watch to the *wazir* that had been given to him earlier. The *wazir* refused to take the watch back on the plea that whatever was offered as a present to a friend could not be taken back in consonance with principles of hospitality.[13]

The population of Yarqand as estimated by Shaw was 80 thousand including five thousand people who lived in the fort of the city. Facility for primary education was available to everyone in a school attached to the mosque. For elder boys between 15 and 20 years, there were 50 to 60 schools in the city, each with a capacity of one hundred students. For the maintenance of schools, land grants were made by the government and Muslim feudal lords, and students also paid nominal fees. But they were taught only reading and writing, and they could read *Qu'ran*. The certificate holders from these primary schools were called *Mullas*. The number of such schools increased under the regimes of Ataliq Ghazi, and he constructed two schools, which attracted large number of students. The canon laws were strictly enforced; there was *Muhtasib* in every locality of the city to exercise supervision over the conduct and activities of people. But Ataliq Ghazi was very lenient and considerate in dealing with complaints against offenders of law; he punished only the mischievous and disturbers of peace, and prisoners of war were not killed. The people in general had no information about geography, history, climate, and polity and society of outside countries, much less any knowledge about development of sciences and learning in Europe. The old idea that the world was divided in seven spheres *(haft aqlalim)* and distorted notion of rise and setting of sun in other lands still persisted. There were no factories or industries in the city of Yarqand. They were so ignorant about their earlier history that they believed that Alexander the Great was a Muslim who conquered the land and spread Islam.[14]

On the eve of the departure from Yarqand to Kashgar, R.B. Shaw was provided with a new fine horse. The royal palace in Kashgar was well guarded, and there he saw for the first time people of Kalmik race who lived near the border of China, all well dressed, and armed with arrow, bow and quiver, standing in rows at the main gates of the palace. The *wazir* conducted him up to the doorsteps of the room where Ataliq Ghazi was sitting alone to receive him. Shaw entered the room and Ataliq Ghazi seeing him stood, greeted, shook hands and asked to sit close to him. He then asked his welfare, enquired his experiences of such a long, exhausting journey and expressed his satisfaction that he at long last arrived safe and well. He related how in the past an Englishman had been murdered on the way to Yarqand by Wali Khan, a highway robber, which had caused them great grief and pain. Shaw informed that though he was a German but their guest in India and we deeply mourned his tragic death. When he excused for his poor Persian, Ataliq Ghazi laughed and remarked that he was well versed in Persian, understood it correctly and spoke very fluently. Shaw told that he was able to defeat and drive out the Chinese from Kashgar and he established his stronghold over it, against the

Chinese, that his country, England, fought over three wars, referring to three opium wars, 1840–43, 1856, 1864. He further informed him that he was not sent by the Governor-General of India, nor he brought any letter from him and he had come of his own will, hearing his name, fame and his achievements.[15]

R.B. Shaw presented to the king some guns manufactured in England which the latter accepted and said, "Exchange of presents among friends was unnecessary, his safe arrival here was for him a great source of satisfaction, and his friendship the fountainhead of strength and confidence." In the subsequent meetings which took place between the ruler of Kashgar and Shaw, the substantive discussion was concentrated on the following issues.

1. Mutual cooperation and harmony between the two countries, India and Kashgar.
2. Encouragement for expansion of trade and commerce.
3. Exchange of envoys between the countries.

Ataliq Ghazi was very eager for the appointment of an envoy to represent British government at Kashgar. He also wanted that traders and merchants should bring their merchandise to his country, and groups of people of every category from this land should visit India without hindrance. He said that his country was very small, and people were poor, there were no industries, and himself was not a hereditary king, surrounded by enemies. He sought the advice of Shaw on what plans and schemes should be adopted to improve the economy of the country. He indicated that he would send an envoy to India without delay. Thus, political matters of any kind were excluded from discussion and both of them studiously refrained from negotiating terms of political alliance or military pact. Shaw responded positively to his proposals, promised to convey his message to the Governor-General and report whatever he saw and experienced to all concerned. He was hopeful that his strategic concerns would be taken into account, problems and challenges confronting him would be favourably considered, and the interaction would pave way to the building of relationship of peace and trust with him. Ataliq Ghazi offered a sum of Rs. 9600 to Shaw to meet the expenses of his return journey from Yarqand to Lahore. He also agreed to appoint a representative at Lahore as suggested by Shaw.[16]

NOTES AND REFERENCES

1. This has now been included in his collection of essays, *Maqalat-i-Sir Syed Ahmad Khan*, (Urdu), edited by Maulana Isma'il Panipati, Vol. VI, pp. 232-63.
2. *Maqalat-i-Sir Syed Ahmad Khan*, p. 233.
3. *Mukatabat-i Allami*, compiled by 'Abu's, Samad, 1606-1607, quoted in S.A. Rizvi, *Religious and Intellectual History of the Muslims in Akbar's Reign*, New Delhi, 1975, pp. 313-14.

4. A detailed history of *Amirs* of Kashgar was given by Mirza Haider Dughlat (1499-1551) in his *Tarikh-i-Rashidi,* dedicated to Sultan Said of Kashgar. He was the son of Muhammad Husain Mirza, son of the Amir of Kashgar, and the sister of Babur's mother, and hence the first cousin of Babur.
5. For details, see Immanuel C.V. Hsis, *The Rise of Modern China,* third edition, OUP, Delhi, 1983, pp. 318-19.
6. Bisheshwar Prasad, *The Foundations of India's Foreign Policy,* Vol. I, Calcutta, 1955, p. 69.
7. *Ibid.*, pp. 71-73.
8. *Ibid.*, pp. 75-76.
9. *Maqalat-i-Sir Syed Ahmad Khan,* pp. 234-35.
10. *Ibid.*, pp. 235-36
11. *Ibid.*, p. 239.
12. *Ibid.*, p. 239.
13. *Ibid.*, pp. 340-41.
14. *Ibid.*, pp. 258-60.
15. *Ibid.*, pp. 243-44.
16. *Ibid.*, pp. 252-57.

15

Afghan Trade with India and Russia, 1880–1901

Bir Good Gill

Afghanistan, the land of rugged Pathans, found itself cramped between British India and Russia in the later half of the nineteenth century. Afghanistan was the only route for Indian goods to reach Central Asia, and its role as an entrepot for transit trade with Bukhara and Russian Turkestan was equally significant. Both the powers were vying with each other to find markets for their products in the region and subsequently to increase their profits and influence. Each tried to outwit the other and establish dominance in the sphere of trade, for they knew well that in the Eastern world, trade often led to the control of the region as well. None of them wanted direct clash and consequently tried to maintain good diplomatic relations on the surface.

The British, besides trade, wanted a buffer that would be serviceable to their interests in the Great Game. The British viceroys in India from time to time sanctioned subsidies to the *Amirs* of Afghanistan to keep them in good humour and to incline Afghanistan favourably towards their interests. In this chapter we study Indian and Russian trade and trade relations with Afghanistan during the reign of Amir Abdur Rahman Khan.

Afghanistan exported fresh and dried fruits, dyes, drugs, tobacco, snuff, wool, furs from Bukhara, raw silk, madder, asafoetida, gold, gold dust, sulphur, lead, zinc, horses, ponies and mules and Bactrian camels. Its requirements consisted of muslin, cambric, velvet, broad cloth, finished piece goods, shawls, brocades of Benares, carpets of Ambala, *lungees* of Multan, Khes, coarse cotton cloth, indigo, leather, salt, sugar, tea and minor items like handkerchiefs, razors, scissors, needles, etc.

The main centre of commercial transaction in Afghanistan was the city of Kabul, being both centrally located as well as the seat of government. As a commercial centre it was at the confluence of trade routes of the Punjab on the one side, and Balkh, Herat, Khiva, and Samarkand on the other. On the Indian side, the major trading centres for trade with Afghanistan were Peshawar and Amritsar. The merchandise dispatched from India went via Peshawar, Khyber Pass, Jalalabad to Kabul and over the Hindukush to Bukhara, Samarkand and other Central Asian *Khanates*. Kabul thus served both as market for Indian goods as well as a vital entrepot for transit trade.

By the second-half of the nineteenth century, Russia was industrialising rapidly and was reaching out the markets of Central Asia. It needed markets for her products. Its nascent industry could not compete with the superior products of the Western world. It directed its attention to developing trade with Central Asia where the demand for her manufactured goods existed. The vast market so readily available naturally enticed Russia. The *Khanates* of Bukhara, Kokand and Khiva were already in close commercial relationship with Russia as it presented an extensive market for their produce and also because they had no other source for procuring iron, copper, gold, hardware, woodwork, dyes, etc.[1] In this pursuit leading to the conquest of these markets, Russia came into collision with a powerful rival, Britain which had stabilised its positon in the Indian subcontinent by now and was trying to expand further into Central Asia.

The Russian expansion into Central Asia resulted in inclusion of Chimkent in 1864, Tashkent in 1865, and Samarkand in 1867. In 1868 the entire *Khanate* of Kokand became a Russian protectorate. The subjugation of Khiva and Bukhara was completed in 1873. To ensure strong commercial relations Russia entered into commercial treaties with these *Khanates* for preferential trade relations.

This swift progress of Russia in Central Asia in a short span of time rang panic bells in British bureaucratic circles both in India and England. In the spring of 1869, Lord Clarendon made a proposal for the recognition of some territory as neutral between the possessions of England and Russia.[2] Prince Gortchakoff agreed in response that Afghanistan shall be beyond the sphere of Russian action.[3]

In England, the pendulum of politics once again swung on the side of Conservative Party. The Party, in 1876, sent Lord Lytton as viceroy of India. His active pursuit of 'forward policy' led to the second Anglo-Afghan War. By 1880, Lord Lytton was as anxious to get out of the mess of his policy, as he was to plunge into it. This was the situation when Abdur Rahman appeared on the scene and his claims to the throne were conceded by the British.

Abdur Rahman had spent twelve years in exile in Tashkent. He had better understanding of British as well as Russian policies in the region. He showed no enthusiasm to grab the throne and knew well that the British had already set a time for the evacuation of her troops from Kabul. In his communication to Lepel Griffin, Chief British political officer in Afghanistan, the Amir said,

> as long as your Empire and that of Russia exist, these two states should find us true and faithful; and that we should rest at peace between them; for my tribesmen are unable to struggle with Empires, and are ruined by want of commerce; and we hope of your friendship that, sympathising with and assisting the people of Afghanistan you will place them under the honourable protection of the two Powers. This is my wish, for rest it is yours to decide.[4]

The Amir wanted total non-interference of the British in Afghanistan affairs. He knew that if he was to gain the respect of his people, he must never appear to be weak. He also insisted on independence in the internal affairs of his country. He refused the appointment of British agent in Kabul or anywhere else in his country. After much persuasion he agreed to a Mohammedan agent of the British government. Col. Mohammed Afzal Khan was the first British Indian agent appointed at Kabul in June 1882. The Amir had all his suspicions about this intruder in his country. Afraid that he could be reporting to the British about the internal affairs of Afghanistan, he kept him isolated from Afghan people. When the latter complained to the Amir regarding such treatment, the Amir minced no words and wrote: "I do not wish that there should be two Darbars—one at my house and the another at your place."[5]

The trade with India, both direct and transit, received his special attention. The Amir was fully aware of his country's position in India's transit trade with Bukhara. The table below shows the value of goods exported from India in the early years of Abdur Rahman's reign.[6]

Indian Exports to Kabul

Items	1882-83 Value in Rs.	1883-84 Value in Rs.	1884-85 Value in Rs.
Piece goods, European	24,75,376	18,63,722	17,09,380
Piece goods, Indian	8,62,730	7,68,187	8,99,965
Indigo	3,98,834	3,95,640	2,90,024
Leather	57,208	94,588	50,138
Metals	48,538	59,478	85,833
Sugar	1,36,397	78,524	1,12,333
Tea	13,24,466	15,23,048	11,75,815

The proportion of these goods sent from Kabul to Central Asian markets however could not be ascertained because no track was kept after they entered Afghanistan. The Amir imposed duties on goods passing through his state. When pressed upon not to do so, he excused himself by stating that he could not part with the custom that had been established by his forefathers. The duties on the goods were levied at almost every halting place in the country, both while entering the territory as well as while leaving it. The goods meant for Bukhara were taxed from the Khyber, right up to Balkh. The Amir showed some leanings towards the Russian goods. The merchandise from India was subjected to heavy imposts. The goods were detained in the custom houses for days and weeks together for the purpose of being examined by Amir's officials and if the slightest suspicion was awakened in the officials' mind, the party was placed under close police surveillance for days and months together. Russian goods and wares, however, brought in from Bukhara and Samarkand were scarcely subjected to any examination at all. *Novoye Vremiya* of 15th of July 1883 observed that Abdur Rahman was not very friendly with Government of India. The paper noted "what his sentiments may be after the receipts of his subsidies we cannot tell", "but the examples set by now deceased and by every other Amir of the past are not encouraging to the English".[7]

Russia tried to make entry of English and Indian goods into Bukhara and the rest of Russian Turkestan difficult. Prohibitive duties were imposed on any import from India into Bukhara. In order to offset this, an appeal was made to the Amir not to tax goods as they passed from place to place in Afghanistan.[8] It was felt that if this was done, there would be greater trade through Afghanistan which would more than compensate for the restriction caused by Russian measures.

The Amir refused point-blank to reduce duties. In an interview with Ataullah Khan, British Agent at Kabul, the Amir stated that he had already suffered a loss of Rs. 20 lakh as revenues (annually). He said: "I am a great loser. I do not know how I shall be able to make up the deficiency."[9]

Russians were also concerned that Indian manufactured goods would not remain confined to Russian Turkestan, but might penetrate deep into European Russia as well, if the flow was not checked.[10] The *St. Petersburg Gazette* believed that there was a cotton textile factory at Peshawar meant only to cater to the needs of Central Asians.[11] But in reality there was no need for any such factory. Textiles of all varieties were collected throughout the Punjab to be exported to Central Asia as they were much in demand. Russia, in order to stop the influx, had to improve her own textiles and then to sell them cheaper. Towards the accomplishment of these ends Russia started construction of railway in Central Asia to bring down the haulage charges. Russian firms were established with the sole purpose to supply the Central Asian markets. Wholesale mercantile houses like those of Koushin (1883) were established at Ashkabad—the trade capital of Russian transactions with Central Asia.[12] Goods were daily dispatched from there to Khorasan, Khiva, Bukhara and Afghanistan too. In 1883, Igmatubu, a Kazan Tartar was dispatched to Herat with samples of Russian goods. Russian trade with the region in prints started from that day. In 1884 this trade touched 1,00,000 roubles. It was a great feat for Russia, as it had managed to penetrate in those markets which had been the preserve of Indian goods so far. The Central Asian market was really hungry for piece goods. If the exports were 1,00,000 roubles in 1884, its sale rose to 5,00,000 the very next year.[13] The reason behind this rise was the durability of Russian fabric, cheap price as compared to the Indian cloth and both colour and designs appealing to Central Asians' tastes. Later, Russian merchants also started competing for the sale of turban material to the Central Asians. The turbans that were sent from India came from Glasgow and Manchester and bore bird patterns and colours that could not be worn by Mohammedans during prayers. The Russian keen eye lost no time in noticing the error and started supplying the checks which were instant success.[14] Once the flow of the trade was turned in favour of Russia, Russian merchants had no problems in getting future orders too. Thus, Russians posed a threat to Indian trade which, since ages, had been India's undisputed monopoly.

Russia was by now confident that it would one day be able to undersell the Indian counterpart. She had studied the native taste and seen that it combined durability with price. The nearness of Russian border with Afghanistan was another reason for the low prices. Indian goods had to undertake long, ardous journeys across the rough and risky passes to reach Afghanistan. Russia further changed its mode of transfer of goods from road-borne to rail-borne trade. The strategic and commercial railway route reached Samarkand in 1888. The British, on their part, could make no such move in Central Asia. The only way that could eliminate or counter-balance Russia's influence was a similar railway to Afghanistan, but Abdur Rahman was strongly against any such thing. He considered that the organism of a Mohammedan state would collapse the moment it was 'pricked by the steel needle', i.e. the railways.

The Amir responded to all suggestions, for the construction of a railway to Kandhar or Kabul with a categoric refusal and declared that if the construction of railway was commenced in his dominions, all work would be immediately destroyed, and those constructing them would be put to death. This he said, was "not of course at his instigation, but in consequence of the fanaticism of the local population".[15] Under the pretext of his people's opinion, the Amir had put stamp on his own decision. His shrewd eye could see the damage that such a railway could do to his land-locked country rendering it a mere entrepot and station on Peshawar-Bukhara highway.

The position of British Indian trade with Afghanistan by the last decade of nineteenth century was considerably weakened. Russian influence in Bukhara and other *Khanates* north of the Oxus had emerged stronger. This was primarily so because the Indian goods could not proceed further beyond the limits of Afghanistan.

Amir Abdur Rahman in an attempt to modernise Afghanistan had established separate departments of education, civil administration and communications. He instituted a Board of Trade and Board of Treasury to modernise the fiscal system of Afghanistan. He felt the need of a systematised currency in the progress of Afghanistan. Under this freshly realised idea, he not only reduced the export of bullion to India, but altogether banned its movement in any form.

The Amir issued a proclamation stating that no gold and silver be exported from Afghanistan. The result was that about one lakh of Kabul rupees, which used to come down to Peshwar every month, ceased to flow in.[16] Soon he started a policy of converting items of trade into a state monopoly. This, he felt, would bring in more revenues to his treasury. In 1891 he forbade all traders from trading in dry fruits, pistachio nuts, asafoetida, cumin seed, and chilghozas.[17] Next year the monopoly of sale of all fruits, from Afghanistan to India was sold to one Nur Mohammad Khan.[18] Dry and fresh fruits and *ghee* were items of regular consumption in northern India. In 1893 the Amir declared the export of *ghee*, grain and tobacco into a monopoly of vend and lease. Such extensive monopolies had serious repercussions on the local trade.

Amir put a ban on export of horses to India. The export of horses in 1896-97 was only 1/3rd of what it was a year earlier. The sale of sheep was turned into a state monopoly in 1895. Even the export of grain was prohibited from Afghanistan by an extraordinary order in 1895.[19] Besides the state monopoly system, the Amir levied duties on goods sent in lumpsum on a pack of goods according to weight.[20] The quality and the price was not taken into account. The cheaper and bulky goods were thus taxed more heavily while finer and precious ones had to pay less taxes.[21]

Not only were Afghan items of trade turned into monopoly, but even those imported into Afghanistan from India. In 1895, the sale of sugar from India met the above-said fate. He ordered that if anyone but the monopolist brought sugar from India a heavy prohibitive fine of Rs. 58 per camel load shall be imposed on him.[22] He further directed his officials to give him the list of tea and cloth consumed in Afghanistan, so that he could appoint his own agents in Kabul to import these articles from India by giving them advances from Kabul treasury.[23]

The silver lining for Indian trade in this dark situation was still the tea. Bukhara served as a depot and agency for distribution of Indian teas. Russia had realised that her *Kiakhta* teas were not at all popular with Bukharans. It was believed that Russian prohibitory duties might shut Indian teas out of Turkestan markets. But both black and green teas from India continued to find markets in Russian Turkestan. In 1885 about 2000 camels laden with the Indian tea went to Bukhara (a camel carried 16 poods. The weight of a pood was equal to 36 English Ibs). Population of Central Asia, in the existing statistics was 6,000,000, but the tea that reached could serve only 2,40,000 (1/3rd of population).[24] This shows that there was lot of scope for Indian teas, since tea was *sine qua non* of Central Asian people. Indian tea, which was so popular in Central Asia, went from Kangra where the plantation had been brought up exclusively keeping in mind Central Asian market. More than ten thousand acres of land was under tea cultivation in 1878 in the Kangra Valley with an annual yield of 1,113,106 Ibs.[25] If Russia closed its markets to Indian tea, it could seriously affect the Indian merchants employed in this trade besides heavy losses to planters. But it was the urgent need of Central Asian people that kept the market alive for Indian tea. The teas sent were mostly of ordinary quality and within the means of Central Asians. The Chinese tea was consumed by the rich people. The ordinary population drank *Kokchi,* the Indian tea. The trade in 1887 amounted to 70,000 poods, and its price varied from 1 to 2-1/2 roubles per pound.[26] According to *Russki invalide* the quantity of Indian tea imported into Bukhara direct through Afghanistan was 46,560 poods in 1889. This was besides the tea that reached Bukhara via Meshed, Persia after paying a duty of 5-1/2%. The total Indian tea into Bukhara averaged 90,000 poods yearly.[27] Definitely, all was not consumed in Bukhara and was further distributed into Russian Turkestan. Russia could not stop the import of tea on two accounts: first, it was the basic need of Central Asians, and secondly, Russia herself supplied none to give competition. She was herself a consumer of large quantity of the leaf, may it be from China, Ceylon or India.

Abdur Rahman was aware of the British need for maintaining Afghanistan as a buffer state to avoid collision with Russia. At the same time he improved relations with Russia, which supplied goods cheaper, better and more conveniently through Bukhara. He even entered into negotiation with Russia to have a trade agreement.[28] It was partly because the transportation of goods from northwestern parts of Afghanistan to Russia was easier and cheaper owing to proximity of distance and railway facilities.

When China reoccupied Eastern Turkestan, Russia entered into treaty engagements with her. Under the terms of the Treaty of St. Petersburg, Russia gained from China many concessions for her trade. The Chinese tea, which started reaching Russia and Russian Turkestan in large quantities, resulted in the decrease of Indian tea trade with Bukhara and beyond. All the more so, as Indian tea had to pay a tax of 25 per cent on entering Russian Turkestan.[29] The decline of Indian teas in Central Asian markets also affected the purchasing power of Indian merchants, as tea was used as a barter for many Bukharan and Central Asian goods like silk, wool, musk, and medicinal herbs.

Russian cotton goods and chintzes, besides being stronger, cheaper and better, were also more durable than the ones supplied by India. They were well suited to the harsh climate of Afghanistan and to rough wear. So they soon became popular among these rugged clans. But at the same time, Indian muslin and calicoes never lost their markets in Afghanistan. These items of cotton goods along with Kashmiri shawls and Indian brocades were not supplied by Russia and found market in Afghanistan as well as Russian Turkestan. The demand of Indian piece goods increased despite the doubling of tax from 2-1/2% to 5% imposed by the Amir.[30] The trade in piece goods to Kabul and Russian Turkestan as compared to 10 years earlier showed the following figures.[31]

Year	Weight in *Maunds*	Value in Rupees
1875-76	34,549	11,51,346
1885-86	28,128	13,30,907

The reduction in volume but increase in value clearly indicates that Indian fine calicos and muslins were still in demand among the comparatively rich section of the population. The value of piece goods exported to Afghanistan in 1893-94 amounted to Rs. 27,00,000.[32]

Russia had thus improved the position of her trade in Central Asia by expansion of railway network. The Indian merchant found himself in a more disadvantageous position because of extremely disturbed situation on the North Western Frontier. The uprising of 1897 affected the Indian trade to Afghanistan and led to the creation of North Western Frontier Province in 1901. The death of Amir Abdur Rahman later in the same year gave a further push to the already declining fortunes of Indian trade with Afghanistan.

NOTES AND REFERENCES

1. Valikhanov M. Veniukoff, *The Russians in Central Asia*, London, Trans., 1865, p. A57.
2. Foreign Department, Secret Branch, Proceedings 180, April 1874, National Archives of India, New Delhi.
3. Prince Gortchakoff to Secretary of State for Foreign Affairs on 19 January, 1874, *ibid.*
4. *Sec, Prog.* 244, June 1880, National Archives of India (NAI).
5. *Sec, E., Prog.* 423, 1883, NAI.
6. *KW, Frontier A, Prog.*, 3-8 December 1885, NAI.
7. *Sec E, Prog.*, 10, September 1883, NAI.
8. *K.W., op. cit.*
9. *Sec. F, Prog.*, 331, February 1886, NAI.
10. *Sec. E, Prog.*, 204, March, 1884, NAI.
11. *St. Petersberg Gazette*, 9th January 1884.
12. *Novoye Vremya* (St. Petersburg), 26th November 1885.
13. *Ibid.*
14. George Dobson, *Russia's Railway Advance into Central Asia*, London, Allen and Co., 1890, pp. 382-83.
15. *Sec. F, Prog.* 98, May 1899, NAI.
16. *Sec. F, Prog.* 340, May 1893. Also Louis Dupree, *Afghanistan*, Princeton, 1973, p. 420.
17. *Sec. F, Prog.* 427, May 1893, NAI
18. Prog. 425, *ibid.*
19. *Sec. F, Prog.* 269, May 1896, NAI.
20. *Sec. F, Prog.* 96, July 1892, NAI.
21. *Ibid.*

22. *Sec. F, Prog.* 493, October 1895, NAI.
23. *Sec. F, Prog.* 496, January 1895, NAI.
24. *Sec. F, Prog.* 187, October 1886, NAI.
25. W.W. Hunter, *Imperial Gazetteer of India,* London, 1886, Vol. II, p. 506.
26. Extract of 11 October 1887, *Frontier A, Prog.* 126-32, April 1888, NAI.
27. Dobson, *op. cit.*, p. 376.
28. M.A. Babakodzhayev, 'Russo-Afghan Trade Relations in the 80s and 90s of the Nineteenth Century', *Historical and Cultural Quarterly*, Kabul, Vol. 22, No. 1, Spring 1969, p. 35; See also, *For, Sec. E, Prog.*, September 10, 1883, NAI.
29. *Sec. F, Prog.* 40, May 1888, NAI.
30. Peshawar Confidential Diary, *Sec. F, Prog.* 91, April 1895, NAI.
31. *Sec. F, Prog.* 40, May, 1888, NAI.
32. *Frontier A, Prog.* 63, Aug. 1895, NAI.

16

Central Asia in Indo-Russian Relations

Devendra Kaushik

Close cultural and economic ties have existed between India and Central Asia since time immemorial. Archaeological excavations of stone and bronze cultures in Central Asia have brought to light a similarity with cultures in northwest India of the same period. Stone implements bearing a close resemblance with those discovered on northwest Indian territory of Punjab have been excavated from sites belonging to the Gissar culture in Tajikistan. More striking are similarities between the finds from Altyntepe in Southern Turkmenistan and the relics of the Harappan culture of northwest India. Harappan type ceramic, seals, and fragments of lazurite have also been found at Shortugai on the southern bank of river Pyanj-Amudaria in Tajikistan. It seems the Harappan settlements received their supplies of lazurite from the mines in Badakshan in the Pamir region of Tajikistan.[1] The relics discovered at Altyntepe in Turkmenistan and Shortugai in Tajikistan indicate existence of extensive trade in art and handicraft products between northwest India and Central Asia and mutual influence in the sphere of development of material culture, subsequently giving rise to interaction in the sphere of religion and spiritual culture. These early contacts from the third and second millennium BC got further strengthened as a result of frequent transmigrations of various ethnic groups on the territories of India and Central Asia and their inclusion quite often in a single state such as the Achaemenian state followed by the state of Alexander the Great and the Seleucids and the Graeco-Bactrian kingdom, the Kushana and the Mughal Empire. Lively contacts with Central Asia were maintained during the reign of the great Mauryan Emperor Asoka whose state extended up to the border of that region. After the decline of the Mauryan Empire various dynasties from Central Asian Scythians—Sakas—ruled in northwest India. These contacts became particularly rich during the Kushana Empire.

Like Indo-Central Asian relations, Indo-Russian relations also go back to the remote past. In a way, they are even much older so far as indirect relations are concerned. However, Central Asia has been continuously a vital link in the relations between India and Russia. And it is but natural, for, being the core of the Eurasian landmass, Russia cannot put up with its exclusion from either Europe or Asia. Because of the absence of a physical barrier on the space between the Urals and the Black Sea resulting in the extension of the Russian Steppe to Central Asia, the latter has ideally served as a bridge between Russia and South Asia. Interestingly, noted British geographer Halford Macinder had called the Eurasian empire of Russia even before World War I, a unique institution representing a "remarkable correlation between natural environment and political organisation unlikely to be altered by any possible social revolution". Historically speaking, there has existed a certain convergence of Russian and Indian geostrategic interests in the Central Asian region which forms the southern portion of the Eurasian landmass separated from the Indian subcontinent by the Pamir and the Hindukush chain of mountains. Developments in this part of the world have shaped the destiny of our peoples more than once in the past and continue to be of great interest even after the disintegration of the Soviet Union.

If contacts between India and Central Asia, as mentioned above, can be traced back to the Harappan culture in the 3rd to 2nd millennium BC, the Indo-Russian contacts also date back to the prehistorical epoch. The closeness in the field of language and mythology points out to a common origin of the ancestors of the Indians and the Slavs and long period of their cohabitation on a common or neighbouring territory. It is a well-known fact that, of all the Indo-European languages, Sanskrit and Russian are the closest. Modern Russian language, so far as grammatical rules and syntax are concerned, strictly follow the great Indian grammarian Panini who lived in the sixth century BC. Tilak's *Arctic Home in the Vedas* contains substantial evidence to show that the ancestors of the Indians and the Russians lived for a long time in close vicinity. A comparative study of Vedic Sanskrit and the languages of the Slav, Baltic and Iranian groups is bound to be rewarding. Research by Soviet archaeologists contains interesting material on the ancient migrations of the Indo-Iranian tribes. Iranian-speaking peoples of Central Asia, such as the Bactrians, Khorezmians and Sogdians long preserved in their material and spiritual culture features, which were common to the Indo-Aryans. Central Asia, of course, underwent large-scale changes during the medieval times as a result of the advent of Islam and the partial assimilation of the Iranian-speaking population by the Turks. But even among the Turkic-speaking and Muslim population of Central Asia it is possible to find beliefs and customs close to those of ancient India.[2]

If one were to count the Tver merchant Afanasy Nikitin's journey to India in the fifteenth century as an isolated event, regular contacts at the popular level between India and Russia became noticeable by the end of the seventeenth century. However, the Russian people knew about the wonderful and prosperous land of India right from the first centuries of the formation of the Russian state of Kiev Rus. Archaeological finds show the existence of active trade relations of Kiev Rus with the Orient. Goods and coins of Oriental origin including Indian have been found in the cultural strata of the eighth and ninth centuries. Gold coins from India dating from fifteenth century have been found in the Volga region. The Russians learnt about India from the Khazars and the Bulgars settled in the southern Volga region. A trade route via the river Volga and the Caspian Sea linking Russia with Central Asia and India started functioning in the tenth-eleventh centuries. A Russian work *Chronicle of Times Past* mention the route to Khwarizm and further to the 'land of Shem', which also included regions of India. Muhammad Aufi, a native of Bukhara who lived in Delhi in the early thirteenth century, writes about the Kievan prince Vladimir sending an embassy to the ruler of Khwarizm. Arab authors record the existence of close ties between the Russians and the Khazars and also associate the Khazars with the Indians on account of good trade routes. Arab author Al-Bakri of eleventh century observes a similarity of customs among the Russians and Indians. "They (Russians) have customs like those of the Indians", Al-Bakri writes.[3]

The Mongol invasion, which devastated parts of Central Asia, disrupted for sometime the trade relations between India and Russia. However, after an interval the Golden Horde itself became a concealing link between Russia and India. In the fourteenth century, the Delhi Sultans maintained close relations with the Golden Horde to whom a number of Russian principalities owed allegiance. Arab traveller Ibn Battuta who visited the Golden Horde in the 1430s writes about its sizeable trade with India mentioning the export of more than thousand horses. India was connected with the Volga region of Russia through two trade routes passing via Transcaucasia (Derbent, Baku, and Shemakha) and Central Asia. According to Ibn Battuta, Mohammad Tughlak encouraged the Indian trade with the Golden Horde and there existed centres of Indian trade in both the capitals of the Golden Horde—the Old and New Sarai. This is confirmed by the discovery of Indian gold coins in the Volga region in a village called Tenishevo.[4] Russian fabrics were priced highly in India in the fourteenth century. Famous poet of Central Asian origin, Amir Khusro Dehelvi, praised the beauty of Russian women. The *Tughlak-Nama* mentions about Russians serving in the army of Ghias-ud-din Tughlak.[5]

After the decline of the Golden Horde the role of the major trading centres in the Volga region was transferred to Kazan and Astrakhan. The latter was linked with Central Asia, Iran, and Northern India. Russian merchants were by now firmly entrenched in Astrakhan. The Golden Horde was destroyed by Timur who invaded both India and Russia. These invasions, however, did not stop the trade routes. The Castilian ambassador to Timur's Court in Samarkand reported that trades with Indian and Russian goods could be found in the city.

Indian traders brought to Samarkand cloves and other spices which found their way to Europe largely through purchases by Russian traders. Shahrukh, son of Timur, sent an ambassador to Tver. The presents brought to the Tsar of Russia by envoys from the Central Asian Khans included, besides precious metals and gems, locally produced items by the Mughal rulers of Delhi. The Tsar's presents consisted of commodities and wares whose trade was state monopoly and which were in great demand at the Mughal court, such as walrus tusk, sable and hawks and falcons.[6]

The establishment of the Portuguese colonies on the western coast of India in the early sixteenth century and the obstruction by the Portuguese navy in other West European countries' trade with India led to proposals by the traders and governments of England, Itlay and Sweden for permission to use the Russian territory for conducting trade with India through the Volga River to the Caspian and thence to India through Iran and Central Asia. The British government made several requests to the Russian Tsar to grant the Muscovy company a monopoly of trade with Bukhara, Persia and India. Sweden, while making peace with Ivan the Terrible, included a provision in the treaty about permitting Swedish merchants to travel to the East via Russia. Giovanni Botero of Italy claimed that the best route to India was through Russia but the Russian Tsar would not allow its use to other European states. While encouraging Eastern trade, the Russian government did not desire to share the profits from this trade with other European traders.

British traveller Ralph Fitch heard of Russian merchants in India in the 1580s, and in the 1590s a Russian merchant, Leonty Yudin, lived for nine years in Bukhara and India. Indian merchants appeared in Russia at the close of the sixteenth century and Russian ruler Boris Godunov extended his protection to them. In 1585, the envoy of Bukharan ruler Abdulla Khan arrived in Kazan to have an audience with Tsar Fyodor Ivanovich. He informed the Russian authorities that he was carrying Indian tents, carpets, wide velvet belts, fine silk cloth and dyes as presents for the Tsar.[7] Thus, the presents from the Central Asian rulers to the Tsars included goods of Indian origin and the return presents from the Tsars to them consisted of typical Russian goods in great demand at the royal Indian court in Delhi. The high profitability of this exchange of Indian and Russian goods through the Central Asian envoys prompted the Khivan and Bukharan Khans to make repeated requests to the Russian Tsars for forging close regular trade relations. The Central Asian Khans did not stop sending frequently their envoys with Indian presents to the Tsars and local goods for trade in spite of widespread acts of brigandage by the nomadic tribes. The growing trade and diplomatic contacts between Central Asia and Russia also reflected the importance of the former as a link between India and Russia.

According to information contained in the *Nikonovskaya Chronicle* in 1532, an envoy from India, Khwaja Hussain, arrived in Moscow in the Court of Great

Prince Vasily Ivanovich with a communication from Babur the Mughal ruler of India who had died in 1530 when the envoy was on his way to Moscow. Opinions differ about this Indian mission to Moscow. It is believed by some that Khwaja Hussain was a private merchant holding a normal safe conduct request from Babur. But others are of the view that Babur being a native of Central Asia was showing interest in the distant northern state which had a long history of relations with his home region. It was not an easy task to establish communication between Russia and India in the early sixteenth century. However, interest in India began to grow in Russia in the mid-sixteenth century during the reign of Ivan the Terrible (1553–84) who seized Kazan and Astrakhan, two long-time important centres of the Eastern trade. In 1557-58, merchants of Khiva, Bukhara and Samarkand petitioned the Tsar for permission to trade in Astrakhan where Indian wares were received via Persia and sent to Moscow.

In the first half of the seventeenth century, Indian goods largely reached Russia through English and Dutch merchants via Archangelsk. During this period, Iran had become an important area of influence of the Indian trading capital. Colonies of Indian merchants came up in the Iranian cities of Isfahan, Shiraz, and Kandahar where thousands of them settled to conduct their business. After the end of the internecine conflict of the 'Troubled Times' in Russia, Indian merchants appeared in Astrakhan in 1615-16 from Iran and Transcaucasia. They extended their trade activities to Moscow and Yaroslav. In Astrakhan, the Indians lived in the company of Armenians, Bukharans, and Persians. By 1647, the strength of the Indian colony of merchants in Astrakhan had grown to 25 and in 1649 they were allowed to set up their independent trading centre. The Russian authorities gave them full protection, permitting free performance of their religious rites. The trade turnover of the Indian merchants was considerable and they paid thousands of roubles as custom duty. Some Indian merchants married the local Tartar girls and had offsprings from them. Indian merchants in Astrakhan received state subsidy for their trading activities. One Sutur, a wealthy Indian merchant, was reported to have received four thousand roubles from the state treasury. Indian merchants from Astrakhan were permitted to stay in Moscow for carrying on retail trade. In the second half of the seventeenth century there were 31 Indian merchants and three priests living in Moscow.[8]

During the reigns of Tsar Mikhail Fyodorovich (1613–45) and Tsar Aleksei Mikhailovich (1645–76) unsuccessful attempts were made to send Nikita Siroyezhin, an inhabitant of Kazan and Vasily Tushkanov, a merchant from Astrakhan, to the court of Indian Emperor Shahjehan. They could not reach India because of the war in Persia. As Russian interest in Indian trade grew, Anissim Gribov was sent to Central Asia in 1646 to explore routes to India from Astrakhan. A plan for an expedition to India by sea was advanced in 1662. Information about India was collected from the Bukharans living in Tobolsk, and Boris Pazukhin was sent to Bukhara to obtain information about routes to India from

Indians settled in Bukhara. Pazukhin's information was compared with the information received from the Bukharan merchants in Moscow. Finally in 1675 a mission headed by Mohammad Yusup Kasimov, a Bukharan settled in Astrakhan, was sent to Emperor Aurangzeb. Kasimov was instructed to bring 'vegetable seeds or small animals and birds which might settle down in the Russian state'. Kasimov could not be received by Emperor Aurangzeb and was turned away from Afghanistan. It was only Semyon Malenky who succeeded in reaching India. He lived there for three years.

Motivated by desire to attain economic progress, the Russian authorities continued their search for dependable trade routes to India with renewed vigour during the first half of the eighteenth century. Fyodor Saltykov's project of 1714 suggested a northern sea route to India to generate additional revenues for the state. He suggested building fortresses in Siberia and setting up trade routes through the territory of the Kalmyks. In 1716 Peter I ordered an expedition to Central Asia in search of new routes to India under Alexander Bekovich Cherkassaky. This expedition despatched a sub-team headed by Lt. Alexander Kozhin to explore the route along the Amu Darya to India by water. Peter also sent an expedition to Bengal in India by sea in 1723 through Madagaskar under David Wilster. Both Kozhin and Wilster failed to achieve their mission. In 1727 an anonymous plan reviewed caravan routes from Astrakhan to India via Central Asia. In the 1730s, Ivan Kirillov proposed a route to India from Orenburg. At the beginning of 1750s the Governor of Orenburg tried to form a company of Russian merchants to trade with India and the Central Asian *Khanates*. This plan proved a non-starter due to lack of response from Russian merchants. In 1760s Russian scholar Mikhail Lomonosov conceived of a plan to set up trade with India through the northeastern route via Siberia and the Central Asian *Khanates*. But the plans to organise a company to trade with India, both overland and by sea through Madagaskar, were not reliable at that time due to the great logistical problems, which the then economically and militarily weak Russia was not in a position to solve. Peter visited Astrakhan in 1722 and received Anbu Ram, the leader of the Indian merchants. By a decree of Peter, Indians in Astrakhan were given freedom to deal with property and inheritance matters. They also received permission to trade outside Astrakhan.

The period between the 1720s and 1740s witnessed a flourishing Indian trade in Russia with a turnover of more than 100 thousand roubles. The strength of the Astrakhan Indian colony rose to 100 and of the Indians residing in Russia to 400-500.[9] An Indian, Sukhanand, who died in St. Petersburg left a fortune of 300 thousand roubles. By the end of the 1740s the Astrakhan colony of Indian merchants began to face difficulties due to the chaotic conditions following the murder of Nadir Shah in Iran. It was about this time that the centre of Russia's oriental trade began to shift from Astrakhan to Orenburg. The political situation in India too began to change with the increasing domination of the British. Yet, despite these unfavourable conditions, casual traffic of travellers and sailors to India did not cease. In the 1760s, four Russian sailors serving on a British ship visited India. They left notes useful for Russia's trade with India. In the 1770s, a Russian, Filipp Yefremov, who had been taken slave in Bukhara, returned to his homeland via India. Yefremov's notes on India published in 1786 ran into three editions during his lifetime. One comes across casual Indian visitors to Russia such as an Indian hermit from Madras in the Trans-Baikal area who is mentioned by the Russian envoy to the Far East. Danil Messerschmidt during his Siberian expedition, met an Indian merchant from Delhi settled in Irkutsk who had married in Russia and embraced Orthodox Christianity. Messerschmidt learnt Hindi and Sanskrit from this Indian merchant. Orientalist George Jacob Kehr got acquainted in St. Petersburg with an Indian merchant from Astrakhan named Sunghara who became a Christian and was elevated to the status of a nobleman. He was called Pyotr Ivanovich Sungur in Russian. He gave lessons to Kehr in Devnagari and Landa scripts.[10]

Russian scholars, journalists and artists also contributed to the development of cultural and scientific contacts with India during the latter half of the eighteenth century. Among them particular mention may be made of Nikolai Novikov whose magazine published information critical of the British rule; Alexander Radishchev, a pioneer of Russian revolutionary democratic movement called the British 'insolent villains'; Nikolai Karamzin published a partial translation of *Shakuntala* by Kalidas into Russian in 1792; in 1788 a Russian translation of *Bhagavadgita* had already appeared. A very prominent place in the history of Indological studies in the eighteenth century Russia belongs to Gerasim Lebedev to whom goes the honour of being the founder of modern Bengali theatre. During the nineteenth century the tradition of studies in Indian culture, language and religon emerged with scholars such as Robert Lenz, Pavel Petrov, Belinsky, Adelung, Kossovich, Minayev, Oldenburg, Shcherbatskoi, Kovalevsky, and Vasilyev. AD Saltykov imparted a romantic hue to the image of India through his work *Letters about India* published in Russian with an album of sketches by the author appended. India occupied an important place in the life and works of the great Russian writer Leo Tolstoy. Mahatma Gandhi, it may be recalled, was a 'follower of Leo Tolstoy'.

Even though the role played by Central Asia as a link in the Indo-Russian relations was considerably reduced by the Tsarist annexation of the region and the establishment of the British colonial rule in India, it was never completely eliminated. The Indian national liberation movement felt the impact of the Russian conquest of Central Asia. As Engels observed,

> ... when a first class European military power asserts itself in Turkestan, endeavours ... to make Persia and Afghanistan into its vassals, and moves slowly but doggedly towards the Hindukush and the Sulayman range – there

> you have a very different state of affairs. British dominion ceases to be inelucable fate and a new perspective appears before the native population. What force has created, force can also break asunder ...[11]

The Russian advance in Central Asia stirred the hopes of the Indian people to throw off the yoke of the British colonial oppression. Soon after the Russian occupation of Tashkent, Maharaja Ranbir Singh of Kashmir sent a mission of four persons. Two of the emissaries were murdered on their way and the survivors Abdur Rahman Khan and Sarfaraz Khan reached Tashkent in November 1865. The mission was not successful as the Tsarist government was not interested in promoting the cause of national liberation of India. This mission was followed by other missions, namely, from the ruler of Indore in 1866, second mission from Maharaja Ranbir Singh of Kashmir in 1870 headed by Baba Karam Prakash, the namdhari mission of Guru Charan Singh reaching Tashkent in 1879 carrying a letter from Baba Ram Singh, and the mission by one Ghulam Haydar Khan who described himself as the envoy of the king of Nepal arriving in Ashkhabad in 1890.

The unwillingness of the Tsarist Russian government to help the cause of Indian independence notwithstanding, the Anglo-Russian rivalry over Central Asia gave a stimulus to the national awakening in India and objectively helped in promoting further the friendly feelings for Russia at the popular level, which had existed over a period of centuries. It was used by leaders of the Indian National Congress to strengthen their demand for greater Indian participation in the armed forces of the country, modification of the Arms Act, increase in the salaries of the Indians serving in the army and higher grades in service, etc.[12] The Indian National Congress opposed the increase in military expenditure to meet the threat of 'Russian invasion'. It opposed the 'forward policy' on the northwest frontier of India. At the 1891 session of the Party, Dinshaw Wacha refuted the government's assertion that the 'forward policy' followed from the advance of Russia in Central Asia. The 1892 session adopted a new approach to the question of increased military expenditure by declaring that this had been caused principally by the military activity going on beyond the natural defence lines of the country in pursuance of the imperial policy of Britain in relation with some of the Great Powers in Europe and urged Britain to bear an equitable portion of this military expenditure.[12]

But if Tsarist Russia had snubbed the efforts of Indian revolutionaries like Raja Mahendra Pratap to forge links with it by not responding to his 'Gold Plate Letter' to the Tsar and handing over two of his envoys sent to Tashkent to the British who executed them, the Soviet power readily welcomed Indian revolutionaries to Tashkent. Apart from Raja Mahendra Pratap, who was given a warm welcome by Red Guards at Termez, other Indian revolutionaries like Abdur Rab, Mohd. Shafiq and Barkatullah among others arrived in Tashkent where they were joined by other Indian revolutionaries from Moscow—M.N. Roy, Abani Mukerji and M.P.B Acharya. The Indian revolutionaries set up a school for political and military training at Tashkent, which was joined by a group of *Muhajirs* (Muslim Khilafat emigrees from India). This school was wound up in 1921 and its 22 trainees left Tashkent for Moscow. Dissensions among the Indian revolutionaries and the Afghan government's refusal to give permission for sending them to India across Afghanistan, besides the trade negotiations with England, were the main reasons for the closure of the Tashkent military school.

The presence of numerous Indians in Central Asia at the time of Russian conquest of Central Asia aroused interest among several Russian orientalists for the study of the history, culture and economy of India. In 1867 P.I. Pashino published his 'Stories about Kashmir as told by the Kashmiris'. This is the first account of this Indian state in Russian based on the author's interviews with Kashmiris living in or visiting Tashkent. Ram Chandra Balaji, a nephew of 1857 uprising leader, Nana Saheb, participated in the Samarkand Russian Scientific expedition for study of Central Asia and helped in organising the Ashkhabad and Tashkent Hindustani courses for Russian military officers in 1897. Russian officers Vygornitsky and Gilferding learnt Hindustani from Indian settlers in Bukhara and published textbooks of Urdu. The Hindustani course at Ashkhabad was merged with the Tashkent course in 1900 and renamed the Tashkent Officers' School for Oriental Languages. Many of the future Russian Indologists were associated with the Tashkent school. Among them mention may be made of A.G. Serebrennikov, A.E. Snesarev, M.V. Grulev, V.P. Polovtsov and V.F. Novitskii. A.E. Snesarev's work *Severoindiiski Teatr* published in Tashkent in 1903 is not only a military-geographical account of North India but also a work related to the history and ethnography of the small states near the Pamir and the Hindukush. The work contains rich information about Gilgit, Ladakh, Baltistan, and Kashmir and the trade of these states with Central Asia.

The process of conversion of India into a British colony was completed by the middle of the nineteenth century. Apart from full political domination of the entire Indian territory, the country also became economically dependent on the metropolitan power. India became a large market for British goods and the main source of raw material and food products for Britain. In the interest of Britain, semi-feudal form of ownership was preserved in the domain of agriculture. The British ruling class fully exploited its monopoly over the Indian economic resources to consolidate its hold over world trade and navigation. Britain earned huge profits by re-exporting Indian agricultural products and raw material to many countries of the world including Russia.[13] Russia's growing capitalist industrialisation, which included development of its textile industry in the first place, aggravated the problem of finding markets for its manufactured goods and sources of raw materials like cotton, indigo and dyes. The world trade being largely controlled by Britain as the main broker, and the long delay involved in receiving raw materials for the growing textile industry and its growing demand for traditional Indian goods like Indian cloth, Kashmir shawls, incense, spices, varnish, and dyes resulted in continuation of its search of new and more reliable trade routes to India.

Thus, one finds nobleman Zubov attaching great importance to trade with India for increasing the wealth of Russia in the report submitted by him in 1802, under the heading 'General Survey of Trade with Asia'. Zubov highlighted the need to acquire more information about the customs of the people through whose land the trade routes passed, the state of roads and the type of rule prevailing there. Other influential Russians like G.S. Lebedev pleaded for establishing direct trade links with India through the sea route around Africa. Lebedev complained that the East India Company of Britain was exporting many Russian goods to India on its ships. The items exported by the British from Russia included mast and sawed timber, wood tar, sail cloth, tallow, hemp fibre, flax, and cran and cow berries.[14] The Russian-American company undertook a round-the-world sea voyage in 1802–1805 to explore the potentiality of trade with India through the sea route. It recommended to Tsar Alexander-I import of sugar, coffee and indigo from the port of Calcutta in Bengal to the port of St. Petersburg directly, bypassing the East India Company.[15] In 1817, Bengali sailors brought a shipload of Indian goods to the eastern Okhotsk port. These goods were exported to Russia by an Englishman Gordon. In the thirties and forties of the nineteenth century, a British firm brought Indian goods directly to the Baltic port of Riga.

The construction of the Suez Canal, which shortened the distance from the Black Sea Russian port of Odessa to Bombay by eight thousand nautical miles in comparison to about five thousand from London, raised hopes about direct Russian trade with India through the sea. The Russian Society for Shipping and Land Trade decided in 1871 to open a shipping line to operate on the Odessa-Bombay route. From Odessa, goods were transported to Moscow and St. Petersburg by rail. The volume of Indian cotton arriving on the Russian vessel *Nakhimov* grew from 400 puds in 1868 to 468,700 puds in 1872. Rivalry with another Russian shipping company and stoppage of subsidy by Russian government along with the obstruction created by the Russo-Turkish war in 1876-77 led to the closure of Odessa-Bombay shipping line run by the Russian Society for Shipping and Land Trade in 1877.[16] With the British monopoly over the overseas trade of India and the inability of the Russian merchant fleet to organise long-distance transport of goods, it was unrealistic to build hopes on direct trade with India through the sea.

Thus, there was again a shift towards the overland route through the south-eastern frontier of the Russian Empire. During the period of Napoleonic wars, on account of the continental blockade, the British started giving priority to the trade routes through Central Asia. Goods hitherto sent by the East India Company to England and from there exported to other European countries including Russia were now brought to Orenburg from Eastern Iran and Northern India through Central Asia. G.F. Gens was an ardent advocate of direct Russian trade with India through the overland Central Asian route culminating at Orenburg.[17] Gens gave great attention to the observation made by traders and travellers who had been to India. He cited the information provided by Tatar traveller Gabidulla Amirov who returned to Orenburg after an extensive tour of India in 1805 and died there a few years later. Gabidulla Amirov wrote about the safe and convenient trade route from Orenburg to Calcutta through Bukhara and Herat. From Orenburg to Bukhara and from there to Herat, Amirov noted the cheap cost of transport by Turkmen caravans. He praised the dependability of the Turkmens and observed that the road from Herat to Calcutta was the safest. Amirov noted that one could go to Calcutta on camels, donkeys, horses or even on carts. "They like the bright Russian goods in Jaipur", wrote Amirov who also noted the availability of Central Asian and Russian goods at the town of Hyderabad in Sind.[18]

Gens also gave great attention to the travelogue of Georgian nobleman Rafail Danibegov's travel to India translated into Russian from Georgian in 1815. Danibegov made his third journey to India in 1822–27. Gens took particular interest in the route of Danibegov's third journey. The Georgian traveller proceeded through the Caspian Sea from Astrakhan to Mazandaran and from there to Tehran, Ispahan, Shiraz and Busher on land and to Bombay on ship. From Bombay, Danibegov travelled to Lahore overland and reached Bukhara through Kashmir and Kabul, finally arriving in Orenburg in 1827. The interesting thing about Danibegov's journeys to India noted by Gens was the different routes taken by him. In 1807 and 1811 he returned from Kashmir to Semipalatinsk through Kashgar and Yarkand. Rafail Danibegov brought with him to St. Petersburg from India goods of considerable value. He was received by foreign minister N.P. Rumyantsev who sent him again in 1828 to Western China and Kashmir for trade purposes along with Madatov and Shargilov. Madatov was received by the ruler of Kashmir who allowed him to carry 20 puds of special wool forbidden for foreign trade. He also brought with him to Semipalatinsk 250 Kashmiri shawls.[19]

The import of Indian yarn and cotton to Russia through Central Asia, however, remained only an unachieved objective. The major trade items imported from India consisted of costly luxury goods like Kashmiri shawls and gold brocades beside indigo and spices. The journey of Rafail Danibegov and Madatov made Semipalatinsk begin to actively participate in this trade. N. Strakhov prepared an interesting manuscript on trade of Russia with Central Asia and India, which looked forward to the realisation of the dream of Peter-I of bringing goods to St. Petersburg through waterways linking the Volga and Don rivers by canal and diverting the Amu and the Syr Darya to the Caspian Sea to facilitate movement of goods in large bulk and reduce the cost of transport. In 1820 the Russian government sent Rafail Danibegov on a diplomatic mission and could not reach Lahore on account of the death of the Russian envoy on his way to India.[20]

In 1820, the Foreign Ministry of Russia despatched a mission to Bukhara headed by its official Negri with Eversman and Meiendorf as other members. The report of Meiendorf on Bukhara and Russia's trade relations with Central Asia and India is of considerable interest. Meiendorf wrote about a rise in trade of Russia with Bukhara on account of growing demand for cotton cloth and Kashmiri shawl.[21] He collected information about the production of Kashmiri shawls. In 1825-26, Russia imported shawls worth 2 million roubles from Kashmir and Turkey. The one-sided trade item of Kashmiri shawls was causing resentment among Russian trading circles, which wanted a change in the pattern of their trade with India. Efforts were made in the Voronezh province by a Russian woman entrepreneur V.A. Yelisyeva to manufacture shawls similar to those from Kashmir.[22] A diversified trade pattern with India was becoming increasingly difficult to achieve because of the elimination of Indian handicraft industries by the British colonial rule. The country which was famous for its high quality textile goods itself became an importer of British cloth.

A change occurred in Russian view of the importance of Central Asia as a flourishing route for overland trade with India against the backdrop of declining prospects of this trade as a result of the British colonial domination by the middle of the nineteenth century. The big trading industrial bourgeoise of Russia and the Russian government now looked to Central Asia as a potential market for its industrial goods and a prospective source of raw material supplies for its textile industry. Meiendorf wrote about purchase of gold and silver coins by Indian merchants in Bukhara. The money received after the sale of these coins was used for lending purposes.[23] The British colonialists by gradually monopolising wholesale internal and external trade of India drove out of business the big Indian merchants who now took to money-lending activities on a large scale both inside India and in the adjacent territory of Central Asia. The British took into their hands the sale of gold and precious stones and diamonds, which were in demand in Russia. The demand for shawls from Kashmir and golden brocade also fell because of their local production in Russia. The persisting demand for Indian indigo and spices was largely met by supplies through the sea route brought by the British firms.

Even then the importance of overland Central Asian trade route for direct trade with India without British brokerage was not completely overlooked in Russia. In this respect, the intimate link between geo-culture and geo-economics served the Indo-Russian trade in good stead. Indian traders engaged in trade with Central Asia were not deterred by frequent closure of the route through

Afghanistan and Iran on account of internal conflicts and wars of succession. Discarding the Afghanistan route, they switched over to transit through Persia before settling down in favour of the Bombay-Batumi sea route and thence by rail to the Caspian and across the Caspian to Krasnovodsk. This sea and rail route became popular because of reduced transport cost and tariff restrictions on goods imported through Bukhara. The drawing closer of the Indian and Central Asian peoples due to millennia-old cultural bonds forged by their inclusion in a common geo-cultural complex imparted strength to them for overcoming the political barriers.

Nevertheless, it will be improper to exaggerate the significance of the geo-cultural ties among India, Central Asia and Russia, which though imparting a tenacity to demand for certain types of traditional goods, could not completely counteract the political barriers created by British and Tsarist colonialism. If the near monopoly of the British over Indian trade and destruction of Indian handicrafts and manufacturing inhibited the development of trade between India, Central Asia and Russia, the restrictions imposed by the Tsarist administration on Indian trade through Bukhara also adversely affected the growth of economic ties between them. The project submitted in 1871 by S.I. Baranovsky, a Russian engineer, for construction of railway line from Orenburg to Peshawar and its later variant of Indo-Volga Railway Line was turned down by the Tsarist authorities fearing penetration of British goods into Central Asia. In 1873 a similar proposal by F. Lesseps for financing construction of a railway line joining Orenburg with Samarkand and Peshawar as an extension of a line from Lisbon to Orenburg was also rejected by Tsar Alexander-II. It was felt that the West European countries would gain more than Russia by the operation of this railway line.[24]

One-and-a-quarter century later the prospects for implementation of such a project have become a possibility, thanks to the forging of strategic partnership between India and Russia to which the growing coincidence of their long-term national interests in the Central Asian region and the urgency for the latter to overcome its landlocked character have contributed in no small measure. The growing trend towards international economic cooperation in the post-Cold War period has further increased the chances of a free flow of agreement between India and Turkmenistan on a trade and transit route through construction of a rail link between Sarakhs and Meshed, thus linking the Turkmen capital Ashgabat with the Persian Gulf port of Bandar Abbas and this was a new milestone in the development of Indo-Central Asian relations. The operation of this route in 1996 provided Turkmenistan and other Central Asian Republics a historic opportunity to gain access to the sea thereby ending their landlocked status. The construction of the missing rail link between Meshed in Iran with

Sarakhs on the Turkmenistan border reduced the distance from the Turkmen capital to Bandar Abbas by 700 kilometres in comparison with the older rail route through Tehran. In 1997, a tripartite pact on transit was signed in Tehran between India, Iran and Turkmenistan. This pact ushered in an era of what may be called the 'New Silk Route'.

During his visit to India in 1999, the Russian Deputy Prime Minister Victor Khrestenko stated that Russia, Turkmenistan, Iran, Oman, India and Sri Lanka were currently working on a project to establish a North-South Transport Corridor by setting up a rail link between them. Work on construction of a 250-kilometre long rail line linking Bekdash on the Korobogozgol Bay on the Caspian Sea in Turkmenistan to Yeralievo in Kazakhstan is being currently planned. From Yeralievo to Russia , the railway line is already functional. Much work, however, needs to be done to further improve the efficiency and management of the existing transport network through Iran and Turkmenistan. The regular maintenance of the existing infrastructure including container terminals on account of their under-utilisation remains a problem. Iran's unwillingness to allow transit of containers carrying spirits and alcohol and meat of certain animals and meat of animals not slaughtered in the Islamic way has also created problem for fuller utilisation of this route. Complaints of delay in getting through the customs clearance and return of containers are often heard from businessmen using this route. Indian companies have not yet been allowed to open their offices in Iran and Turkmenistan and ply the Indian registered vehicles on this route. India has yet another option for reaching Central Asia through an overland route besides the already operational Bandar Abbas sea and rail-road route through Iran and the still problematic route through Afghanistan. New Delhi could explore the possibility of reaching an agreement with Beijing for use of its road to Kyrgyzstan through Xinjiang province. India can use this road by constructing a small link road in Ladakh joining the Tibet-Xinjiang road passing through the disputed Aksai Chin territory. Ladakh is already linked with the other Indian state of Himachal Pradesh. The Central Asian Republics can gain access to the Indian sea port of Kandla in Gujarat through this overland route through Xinjiang and Ladakh.

NOTES AND REFERENCES

1. Works of V.A. Ranov, M.N. Pottier *et al.*, cited by B.A. Sitvinskii in N.A. Khalfin and P.M. Shastitko (eds.), *Rossiya I Indiya*, Moscow, 1986, pp. 10-12.
2. G. Bongard Levin and A. Vigasin, *The Image of India*, Moscow, 1984, pp. 45-46.
3. *Ibid.*, p. 24
4. *Ibid.*
5. *Ibid.*

6. See, K.A. Antonova's contribution based on material provided by I.G. Nizamutdinov in N.A. Khalfin and P.M. Shastitko (eds.), *Rossiya I Indiya*, Moscow, 1986, pp. 42-43.
7. M. Iu. Iuldashev, K. Istovii Torgovykh I Posolskikh Sviazee Srednei Azii c Rossiei v. XVI–XVII v., Tashkent, 1964, p. 75.
8. G. Bongard Levin and A. Vigasin, *op. cit.*, p. 32.
9. *Ibid.*, p. 35.
10. *Ibid.*, p. 38
11. Marx and Engels, *Works*, Vol. 22, p. 45 (in Russian).
12. Bimal Prasad, *The Origins of Indian Foreign Policy*, Calcutta, 1960, pp. 37-39.
13. Report of the Seventh and Eighth Sessions of the Indian National Congress, pp. 28-36.
14. N.A. Khalfin and P.M. Shastitki, *Rossiya I Indiya*, Moscow, 1986.
15. *Ibid.*
16. N.A. Khalfin and P.M. Shastitko, *op. cit.*, 1986, pp. 173-78.
17. GAOO, F. 166, 'G.F. Gens, Predsedatel Orenburgskoi Pogranichonoi Komissie'; also Ye. Ya. Liusternik, Russko-Indiiskie, ekonomi-cheskie, nauchney I Kulturnye sviazi v XIX v., Moscow 1996, pp. 7-11, 49, 55-58, 61.
18. Ye. Ya. Liusternik, *op. cit.* (appendix); also N.A. Khalfin, Stranstovovaniya Gabaidully Amirova po Indii, Zvezda Vostoka, Tashkent, 1956, No. 7.
19. N.A. Khalfin and P.M. Shastitko (eds.), *op. cit.*, p. 101.
20. P.M. Shastitko, 'Missiya Mekhti Rafailova K. Ranjit Singhu', Sovetskoe Vostokovedenie, 1957, No. 4, pp. 129-30.
21. N.A. Khalfin and P.M. Shastitko, *op. cit.*, p. 104.
22. *Ibid.*, p. 105.
23. *Ibid.*, p. 107.
24. Izvestia Imp. Russkogo Geograficheskogo Obshchestvo, T.X, 1874, No. 4, pp. 149-70; also AVPR. Glavny Arkhiv, 1-9, 1873-1875, d.5, 1. 15, 16.

17

The Emirate of Bukhara and Its Relations with India and Russia of Nineteenth Century

Iqtidar Husain Siddiqui

The countries of Central Asia and India appear to have had close cultural and trade relations since ancient times. These relations became closer during medieval times because the founders of the Delhi Sultanate and the Mughal Empire in the thirteenth and sixteenth centuries respectively hailed from Central Asian lands. Along with the conquerors and the founders of the ruling dynasties came the scholars, poets, scientists, and Sufi saints. Religious influences spreading from one direction to the other set in motion a process of reciprocal cultural enrichment. There was also unhindered overland trade carried on by merchant caravans. Its progress served as a catalyst of change. The foreign merchandise introduced new crafts as well as helped the modification of indigenous ones; the information of important developments and rise of new trends in different countries visited by the merchants found its way with them. However, the decline and break up of the Mughal Empire during the latter half of the eighteenth century disrupted relations between India and Central Asian kingdoms, including the Emirate of Bukhara. Only a few regional rulers, such as Najib ud-Daula in the north and Nizam of Hyderabad Deccan in south India, maintained trade and cultural relations with the rulers of Transoxiana. This chapter seeks to discuss briefly first the emergence of the Mangit ruling dynasty under Shah Murad and then the socio-economic conditions in the Emirate of Bukhara as well as its relations with India and Russia during the nineteenth century.

With the establishment of the Mangit dynasty of Shah Murad, the son of the Ataliq (regent) Daniyal in Bukhara (reigned 1785–1789-90), a fairly stable order was established. Shah Murad, having ascended the throne, changed the *Khanate* of Bukhara into Emirate through the centralisation of state. He assumed the title of Amir while his son and immediate successor Mir Haider Khan was called Amir ul-Muminin. The latter's title implied that the ruler considered himself the leader of all Muslims and had nothing to do with the early tribal tradition. His father, Shah Murad had already reduced the Uzbek tribal chiefs to subservience to the state. A central army was established and urban support sought against the tribal chiefs. A bureaucratic apparatus was set up in place of the chiefs. The new bureaucracy was composed of the non-Uzbek Turkomans, Tajiks and even slaves, all tied to the monarchs by loyalty. They were posted on key positions in the capital and the provinces. Efforts were also made for the extension of cultivation through the construction of new irrigation canals. The friendly policy adopted by Shah Murad towards the foreign merchants gave boost to trade and commerce. The minting of a gold coin, named *tilla,* reintroduced after a long time does point to the economic development that had followed the dynastic change.[1]

Mention made by the contemporary Indian traveller, Hafiz Muhammad Fazil Khan, of the foreign merchants in Bukhara provides us with insight into trade relations between Bukhara and the neighbouring countries, Afghanistan, India, Russia and China. Besides the merchants from foreign countries, the merchants of Bukhara also moved in caravans with their merchandise and returned loaded with foreign products.[2] Among the exports from India, sugar, indigo, cotton cloth and shawls of Kashmir were in great demand. Besides European products in general and English goods in particular, these were also supplied from India to Bukhara.[3] The trade in Kashmir shawls was quite profitable. Regarding its popularity in Russia, Mohan Lal Kashmiri states:

> Kabul supplies Bukhara with valuable shawls of Kashmir ... Mulla Rahim Shah, a respectable merchant, bought Kashmiri shawls for 17,000 rupees, and with them from Bukhara he made forty-seven marches to Orenburg, and from thence, after eleven days, he arrived at the celebrated market of Makra in Russia. When he was acquainted with the rates of merchandise, he hurried down to Moscow with loads of shawls, where he realised 34,000 rupees besides paying the transit duty, amounting to 200 rupees, which is taken in Russia as a duty upon a single piece of shawl, whether it values Rs. 100 or Rs. 1000.[4]

As regards India, it still imported war horses from Central Asia. According to Hafiz Muhammad Fazil Khan, the price of a war horse in the *bazaar* of Bukhara ranged between rupees one hundred thirty and nine hundred. The sale of horses in Bukhara was held on Monday and Friday every week. He writes:

> On Mondays and Fridays the horses are brought near the gate of Imam outside the city walls. There are two types of famous horses, one called

> Quralghi (also known Uzbeki) and the second Turkoman horse. The former is of middle height, well-built and it fetches from seven to twenty *tilas* (gold coins) or even forty *tilas*. The Turkoman horse is of a large height, attractive and swift-moving. Its price ranges between twenty and hundred *tilas*. Besides the supply of horses, precious stones, such as munga and turquoise, silk fabric, fur and musk bladders were also imported from the Emirate of Bukhara to India.[5]

Like their countepart in India, the people of the Emirate of Bukhara also appear to have got frozen in their medieval cultural moorings. They were not able to meet the challenge of time, in spite of their encounter with Russia. No doubt, Shah Murad and his successors succeeded in centralising state-power; the state apparatus was modelled by them on the traditional medieval pattern. Unaware of the important changes that had taken place in war technology in Europe, including Russia, the Bukhara army still fought with medieval weapons. Hafiz Fazil Khan from India who visited Bukhara in the beginning of the nineteenth century could not find any difference between the political system of an Indian princely state and the Emirate of Bukhara.

As a religious-minded Muslim, he rather seems to have been impressed by the Bukharan society, which he calls an ideal one. Describing the peace, communal harmony and the judicial system under Mir Haider (reigned AD 1800-1826), he states that justice was administered impartially; that the legal system based on *Sharia* (the Islamic canon law) made no discrimination against anyone on account of birth or creed.

All were equal in the eyes of law. Mir Haider, the king strictly enforced the *Sharia's* law and he himself acted as the chief justice of his kingdom. He allowed the collection of taxes permitted by the *Sharia*, the innumerous non-Islamic taxes were abolished. Thus the people were relieved of the heavy burden of taxes, not allowed by the *Sharia*. He also noticed the diaspora of Indian merchants in Bukhara. According to him, the Jews and the Hindu merchants enjoyed full religious freedom. He writes:

> the *Jaziya* (poll-tax) is collected from the Jews and Hindus in accordance with the canon law. It is levied from one *tanka* (rupee) to four *tankas* on individuals in accordance with their capacity of payment. The Shikarpuri Hindus go to Bukhara in connection with their trade, some stay there for six months, while others spend the whole year and then return to Shikarpur via Kabul after they had done their business. No Hindu owns a house in Bukhara. The Jews own one thousand houses in their locality near the gate of Salah Khana (Magazine). They are engaged in the trade of silk, the profession of dyer, carpentry, slaughtering of animals and selling meat.[6]

Alexander Burnes and Mohan Lal supplement the information about the Jews. The former adds that the Jews "are a race remarkably handsome: they are four thousand and had migrated from Mashad (Iran) and generally worked as dyers."[7] Mohan Lal says: "I passed through the famous street of the Jews. The eyes of women are alluring and their persons enticing, though everyone looked half Scotish. No fewer than 3,000 Jews are said to inhabit Bukhara."[8]

It was also in the beginning of the nineteenth century that the competition began between Russia and Britain over the establishment of political hegemony in Central Asia. After the establishment of their supremacy in India, the British rulers became obsessed with the fear of Tsar's invasion of their Indian Empire through Central Asia and the English officers of the East India Company began to send their agents to Afghanistan for obtaining information on the life and condition in those regions. Their aim was to establish friendly relations with the rulers of Afghanistan and Central Asia or conquer them, in case diplomacy was not successful. In AD 1811, Saiyid Izat Ullah Khan and Hafiz Muhammad Fazil Khan were sent by Charles Harper and Charles Metcalf to Bukhara.[9] But these envoys could not gain any success in their mission. On their arrival in Peshawar, Bahadur Khan, the Afghan governor arrested Saiyid Izat Ullah Khan and sent him to the fort of Attuck. Muhammad Fazil Khan, who did not disclose his identity, proceeded to Bukhara. In Bukhara he visited the ruler Mir Haider Khan and presented the bag and petition that he had carried. After forty days he was asked to leave Bukhara. He had to return empty handed.[10] Later, Alexander Burnes went to Bukhara in 1832 and returned without any success.

In fact, England sought the friendship of the ruler of Bukhara in order to use his kingdom as a buffer between India and the Tsar's Empire. At this time, the ruler of Bukhara, Nasr Ullah Khan, did not trust the Christian rulers and was opposed to developing friendship with anyone of them. At times, the English envoys excited his anger by refusing to submit to ceremonies customary at court. Colonel Stoddart was thrown into prison for this reason. In 1840, Captain Arthur Conolly visited Kokand at a time when its ruler was at war with Bukhara. Unsuccessful in Kokand, Conolly moved to the camp of Nasrullah Khan at Mehran. He was put in jail. He was executed on 17 June 1842 after the English army had been defeated in Kabul.[11]

Unlike the English rulers, the Russians were successful in their diplomacy. The Russians had disputes with the *Khanates* of Kokand and Khiva over boundaries. They cultivated friendly relations with the Amir of Bukhara until they had subdued Khiva and Kokand. In 1866, the Khan of Kokand acknowledged the overlordship of Russia and then the ground was prepared for Russia to advance as far as the Emirate of Bukhara. In 1868 the Russian army moved towards Samarkand and captured it without any difficulty.[12] The Bukharan army was no match against the Russians. It was put to route. It was totally useless on account of its lack of discipline, absence of martial qualities and the absence of modern armament. The infantry was equipped with outmoded flint-locks and matchlocks. There was also inadequate supply of artillery shells.[13] Generally, the soldiers fought with javelins. Mohan Lal observed in 1830:

> four regiments of Russian infantry might easily subdue the whole of the country, if it had not got natural obstacles: but I venture to say, it would be retained in subjugation with great difficulty, owing to the obstinacy of the people.[14]

In short, the social system in the Emirate of Bukhara and its neighbouring *Khanates* was medieval; the wind of modernism had not blown in this part of the world. Even the institution of slavery was intact. Hafiz Fazil Khan, Alexander Burnes and Mohan Lal refer to its existence. They also testify to the good treatment meted out by the master to his slave. Alexandar Burnes writes: "In circumstances of so many of them continuing in the country after they have been manumitted, seems to establish this fact (i.e., good treatment)". As regards the toiling people or daily wage-earners, our sources do not yield any details. Incidentally, lower class people receive a passing mention in the details furnished by Hafiz Fazil Khan about the dress of people. He says that the rich people put on clothes from head to foot embroidered. Even their shoes were of leather or they wore Uzbek slippers.[15] As for the Kazakh nomads, they lived in primitive conditions in their region. They reared sheep, horses and camels and lived on their milk and meat. They sold horses, camels, sheep and also earned money by rowing boats.[16]

As the Bukharan society survived with its cultural stagnation, its army failed to defend the country against the Russian invasion. In 1868, Amir Muzaffar al-Din's army was defeated and he had to acknowledge Tsar's suzerainty. The city of Samarkand and its province were annexed to the Russian Empire. Since then the Amirs of Bukhara remained the faithful allies of Russia. None of them tried to modernise his army; the last Amir, Saiyid Alam Khan (reigned: 1910–1920) was given military training in Russia, but he was fond of pleasure. He could not mend his ways even after the fall of the Tsar. The communists occupied Bukhara in 1920 and the Amir of Bukhara had to run away. He got shelter in Kabul.[17] After the abolition of the Amir's institution, Bukhara and its people were exposed to modern influence.

NOTES AND REFERENCES

1. Hafiz Muhammad Fazil Khan, *Tarikh-I-Manazil-I-Bukhara*, Persian text, edited with English translation by Iqtidar Husain Siddiqui, Khuda Bakhsh Oriental Public Library, Patna, 1993, pp. 41, 43, Eng. tr. 37, 38, 39; V.V. Barthold, *Four Studies on the History of Central Asia*, Eng. tr. by V and T. Monorsky, Leiden, 1962, 1, 66-67.
2. Alexander Burnes found the shopkeepers in Bukhara using large European urns instead of teapots for making tea. Mohan Lal Kashmiri also found the shops in Bukhara bazaar, called Ragistan full of foreign merchandise. He writes, "The shops, which succeed each other in a straight line, present a splendid sight. They are ornamented with beautiful China ware and Russian bottles". Cf. Alexander Burnes, *Travels into*

Bhukhara, OUP, Karachi, 1973, Vol. I, p. 277; Mohan Lal Kashmiri, *Travels in the Panjab, Afghanistan and Turkestan*, Calcutta reprint, 1977, p. 81.

3. *Tarikh-I-Manazil-I-Bukhara*, pp. 41 (text), p. 37 (Eng. tr.).
4. Mohan Lal, *op. cit.*, p. 28.
5. *Tarikh-I-Manazil-I-Bukhara*, p. 25 (text), Eng. tr. 26.
6. *Tarikh-I-Manazil-I-Bukhara*, p. 28-29. Eng. tr. Fazil Khan is corroborated by Mohan Lal about the nature of State. He writes: 'King is the head and in his name all business managed. Notwithstanding, his authority is limited by the law of Muhammad called shariat', Cf. Mohan Lal, p. 77.
7. Alexander Burns, pp. 274-75.
8. Mohan Lal, pp. 75-76.
9. *Tarikh-I-Manazil-I-Bukhara*, p. 1 (text), 11 (Eng. tr.).
10. *Ibid.*, p. 47.
11. Arminius Vambery, *History of Bukhara*, Karachi reprint, 1990, pp. 379, 381-85.
12. *Ibid.*, p. 410.
13. Seynour Becker, *Russian Protectorates in Central Asia, Bukhara and Khiva, 1865-1924*, USA, 1868, pp. 117.
14. Mohan Lal, p. 82.
15. *Tarikh-I-Manazil-I-Bukhara*, p. 36-37 (text).
16. *Ibid.*, p. 24.
17. Cf. *Encyclopaedia of Islam* (New Edition, Leiden, 1991), Vol. VI, pp. 418b-419a.

18
Kashmir and Russian Turkestan during the Nineteenth Century

K. Warikoo

Kashmir has played an important role in India's relations with Central Asia on account of its geographical proximity and cultural affinity with that region, since ancient times. Due to its linkage with the Silk Route, Kashmir and particularly its frontier territories of Ladakh, Baltistan, Gilgit, and Hunza became a major gateway in the Indo-Central Asian exchange of men, materials, and ideas. These contacts, however, received a setback in the wake of the Anglo-Russian colonial rivalry during the nineteenth century, as movement between British India and Russian parts of Central Asia was subject to several inhibiting influences. The Russians were expanding southwards in Central Asia till they consolidated their position with the establishment of Russian Governorate General of Turkestan in 1867 with headquarters at Tashkent. On their part, the British used Kashmir and its frontier territories of Ladakh, Baltistan, Gilgit, Hunza, Nagar, Yasin, Chilas, Puniyal, Chitral, and Ishkoman as frontier listening posts to monitor the Russian movements in Central Asia. Notwithstanding the restrictions imposed by two rival powers on mutual exchanges between Central Asia and British India, contacts between Kashmir and Russian Turkestan continued to be both of general and commercial nature, though much less in scale. However, this period is marked by important visits by intelligence agents, political emissaries and even official missions from Russian Central Asia to Kashmir and vice versa, which is the focus of this study. This not only constituted an extension of the 'Great Game' to Kashmir frontiers, but even influenced the formulation of British policy towards Kashmir and its frontier dependencies during this period.

In modern times, the earliest Russian interest in Kashmir affairs can be traced back to the travels of numerous Russian and Central Asian travellers like Yefremov, Danibegov, and Abdul Karim, all of whom visited Kashmir in the late eighteenth and early nineteenth centuries.[1] Filip Yefremov travelled via Bukhara-Kokand-Yarkand-Leh-Srinagar-Jammu route to the Indian mainland (around AD 1774-75) and returned to Russian Empire on November 5, 1782.[2] Yefremov can safely be described as a pioneer in bringing to notice of the then Tsarist Russian government the state of affairs in Ladakh, Kashmir, and Jammu during the later years of the Afghan rule. Refail Danibegov of Georgia made his return journey to Russia overland from Calcutta via Murshidabad, Patna, Garhwal, Delhi, Kashmir, Ladakh, Yarkand, Aksu, Turfan, Semipalatinsk, Omsk, Makaria (Novgorod) and Moscow (in around AD 1795-96). His travelogue touches upon the situation in Kashmir and Ladakh, besides highlighting the rich shawl industry of Kashmir.[3] Round about the same time one Abdul Karim, resident of Bukhara, travelled through Kabul-Peshawar-Muzaffarabad-Srinagar route to Kashmir.[4] The travelogues of these three visitors shed interesting light on the political and socio-economic conditions in Kashmir during the Afghan rule. The elaborate description of shawl industry and its problems in the accounts of these foreign visitors shows the great attraction Kashmir shawls held for the people in Central Asia and Russia.

The presence of Russian and Central Asian merchants in Kashmir during the eighteenth and nineteenth centuries for purpose of shawl trade is testified by such eye-witness accounts as that of Bernier, Yefremov, Abdul Karim, Forster, Moorcroft and other sources. In fact, the shawl goods of Kashmir and the *pashm* (fine wool) yielding goats of Ladakh stimulated the Russian interest in developing trade with adjacent countries in Asia, which was particularly intensified in the wake of enforcement of the continental blockade by Napoleon in Europe. Tsarist Russia sent several missions to the *Khanates* of Bukhara and Kokand to secure their consent in the free movement of Russo-Chinese trading caravans from Russia to Kashgar via Bukhara and Kokand and vice versa.[5] Once this was achieved, Russia could and did think of extending her commercial relations with Ladakh, Kashmir, and Punjab.

AGHA MEHDI'S MISSIONS TO LADAKH

Agha Mehdi Rafailov who had established himself as a shawl trader, was instrumental in arousing Russian interest in Kashmir and its shawl goods. According to a Russian scholar, O.F. Solovyev, the then Russian Foreign Minister, Rumantsev had commissioned in 1808 Mehdi Rafailov (the same Agha Mehdi as mentioned by Moorcroft), Zakhar Shargilov of Tajlis and one Armenian, Egor Artemov to ascertain the trade route between Russia and India.[6] Apparently, Russia sought to prepare the ground for opening its commerce with Ladakh and Kashmir via Kokand, Kashgar, and Yarkand. According to Moorcroft, Agha Mehdi was son of a Jew settled in Kashmir who had lost his parents at an early age. He started his career early in life as a mere peddler and rose to be one of the leading shawl traders well established in Russia and was operating from Kabul.[7] After embracing Christianity, his access to the ruling circles in St. Petersburgh was facilitated.[8] Agha Mehdi is reported to have been duly honoured by the Tsar Alexander-I with presents of gold chain and a medal for his successful mission to Ladakh.[9] He was awarded the title of Counsellor of Commerce by a decree of a Senate on 27 January 1817 and was elevated later as *Nadvornyy Sovetnik* (Court Counsellor) with a civil rank of seventh class.

Soon after the Sikhs acquired their control over Kashmir in 1819, Russia decided to send Agha Mehdi Rafailov in January 1820 on yet another mission to Ladakh and Punjab via Chinese Turkestan. Under orders of the Russian Emperor, Agha Mehdi was to deliver friendly communications to the Raja of Ladakh and Maharaja Ranjit Singh at Lahore. That this mission was carried out after due preparations, is borne out by the following information left to us by Moorcroft who was at that time in Ladakh.[10]

(a) Agha Mehdi had been tutored at St. Petersburg for about a year by a trained British artist in the use of various dyes for applying to shawl goods.
(b) He was provided with several packages of dyes such as cochineal, indigo wood, berbery root and other mordants like acetile of lead, aluminic potash, soda lime, etc. for use in Kashmir shawl-making.
(c) He was carrying several emeralds and rubies meant as presents for the chiefs of Ladakh and Punjab, besides gold ducats in considerable quantities.
(d) He was escorted across the Kyrgyz territory to the borders of Chinese Turkestan by a troop of Russian cavalry.

Agha Mehdi carried letters from the then Foreign Minister of Russia, Nesselrode to the Raja of Ladakh and Maharaja Ranjit Singh of Punjab. As per the Russian sources, Nesselrode had signed the letters on January 17, 1820.[11] Written in Russian language and transcribed in golden ink, the letter introduced Agha Mehdi, as one of the 'counsellors of the State of Russia.'[12] Nesselrode conveyed the Russian Emperor's desire to open the 'gates of friendly intercourse' and to clear "the road to traffic between the merchants of Russia and Punjab from all impediments."[13] Ranjit Singh was further assured that any of his subjects whether merchants or travellers would receive "the most friendly manner and a consideration exactly proportionate to their rank and station" on their visit to Russia.[14] But Agha Mehdi was not destined to fulfil his mission as he died near the Karakorum Pass. Though Soviet scholars attribute his death to illness,[15] it can more probably be assigned to treason rather than natural circumstances. Some of his fellow travellers might have been tempted to appropriate the treasure (charged to Agha Mehdi in the form of gold ducats, emeralds, etc.). That the noted Hungarian orientalist and traveller, Alexander Csoma de Koros informed one Englishmen, W. Murray, that the Russian Ambassador was murdered by his followers at a pass several days' journey from Leh and his property plundered,[16] further substantiates this view. Besides, Agha Mehdi's companion Mohammad Zahoor was seen by Moorcroft selling off the dyes, emeralds and rubies, which he later invested in the purchase of shawls for resale in Bukhara.[17] It becomes obvious that Agha Mehdi Rafailov was commissioned by Russia to explore the possibility of establishing a friendly political and regular commercial intercourse with Ladakh, Kashmir and Punjab via Central Asia and Chinese Turkestan.

KOKAND ENVOYS VISIT LADAKH AND KASHMIR (1837, 1854)

In a bid to meet the growing Russian threat to the Central Asian *Khanate* of Kokand, the Khan of Kokand despatched his emissaries to India for securing British support. Since the Kashgar-Yarkand-Leh route was practically free from robbers, Central Asians preferred it to the troublesome Kabul route for coming to India. It was in 1837 that an envoy from Kokand arrived at Ladakh. He had been deputed by the Khan of Kokand to present a pair of rubies and horses to the Governor-General of India with a view to establishing friendly relations with the British government.[18] It was a strange coincidence that at about the same time one Haji Mohammad Ali of Yarkand had been maltreated by Raja Gulab Singh's representative at Leh for his friendly conversations with Vigne, a British traveller.[19] The Dogra Chief was keen to prevent the friendly interaction of the British travellers with any visitors from the neighbouring Central Asian *Khanates*. Alarmed at the treatment meted out to the Yarkandi visitor, the Kokand envoy sold off his property in Leh and burnt the letter charged to his custody, returning to Kokand through Yarkand and Kashgar without attaining his objective.[20]

Finding himself unable to resist the Russian occupation of Ak Masjid (in 1853), the ruler of Kokand Khuda Yar Khan, made a renewed attempt to secure British assistance for safeguarding the remaining portion of his *Khanate*. It was in August 1854 that an accredited envoy from Kokand, namely, Shahzada Sultan Mohammad Khan arrived at Peshawar through Oxus-Badakshan-Zebak-Chitral route, bearing letters for the Governor-General of India and the Commissioner of Peshawar Division, H.B. Edwards.[21] The Kokand ruler requested the British Indian government to "loan the services of some officers for training his undisciplined forces to withstand any further Russian onslaught".[22] The Kokandi envoy returned to Kokand via Kashmir, Yarkand, and Kashgar. Shehzada's visit to Kashmir while on his way to Kokand enabled Maharaja Gulab Singh of Kashmir to establish direct rapport with the Kokandi authorities and also to make a show of his strength before his Central Asian guest. When Shehzada Sultan Mohammad Khan arrived at Srinagar on 10 September 1855, he was received personally by the Kashmir ruler and also presented a purse of five hundred rupees.[23] Gulab Singh was keen to extend his direct friendly relations with the neighbouring Central Asian *Khanates*. He wished to restrict the British activity in his frontier territories in order to maintain his high political stock in Central Asia and to prevent its erosion in the face of British paramountcy in India.

KASHMIR DURBAR'S EMISSARIES IN RUSSIAN TURKESTAN

After the mid-nineteenth century when the Anglo-Russian rivalry gained its intensity, Britain became restive to use Kashmir as a listening post for monitoring the Russian movements in Central Asia. With this end in view, sustained pressure was brought upon Maharaja Gulab Singh and his successor Ranbir Singh to secure a foothold in this frontier outpost. Whereas the British were keen upon acquiring firmer control over the conduct of domestic and external politics of the State, the Dogra rulers were not prepared to allow any erosion of their authority over their subjects or to see their prestige wane in the eyes of their Central Asian neighbours. Yet the Dogras played safe and lent armed assistance to the British Indian government during the second Anglo-Sikh war and the 1857 uprising. At the same time, both Gulab Singh and his successor Ranbir Singh permitted such staunch anti-British fighters as Bhai Maharaj and Kukas to operate covertly from their territory. The Dogra strategy was focussed on the aim of keeping the British at an arm's length from Kashmir. But the British could not bear that Kashmir being their subsidiary ally, should prove to be a bottleneck in their policy of extending commercial and, thereby, political influence in Central Asia. They mounted pressure on Maharaja Ranbir Singh to allow free movement of Indian trade to Central Asia. Further to keep a vigil on the Central Asian developments, British officers were stationed in Kashmir. The increasing British interference in Kashmir made the Dogra rulers bitter.

When the Russians occupied Tashkent in 1865, Maharaja Ranbir Singh was the first Indian prince to send secret emissaries to convey his greetings to the Russian General Cherniaev on his success. Soviet scholar, N.A. Khalfin, on the basis of Russian archival records, has given details about this mission and also about the Russian response to Kashmir overtures. According to Khalfin, two emissaries, namely, Abdul Rahman Khan and Sarfaraz Khan ibn Sikandar Khan arrived in Tashkent on November 24, 1865.[24] They came via Peshawar, Balkh, and Bukhara. The Kashmir emissaries were accorded a kind reception by the Russian Governor of Turkestan Oblast, Major General M.G. Cherniaev.[25] Drawing the Russain attention to the general discontent with the British rule, the Kashmir emissaries told Cherniaev that the Maharaja had commissioned them to convey his declaration of friendship and also to explore the prospects of developing Russo-Kashmir relations.[26] They also informed Cherniaev about the intention of the Kashmir ruler to send another mission to Russia via Leh-Yarkand-

Farghana route.[27] Cherniaev promptly reported the arrival of Kashmir emissaries to his superior, N.A. Kryzhanovsky, the Governor-General in Orenburg.[28] On his part, Kryzhanovsky instructed Cherniaev to obtain information about the political situation and cautioned him not to make any commitment before the envoys. While transmitting the news of the arrival of a Kashmiri mission at Tashkent to the Russian Foreign Minister, A.M. Gorchakov on December 30, 1865, Kryzhanovsky observed that it would not be in the Russian interests to cold-shoulder any request for help from such people as could prove useful later especially for trade purposes.[29] But his remark that,

> a positive promise of aid with no means to proffer it to the populations of countries cut off from us by the Himalayas would be pointless and merely injure Russia's prestige in Central Asian eyes,[30]

was an open admission of the Russian inability to go beyond the Himalayas. Besides, Kryzhanovsky's advice to Cherniaev not to make any hostile remarks against the British in his talks with the Kashmir envoys,[31] indicated the Russian desire to be inoffensive to the British. Not wishing to jeopardise the Anglo-Russian relations, Kryzhanovsky proposed to reply to the Kashmir envoys or similar other missions that might arrive in further in the following terms:

> The Emperor of all the Russia is on terms of complete amity with the Queen of England, and so long as no hostile gesture is made by the British Government, it is not proposed to move out troops to the banks of the Amu Darya.[32]

That both the Russian Emperor and his Foreign Office approved the proposals made by the Governor-General of Orenburg,[33] showed that Russia did not want to pick up any trouble with the British. But for treating the Kashmir emissaries well and allowing them to stay at Tashkent for another six months (though they were put under surveillance), the Russian authorities in Central Asia promised nothing in return[34] for Maharaja's offer of friendship. On June 23, 1866, the new Governor-General of Turkestan Oblast, D.I. Romanovsky reported to his superiors that he had no reason to suspect the genuine desire of the Kashmir emissaries to be the first of the inhabitants of India to congratulate Russia on her military successes.[35] They had also assured the Governor at Tashkent that trade could easily be developed between Kashmir and Tashkent via Kokand since the intervening territory of Kashgaria was on friendly terms with the Kashmir ruler. The Kashmir envoys left Tashkent around June 1866 for their return journey to Kashmir.[36] They were fairly successful in impressing the Russian authorities in Central Asia about Maharaja Ranbir Singh's sincere intention to develop Kashmir's cordial relations with Russia, which in their view would have facilitated direct overland trade between Kashmir and Central Asia.[37]

One year later, Maharaja of Kashmir sent his trusted agent Mehta Sher Singh to Bukhara, Samarkand, Tashkent, and Kokand. The British Indian authorities were alerted by Cayley, the British Officer on Special Duty, about the arrival of Sher Singh, an agent of the Majaraja at Leh in October 1867 and his departure for Jammu in a secret manner.[38] Though Cayley's information was correct, his presumption that Sher Singh acted as Maharaja Ranbir Singh's emissary to the Russian Governor at Khodjent,[39] is not borne out by fact. Mehta Sher Singh was actually deputed by the Kashmir ruler at the behest of British Indian government to Russia and Central Asia for obtaining political intelligence.

Mehta Sher Singh's report of his travels in Central Asia,[40] which he submitted to Maharaja Ranbir Singh, throws interesting light on the nature of Ranbir Singh's policy towards Central Asia. The Kashmir ruler had sent Sher Singh on a secret fact-finding mission to Central Asia. The Kashmir agent had left Kashmir on July 28, 1866 to travel through Muzaffarabad, Hazara, Attock, Peshawar, Kabul, Balkh, Bukhara, Samarkand, Tashkent and Kokand.[41] Mehta Sher Singh who remained away from Kashmir for about sixteen months, spent about a fortnight in Bukhara during November-December 1866 and more than a month (March-April 1867) in Tashkent.[42] He returned to Kashmir on October 24, 1867.[43] In his report, Sher Singh reproduced the contents of a letter addressed by the British Indian authorities to the Maharaja of Kashmir, whereunder the latter was asked to collect detailed information about the Russian movement in Central Asia, the strength of Russian troops, conditions of Kokandi defences, arms, ammunition and fortification on the two sides, relations between the rulers of Kokand and Bukhara, etc.[44] The Maharaja was impressed upon to get the said intelligence collected through "a most trusted person who should take extraordinary care in verifying the reports obtained."[45] That explains as to why Sher Singh avoided any contact with the Russian officials during his travels within Russian parts of Central Asia. Sher Singh's report gave a detailed account of the Russian troops, their arms, positions and fortification.

A second mission from Kashmir led by one Baba Karam Prakash was despatched in October 1869 and it reached Tashkent in June 1870.[46] According to the Russian archival records, Karam Prakash was commissioned by Maharaja Ranbir Singh to ascertain whether the Governor of Russian Turkestan was the proper authority to correspond with the ruler of Kashmir and as to which route would be advisable for developing Kashmir's commercial and political relations with Russia.[47] The Maharaja also wanted to convey his desire to establish friendly ties with Russia as his relations with the British were not satisfactory. According to Khalfin, this mission failed in evoking any response from the Russian ruling circles. Though the British Indian authorities failed to keep timely track of this mission, yet they learnt about it soon after. As per records available in the National Archives of India, the Punjab government was informed by its agents which were active in Russian Central Asia gathering intelligence, about Karam Prakash's mission to Samarkand. He was reported to have presented a shawl to the Russian-Governor General on which was inscribed a Persian couplet to the effect: "Every person looks out for a big tree in order to obtain rest under its cool shade."[48]

Alarmed at the receipt of such news reports from its agents posted in Kashmir, Punjab and the neighbouring Central Asia, the Government of Punjab cautioned the Viceroy, Lord Northbrook in early 1873 about the dangers implicit in Maharaja's direct communications with the Russian authorities in Turkestan. Startling disclosures made by one Gulab Khan (a native of Rawalpindi who shifted to Katta Kurgan in June 1881), which earned him much distinction in the British ruling circles, provide specific instances of the overtures made by the Kashmir ruler to Russian authorities in Turkestan. Gulab Khan used to communicate his reports to the Punjab government from Katta Kurgan during the years 1881-84, through his trusted courtiers.[49] While reporting Karam Prakash's mission to Russian Turkestan, Gulab Khan clarified that it was preceded by another Kashmiri mission led by Sher Singh.[50] Gulab Khan also reported about the despatch of one Ganga Ram, a Brahman of Danisal (in Raisi, Jammu) to Samarkand after Karam Prakash and his stay there for a period of four years to learn Russian language.[51] Maharaja of Kashmir had employed several Hindu, Kashmiri and even Afghan news-agents who used to travel to Central Asia in the guise of mendicants or traders to collect intelligence or to carry messages for Russian authorities in Central Asia. The Kashmir agents preferred to travel via Peshawar-Kabul-Bukhara route to avoid detection at the hands of the British agents posted at Ladakh and other stations within Punjab. The reports that were received by the British from their secret agents operating in Central Asia, were also corroborated by the information provided by their agents planted within the Amir's court at Kabul. It was in 1880, that the Amir of Kabul was reported to have informed a select gathering of his nobles that "during the last five years out of eleven years he passed at Samarkand, General Kaufmann received at least four letters from the Maharaja of Kashmir sent through Hindu agents."[52]

Contemporary evidence like official diaries, intelligence reports and proceedings of the British Indian and Tsarist Russian governments available in the Indian and Russian archives all point to the fact that Maharaja Ranbir Singh of Kashmir maintained contacts with Russians in Central Asia by sending his emissaries. Recorded statements of Gulab Khan, Syed Khan, Aziz-ud-Din, Mian Rahat Shah and other British news-agents leave no doubt about the frequent trips made by Ganga Ram, Mansukh (both natives of Jammu) and also of Jas Ram and other Kuka fighters to Russian Central Asia as emissaries of the Kashmir *Durbar*. Secret diaries received from Kabul, which quoted the Afghan ruler as being a witness to the passage of such agents through his territory, further corroborate the same.

Judging from the conditions existing in India during the period of British paramountcy, Ranbir Singh's attempt to move away from the British stranglehold was daring and unique. His success in maintaining a friendly liaison with the Russians in Central Asia by means of regular exchange of emissaries thus outwitting the alert British intelligence network, speak of Ranbir Singh's acumen in diplomacy. He usually entered into oral rather than written communications with the Russians to avoid detection by and consequent involvement with the British Indian government. All these emissaries invariably took Srinagar-Muzaffarabad-Peshawar-Kabul-Central Asia route rather than the Leh-Yarkand-Kashgar-Kokand route, in order to escape detection by the British officer posted in Leh. Ranbir Singh had even established a school for the teaching of Russian language in Kashmir with a view to training his agents in that language.[53] By doing so, Ranbir Singh sought to overcome the language barrier in his free communication with the Russian authorities in Central Asia. His contacts with the Russian authorities had developed into a warm relationship. In 1877 General Kaufmann, the Russian Governor-General of Turkestan sought Maharaja Ranbir Singh's help in recovering the treasure of the dethroned chief of Kashgar, Beg Kuli Beg, who had taken refuge in Russian Turkestan.[54] It may be recalled that Beg Kuli Beg while fleeing towards Kokand after the re-occupation of Kashgaria by the Chinese in 1877, had sent his treasure (gold and silver worth 12,000 pound sterling) through his trusted servants to Kashmir, for safe custody.[55] But one of his servants had misappropriated large part of this treasure.[56] Kaufmann's successor, General Rosenbach maintained this liaison and was prompt in sending his condolences to Maharaja Pratap Singh on hearing the death of Ranbir Singh in 1885.[57] Such mutual friendly liaison between any ruling Indian prince and the Russian authorities in Central Asia was not to be seen any more after Maharaja Ranbir Singh's death.

RUSSIAN RESPONSE TO KASHMIR OVERTURES

While measuring the Russian response to the overtures made by Maharaja Ranbir Singh of Kashmir, we need to bear in mind that the Russian policy was not to get involved in the internal affairs of British India. Although Ranbir Singh's attempt to forge links with the Russians in Central Asia did not bear any political fruit, it helped in promoting the socio-economic interaction between the two regions. Russians consented to the free import of Kashmir shawls into the Russian territory, as per Faiz Buksh's report submitted to the British authorities in Punjab in 1871.[58] Russian sources also confirm that Gorchakov had consented to provide adequate protection to Kashmir merchants in Russian territories.[59] Numerous Kashmiris began to reside in Russian Central Asia, some learning Russian language and some running shops.

Russian authorities also reciprocated by sending some envoys in disguise to meet the Kashmir ruler. Pachino, an officer in the Russian Foreign Service having knowledge of Arabic, Persian, and Turki, made several attempts in

1870s to meet Maharaja Ranbir Singh of Kashmir. Each time he failed to penetrate the fence of British intelligence network and had to return without having attained his objective.[60] When Pachino repeated his visit to India and reached Lahore in 1875, he was prevented by the British authorities from crossing the border towards Kashmir.[61] They also asked the Maharaja of Kashmir to forbid Pachino from entering his territories.[62] Similarly, in mid-1872 when a high power Russian embassy headed by General Kaulbars was negotiating a treaty with Yakub Beg in Kashgar, one of its members tried to establish contact with the Kashmiri ruler through the medium of some Kashmiri traders residing in Yarkand to find out if the Indian exports to Yarkand via Kashmir included arms and ammunition. At Yarkand the said officer contacted a Kashmiri trader, Khaliq Dar, who was also a trusted agent of the Maharaja in Yarkand, and sent through him a message of friendship and alliance with the Maharaja of Kashmir.[63] In early 1873, Khaliq Dar proceeded to Kashmir and informed the Maharaja accordingly. But Ranbir Singh forwarded to the British Indian authorities the information regarding Russian interest in Kashmir, which was received from Khaliq Dar. It appears that the Kashmir ruler wanted to reaffirm his loyalty to the British, which became increasingly alarmed over the prospects of Russo-Kashmir alliance. Now the British decided to have a full-fledged permanent Residency in Kashmir, which could put check on any flirtations of the Kashmir *Durbar* with the Russians.

Kashmir's overtures to the Russians in Central Asia need to be viewed in the context of Anglo-Russian rivalry. Though Russia was not strong enough to move beyond the Oxus in the south and Pamirs in the east, yet its military successes in Central Asia had earned it a definite advantage in respect of the psychological influence created on Asian peoples. The disgruntled Indian princely rulers who were already annoyed with the increasing British interference in their domains, derived a sort of moral encouragement from the appearance of Russia close to the British Indian frontiers, which stimulated their anti-British aspirations. On their part, the Russians reciprocated Ranbir Singh's friendly sentiments, but they steered clear of any active involvement in the internal affairs of British India, which could have led them to a direct conflict with the British. The entire Tsarist administration, from the Governor-General of Orenburg to the Foreign Minister, Gorchakov, or even to the Tsar Emperor himself, was unanimous in the view that Russia should not use the opportunity provided by Kashmir ruler's friendship for making any hostile gesture towards the British. This was also due to the Russians being not sure of their capacity to offer any help to remote territories lying beyond the Himalayas.

NOTES AND REFERENCES

1. P.M. Kemp (ed.Q), *Russian Travellers to India and Persia, 1624-1798,* Delhi, 1959.
2. *Ibid.*, p. 63.
3. *Ibid.*, p. 119.
4. Charles Schefer, (ed. and tr.), *Histoire de L'Asie Centrale par Mir Abdoul Karim Boukhary,* Paris, 1876.
5. *Foreign Political*, 9 January 1824, p. 23.
6. O.F. Solov'yev, K. Voprosu obotnoshenii tsarskoy Rossiik Indii XIX nachale XX veka. *Voprosy Istorii* 1958, No. 6. pp. 96-109.
7. William Moorcroft, *Travels,* Vol. I, p. 385.
8. *Ibid.*
9. D. Kaushik, *Indian and Central Asia,* New Delhi, 1985, p. 83.
10. W. Moorcroft to Metcalfe, Government of India dated 6 May 1821, *Foreign Political,* 10 October 1823, p. 25. See also Moorcroft, *Travels*, Vol . I.
11. O.F. Solov'yev, *op. cit.*
12. Moorcroft to Metcalfe, May 6, 1821.
13. *Ibid.*
14. *Ibid.*
15. O.F. Solov'yev, *op. cit.*
16. *Foreign Political*, January 7, 1825, p. 32.
17. Moorcroft to Metcalfe, May 6, 1821.
18. *Foreign Political*, August 1, 1838, pp. 32-33.
19. *Ibid.*
20. *Ibid.*
21. *Foreign*, S.C. November 24, 1854, pp. 1-25.
22. *Ibid.*
23. *Foreign*, S.C., November 30, 1855, pp. 33-4.
24. N.A. Khalfin, *Russia's Policy in Central Asia, 1857-1868.* Translated from Russian into English by Hubert Evans, London, 1964, pp. 67-68.
25. *Ibid.*
26. *Ibid.*
27. *Ibid.*
28. *Ibid.*
29. *Ibid.*
30. *Ibid.*
31. *Ibid.*
32. *Ibid.*
33. *Ibid.*

34. *Ibid.*
35. *Ibid.*
36. *Ibid.*
37. *Ibid.*
38. *Foreign Political, A.* November 1867, pp. 64-67.
39. *Ibid.*
40. *Safarnama Mehta Sher Singh, Samvat* 1923-24 (Urdu MS, in Jammu and Kashmir archives).
41. *Ibid.*
42. *Ibid.*
43. *Ibid.*
44. *Ibid.,* folio 75-77.
45. *Ibid.,* folio 76.
46. N.A. Khalfin, *op. cit.*
47. *Ibid.*
48. *Foreign, Secret,* March 1880, p. 251.
49. *Foreign, Secret,* August 1882, pp. 349-59.
50. *Foreign, Secret,* August 1882, pp. 349-59.
51. *Ibid.*
52. *Foreign, Secret Supplement,* November 1880, pp. 127-28.
53. K. Warikoo, *Central Asia and Kashmir: A Study in the Context of Anglo-Russian Rivalry,* New Delhi, 1989, p. 39.
54. *Ibid,* p. 37.
55. *Foreign Political, A.* May 1878, pp. 256-75.
56. *Ibid.*
57. K. Warikoo, *op. cit.,* p. 38.
58. *Foreign Political, A.* December 1872, pp. 592-93.
59. U.F. Solov'yev, *op. cit.*
60. For further details on the Pachino mission, see K. Warikoo, *op. cit.,* pp. 43-45.
61. *Foreign, Secret,* May 1875, pp. 151-63.
62. *Ibid.*
63. For further details, see K. Warikoo, *op. cit.,* pp. 41-43.

19

The Anglo-Russian Setting in the Pamirs

Sneh Mahajan

A glance at the map of Central Asia shows that Afghanistan is shaped like a leaf with a stem jutting into the Pamirs in Central Asia. This part of Afghanistan is known as the Wakhan (or Vakhan) corridor. Its borders touch Pakistan, the heart of Pak-occupied Kashmir, China, and Tajikistan. This Wakhan corridor was established as a result of two agreements regarding frontiers of Afghanistan signed in 1890s – one between Sir Mortimer Durand on behalf of the Government of India and Abdur Rahman, the Amir of Afghanistan, in November 1893 and the other between London and St. Petersburg in March 1895. These agreements were made to decide on the eastern, northern and northwest boundaries of Afghanistan. These boundary lines were worked out after hard bargaining and a series of compromises among the countries involved. These had no ethnic basis. These lines, at places not even marked, are still there though in 1917 the Tsarist Empire ceased to exist and the British Indian Empire was dismantled thirty years later. Even the USSR has disintegrated. It was never envisaged that these frontiers would remain de jure international frontiers for so long.

The issue centering on frontiers is interesting as well as significant for a number of reasons. Any issue relating to boundaries of nations is, in any case, significant. Until the days of 'the fault-line wars', the frontiers have been the razor's edge on which have hung suspended the issue of life and death of nations. This particular frontier in this politically sensitive region is a curious configuration. It was deliberately created for very practical reasons. Yet it has lasted to this day. Moreover, it has lasted in a region that has remained an arena of super power rivalries. USSR, the super power of yesteryears, spent ten years trying to subdue the Afghans and the first war in twenty-first century was fought here. It is also noteworthy that this border has lasted despite the emergence of a vociferous movement for change of frontiers among the ethnic groups inhabiting this region.

The issue of constructing frontiers in Central Asia has to be situated in the context of what is often described as 'the Great Game in Asia'.[1] The Durand and the Pamirs agreements marked the culmination of efforts on the part of the British government to ensure the defence of India. The negotiations to establish acceptable frontiers had extended over a decade. This study seeks to answer the question why Britain was so keen to have a corridor between the Russian Empire and its Indian Empire.

There has been an ongoing debate among scholars on the issue as to whether, for Britain, the Indian Empire was an asset or liability. But there had been no doubt whatever at any stage, not even during the Second World War, that the control over India had to be retained. This implied that frontiers of India and the routes to India had to be defended and this influenced Britain's relations with European countries decisively. But official documents do not convey the idea of importance of India for Britain's policy-makers. In these, expression like 'the eastern empire', 'the Asiatic Empire', 'our possessions in the East', etc. are generally used. But such expressions were mere euphemisms for the Indian Empire. These do not convey the fact that the Indian Empire covered 97 per cent of Britain's Asiatic Empire.[2] In terms of population, even in 1912, that is to say, of all the acquisitions of 'the age of imperialism', in Britain's Empire, 10.2 per cent population lived in the United Kingdom, 5.4 per cent lived in the dominions with responsible government, 11.7 per cent lived in the dependent empire excluding India, while 72.6 per cent lived in the Indian Empire alone.[3] Britain wanted to be left unmolested and enjoy alone this vast and opulent possession. The British government did not perceive any danger to the Indian Empire from any state in the vicinity of India. Given Britain's maritime hegemony it could put pressure on any state anywhere with a coastline. However, Russia was not amenable to naval pressure. In the second-half of the nineteenth century, it was a common assumption in Europe that the next great war would be fought between Britain and Russia.[4] These two countries also identified each other as enemies.

Why were these powers perceived as enemies? They did not have any common frontier. Russia's naval power was no match for Britain's while Britain's military power was considered negligible. The reason was that Russia was expanding in the entire region from the Aegean Sea in the west to the Sea of Japan in the east. Russia's expansion in Central Asia seemed to threaten the frontiers of India while its expansion towards the Mediterranean seemed to threaten the short routes of India. Russian statesmen and historians have tended to argue that Russia had no ambition to conquer India, that it did not entertain appeals for help that poured from rulers of 'native' states, and that expansion resulted from ambitions of 'men on the spot'—the 'irresponsible' governors of frontier provinces.[5] But there is sufficient evidence to the effect that plans of expansion got full support from St. Petersburg. Whether Russia planned to invade India or not is not the issue here. The real factor is that the British thought it might. To the British, Russia seemed to be a sprawling land power with unlimited human resources. During 1830-80 Russia had advanced some 2000 kilometres from the Caspian towards Herat and during the next four years it had expanded by another 1000 kms. in the direction of Kabul. Russia had occupied Tashkent in 1865, Bukhara in 1866, and Samarkand in 1868. To unsettle the Raj, the Russians did not even have to conquer India. The Raj was based on the prestige of Britain's power. Any defeat even on the remotest frontier in mere skirmish could create, as Salisbury noted, "a spasm of sedition from the one end of India to another".[6] The British never forgot 1857.

Where could Britain exercise pressure on Russia to prevent it from expanding in the direction of the Indian Empire? The answer seemed to elude British statesmen and strategists. The British navy could not move on wheels. Naval blockade could not inflict significant damage on Russia's economy. There was little hope of penetrating Russia's defences from the side of the Baltic Sea. Throughout the nineteenth century a lively debate continued as to how, where and by whom Russia's advance should be checked. The attitude of the ruler of Afghanistan could be of decisive importance. But Afghans had refused to cow down to the British pressure. Two invasions of Afghanistan to install a friendlier ruler had ended in bloody failure. No Amir ever agreed to take responsibility for the safety of a British resident. To prevent Russia from entering India many strategies were advocated. The Close Border School wanted to meet Russia at the foot of the Hindukush while the forward school advocated that Kabul-Kandahar line should be occupied. To meet Russia in superior force on the northwest frontier of India, the British strategists calculated their resources to the last man (even animal) available and to the last penny available. But a winning combination eluded them.[7] To prevent Russia from advancing towards India, many strategists in Britain advocated Black Strategy. They wanted Britain to send an expedition to Caucasus through the Black Sea where it would get support from local people and thus strike at Russia's underbelly.[8] But, for entering the Straits of Bosphorus and Dardenelles it was essential to get permission of the Ottomans. As we shall see, that was not always possible.

All these issues came to the forefront in 1855 during the Penjdeh 'Incident'. After the Second Anglo-Afghan War, Amir Abdur Rahman had accepted that the British would control the foreign policy of Afghanistan. Thereafter, he was very keen that the frontier between Russia and Afghanistan should be demarcated. But the British were reluctant because they relied neither on the word of the Russians nor on Amir's fidelity. But, in 1884, Russia occupied Merv. This brought the Russian almost to the Afghan frontier. Any further move would have brought Russia face to face with Britain. When Granville, the British Foreign Minister, protested Giers, the Russian Chancellor, replied that Russia, having abstained from concerning itself with the transaction by which England at different periods had extended her sphere of action along her Indian frontier, had a right to expect the same consideration.[9] Giers' sharp reminder made the British accept the proposal for delimitation of Russo-Afghan frontier. The Boundary Commission was appointed in June 1884 on which Col. Ridgeway represented Britain and General Zelenoi represented Russia. Both sides tried to strengthen their respective positions. Kimberley, the Liberal India Secretary, advised Ripon to strengthen the defence by completing the Quetta railway. Similarly, the Russians tried to delay the negotiations so that they could bring all 'Turkoman tribes' under their umbrella.[10] Afghanistan was not represented on the Commission. But the Amir was aware of the advantages of delimitation. In his *darbar* he is reported to have said that once the frontier was fixed, the British would be forced to come to his aid in case of any aggression on the part of Russia. At this stage, on 30 March 1885, the Russian and Afghan troops fought at Penjdeh, a little known place in Central Asia, to the northwest of Afghanistan. The Afghan army suffered heavy losses and retreated. The British cabinet took a very serious view of the matter. Britain's position in India seemed threatened. The Sudan expedition was recalled. Numerous dispatches were exchanged between London and St. Petersburg and the generals on the spot. Gladstone, the man who was known for opposition to war, asked the Parliament to sanction a grant of eleven million pounds and got it.[11] This was the biggest grant for military purposes sanctioned after 1815 leaving aside the years of the Crimean War. In early April, the Foreign Office dispatched telegrams to major embassies warning them that situation of utmost gravity had arisen.[12] In the pacific, Port Hamilton was occupied.[13] Even documents announcing a state of war between Britain and Russia were printed.[14] Reinforcements were promised to the Government of India though only 36,000 men were available for reinforcing the army in India.[15] It was decided to call up the reserves. Even Russia urged Bismarck to put pressure on the Ottomans not to give permission to the British to send their army through the Straits. For Bismarck it was more important to maintain the Dreikaisersbund, which he had renewed in 1884 at Kremsier. He agreed.[16] In the diplomatic correspondence and exchanges between London and Calcutta at this time one constant theme was that Britain was hovering on the brink of war.[17] The situation eased only when Russia agreed to accept arbitration. The whole episode shows how sensitive Britons were about the security of India and the extent to which they were ready to take risks for the purpose.

After Penjdeh, the Boundary Commission resumed work. Its task became easier as the Amir did not show any attachment to Penjdeh. After prolonged and intricate negotiations, he took Zulfikar Pass instead. The boundary from Zulfikar to Oxus between Afghanistan and Russia was demarcated. The Amir expressed a desire to demarcate the rest of the boundary to the northeast of this state also.

In the mountainous and desolate region of Pamir to the northeast of Afghanistan, there were territories, which were virtually no man's lands. The British Government did not want Russia to fill this vacuum. It was very keen to prevent the establishment of coterminous frontier between the Russian and the British Empires in Central Asia. It wanted either Afghanistan or China to fill the gaps. Russia wanted to annex Roshan and Shighnan. This was an area where, at the time of Clarendon-Gorchakov talks of 1869-73, Britain had recognised Russia's claim because of some oversight, while the Amir was not called upon to vacate it.[18] The increasing interest taken by Russia in this region was becoming a source of anxiety for the British government. In the summer of 1890 the Government of India sent Captain Younghusband to the Pamirs to survey the Afghan and Russian frontiers and to ascertain the exact limits of Chinese authority. Colonel Yonoff expelled him from there. Meanwhile, there was a skirmish between Afghan and Chinese forces over Smoatash. Later, in July 1893 Afghan contingent at Somatash was defeated by Yonoff. It became clear that China and Afghanistan did not have resources to offer resistance to Russians. At the same time both Britain and Russia worked to expand their empires in Central Asia. Russia showed a determination to occupy Roshan and Shighnan. To keep Russia away from the Indian frontier, London instructed Sir R. Morier, the ambassador at St. Petersburg, to make efforts to obtain at least a part of Shighnan.[19] At the same time, to prevent Russia from gaining a footing on the southern slopes of the Hindukush, the British government too, adopted a bold, forward policy. In early 1980s it established control over Hunza, Nagar, Gilgit, and finally, Chitral.[20] It was, however, becoming clear that the extension of the Indian Empire on the northwest would not ensure the safety of the Indian Empire. The Amir remained resentful. He resented the acquisition of territory as well as the construction of railways by Britain to new Chaman in the vicinity of his state. He refused to permit communication between the British agency at Gilgit and the governor of Badakshan. Many other rail developments were also causing up to Samarkand and its branches connected it to Tashkent and Adijan in the vicinity of the Chinese frontier. The Trans-Caucasian railway to Julfa was also commenced. By obliterating distance between the Russian and the Indian frontier, these railways seemed likely to increase the vulnerability of India. By 1992, signs of emerging Franco-Russian combine could also be discerned. To Britain it seemed that its two enemies were joining hands. France had surplus capital to invest and agreement between them was likely to encourage Russia's railway building projects. Moreover, because of its naval strength France could delay the dispatch of army contingents from Britain in case Britain became engaged in a war against Russia in Central Asia.[21]

In view of the weakness of its own position and the intransigence of Russia, the British government was not ready to indulge in any serious quarrel with Russia. It thought it advisable to make the Amir evacuate Roshan and

Shighnan of his own free will than be turned out by Russia.[22] Russia's pressure made the Amir also accept British proposal for dispatch of a British officer to Kabul to discuss the issue of boundary on the upper Oxus in the Pamirs. Sir Mortimer Durand, Foreign Secretary in the Government of India, was sent. He went without a military escort. He was empowered to make considerable concessions. On his part, the Amir agreed to withdraw his forces from Roshan and Shighnan. The Government of India got a free hand in dealing with people in Chitral, Bajaur and adjoining areas.[23] The agreement was signed on 12 November 1893. Subsequently, commissions were appointed to demarcate the boundary line between the Indian Empire and Afghanistan. This became known as the Durand Line.[24] In March 1895 the Anglo-Russian agreement on the Pamirs issue was signed.[25] A commission of British and Russian representatives was appointed to mark the boundaries precisely.

Colonel M.G. Gerard was Britain's representative. He was instructed not to leave any points undiscussed between Chinese and Afghan territory. This could make the Russian and British Indian Empires contiguous at some future date. Russia followed to annex the plateau of Pamir. A corridor going right up to the Chinese territory was created. It is significant that the Amir was reluctant to occupy Wakhan because, after the surrender of Shighnan, it was like an arm extended into the desert which could be shorn off by Russia any time.[26] The Commission was also charged to come to an agreement with the Chinese Government to limit Chinese territory in the vicinity of this line.[27] Britain and Russia formally accepted this line in August 1896.

It is perhaps not wrong to describe the northeastern frontier as an 'erractic' frontier. The Wakhan corridor is perhaps rightly described as 'a curious configuration'. But this frontier certainly was not an outcome of 'accident' of history. The lines were drawn and accepted by each of the powers after a very cool calculation of their interests. Russia was expanding its empire in Central Asia. The British were not able to work out any viable strategy for the defence for their Indian Empire, while, as the Penjdeh crisis showed, they were determined to keep their hold over India. Even expansion of their control to the northwest did not provide any solution, for it could not increase human and material resources at Britain's disposal. It was to avoid the eventuality of having coterminous frontier in Central Asia that this corridor was created. However, British statesmen had little faith in the promises of Russia.[28] They could never imagine that this frontier would last for so long. It also becomes obvious here that the issue of defence of India was not a matter between Britain and Russia but was an integral part of Britain's relations with European countries.

Incidentally, it might also be pointed out that this issue throws light on the ongoing debates in the fields of diplomatic history and also imperial history. In diplomatic history, the battle between *Innen-* and *Aussenpolitik* has raged for decades. The British historians have tended to argue that the British foreign policy was relatively free from domestic constraints.[29] Here it has been argued that the commitment to maintain the Indian Empire was an important determinant of British foreign policy. If need to maintain this empire was felt for economic benefits, for prestige, for maintaining the imperial system or for any such reason, the relevance of domestic considerations cannot be negated. In imperial history scholarly literature has yet to resolve the question whether empire was valuable or expensive. If far-fetched precautions were taken for the defence of this 'jewel in the crown', "if Britain was ready to take the risk of war without even having the resources to win it, as shown in this paper, then their valuation of this jewel must have been very high". One more point must be made. Historians writing even in the twenty-first century, tend to refer to the role of the 'man on the spot' in discussing territory expansion of empires. The policies of the Government of India—annexation of territory on the northwest, military operations, frontier negotiations, settlement with tribes—were all conducted under instructions of the 'Home Government' and were warmly approved by the cabinet.

NOTES AND REFERENCES

1. See G. Alder, 'Big Game Hunting in Central Asia', *Journal of Imperial and Commonwealth History*, 1981: 9/2, 318-29, and D. Fromkin, *The Great Game in Asia*, Foreign Affairs, 1980, 58/4, pp. 936-51.
2. See tables in L.E. Davis and R.A. Huttenback, *Mammon and the Pursuit of Empire*, Cambridge, 1986, pp. 27-28.
3. Sneh Mahajan, *British Foreign Policy, 1874-1914: The Role of India*, Routledge, London/New York, 2002, p. 4.
4. P.M. Kennedy, *Anglo-German Antagonism*, London, 1980, p. 411; and D. Fromkin, *The Great Game in Asia*, p. 936.
5. For a discussion of Russia's motives, see N.A. Khalfin, 'Indian Missions in Russia ...', *Modern Asian Studies*, 1988, 4/1&2, pp. 157-297.
6. Quoted in J.A.S. Grenville, *Lord Salisbury and Foreign Policy*, London, Cab. 37/13.
7. See Sneh Mahajan, 'The Defense of India and the End of Isolation', in *The Journal of Imperial and Commonwealth History*, 1982, 10/2, pp. 168-93.
8. See Memorandum by Rothwell, 7 July 1884, Public Records Office, London, Cab. 37/ 13.
9. Quoted in D.P. Singhal, *India and Afghanistan*, Delhi, 1960/1982, pp. 113-17.
10. *Ibid.*, p. 117-18.
11. For Gladstone's speech, see Parliamentary Debates, House of Commons, 27 April 1885, Cols., pp. 855-60.
12. For these telegrams see PRO. F. O. 65/1239.
13. See R.L. Greaves, *Persia and the Defence of India, 1884-1892*, London, 1959, pp. 72-73.

14. *Ibid.*, p. 72.
15. Mahajan, *British Foreign Policy*, p. 15.
16. See letters in Dugdale, pp. 197-201.
17. See Kimberley to Dufferin, 10, 17 and 24 April 1885, Dufferin Papers, Correspondence with the Secretary of State; Graville Papers, PRO, 30/29/186. Also see Robert Morier, British ambassador at St. Petersburg to Salisbury. Confdl. no. 146, 18 April 1888, PRO, F.O. 65/1348.
18. Mahajan, *op. cit.*, p. 24.
19. See NAI, *Foreign Department Secret Proceedings*, July 1893, Nos. 493-570 and August 1893, Nos. pp. 274-332.
20. However, in 1897, the Government of India had to face fierce revolt in this region. The situation improved after administrative changes were introduced.
21. See Mahajan, *op. cit.*, pp. 103-05.
22. See NAI, *op. cit.*, December 1891, pp. 206-91.
23. See India Office Library, *Political and Secret Letters and Enclosures*, Vol. 73. Also given in Singhal, *India and Afghanistan*, Appendix H.
24. Durand was not a member of any commission.
25. British Parliamentary Papers, Vol. 109, 1895, pp. 159-60.
26. PDSE, Vol. 73, p. 16.
27. See NAI, *op. cit.*, June 1895, pp. 340-95.
28. Salisbury wrote to Ridgeway in 1887 that demarcation was not worth the paper it was written on. Singhal, *India and Afghanistan*, p. 113.
29. Z. Steiner, *Britain and the Origins of the First World War*, London, 1977, p. 24.

20

Russia's Threat to British India: The Tibetan Dimension

T. Shaumian

Situated in the heart of Asia and bordered by the mighty Himalayas, Tibet is a junction between the largest Asiatic civilisations. Here is preserved a unique socio-political and economic structure with political and economic supremacy of the Lama church. The religious head—the Dalai Lama—is the living divine being and also the temporal ruler of Tibet.

Important as the residence of the Lamaist religious head, Dalai Lama, Tibet was visited by many pilgrims not only from neighbouring India, Nepal, Sikkim, and Bhutan, but also from Mongolia, Trans-Baikal area and Kalmyk Steppe of Russia. That a large number of Buddhists lived in India and led the British colonial authorities to establish firm connections with Lhasa. The Government of Great Britain and Russia used these facts to conceal the true motives of their interest in Tibet, its favourable strategic position in the heart of Central Asia, in the first place, under the disguise of their care about their Buddhist subjects.

Since the end of the eighteenth century Great Britain actively and regularly attempted to penetrate into China from the Indian territory across the Himalayas, gradually seizing parts of the Himalayan principalities—Bhutan, Sikkim, and Nepal—to go nearer and nearer the Tibetan borders.

In 1898 Lord Curzon became the Viceroy of India. It is well known that the British government in London only broadly determined the policy of Great Britain in Central Asia. Concrete implementation of it lay in the hands of the Viceroy of India. It is not surprising that by the end of the nineteenth and beginning of the twentieth centuries, Asia policies of Great Britain reflected the political views of nationalist circles of the British establishment whose worthy spokesman was Lord Curzon.

The principal task of Lord Curzon in India was to further expand and strengthen the British possessions. Russia's active penetration into Central Asia was used by Curzon to come out with the theory that conquest of India was the principal objective of Russia, and Central Asia was springboard for attacking that British colony.

As is known, there were no common borders between Russian possession in Asia and India. They were divided by Sinkiang and Tibet which were in the sphere of the influence of Ch'ing China. Curzon therefore was extremely watchful of the success of Russian policy in Sinkiang and of the signs of the growing Russian influence in Tibet.

Lord Curzon accelerated his efforts to establish relations with the Government of Tibet, and unfriendly attitude of the Tibetan ruling circles produced sharp displeasure of the Anglo-Indian administration, particularly as British agents and later the Russian press reported that the Dalai Lama had sent letters to the Russian Tsar through special Tibetan missions. Lord Curzon was at the end of his tether when the Russian government newspaper, *Journal de saint-Petersburg*, in October 1900 published a brief news item that on 30 September 1900, Russian Emperor Nicholas-II had received in the Livadia summer palace Ngawang Lozang Dorjieff, the first Tsenyi Khenpo, attached to the Tibetan Dalai Lama. A Russian Buryat by origin, Dorjieff was in the service of the High Priest in Tibet; in future became not only the ideologue, but a direct performer of the basic measures connected with the implementation of the policy of rapprochement between Russia and Tibet.

The British, justifying their expansion in the Central Asia to the northeast of the borders of India, as a measure to protect the Indian borders, faced Russian interests seeking to strengthen Russia's position in Central Asia. Thus the relations of the Anglo-Indian colonial authorities with the borderland territories greatly exceeded the limits of local border conflicts and were determined by the terms of the so-called 'great game', the Anglo-Russian rivalry in Central Asia, directly affecting also the European interests of both the powers.

According to the British version, Britain was only defending her Indian possessions, while Russia, by seizing one Central Asian region after another sought also to add India, 'the Jewel in the British Crown' to their possessions. This viewpoint is at least disputable. It appears that Russians and Britain pursued offensive policies from the strategic point of view, in the interest of developing trade and acquisition of new sources of raw materials and market for the growing bourgeoisie of these countries. And it was in Central Asia that these two streams of expansion clashed.

One of the episodes of that 'great game' is dealt with in this chapter. The study makes use of original sources from the Foreign Policy Archives of the Russian Empire (Arkhiv Vneshney Politiki Rossiyskoy Imperil, AVPRI) and the National Archives of India, including reports and letters from Russian and

British diplomatic representatives and agents from London, Petersburg, Calcutta, Peking and Urga.

The reported reception of the Tibetan representative Dorjieff, by the Russian Tsar in September 1900, caused great anxiety in London and Calcutta. The British diplomats in Petersburg were instructed to ascertain its implications on the spot.[1] The charge d'affairs of Great Britain in Petersburg, C. Hardinge, got in touch with Tibetan doctor P.A. Badmaev, who played a role in Tibetan orientation of Russian policies, and in report to Marquis Salisbury in the Foreign Office on 31 October 1900 made it known that after talking with him, he came to the conclusion that the mission was of an official nature, although Badmaev asserted that it was a courtesy visit by Dorjieff. Hardinge himself considered it possible that Dorjieff had visited Petersburg to clear up purely religious issues between Lhasa and the Russian Buddhists. However, Hardinge wrote, "whatever might have been the aim of the mission, the Russian government would benefit from it and seize the opportunity to propagate the opinion that it would be natural for Asiatic peoples to be under the Russian patronage."[2]

Curzon, at first had received the report of the mission critically and even stated that Dorjieff was swindler and his mission to the Tsar was a 'fraud' and entirely fabricated. Of course, Curzon knew that Russia for a long time had been attempting to penetrate into Lhasa, but the presumption that the Tibetan Lamas might have shed their usual suspicious attitude towards the Europeans and openly sent a direct mission to Europe, was from his point of view unlikely. Curzon was also convinced that Tibet would sooner ask for support from Great Britain, than from Russia. Besides, believing that it would take not less than ten years for Russia to make Tibet her protectorate, he considered that the British still had sufficient time to drive Russia away from Tibet. To achieve that time, it was first necessary to establish direct relations with the Dalai Lama. "A Russian protectorate over Tibet is to be stopped, and the only way to stop is by being in advance ourselves".[3] In case, it would be done by friendly correspondence, which Curzon's persistent effort had tried to establish, albeit without any result, future use of force might not become necessary. It must be said that even these attempts of Curzon to establish correspondence with the Dalai Lama were regarded by the Foreign Office as needless, justly being afraid that harder pressure on Tibet could make the latter come closer to Russia.

Curzon, in his letter to Hamilton, wrote that for British it would be a madness to cross the Himalayas and occupy Tibet. But it is important that nobody else captures it; so it is necessary to convert it into a buffer between the Indian and the Russian Empires.[4]

From the correspondence of Curzon and Hamilton on the question of Tibet, it is evident that there were serious disagreements between the Anglo-Indian government and the London Cabinet, which manifested themselves whenever any matter of external policies concerning India cropped up. Thus, in the case of Tibet, what Curzon could not secure by negotiations, he was prepared to secure by force while the London government was more cautious and dealt with the matters of foreign policy along with the consideration of the interest of the British Empire as a whole.[5] As regards relations with Russia, the foreign minister Salisbury wrote that Curzon wanted him to negotiate with Russia, pretending as if they (the British) had '500000 soldiers' to back them up, which in fact they did not have.[6]

Meanwhile rumours about Russia's penetration into Lhasa were becoming more and more persistent. The reports of the Russian press about a new Dorjieff's visit to Russia in June 1901, this time with a whole group of Tibetans, greatly increased the interest in the situation in Tibet.

Having learnt that on 23 June 1901, Tsar Nicholas-II had received the extraordinary ambassadors of the Dalai Lama in his summer residence, Peterhof the British Ambassador in Petersburg tried to find out the details of the reception. He informed his government that according to Dr. Badmaev, the Tibetans had requested Russia to help them in case of British aggression. The Chinese Charge d'affaires in Petersburg supposed that Dorjieff came to Petersburg to request the Tsar not to prevent Russian subjects to penetrate into Tibet.

The British Ambassador in Petersburg, Scott, received an instruction from London to meet the Foreign Minister of Russia, Lamsdorff. During their talk on 3 July 1901, Lamsdorff characterised "the Russian press conclusion that the Tibetan guests had come on some diplomatic mission, as absurd and absolutely baseless".[7] According to him, Dorjieff came to Petersburg "probably to collect money for his order" from the numerous Buddhists of the Russian origin. Lamsdorff stated that during Dorjieff's first visit the Emperor had received him in Yalta with the aim of learning the facts about life in Tibet, which was of interest to him. The Russian Imperial Geographic Society also displayed great interest in this visit which, however, was not of an official nature.[8]

After the Russian press reported that Dorjieff had paid visits to Lamsdorff and Witte, the Russian Finance Minister, Scott again had a talk with Lamsdorff and was reassured by the latter that the mission was not official and could not be regarded as political or diplomatic. It was similar to missions sent by the Pope of Rome to other countries, said Lamsdorff. In the letter of the Dalai Lama, sent to him through Dorjieff, he only wished him good health and wrote that he himself was in a good state.[9]

However, the reports of Britain's Ambassador in Petersburg, did not satisfy the Foreign Office. Hamilton, the Secretary of State of India, emphasised his surprise that Russia publicly welcomed the Tibetan mission, when the Dalai Lama ignored the Viceroy of India and returned his letters without even opening them. On 2 September 1901, Scott again visited Lamsdorff and conveyed to him that the British government could not be indifferent towards any actions, which might violate or change the existing status of Tibet. At that, the Russian Minister once again reiterated his earlier statement that the mission dealt "with purely religious matters and had no political aims or diplomatic nature".[10]

While the London government was still hesitant about the nature of Dorjieff's mission, Lord Curzon openly expressed the doubts that "the Tibetan mission to Russia represented only monasteries"[11] and demanded the Foreign Office to conclude a treaty in Lhasa guaranteeing permanent relations between England and Tibet. For this Curzon was willing to take any measures, including even an armed invasion of the Tibetan territory. Hamilton wrote that the way proposed by Curzon "may boomerang. It may place Tibet in the Russian hands". Besides, according to the London Cabinet, Britain had no material prerequisites to organise any expedition beyond the Indian borders.[12] However, Curzon ignored these arguments and continued to assert that Dorjieff was a Russian agent.

Curzon and the London government, realising the importance of the events in Tibet, still did not assess identically the seriousness of the events and the methods to be applied in Tibet. The differences on the Tibetan issue between Calcutta and London further aggravated.

As far back as August 1901, Hamilton wrote to Curzon that "the Tibetans are but the smallest of pawns on the political chessboard, but castles, knights and bishops may be all involved in trying to take that pawn".[13]

The spread of rumours in the press and in some diplomatic circles about the Russo-Chinese Agreements on Tibet, about Russian agents in Lhasa, etc. gave the Curzon government a new pretext to intensify the anti-Russian propaganda and for the justification of the 'offensive policy' provoked by the Russian threat to India.

In May 1902, V. Klemm, the Russian Consul-General in Bombay, reported to the Russian Foreign Ministry that the Anglo-Indian newspapers were almost daily printing "cock and bull stories of war and outrageous slanders about Russia." All Indian libraries contained books "which wrote with suppressed fear and undistinguished spite of Russia's intentions vis-à-vis India, the possible outcome of this allegedly inevitable struggle of the whale and the bear for approaching that treasure".[14]

During a talk with Klemm, a British officer acknowledged that false information about Russia, especially about the Russian civil and military authorities and about their treatment of people, was a part of programme to train the Indian native troops. According to Klemm, the editor of a native newspaper told him that "malicious attack directed at the Russians are welcome to the government and to place the British public as a means to strengthen the British charm and the sympathies of native Indians for the British regime".[15]

Despite the stepped-up anti-Russian propaganda, the Indian public opinion believed that Russian threat to India was being greatly exaggerated. For example, *The Times of India* wrote on 4 September 1902, that "Russia for many years will be busy with the assimilation and development of its acquired territory. Therefore, British Indians should not think that Russia would dream of invading India during the life of present generation". A distinguished member of the Anglo-Indian government, a well-known expert on Asiatic problems, Henry Cotton, in an interview on 3 December 1902, stated that he did not believe that,

> Russia has any plan regarding Tibet. Tibet is located at a distance of 1500 miles from the nearest point in the Russian territory and has nothing in common with the Russian sphere of activities in the Chinese territory .... In the present case, again the old slogan 'Russia is interested in India' is repeated. I do not believe that this really is the case; but even if it were, I am sure that Russia could never do this.

Cotton thought that Russia could never cross the Himalayas at the present level of technological development.[16]

Although the British Defence Ministry was anxious over the development around Tibet, nevertheless the British army strategists at times showed sobreity and realism appraising the real situation in connection with the rumours about the 'Agreement' of Russia with China and Tibet. Lieutenant-Colonel V.R. Robertson prepared a "Memorandum on the alleged agreement between Russia and China concerning Tibet",[17] in which the position at the northeast border was discussed. He wrote that from the purely strategic point of view, it is difficult to believe that some day, the Russian protectorate over Tibet may convert the Himalayan principality of Nepal 'sandwiched' between British India and Tibet, into a 'second Afghanistan'. Irrespective of strengthening of Russia's position in Sinkiang and Mongolia, "the distance from Tibet is too complicated and the roads from Tibet to Nepal are difficult to access". 'Hence,' continued V.R. Robertson,

> Russia will never move as many soldiers across the Tibetan border as she may move across the border of Afghanistan. So it might be considered that the threat to Tibet from the Russian side lies not in the intention to capture their firm strategic position, but in the desire to divert the attention of British from the regions where they were really trying to concentrate their efforts, i.e. from Afghanistan and Persia.

Besides, Robertson wrote, after achieving a nominal protectorate over Tibet, Russia would do everything possible to complicate the political situation, create disturbances among the local tribes and prevent the development of trade. So it was necessary, according to V.R. Robertson, to take steps to prevent Russia for making Tibet its protectorate.

Thus, it was clear that the London Cabinet, the representatives of the Defence Ministry and the Indian press soberly evaluated the new situation realising that the Anglo-Indian government need not fear the Russian threat to Tibet. At the same time, the idea of Russian penetration into Tibet justified the plans of the most bellicose representatives of British colonial circles, who used it as a pretext for the armed invasion into the Tibetan territory.

Curzon and the Anglo-Indian authorities did not have any comprehensive proof of the existence of a treaty between Russia and Tibet; however, Curzon, Lansdowne and Hamilton conjectured that there must have been some sort of negotiations or, if not a secret treaty, then surely a secret agreement between China and Russia, concerning Tibet.[18] Curzon considered it his duty "to foil this petty game, while there is still time". On 28 May 1902, he wrote to Hamilton: "As you probably know my open answer to any such action of Russia will be very simple. Without the slightest difficulty, I would put a British army into Lhasa".[19] Thus, Curzon only looked for a pretext to fulfil his plan to invade Tibet.

On 8 January 1903, the Viceroy of India sent to Hamilton, Secretary of State for India, a letter in which he formulated the main principles of the Indian Government policies vis-à-vis Tibet. He enumerated the main developments in Anglo-Tibetan and Russo-Tibetan relations. He reminded that

> the Russian border nowhere even touches that of Tibet, and the nearest point of the Russian territory is considerably more than a 100 miles short of the Tibetan capital, which is situated in the extreme south and in close proximity to the northern frontier of the Indian Empire.[20]

On 2 February 1903, the Russian Embassy in London sent a memorandum to the Foreign Office saying that the Russian government had learnt from a reliable source that the British military expedition had reached Komba-Ovaleko on the way to the northern part of the Chumbi Valley. The Russian government drew serious objection to this and stated that it might take suitable measures to safeguard its interests in that region.[21]

Thus, it, attempted to use the threat of the British invasion in Tibet to put pressure on the ruling circles of Great Britain to gain concessions on other controversial matters.

On 6 February Curzon replied that the information of the Russian Ambassador had no ground and that the matter concerned only the discussion of the border issues (between Indian and Tibet) with the atmosphere of mutual understanding and friendship prevailing during the discussion.[22]

On 11 February 1903, a talk took place between Lansdowne and Benkendorff, Russian Ambassador in England, on the Russian memorandum of 2 February 1903. Lansdowne said that in his opinion the memorandum was written in somewhat unusual threatening tone that it dealt with the country in direct vicinity of the Indian borders and it was strange enough that Russia had so resolutely spoken of immediate defence of her interest in that region. Lansdowne suggested that in case the Russian government wanted information on that matter, it could directly approach him. He repeated that the information was baseless and pointed out that the Chumbi Valley was situated close to the Indian border, and always served as a trade route between the two countries. Benkendorff, on his part, remarked very cautiously that all the rumours of such kind were possibly being spread to aggravate relations between Russia and Great Britain. He did not see any reason, why the two countries should quarrel because of Tibet.[23]

On 18 February, Lansdowne and Benkendorff met again. The British minister stated that the Indian Government was extremely perturbed by the Russian memorandum. Indian interests in Tibet were of special character, he reiterated. Lhasa was in close proximity to the northern borders of India, while the Asiatic possessions of Russia were more than a thousand kilometres away from Lhasa. So, any manifestation of Russia's interests or activities in that region might perturb population or create an impression that the British influences were being pushed into the background and that Russia was quickly moving into the regions, which never had been within the sphere of her interests.

Curzon believed that Great Britain did not have such serious reasons for taking extreme action in any other part of Asia. If Great Britain delayed, declared Curzon, then in future "some gross and irrelevant insult is offered to our honour or our flag." He maintained that resolute actions would serve the interests not only of India, but of the British Empire as a whole, that England's prestige should be unconditionally recognised in any point of the 'glacis', which surrounded it.[24]

In 1903 the Anglo-French negotiations started regarding all colonial problems. Great Britain was preparing for an open encounter with its main rival—Germany. During that period, England showed the tendency to come closer to Russia, which was actively supported by France. With the start of 1903, the discussions between the Russian Ambassador in London, Benkendorff and Lansdowne became regular.

On 20 March 1903, Russian Minister of External Affairs, in a letter to his Ambassador in London, Benkendorff, formulated the principles of Russian policies in relation to Tibet. He wrote, *inter alia*, that

> the Imperial government considers that it is necessary to maintain status-quo in Tibet and, if the English would somehow violate that, Russia will not fail to protect her interests, of course, not by taking any direct measures in Tibet herself (as she is removed from us by Anglo-Indian possession), but probably in other proper parts of Asian continent.[25]

On 24 March and 8 April 1903, Lansdowne met the Russian Ambassador Benkendorff in London, who assured the British minister that the rumours about the secret treaties between Russia and Tibet and between Russia and China regarding Tibet were unfounded. Benkendorff stated that Russia had not had any agents in Lhasa, nor did she intend to despatch any mission there.

He further said that although the Russian government did not have any plans regarding Tibet, it could not remain indifferent to any attempt to violate the status-quo in Tibet. Russia would protect her interests in Asia, not only in Tibet, but also in any other place. The Russian government considered Tibet as a part of the Chinese Empire and was interested in its integrity.[26]

Thus, it seemed that Great Britain and Russia exchanged commitments regarding Tibet. Nevertheless, the British continued their military preparations at the Tibetan border, moving in their forces, etc. Younghusband explained that the English still were apprehensive of Russian influence in Tibet, believing that even if Russians did not intend to help the Tibetans, the latter "might and did think they could count upon Russian support". He further stated that Tibetans might expand 'ordinary amenities' from the Russian side "into a promise of thick-and-thin support against the English."[27] However, it was clear that the Anglo-Indian government would not like to miss such a convenient chance to capture Tibet, which ultimately arose in 1903.

The British Government in London made a close scrutiny of the messages of the Viceroy of India of 7 May 1903, and agreed upon the need to conduct negotiations in Khamba-Dzong regarding the border. Lansdowne and Hamilton did not consider it advisable to put on the agenda the question of the residence of the British Agent (either in Lhasa or in Gyantse). Hamilton wrote to Curzon that complications, which might arise due to such step, might in the existing conditions overweigh the probable advantage of the sort of arrangement,[28] as the proposed measure, according to Lansdowne, might lead to a serious breach of status-quo in Tibet to which, as it was expressed, the Russian government would not remain indifferent.[29]

The British press continued to spread rumours about Russian penetration into Tibet and of 143 Russian engineers who had arrived in army uniforms in the eastern border of Tibet and of Kazak detachment coming to Tibet from the north and so on.[30]

The British government informed China that its aim was to establish friendly relations with Tibet and expected that the Chinese government would put immediate pressure on the Dalai Lama so that he would send a plenipotentiary emissary to negotiate without delay; otherwise, Britain would be compelled to take necessary measures to ensure the security of the mission.[31]

Thus, Tibet's fortune was decided. The British colonial authorities using the weakness and unpreparedness of the country to resist such a powerful and highly experienced neighbour, the inability of China, due to the complexity of her internal situation, to defend her vassal, and the further aggravation of the situation in the Far East, diverting Russia's attention from Tibet, sent their heavily armed forces to the territory of Tibet.

NOTES AND REFERENCES

1. National Archives of India (NAI), January 1901, Ns. 80-95, Doc. 90.
2. NAI, Doc. 95.
3. A. Lamb, *Britain and Chinese Central Asia*, London, 1960, p. 225.
4. *Ibid.*, p. 260.
5. Lord Ronaldshay, *The Life of Lord Curzon*, London, 1928, Vol. II, p. 205.
6. *Ibid.*, p. 206.
7. Great Britain, Foreign Office, Papers relating to Tibet, Cd. 1920, p. 116.
8. *Ibid.*, p. 116.
9. *Ibid.*, p. 117.
10. *Ibid.*, p. 123.
11. A. Lamb, *op. cit.*, p. 256.
12. Lord Ronaldshay, *op. cit.*, Vol. II, p. 207.
13. A. Lamb, *op. cit.*, p. 262.
14. AVPRI, Fund Central Asia Desk, file No. 920, list 81.
15. AVPRI, *Ibid.*, list 81.
16. *Amrita Bazar Patrika*, Calcutta, December 3, 1902.
17. National Archives of India, February 1903, Ns. 1-88, Doc. 61.
18. A. Lamb, *op. cit.*, p. 275.
19. *Ibid.*, p. 276.
20. National Archives of India, February 1903, Ns. 1-88, Doc. 82. Papers relating to Tibet, Cd. 1920, pp. 150-53.
21. National Archives of India, April 1903, Ns. 130-172, Doc. 145, Enclo. 1.
22. Papers relating to Tibet, Cd. 1920, p. 179.
23. National Archives of India, April 1903, Ns. 130-72. Doc. 142, Enclo. 2.
24. Lord Ronaldshay, *op. cit.*, Vol. II, p. 275.
25. AVPRI, Fund Chinese Desk, file No. 1455, lists, pp. 37-38.
26. National Archives of India, July 1903, Ns. 38-95, Doc. 42.
27. F. Younghusband, *India and Tibet*, London, John Murray, 1910, p. 82.
28. NAI, Doc. 55.
29. NAI, Doc. 77.
30. P. Fleming, *Bayonets to Lhasa*, New York, 1961, p. 82.
31. NAI, November 1903, Ns. 159-234, Doc. 201.

21
Indians in Central Asia in the First Two Decades of the Twentieth Century

Surendra Gopal

Historical records show continuous exchange of visits by Indians and Central Asians to each other's territories at least for the last six centuries. Visitors included traders, scholars, artists, artisans, job-seekers, soldiers, adventurers, common men, etc.

Indians travelling to Central Asia were adherents of different faiths, such as Hinduism, Islam, Sikhism, Jainism, Zoroastrianism, etc. They hailed from different regions of the Indian subcontinent, though it is clear that the majority of our countrymen visiting Central Asia belonged to the geographically contiguous area of the northwest, i.e. Kashmir and its adjoining areas of Ladakh, Baltistan, Chitral, etc. and the Punjab, the North West Frontier Province and Sind. Dmitriyev puts them by number between six and eight thousand at the beginning of the twentieth century.[1]

From the second-half of the nineteenth century, the nature of Indo-Central Asian contacts underwent qualitative changes. European colonial powers became entrenched in both these areas: Great Britain in India and Tsarist Russia in Central Asia. A stable monarchy in Afghanistan and fluctuating political situation in Eastern Turkestan shaped this relationship. Russia and Great Britain began to view each other's moves with suspicion; mutual fear and rivalry shaped their policies. Eventually it affected the nature of contacts between Central Asians and Indians.

Throughout the nineteenth century, British and Tsarist agents, travellers, intelligence gatherers, political analysts, variously disguised, entered each other's territories and the arena was transformed into a hotbed of intrigues. The two European powers had started the 'Great Game'.[2]

Both the Central Asians and the Indians were not unaware of the attitudes and conflicting ambitions of the two imperialist powers; the activities of Indian immigrants to Central Asia bear clear imprint of the changed situation at the dawn of the twentieth century.

The functioning of Indian traders should now be considered in two zones: (a) in the nominally independent *Khanate* of Bukhara and (b) in the Russian-occupied Turkestan, which included the former *Khanate* of Kokand including the Farghana Valley and the Badakshan region in the upper reaches of the Oxus River (modern Tajikistan). Afghanistan and Eastern Turkestan were the major corridors through which Indians entered Central Asia.[3]

Bukhara, the greatest distributing centre of goods in the Mawra-un-Nahar had been since the past several centuries, a major concentration point for Indian immigrants. Growing Russian influence over the *Khanate*, especially after the Tsar had annexed the contiguous territories covered by Samarkand, Tashkent, Farghana Valley, etc. in 1860s, added to the problems of Indian merchants.

In order to promote the interest of her mercantile community, Russia had begun dictating Bukharan customs policies. At one point of time Russia laid down that the duties on imported goods would be as prescribed by all-Russian Customs Union. This hurt Indian merchants who were basically importing fine Indian cotton textiles, indigo, tea, spices, etc. and paying taxes at rates less than the West Europeans. They were reduced to the position of small-time retailers.[4]

Earlier with their base in Bukhara, Indian merchants could freely travel all over the region with their goods but now Russia started imposing restrictions. Indians were not allowed to enter the Russian-held territory without prior permission. They had to spell out the routes they expected to take while applying for permission and were not permitted to deviate from the itinerary they had outlined.

Furthermore, by the end of the nineteenth century new powerful technological forces shaping the course of trade had emerged. With the construction of Trans-Caucasian and Trans-Caspian railways, the region had become easily accessible to industrialised nations of Europe whose steamships carried goods to the shores of the Black Sea, which were then transported all over Central Asia by the rail network. The emerging Russian bourgeoisie was keen to exploit the new transportation system; the Indians tried to counter them by boosting their exports; they began sending goods from the port of Bombay to Batumi (Poti) on the Black Sea.[5] The reduced transportation cost helped Indian merchants to bring down the prices of their goods and survive.[6] They could not, however, offset the advantages enjoyed by the merchants of industrialised nations. The inclusion of Bukhara in 1895 in the All Russian Customs Union meant a hike[7] in the taxes paid by Indians who were put to a disadvantage in comparison to their Russian counterparts. Hence in Bukhara, Indians became immigrants.

As moneylenders, non-Muslim Indians, especially those hailing from Shikarpur in Upper Sind became a well-identified group. However, it may be noted that Shikarpuri was a common connotation for all the non-Muslims from the Indian subcontinent. The Russian traveller Novitski noted this fact towards the beginning of the twentieth century.[8]

At the turn of the twentieth century there is a likelihood that the number of Indian moneylenders increased because the Tsarist authorities had actively adopted the policy of suppressing and driving out Indian moneylenders from territories ruled by them accusing them of exploiting the common peasants and artisans in Turkestan. In Bukhara the Emir did not discriminate against Indian moneylenders who survived there till its incorporation into Russian Turkestan in 1920.[9]

Indian traders residing in Bukhara sent a petition to the Tsar requesting him to allow them the right of free travelling on the territory of Russian Turkestan. Their request was turned down.[10] In pursuit of this policy several restrictions were imposed on the movements of Indians in Central Asia and they were barred from entering certain areas.[11]

The Khan of Bukhara, however, realised that the Indian moneylenders performed a socially useful economic function by providing for small credit needs of the common man in his *Khanate*. Hence, he refrained from excluding Indian moneylenders from operating in his dominion. This comes out very clearly from the description of Indian moneylenders in Bukhara given by the Tajik author Sadriddin Aini who had intimate personal contacts with them.

Sadriddin Aini while studying in Bukhara in 1890s found out that the Hindus resided in the serai named Alimjan.[12] In three other big caravan-serais there lived more than three hundred Hindu moneylenders.[13]

Indians loaned small sums ranging between ten and twenty tenegs to the poorest section of the population or the peasants and the soldiers of the Khan for short periods.[14] They charged a very high percentage of interest with the result that only those who were extremely needy and could not get any loan elsewhere turned to them.[15]

The high rate of interest charged by the Hindus is evident from the description of Aini. The loan was advanced for either six weeks or for two months and the amount to be returned was either twice or one-and-a-half times of the original capital advanced.[16] Aini also throws light on the manner in which these loan transactions took place. The moneylender stays in his room in the caravan-serai. When someone borrowed, the moneylender wrote down the name of the borrower at the top of a page around fourteen inches long and two inches broad in an Indian language along with the sum borrowed by the loanee. The transaction was never registered with the administration and these pages served as the account book for the moneylender.[17]

For the purpose of accounting, the moneylender, if he had lent twenty tenegs for two months, wrote down thirty tenegs to be paid by the borrower. He then divided the thirty tenegs in eight equal in accordance with the eight weeks; the process of returning the loan commenced from the coming week.[18]

The moneylender dressed himself in a black gown which was tied round his waist by a string. He sat in his room in the serai till noon. He had an embroidered square cap on his head. This was the dress prescribed for the Hindu moneylender by the Khan of Bukhara so as to distinguish him from the local population.[19]

In the afternoon the moneylender went out to collect money from his borrowers. He put from forty to fifty slips in a solid bag with the name of the borrower sticking out and walked all over the city till evening visiting different serais, bazaars and streets and collected money from his loanees.[20] Then he came back to the serai.

In the serai, the moneylenders generally prepared a drink from green herb called *Ab Sabz* or green water. The herb was first soaked in water and was then crushed in a mortar. Thereafter, it was poured over a piece of cloth and drunk. It was intoxicating for in the aftermath there were quarrels and fights.[21] Indian readers of this piece will immediately recognise that the drink was *bhang*, a mild narcotic very popular among different sections of the population. As Sadriddin Aini notes, such a conduct created aversion for the Hindu moneylender among the local population.

The Khan of Bukhara had appointed a special officer, Esaul Hindu, to keep watch over the Hindu moneylenders.[22] This officer had under him a number of other junior officers who helped him in his work. He kept a close watch over the activities of Hindu moneylenders.[23] Through these officers the Khan of Bukhara had an exact knowledge of the property owned by each of the moneylender. The officers knew the wealth of each moneylender with such an exactitude that on the point of death he could not clear each heir, and the money was transferred to the treasury of the Khan. This was an important reason why the Emir of Bukhara did not interfere with the activities of the Hindu moneylenders, whose wealth eventually found its way to his chests![24]

In addition to Bukhara, Hindu moneylenders were also found in other cities of the Emirate—Gizhduvan, Karshi, and Babkent, etc.[25] Hedged in with so much uncertainty, oppressed by the authorities and despised by the native populace, life for the Hindu moneylender was trauma and the evening drink of *bhang*, helped him to forget his miseries at least temporarily.

However, there are other sections among the Indians whose members were traders and bankers and they consisted of both Hindus (including Sikhs and Jains) and Muslims. Broadly speaking, these traders came from Sind (Shikarpuris), North West Frontier Province (Peshawaris), Punjab (Multan and Lahore), and Kashmir.

On the territory of the Bukharan *Khanate*, Hindu moneylenders remained active till the Bukharan *Khanate* was absorbed by the Bolshevik regime of Russia in 1920.

Hindu moneylenders also plied their profession in Badakshan in the upper reaches of Oxus, now a part of Tajikistan. There was no clear-cut dividing line between moneylending, banking and trading. One could ply all the occupations simultaneously or concentrate on one or two of them.

The scale of operation of these traders varied considerably. Some of them were wholesalers and others were peddlers. The capital at their command showed great fluctuation; the items they traded in showed wide variation. The description given by Sadriddin Aini again is enlightening.

Aini refers to a Hindu, Bairaji, resident in the same serai Alimjan where the Hindu moneylenders lived. He did not practise usury; he sold semi-precious stones, which were purchased by jewellers and coppersmiths for beautifying objects crafted by them.[26] However, he was treated as a connoisseur of precious stones and even the Emir of Bukhara sought his advice while making purchases of jewels. Others also called upon him and sought his opinion regarding the value and quality of gems they intended to buy. He was given a certain amount for the services he rendered.[27] But what is important is the fact that he was a well-educated person and had a clear worldview.

Aini writes that he possessed a personal library which had a number of books, printed as well as in manuscript form, in Indian and Tajik languages. The printed Tajik books were published in India. Baiarji could freely read and write in Tajik. Aini stuck friendship with him and borrowed his Tajik books.[28] Bairaji was better dressed than his compatriots and spent his entire time reading books.[29]

When Aini expressed his anguish at the fate of Hindu moneylenders, Bairaji explained to him that the British rule had brought miseries on Indians; in their homeland they were starving. Hence, they had to emigrate and earn their livelihood in foreign countries. In Bukhara, Hindus had discovered moneylending to be the easiest employment. He also noted that if the Amir stopped usury by the Hindus, they would be forced to work as hired labourers. At the same time, he noted, cessation of the moneylending operations of the Hindus, will spell ruin for the ordinary poor Bukharans.[30]

The opening of the Suez Canal in 1869 established direct voyages between the port of Bombay (now Mumbai) and the Russian-controlled ports on the Black Sea. The Black Sea ports were linked to Central Asian markets by railways by the opening of the twentieth century. This development affected the land-based trade between India and Bukhara. It was noted in 1911 that this tendency was evident in decreasing collection of customs duties by the Russians and the Afghans.[31] Faced by the competition mounted by the emerging Russian capitalist class, Indians entered into a compromise: they also became exporters of factory-made Russian goods to Eastern Turkestan, Afghanistan and India.

In the Bukharan *Khanate* they combined usury with trading operations despite constraints and handicaps. As non-Muslim, every Indian paid *jiziya* or poll-tax and twice the customs duty paid by a Muslim.[32]

The situation was different in the Russian-held Turkestan. Russia had consciously suppressed usury by Hindus and a law to this effect was promulgated as far back as in 1877.[33] The government policies immediately affected Indians adversely.

Russians also obstructed Indian traders in other ways. Indians were required to have passport and Russian visa for visiting Russian Turkestan.[34] For a time Russian authorities asked the police to report on the activities of Indians as they suspected them of being spies of the British.[35]

Indian residents of Bukhara, Muhammad Sadyk and Sultan Muhammed, appealed to the Tsarist authorities to lift the ban on free movement of Indian merchants in Russian-held Turkestan.[36] The Russian Counsel in Bombay was specially advised in 1902 to inform the names of such persons visiting Central Asia who could be suspected of taking up moneylending after their arrival. They were to be put under police surveillance.[37] In 1908 specific instructions were issued that Indians suspected of indulging in moneylending should be denied visa.[38]

The law forbade Indians from acquiring land in villages. This led to a sharp reduction in the number of Indians in Tashkent.

The Hindu moneylenders who could not adjust to the new situation either left for the Bukhara *Khanate* or for Eastern Turkestan where they were permitted to ply their trade, though here again the local population looked down upon them. In fact, Eastern Turkestan became a major theatre of their activities.[39]

In 1907-08, according to a Russian officer M.S. Andreyev, there were around 200 Hindu Shikarpuris engaged in moneylending.[40] The presence of Hindu moneylenders is noted in twenties and thirties as well in Chinese Turkestan after they had been forced to stop their activities, both commercial and usurious, following the consolidation of the Bolshevik power in 1920 in Central Asia.

In face of government restrictions, Indian traders in Russian Turkestan opted for cooperation with the Russian bourgeoisie. When the Russians established factories they became suppliers of raw-material. Some Indians opened their own factories. During 1907–10 Indians owned three factories.[41] But it was clear that this could not be their mainstream activity.[42] Indians had basically turned into sellers of local handicrafts or goods manufactured in Russian factories in the bazaars of Central Asia.[43]

The changes in the transportation system following the introduction of railways and steamships enabled the Russian bourgeoisie to bring their goods to Central Asia at cheap rates. Having consolidated its rule in Central Asia during the three decades of the nineteenth century, the Russian state policies openly promoted the interest of the emerging Russian capitalist class. The Indian traders devoid of political support and lacking direct links with India had no option but to face decline.

Both in the Bukharan *Khanate* and the Russian-held Turkestan, Hindus were allowed to follow their own socio-cultural and religious norms. Though not allowed to construct a temple, they were permitted to set up their idols and icons in the serais where they lived.[44]

Contemporary sources indicate that the Hindus celebrated at least two of their religious festivals—*Diwali,* the festival of light and *Janmasthami*, the birthday of Lord Krishna—in full view of the public. Local dignitaries and authorities were present as their honoured guests. *Mir Shab*, the Bukharan officer was, by custom, always invited to attend the *Diwali* festivities and he made it a point to be with the Indians.[45]

In Tashkent, the administrative centre of Russian Turkestan, a school for teaching Indian languages to Russian military officers was established after it had functioned for a short while in Ashkhabad. Local Indians were recruited to teach spoken Hindustani; some teachers were also recruited from India to teach the language. A Kashmiri, Kabirshah Mustafin, resident in the village Bikabad in Pskentski region of Tashkand, proved to be very popular teacher. He could teach even through the medium of Russian.[46]

When Indian teachers went to their homeland during vacations they were asked to bring in textbooks when they returned. A number of books and dictionaries were published from Tashkent, which emerged as an additional centre for the development of Russian Indology.[47]

It might also be noted that Indians in Turkestan began to learn the Russian language and they acted as interpreters for their compatriots before Russian authorities in the nineteenth century.

The Anglo-Russian Convention of 1907, which ushered in an era of Anglo-Russian cooperation temporarily ended visits by Indian patriots seeking Russian aid to overthrow the British rule, as was the case in the nineteenth century.

The outbreak of the First World War in Europe in 1914, the emergence of a pro-German regime in Afghanistan, and the German support to Indian freedom fighters provided an opportunity for Indians to renew their political activities in Central Asia.

Mahendra Pratap formed a Provisional Government in Afghanistan in 1915 and sent his emissary twice to the Tsarist Governor in Tashkent in 1916. On the first occasion, the Indian mission was not entertained. Mahendra Pratap and his foreign minister Barkatullah took another chance and this time their emissaries were handed over to the British officials who shot them dead.[48] But things changed after the Bolsheviks came to power in Russia following the November Revolution of 1917.

Some Bolshevik revolutionaries, especially Weltman, during their exile in Paris had been in touch with Indian revolutionaries. After the Bolsheviks became rulers of Russia, the Indian patriots knowing their aversion for capitalism, colonialism and racialism, turned to them for support in their struggle against the British rule.[49]

The Bolsheviks responded positively. When the Third Communist International (Comintern) was established and the new regime decided to actively promote fight against colonialism and to support freedom struggles in the colonies, a section of Indian patriots aligned themselves with the new regime. In December 1919, Indians in Tashkent formed the Indian Revolutionary Association.[50]

The third congress of Comintern was held in Moscow in 1920. It decided to use Tashkent as a base for waging war against British imperialism in the East. A group of Indian participants in the 3rd Congress at Moscow headed by M.N. Roy was sent to Tashkent.[51] They tried to recruit Indians residing in Tashkent for their cause. They were joined by a group of Indians headed by Acharya who had arrived from Kabul.[52] The first Indian Communist Party was formed in exile in Tashkent.

The Soviet regime needed legitimacy in the Muslim-dominated Central Asia. It also needed the support of the local populace because the White Army was trying to stir up trouble. The British in India had not kept quiet. They had also sent Bailey to make things hot for the Bolsheviks.[53] The services of Barkatullah, an Indian revolutionary and a Pan-Islamist and a diehard anti-British, were used for conducting anti-British propaganda. He wrote pamphlets in Persian, which were printed and extensively distributed in Central Asia.[54]

The morale of Indians received a boost when hordes of Indian Muslims arrived in Tashkent via Afghanistan. Their journey was facilitated by the new Afghan king, Amanullah who succeeded his father Habibullah after he was assassinated in 1919. The new king followed 'ultra-nationalist and un-British policies'.[55] The Indian Muslims had left the country with the aim of fighting against the allied powers in defence of the Caliphate.

Among the important leaders who arrived in Tashkent was Maulana Obaidullah Sirhindi, a proponent of Pan-Islamism. He left for Moscow and thereafter for Constantinople.[56]

The political activism of Indians in Tashkent was short-lived. Their internal bickering compelled the Comintern to order them back to Moscow; the Military School was closed in 1921 as a sequel to the Anglo-Russian agreement[57] and the students were advised to proceed to Moscow and get admitted to the newly established Communist University of the Toilers of the East.[58]

The Bolshevik regime succeeded in consolidating itself by instigating a rebellion in Bukhara which forced the Khan to flee and Bukhara was thereafter united with Russian Turkestan.

The British military intervention in trans-Caspia and trans-Caucasus also came to nought; the presence of the Indian armed forces only aroused local hostility. On May 1, 1920 the Red Army occupied Baku and Azerbaijan became a part of the Soviet Union. Lenin described Baku as 'a Marxist window on the Mostem East'.[59]

British spies, such as Bailey, Blacker, Etherton, and Macartney had sneaked into Tashkent[60] to oust 'the Bolsheviks who were described as pro-German'. The British agents were instructed to align with the anti-Bolshevik groups, and if possible try to bring about rising in Tashkent similar to that they had engineered at Baku and Ashkhbad against the Bolsheviks by rendering financial assistance, which might sound the death knell of the Bolshevik power in this region.[61] Soon they realised the futility of their efforts to overthrow the Bolsheviks and they gave up.[62]

The British in India, however, did not cease sending their agents to Central Asia for inciting local population against the Bolsheviks; but even the revolt of Bachcha Saki in Kokand failed to roll back the wheel of history. Bolsheviks remained in firm control of Turkestan from the shores of the Caspian to the borders of Sinkiang.

With Bolsheviks pursuing a policy, which aimed at abolishing private control over means of production and eliminating private commerce, Indian traders and moneylenders became redundant. Some returned to India, some went to Chinese Turkestan to which, because of porus borders, access was not difficult. Private commerce and usury still prevailed in Chinese Turkestan and caravans between Srinagar in Kashmir and Kashgar in Sinkiang continued to travel.[63] Usury was condemned by the locals and it was noted, "Moneylending by British subjects is not encouraged by his Majesty's Consulate-General at Kashgar ... moneylenders get no support from British consular officials in Turkestan".[64] Still Indians could practise usury and carry on trade.

Indians in Chinese Turkestan maintained a very fragile relationship with the Soviet Central Asia. Indian traders in Central Asia had passed into history.

Rest of the Indians who could neither return nor go to Sinkiang became integrated in the local population. The Census conducted in Uzbekistan in 1926 recorded all Indians as permanent residents of the USSR and hence, it is difficult how many of them were there.[65]

Along with scholars, travellers, traders, soldiers from India who went to Central Asia, groups of Indians belonging to the lowest rung of the social order also entered Central Asia. The Soviet indologist Oranskii discovered a collection of *Paria* in Tajikistan who spoke in a language akin to Punjab and who with great zeal had preserved their language. Of course, they had forgotten from where their forefathers had originally arrived.[66]

In the Soviet regime the nature of Indians entering Central Asia was entirely different from the preceding centuries. In the thirties and the forties occasional visitors made their way. Only after Khrushchev opened up the Soviet Union and free India became a friend of the Bolshevik regime that Indo-Central Asian contacts were revived: Central Asia now welcomed Indian scholars, students, and cultural workers.

NOTES AND REFERENCES

1. G.L. Dmitriyev, *Iz Istroii Sredneaziatsko-Indiiskikh Otnoshenii Vtoroi Poloviny XIX-Nachala XXV, (Indiiskiye Vykjodsty V Srednei Azii), Avtoreferat*, Tashkent, 1965, pp. 6-7.
2. Devendra Kaushik, *India and Central Asia in Modern Times*, New Delhi, 1985, Chapter 5; P.M. Shastitko (chief editor), *Rossiiskiye Puteshestvenniki V Indii XIX*, Moscow, 1990, pp. 235-44. The article deals with the visit of A.E. Snesarev to India in 1899; K. Warikoo, *Central Asia and Kashmir*, New Delhi, 1989, ch. 1.
3. B.I. Iskandrov, *Srednyana Aziya Indiya*, Dushanbe, 1993, p. 91.
4. Dmitriyev, Avtoreferat, 1965, *op. cit.*, p. 11.
5. *Ibid.*, p. 9.
6. *Ibid.*
7. *Ibid.*
8. *Ibid.*
9. Avtoreferat, p. 11.
10. T.N. Zagorodnikova and P.M. Shastitko (chief editors), *Russko-Indiiskiye Otnosheniya V 1900-1917*, Moscow, 1999, p. 250.
11. *Ibid.*, pp. 243-44.
12. Sadriddin Aini, *Sobraniye Sochinenii*, Vol. V (Bukhara), Moskava, 1974, p. 44.
13. *Ibid.*, p. 46.
14. *Ibid.*, p. 44.
15. *Ibid.*
16. *Ibid.*
17. *Ibid.*, p. 44.
18. *Ibid.*
19. *Ibid.*, p. 45.
20. *Ibid.*
21. *Ibid.*
22. *Ibid.*, p. 46.
23. *Ibid.*
24. *Ibid.*
25. *Ibid.*
26. *Ibid.*, p. 45.
27. *Ibid.*, p. 45.
28. *Ibid.*

29. *Ibid.*
30. *Ibid.*, p. 46.
31. Iskandrov, 1993, *op. cit.*, p. 45.
32. Avtoreferat, p. 13.
33. *Ibid.*, p. 15.
34. *Ibid.*
35. *Ibid.*
36. Tatyana and Shastitko, pp. 244-48.
37. *Ibid.*, p. 86 and doc. no. 61.
38. *Ibid.*, pp. 86-90.
39. Zagorodnikova and Shastitko, *op. cit.*, p. 239.
40. P.T. Etherton, *In the Heart of Asia*, London, 1925, p. 131. He noted, 'Yangi Hissar [51 miles from Kashgar] is the happy hunting ground of Hindu moneylenders hailing from Shikarpur.'
41. G.L. Dmitriyev, 'Iz Istorii Indiiskikh Kolonii V Srednei Azii', in D.A. Olderogge (chief editor), *Strany I Narody Vostoka Indii-Strana I Narod*, Book 2, Moscow, 1972, pp. 235.
42. *Ibid.*, pp. 238-39; Avtoreferat, p. 12.
43. *Ibid.*, p. 238.
44. *Ibid.*, pp. 239-41.
45. *Ibid.*, pp. 242-43.
46. *Ibid.*, pp. 246-47.
47. *Ibid.*, pp. 246-47.
48. Zagorodnikova and Shastitko, pp. 444-58.
49. M.P. Pavlovich (Weltman), *India V Borbe Za Nezavisimost*, Moscow, 1925.
50. Avtoreferat, p. 21.
51. Purabi Roy, Dutta Gupta and Vasudevan (eds.), *Indo-Russian Relations, 1917-1947*, Part I, Calcutta 1999, pp. 38-43.
52. *Ibid.*, pp. 57-9; pp. 62-67.
53. F.M. Bailey, *Mission to Tashkent*, London, 1946, pp. 30, 55, 78.
54. Etherton, p. 155.
55. *Journal of the Royal Central Asian Society* (*JRCAS*), 1933, p. 470.
56. During Obaidullah Sindhi's stay in Moscow in 1923, he was received four times by the Soviet Foreign Minister Chicherin. Zafar Hassan, *Ap Beeti*, (in Urdu), Lahore, 1955, p. 257.
57. Warikoo, 1989, *op. cit.*, p. 118.
58. See my unpublished paper, 'Comintern and the Indian Communist Party: The Early Years.'
59. *JRCAS*, 1936, p. 155.

60. T.R. Sarren, *British Intervention in Central Asia and Trans-Caucasia*, New Delhi, 1989, p. 99. Bailey in 1922 was Political Officer in Sikkim. Warikoo, p. 117; P.T. Etherton, *In the Heart of Asia*, London, 1925, p. 124.
61. *Ibid.*, p. 101.
62. *Ibid.*, pp. 104-07.
63. *JRCAS*, 1933, p. 533.
64. *JRCAS*, 1933, p. 486.
65. G.L. Dmitriyev, 'Is Istorii Indiiskikh ...', p. 234.
66. I.M. Oranskii, 'K Etnografii Indoyazychnoi Gruppy Parya', in *Strany I Narody Vostoka India-Strana I Narod*, pp. 219-33.

SECTION IV

CONTEMPORARY PERIOD

22

India and Central Asia: An Overview of Relationship

Tabasum Firdaus

Indo-Central Asian relationship is traceable to the hoary past. If the theory of the rise of the Aryans from the Central Asian Steppes and their subsequent movement southward is to be accepted, then the first significant link between the two peoples is traceable to the times of the migration of the Aryans.[1]

In the course of history, not only great warriors but also great missionaries and Sufis rose from Central Asia and carried their respective mission to the land of Hindustan. Chingiz Khan, Timur and Babur were well-known conquerors that established empires and gave an efficient administrative system to the lands they had conquered.[2]

During the Soviet power, Central Asia remained somewhat out of focus. Under Stalin's plan of constructing of linguistic states [3] five states were created. Besides two more trans-Caspian republics were also loosely included in the Eurasian part of the Soviet Union.

Owing to the nature of very close relations between India and erstwhile Soviet Union, New Delhi did not strictly focus on Central Asia and did not venture to build closer relationship with any one of the five Central Asian republics of Soviet days. This perhaps reflected the fallout of cold war mentality when the superpowers continued to remain at loggerheads.

After the break up of the Soviet Union, India took her time to open embassies in the newly independent states of Central Asia.

India's Central Asia policy at that point of time was markedly different from the policy of other neighbouring states like Pakistan, Iran, Saudi Arabia and Turkey. Indian Deputy Commerce Minister Salman Khurshid visited Central Asia in the summer of 1992 and announced credit of $10 million each to Uzbekistan and Kazakhstan and $5 million each to the other republics. India would also help Iran build the railway link between Ashkhabad and Meshed.[4]

Above mentioned countries were under an illusion that the collapse of the Soviet Union and decentralisation of political and military power had created a vacuum and they could fill it using strategies suiting their interests. Looking in retrospect, we find that these rather impetuous neighbours tried to manipulate Central Asian people for their own interest without committing themselves to any real assistance to them in their hour of need.[5]

For example, Turkey came forward with the pan-Turkism programme. She thought that these could become the satellite states and thus Turkey would emerge as a crucial factor in deciding the future course of foreign and home policies in these states.

Saudi Arabia, being the fountainhead of Sunni-Wahhabism, came along with the agenda of sharpening of religious sensitivity of the people of Central Asia who were of mostly of Sunni faith. A large number of copies of the holy book running in hundreds of thousands were distributed among people in Central Asia. Saudis provided big amounts for the construction of mosques in the length and breadth of Central Asia, particularly in Uzbekistan and Tajikistan. Funds were also provided for assistance to the clerics (*mullahs*) who were appointed to lead the praying congregations in the mosques. Pakistan also towed the same line and many Pakistani *mullahs*, mostly the *Jamaat-e-Islami* activists, were found roaming the lands of Central Asia and making prolonged halts at the newly constructed mosques. Thus the two countries in tandem tried to induct fundamentalist ideology among the Central Asian people besides others in other parts of the world.[6]

The case of Tajikistan was somewhat different. Tajiks are neither linguistically nor ethnically affiliated to the Turkic stock. As such, Pan-Turkism did not work in that case. But it was Iran that tried to create a strong clout for herself in Tajikistan. The Tajiks and Iranians are of the common stock and Tajik and Farsi are two sides of the same coin. This was the powerful instrument for Iran to make her presence felt in Tajikistan. But unfortunately, adding the extremist religious element to the cultural lever, particularly when the Tajiks were Sunnis and the Iranians were Shias, Iran made herself a suspect in the eyes of the Tajiks who sooner than later rejected the ideology of export of Islamic revolution.

Tajikistan was already involved in a fierce struggle against the fundamentalists at home and was in no way prepared to exacerbate the already tense situation. In this way, Iran had to drag her feet and restrain herself to cultural activities only, that too of somewhat superficial nature.

In comparison to this, the first thing India did was to be slow on opening her embassies in Central Asian Republics. The Indian embassy in Tajikistan was opened six years after the declaration of independence by that state. This gave New Delhi sufficient time for understanding the situation in Central Asia in a new set of circumstances. It also helped her assess in what ways India should assist these nascent Republics to stand on their legs.[7]

It has to be remembered that India does not favour creating power blocs. Her thinking is that these blocs, when created, naturally make others suspicious about them and thus instead of developing friendly relations, an atmosphere of animosity and antagonism is created.

After establishing formal diplomatic relations with the Central Asian States, India entered into bilateral agreements with some of them, which essentially provided for support to all the states in scientific and technological fields in order to provide for the development of industries. Strengthening of industrial base of these states has been the primary concern of India. In the areas of tourism, hotel industry, banking, accountancy, agro-industries, pharmaceuticals and textile industry, India offered her expertise and assistance.

India opened admission in higher and technical education for more students and researchers from the Central Asian States, in almost all big educational institutions in the country. We find students from Central Asia receiving education in various branches of learning. This has endeared India to these States more than anything else has.

Trade and commerce between India and the Central Asia have been made less complicated. India has also contributed funds for various projects in Central Asia. We find hotels in New Delhi packed with individual and small-scale traders from Central Asia who make on the spot purchases in bulk and dispatch the goods to their destinations. India has an agreement with Iran by virtue of which Indian merchandise is unloaded at Bandar Abbas in Persian Gulf and then carried through railway freight to Sirakhs on Iran-Turkmenistan border wherefrom it is carried to different destinations in Central Asia. India had helped Iran build the Bandar Abbas-Sirakhs rail link. At present this is the only viable trade route between India and Central Asia.[8]

In the area of political relations, India has never tried to tie down these states to any particular political parameter that might suit India's interests.

However, India has been, by and large, satisfied with the security arrangements made by the Central Asian States, either bilaterally or multilaterally, in which Russia has been an important partner. By and large India has accepted the ground reality that Russia has still a very significant role to play in the affairs of Central Asia. Even the Americans and European Union, are of the same opinion. There is strong justification for that.[9] In this context the Russian mind can be understood from the following small passage from the Great Russian novelist Dostoevsky written in 1881:

> ..the Russian is not only European, but also an Asiatic. Not only that in our coming destiny, perhaps it is precisely Asia that represents our main way out. In Europe we were Asiatic, whereas in Asia we, too, are Europeans. Our civilizing mission in Asia will bribe our spirit and drive us thither.[10]

In the context of the prevailing situation in Afghanistan, Central Asia has also come under focus. Since Uzbekistan and Tajikistan both apprehend the rise of fundamentalists in their states, they have agreed to contribute their bit in the US fight against terrorism. Tajikistan has hundreds of kilometres of common border with Afghanistan, which, as the history of last one decade shows, the fanatical Afghan Taliban invariably violated. They tried to indoctrinate the Tajiks with fundamentalist ideology and to supply them with arms and training to destabilize the regime in Dushanbe.

India has endorsed the security arrangement between Tajikistan and the CIS in which Russia is playing the leading role. She had also indirectly expressed her support to the Northern Alliance forces as long as they accepted the policy of secularism and democracy as the political dispensation.

India has always been supportive of Tajikistan in her fight against religious extremism. Twice did the Tajik President Imomali Rahman pay visits to New Delhi during 1999- 2001. The most recent visit was in July 2001 when several bilateral agreements pertaining to the flow of trade and commerce between the two countries were signed. These protocols are the cornerstone of good bilateral relations. Likewise with other Central Asian States also India has signed bilateral agreements and protocols that would further consolidate good friendly relations with them. Uzbek president, Islam Karimov also paid a couple of visits to New Delhi to further strengthen ties with India.

Finally, India has an important role to play in the context of Central Asia. India is going through a charcoal phase of political history. Wedded as she is to democracy, secularism and pluralism, she is managing a vast population of varying shades, ethnicity, language, religion and culture. Central Asia will have to learn a lot from India's experience in dealing with political opponents and internal subversion. It is true that the present leadership in Central Asia is the same leadership of the communist days. Central Asian States have to learn about party system, the functioning of opposition, free and fair elections, the rights and duties of citizens, the enforcement of constitution and respect for judiciary, freedom of press etc. In all these matters, these republics have to learn from India. Above all Central Asian States and India are in full agreement on the questions of necessity of peace in the region so that economic backwardness can be overcome. Hopefully greater interaction and co-operation between the two will take place in years to come.

To sum up, India as a rising economic and regional power in South Asia has vital interests in Central Asian region. She can find a vast market for her goods of all denominations from household and consumer goods to heavy machinery, air crafts, weaponry, and vast electric and electronic equipments. India is in need of energy resource which Central Asia, particularly Kazakhstan and Turkmenistan has in abundance. India needs overland connectivity with Central Asia that is secure and viable. For this purpose India needs friendly relations with Pakistan and Afghanistan. The TAPI gas pipeline could become a model for India-Central Asia connectivity. India and Central Asia both are vulnerable to religion-based terrorism and the CARs are the components of Shanghai Co-operation which has vowed to fight terrorism, fundamentalism and conservatism.

Central Asia stands at the junction of two major Asian powers, Russia and China. Their strategy in Central Asian region will have direct impact on India's foreign policy. India has good relations with Afghanistan and its contiguous Central Asian state of Tajikistan. The end game in Afghanistan will have direct bearing both on Central Asia as well as Pakistan and India. Therefore India will be closely watching the developments in Afghanistan particularly when the US and NATO troops intend to leave the war-torn region in 2012. The entire region is passing through a crucial period. China is extending her sphere of influence in Gilgit-Baltistan, the part of the original state of Jammu and Kashmir now under Pakistan. Neither India, nor Russia and nor the US can close her eyes on this new dynamics of Sino-Pak strategy in the region.

NOTES AND REFERENCES

1. G.Bowles, *The People of Asia*, USA, 1977.
2. F. Al-Din, Attar, *Muslim Saints and Mystics: Episodes from the Memorial of the Saints*, Arkana, penguin, London, 1990, see also *Baburnameh, translated by Annette Beveridge, reprinted by Sang-e-Meel, Lahore.*

3. J.Stalin, *Marxism and National Question*, Proletarian Publishers, USA, 1975.
4. Rashid , Ahmad, *The Resurgence of Central Asia, Islam or Nationalism*, Karachi, 1994, p. 220.
5. Rumer, "The Gathering Strom in Central Asia", *Orbis*, winter 1993.
6. M.Brill Olcott , "Central Asia's Post Empire Politics," *Orbis*, Spring, 1993.
7. Rashid Ahmad , p. 220.
8. M.Jiali, "Central Asia :Geo-Strategic Situation and Big Power Politics," *Contemporary Central Asia*, Vol. 3, no 1, 1999.
9. G.G.Hosking, A History of the Soviet Union, Fontana, London, 1990.
10. M.Hauner, what is Asia to US? Russian's Asian Heartland Yesterday and Today, Unwin Hyman, London, 1990. He quotes an article by Dostoevsky on the Russian victory at Goek, Tepe, where thousands of Turkomen were massacred by Russian Force.

23

A Secret Report by the First Soviet Ambassador: India's Early Years of Independence

V.P. Kashin

K.V. Novikov,[1] the first Soviet Ambassador to India, presented a report on July 5, 1949, to the Foreign Policy Commission of the Central Committee of the Communist Party. The document has a 'top secret' classification. At present, it is available in the Russian Centre for Maintenance and Research of the Modern History Documents (RCMRMHD), where the main part of the archives of the Central Committee of the CPSU was preserved. The shorthand record of the account is done in 26 typewritten pages. The account itself is 9 pages and includes the Ambassador's answers to the questions of the Commission's members. There were 28 such questions: 9 were connected with the situation in the CPI, 8 dealt with the political situation in India, 7 on the British-Indian relations, and 4 questions concerned the spread of the Soviet publications in India.

The main task set before the Ambassador by the Commission was to give a detailed analysis of the situation in India and simultaneously to discover the presence of the revolutionary crisis sign in the country. Quite understandably a considerable part of the report dealt with the position of the working class and the peasantry as well as the role of the CPI. But to a great disappointment of the Commission members the Ambassador could not discover a revolutionary situation in India. In his opinion, the struggle of workers and peasantry was exclusively under economic slogans and did not touch the basis of the present political formation. The report says:

> There has been no improvement in the economic status of the working class and peasantry in comparison with the British period. Moreover, the progressive

> deterioration is taking place. While under the English rule, till August 15, 1947, a qualified worker earned 50-60 rupees and was also getting, in different branches of industry and various princely states, roughly speaking, about 20-30 rupees a month as high prices addition. From August 15, 1947, to the present time, the subsistence level index grew from 150 to 200 points. For the period the Indian government is in power it has grown from 200 points to 360 in 1948 and to 560 in this year (1949). The development is not towards the wage increase but towards the abolition of high prices bonuses and secondly, towards the liquidation of fair price shops where the workers could buy cheap products. It was planned to organise a general strike of railwaymen on March 9. One of the main points of the strike was the question of abolition of high prices bonuses and liquidation of the fair price shops.[2]

While the workers were dissatisfied with low wages, bonuses addition, etc., the peasantry was angry with the revenue policy of the government as a whole. The report continued:

> The situation now is that the Indian government has to import 4 million tones of grain this year. The Indian government has now to spend all the export profits mainly for the grain import payments. Finding it necessary to cut down expenses and to reduce the import of grain, it introduced a tax in kind instead of the cash one. The Indian officials began to tour the villages and extort grain from the peasantry, which has grain left neither for sowing nor for subsistence; this has inevitably provoked a repulsive reaction against the Indian authorities: separate, uncoordinated, spontaneous peasant revolts against various government grain collectors, landowners, feudal lords and especially against usurers take place here and there. The minister of the Interior of the Madras province was questioned in the Parliament about the number of recent mass shootings in the Madras province. He answered that from the beginning of 1947 till the September 1, 1948, the government recorded 52 mass shootings of the peasant and workers' campaigns.[3]

Nevertheless, severe measures against the strikers hardly caused any serious protest from the democratic-minded circles and the repression victims themselves. "The press features these shootings like order of the day", the report stressed.[4] The reason for this apparent paradox is rightfully described by the reporter as the simultaneous impact of the following three factors: firstly, the organisational weakness and insufficient political orientation of the Indian proletariat and the peasantry; secondly, in the spontaneous, local and defensive character of the workers' and peasants' actions, and thirdly, in the absence of a co-ordinating work among the Indian communist masses.

> A great shortcoming and misfortune of the democratic movement is in that in the overwhelming majority of cases spontaneous actions take place without any co-ordinating or guiding activities of the Communist Party.[5]

A temporary prohibition of the CPI and its underground work even more weakened the links between the party and the people. Emphasising this circumstance, Novikov at the same time declined the supposition of those Commission members, who regarded the anti-Communist repressions as a result of police provocation and put forward his own version:

> At present both the working class and the peasantry of India are in a somewhat awakened mood. Strikes of the working class and armed revolts of the peasantry take place around the whole country. To tell the truth, these actions of the working class and the peasantry are separate and spontaneous; they are rather of a petty character, but the main thing is that the whole country is engulfed in this movement. Under these conditions many local Communist Party organizations apply persistently to the Central Committee asking for help with arms and munitions.[6]

> Until the Second Congress held in March of the previous year, the Communist Party of India thought that Nehru could turn to the left. Before this Congress of the Communist Party, the Central Committee supported the Nehru's government and made the main emphasis upon the struggle against British imperialism. The Communist Party considered that the Indian government could, as a result of criticism and outside pressure, turn not towards the further new-form of rapprochement with the British imperialism, but towards the left for the sake of the establishment of a certain kind of democratic government.[7]

But during its Congress,

> the Communist Party rejected the policy of supporting the Indian government and proclaimed the struggle against the British imperialism on par with the struggle against the present regime in India.[8]

Thus, the Ambassador considered the change in the CPI's attitude to the government as the main reason for the ruling circles' 'displeasure' with the Communists. In its turn a cardinal revision of the party's home policy line implied an inevitable change in its leadership.

> The Second Congress of the Communist Party of India condemned the position of the previous Central Committee (CC) including the position of the General Secretary Joshi as a reformist one. Joshi was relieved of his General Secretary post and the staff of the Central Committee was almost wholly renewed. The present CC is not known to us. It was published that Ranadive was elected General Secretary. From the conspirative point of view the Indian Communist Party took the right decision not to publish the names of the new CC members. I am a little bewildered by the fact that they could not inform us even of the head person of the Central Committee.[9]

The report goes on:

> At its December meeting Political Bureau carefully analysed the work of provincial Party organisations, in accordance with the decisions of the Second Congress of the Communist Party. In these decisions the Political Bureau strictly underlines that a reformist tilt still exists in the ranks of the Communist Party, that Joshi despite his speech at the Congress, in which he has admitted his mistakes and approved the decisions of the Second Congress of the Indian Communist Party, in reality pursues in essence the old reformist policy. Moreover, these decisions point out that he supported and tried to establish close links with the reformist groups and groupings in provincial party organizations and princely states. A problem of treason in the Communist Party ranks was discussed at that Political Bureau meeting. The treason came to such a level that the underground organization network of the Indian Communist Party was discovered by a policeman, so the CC had to re-establish the whole underground organization network to prevent itself from new failures.[10]

Later, while considering the political situation in India, Novikov made some principal observations that were not only far from the essence of Stalin's estimates but were in absolute contradiction with them.

> Before my arrival to India, I was instructed by Comrade Stalin to bear in mind that the Indian government came to power on August 15, 1947, as a result of the deal between the Indian national bourgeois-feudal circles and British imperialism,[11]

the Ambassador said in the preamble of his speech. As a result, he came to the conclusion that after the achievement of independence, the absolute power was in the hands of the national bourgeoisie. So, the establishment of Nehru government, the act of transfer of power to the Indian side by the British, the partition of India and the positive action of the Indian government, which were directed towards the establishment of diplomatic relations with the Soviet Union and development of the Soviet-Indian cooperation least of all corresponded to the classification of 'political farce'.

At the same time the reporter made it clear that the British have changed the form of their participation in the economic life of the country.

> They sell a portion of shares to the Indians, 25 per cent, make the management boards [of the companies – Kashin] Indian, thus the company becomes Indian too. From the other side, they purchase the shares of the companies which are purely Indian.[12]

The Ambassador observed,

> The Communist press published only the information that at the present 75 per cent of investment profits are appropriated by the British bourgeoisie and

> only 25 per cent by the Indian one. A part of the leading bourgeoisie circles is ready to reconcile to such distribution, but a part of the same circles would like to change the situation so that 75 per cent of profits would come into the hands of the national bourgeoisie and 25 per cent into the hands of the foreigners. Such is the position of Socialist Party of India.[13]

Novikov's estimation of Jawaharlal Nehru's political role was even more independent and farsighted. Contrary to Stalin's views he described India's first Prime Minister as the leader of liberation movement, a subtle politician, a wise parliamentarian and a faithful Congress member, able to skilfully assess public mood, as a man enjoying great authority and respect in his country. Discussing Nehru's views, he unintentionally forerun his time and made theoretical statements concerning the variety of methods of transition to socialism in accordance with the concrete conditions of this or that country.

> He [Nehru – Kashin] sometimes opposed Gandhi, styled himself a Socialist and in some cases assessed in a positive way the Soviet system, Communism and stated that India had the same problems as Russia had had. At present Indian national bourgeoisie and the Congress intentionally propagate the view that within the Congress and the government, Nehru is progressive figure. This is corroborated by Nehru's repeated statements that he is a supporter of Socialism, but under the conditions of India ways and methods of socialist transition must be different from those of the Soviet Union.[14]

Paying homage to Mahatma Gandhi as a recognised leader of liberation struggle of the people of India, the Ambassador informed that the next day after Gandhi's assassination he offered his own and the Soviet government's condolences to Nehru and after a few days condolences on behalf of the Foreign Ministry and the Soviet government were expressed by the special note of the USSR Foreign Ministry. Moreover, the Ambassador behaved as a courageous man of principles and criticised the position of Stalin who did not publicly react to Gandhi's tragic death.

> Comrade Molotov asked me if Comrade Stalin was right not to offer his condolences on the occasion of Gandhi's death. I answered that from a practical point of view it was harmful as Truman, Churchill and other government and state leaders of the world sent their condolences while Comrade Stalin did not. From a conjectural point of view it was harmful for us.[15]

As part of the report testifies to the fact, winds of the 'cold war' did make an impact upon the initial phase of Indo-Soviet relations. It could hardly be otherwise in the period under review, when sharp ideological confrontation ruled supreme. According to the Ambassador, the Indian censorship board prohibited to show a number of Soviet films in India. He cited the examples of some films like *She Fights for Her Motherland*, which had been permitted by the British colonial authorities and prohibited in the independent India. This film pictured the heroic deeds of a woman guerrilla during the war against fascism and therefore was viewed by the Censorship Board as a guerrilla war instruction. Another prohibited Soviet film, *The Stone Flower* was just a fairy tale which was proclaimed dangerous due to the scene of a landlord's cruelty towards a stone cutter: it was supposed to fan popular wrath against the landlords. The Ambassador concluded:

> I must say that there is a document, the instruction of the Indian government which has fallen unofficially into our hands. It instructs the provincial governments to see to it that a minimum of the Soviet propaganda reaches India. It is openly stated there that there is a TASS publishing agency in India, so be expedient that your propaganda authorities do not allow the TASS information to be published with the exception of those articles and materials that are contradictory to themselves.[16]

K.V. Novikov's objectivity, sagacity and personal courage as evident from his interpretation of the social and political situation in the newly independent India were not unnoticed by the Commission and had a negative impact upon his further career. After the commencement of his Ambassadorial term in India, he was occupying some secondary posts in the Foreign Ministry and retired in 1973.

Nevertheless, in spite of Stalin's unfriendly and preconceived attitude to India and its leaders at the end of 40s, there were some positive tendencies in the Soviet-Indian relations towards a certain rapprochement and establishment of trade and economic contacts. After Nehru's unsuccessful 1949 visit to the USA and the American side's refusal to offer India food aid, the government of India made an analogous request to the Soviet Union. In 1951 a contract was signed for the delivery of 100 thousand tonnes of Soviet wheat to India in exchange for the traditional goods of the Indian export.[17] The next year India agreed to participate in the international economic conference organised in Moscow and the Soviet Union from its side took part in the international industrial exhibition in Bombay. Simultaneously, Moscow offered to deliver industrial equipment to India.

The Soviet leadership's growing interest in India was corroborated by the fact that on 5 March 1952, Stalin received S. Radhakrishnan, the Ambassador of India to the Soviet Union and on 18 February 1953 his successor K.P.S. Menon was also received by the Soviet leader. It is to be noted here that during the last years of his life; Stalin personally received only three ambassadors, among them two were of the Republic of India. As a result, at the initial stage of the Soviet-Indian relations, in spite of the obvious difficulties, the necessary foundation was laid for development and intensification of mutually beneficial co-operation between the two countries.

NOTES AND REFERENCES

1. Kirill Vasilyevich Novikov, 1905-1983, was in diplomatic service since 1940. In 1940-42, he was counsellor in the Embassy of the USSR in Great Britain, and in 1942-47, he was head of the 2nd European Department of Foreign Ministry, and Member of the Foreign Ministry Board. He participated in a number of international conferences like the Yalta 1945, Potsdam 1945, San-Francisco 1945, and Paris Peace conference 1946. K.V. Novikov was the Soviet Ambassador to India during 1947-53.
2. RCMRMHD, F. 17, 1. 128. D. 1187, P. 39.
3. *Ibid.*, p. 29.
4. *Ibid.*
5. *Ibid.*, p. 30.
6. *Ibid.*, p. 28.
7. *Ibid.*, p. 21.
8. *Ibid.*, p. 28.
9. *Ibid.*, p. 25.
10. *Ibid.*
11. *Ibid.*, p. 20.
12. *Ibid.*, p. 34.
13. *Ibid.*
14. *Ibid.*, pp. 20-21.
15. *Ibid.*, p. 22.
16. *Ibid.*, p. 36.
17. P. Shastitko *et al.* (eds.), *The USSR and India*, Moscow, 1987, p. 167.

24

Indo-Russian Trade: Soviet and Post-Soviet Trends

V.V. Chernovskaya

The Indo-Russian trade and economic relations reflects a new trend. In recent years, the two countries have realised that the level of trade does not correspond with the potential and looked for ways to boost this. They realised that in the changed situation in Russia in the nineties, strengthening cooperation at the regional level could catalyse bilateral ties.

As we tackle some questions concerning the presence of Indian business in Russian regions, it should be noted that in Soviet-era the status of Indo-Soviet trade was rising. As the largest exporter of tea together with other products like rice, tobacco, pharmaceuticals, textiles and leather garments, Indian business had a protected consumer market that was growing rapidly in demand. So, we have to look upon its present position in Russian regions, in this context.

SOVIET PERIOD

Since 1953, when the first long-term trade agreement took place, seven long-term agreements were signed between the two countries up to the collapse of the USSR. This bilateral trade through a specific system called Rupee Trade system, based on annual plans, made the Soviet Union India's second largest trading partner. The trade turnover between the two countries increased from Rs. 2 crores in 1953 to about 8,000 crores in 1990-91.[1] It has been pointed out that over 80 per cent of Indian exports were to the Soviet Union. Many industrial units in India were producing only for the assured market of the Soviet Union.[2]

In the Soviet period major actors in Indo-Russian trade and other economic relations were public sector units and state trading corporations. Only in the eighties a few Indian private houses slowly moved to the Soviet market. Such terms as 'tatachi', 'birlachi', that is, the Tata and the Birla people, operating in it became a part of lexicon used in ministries and departments responsible for importing goods from India.

When the trade between the two countries was under absolute state control, on all buying and selling there was no need for Indian companies to advertise or promote their goods. As it was mentioned, the Soviet Union has been the largest importer of tea, rice, tobacco, pharmaceuticals, textile, leather garments from India. It accounted for 50 to 66 per cent of total Indian exports. There was, of course, a high degree of instability in the Soviet demand. However, Indo-Soviet trade led to diversification of Indian export markets and better terms of trade. In the nineties the situation changed drastically.

DECLINE IN TRADE DURING POST-SOVIET PERIOD

Following the break-up of the USSR, rupee trading system based on annual plans was abandoned. Coupled with dismantling of the central buying and selling system in Russia, restructuring of its economy, growing contact between Russian and Western markets, Indo-Russian trade has declined substantially in the last one decade. As compared to 1991 when the trade turnover between the two countries stood at $ 5.5 billion it dropped to $ 1.9 billion in 1995-96 and slumped to $ 1.3 billion in 1998-99. Only in 1999-2000 it registered a positive growth of 25 per cent over the previous year reaching $1.57 billion.[3]

In fact, these figures do not reflect the true picture. A substantial amount of Indian goods enter Russia via 'shuttle trade' or through third countries.[4] Brought by Russians visiting India in large numbers and looking for quick returns as well as dealers treating the Russian market as a place for shoddy sub-standard goods, such trade was working against Indian brands. Unfortunately, Indian consumer goods acquired a name for poor quality. Much of the goodwill that existed for them in the eighties seems to have been wiped out. Added to this, the large number of fakes swamping the Russian market such as, Polish coffee, Uzbek rice, Georgian tea, etc. in Indian pack made Russian buyers suspicious.

There are other difficulties too. When our state-regulated economy moved towards a market-oriented system, it was difficult for many Indian companies to adjust to rapidly changing economic and commercial environment, driven by market forces. State trading was restricted to defence and some other items. Trade had to be conducted through private companies and joint stock companies set up by Russians. Indian goods faced increasing competition with Western and cheap Southeast Asian goods. High cost and long time in transportation of goods from India added to their cost and made them less competitive in the market as compared to exports from European countries and such neighbouring countries as China and Turkey. The cumulative effect of all this was lack of confidence in India's business and trading community. And it did not inspire the private sector to go to the Russian market in a big way.[5] In 1998, some of the Indian companies that had operations or representative offices in Russia have closed shop; yet more were on borderline, and others—Cadila, Balmer Lawri, Larsen and Toubro, and Bharat Forge—were reported to have lost faith in their Russian operations.

Meanwhile, Russia provided a large market for Indian business. The market size is estimated at $ 18 billion. It is growing by 4 to 6 per cent every year especially for foodstuff, beverages, textiles, leather goods, consumer electronics and cosmetics.[6] Addressing a meeting of Indian businessmen and entrepreneurs in Bombay on 5 October 2000 President Vladimir Putin stressed: "One of the main tasks is to bolster economic and trade cooperation, which now do not correspond to the potential of our countries".

Russian regions are viewed as permanent factor determining the future of Indo-Russian trade and economic relations.

INDIAN BUSINESS IN REGIONS

Taking advantage of Russia's new free-market policies, the regions were trying to recover lost ground in India in the aftermath of Soviet collapse. Sverdlovsk oblast, where the giant machine building factory Uralmash that once supplied machinery and equipment to India is based, was the first among them. In 1994 a 'Days of Sverdlovsk' fair was organised in Delhi to introduce this region to Indians. During the fair a decision was taken to set up joint ventures in the region with participation of Indian companies.

In a similar way Sverdlovsk was followed by Voronezh, a hub of Russian heavy industry. Then governors of several industrially developed regions of Central Russia (Ryazan, Tula), Siberia (Omsk, Irkutsk), Far East (Vladivostok) as well as presidents of republics (Bashkortostan, Tatarstan, Saha) showed their keen interest in reviving economic links with India.

The Indian Embassy in Moscow took several initiatives to get Russian regions interested in India. A working group to promote cooperation with the regions was set up under the Intergovernmental Joint Commission, the apex body for shaping bilateral ties. Under patronage of the working group Indian businessmen established direct contacts with a few regions. Part of them resulted in signing of memoranda of understanding and protocols on trade, economic, scientific and cultural co-operation. An example of stable collaboration up to 2003, is the protocol on co-operation in these fields signed in 1997 between Bashkortostan and the Indian embassy.

There are 89 regions in the Russian Federation. With a view to increasing co-operation at the level of regions the Indian embassy launched informative programmes, including organisation of seminars, conferences and round tables. Coordinated through the Institute of Oriented Studies, RAN, they have succeeded in St. Petersburg, Vladivostok, Ufa, and Ryazan. In total, 17 Russian regions are reported to have involved in different programmes initiated by the Indian embassy throughout the nineties.

Practically these programmes helped to identify areas of mutual interest including business and trade. Now there are about hundred Indian firms and 15 Indo-Russian commercial organisations that step up co-operation at the level of regions. Hindustan Lever and Ganpati Exports are increasing their exports substantially; Lupin laboratories, Nirma, Alfa Group, and Procter & Gamble are setting up their manufacturing units. There are also 74 entities with Indian participation mostly in trading.[7] And what is more important is that the presence of Indian business in Russian regions has begun to exhibit a new trend. Some big Indian corporations expressed their willingness to invest in regional projects, including factory on shaping rough diamonds and pharmaceutical plant in Jakutsk (Saha), Sakhalin oil-gas industrial goodwill and in other regions in joint ventures with local authorities.

But there are many problems too. The Russian regional market needs long-term commitment. It requires an intimate understanding, complete information about changing dynamics, and aggressive market techniques. Converted into real commercial and economic gains, the above mechanism would provide a stronghold for Indian companies not in a few but in many regions. The present situation corresponds to neither the potential nor the possibilities of Indian corporate sector to compete for share in regions. While American, German, and French companies are proceeding aggressively, consumer and luxury goods from across these countries are advertised, promoted, and made available in plenty.

By way of conclusion, it can be said that the two countries face the challenge of globalisation and adjusting their economies to new conditions; they can benefit immensely by accelerating their co-operation. Coincidence of their geopolitical interest is also lending an urgency to expansion of co-operation in economic, trade, technological, scientific, and cultural fields. Strengthening cooperation at the regional level is catalysing bilateral relations in these areas.

NOTES AND REFERENCES

1. G. Sachdeva, 'Indo-Russian Economic Relations, An Assessment', India and Russia: Towards Partnership, Round Table, JNU, New Delhi, 21.09.2000, p. 2.
2. J. Bakshi, *Russia and India: From Ideology to Geopolitics*, New Delhi, 1999, p. 132.
3. R.L. Varshney and R.K. Wadhwa, 'Economic and Trade Relations between India and Russia', Indo-Russian Relations, Prospects and Problems and Russia Today, Seminar, International Institute for Asia-Pacific Studies, New Delhi, 24.09.2000, p. 4.
4. G. Sachdeva, *op. cit.*, p. 5.
5. *The Times of India*, New Delhi, 10.08.1996.
6. R.L. Varshney and R.K. Wadhwa, *op. cit.*, p. 5.
7. *The Hindustan Times*, New Delhi, 07.12.1998.

25

Security Issues in New Central Asia: India's Concern, US Perception and International Perspectives

S.P. Singh

The central theme of this paper is to critically examine the various challenges from the forces of political Islam in Central and South West Asia during the last decade. The brief discussion reflects upon various security issues in new Central Asia: India's concern, US perception and international perspectives.

INTRODUCTION

Central Asia, which was well known to the classical world of the Greeks and the Romans, remained for quite a long period the home and cradle of an ancient and a highly developed civilisation. This sprawling area was eloquently mentioned in Homer's *Odyssey* and copiously referred to by Herodotus in his *History*. Depicted by geographers as the 'mother of all the continents' and by historians as the 'originator of human civilisation', the Central Asiatic Region (CAR) has played an important role in the various epochs of world history. In modern times, however, this region remained dormant for pretty long time, more particularly during the Russian and the Soviet rule.

But the dramatic demise and dismantling of the Former Soviet Union (FSU) in December 1991 catapulted this area again on the map of the world practically out of nowhere. The five countries of this area, which the foreign policy community in the USA used to brush aside as 'the stans' only a decade ago, captured the attention of the strategic thinkers and policy-planners all over the world. It is true that they had no historical roots as modern nation states and no track-record of separate political entities. But due to their sudden appearance from the wreckage of the FSU, these countries have been thrust upon the world atlas. They were born on the ashes of the former USSR, and they did not fight for separate nationhood like the brave Balts, the Caucasians, the Moldavians as well as the Ukrainians. Statehood and nationality were imposed upon them.

The dissolution of the FSU, which is a watershed event in modern world history, heralded the advent of a new era of incalculable possibilities. It put an end to the bipolarity of the world and overhauled the contours of international security. The dramatic disappearance of the FSU seriously impacted the all too formidable issue of the security of the two distinctively separated areas of Central Asia and South West Asia, which have merged into one single arc of a grave crisis with the gradual destabilisation of centuries-old buffer state of Afghanistan and the erosion of the failed state of Pakistan.

The instantaneous exit of the Central Asian States (CAS) from the backyards of the FSU has thrown out several challenges and opportunities in this highly volatile region out of which the emergence of political Islam is the most significant. The sudden developments in this area has thrown out the well-established politico-military equations from the eastern fringe of the Muslim-dominated Xinjiang province of China's Eastern Turkestan region to the whole of the Persian Gulf and further beyond to the Adriatic Sea in the vicinity of Turkey.

SECURITY ISSUES IN THE NEW CENTRAL ASIA

The recent upsurge in the forces of political Islam and in the subsequent Taliban threat as well as its cumulative impact on the geo-strategic environment in this area has far-reaching consequences for the security of the vast region lying between the Caucasus in the Russian Federation and far-flung Kashmir in the Indian subcontinent.

The heterogeneous complex of the CAS has long been characterised by forced statehood, flexible frontiers, numerous border disputes, artificial nationalities, ethnic mix, cultural diversity, linguistic varieties, clan affiliations and sub-national loyalties. All these features, which are anything but unifying, have weakened the foundation of these newly born political entities. All along, Islam has been the only unifying factor in this region.

But in the recent years, Islam has been used as a competing ideology to fill up the vacuum left over by the FSU. The protagonists of political Islam have toiled hard in this area to destabilise the established secular regimes in this vast area. As a consequence of it, the processes of social engineering, political formations and economic transformation of this conflict zone have been grossly impaired.

Several factors have been responsible for the emergence of political Islam in the Central Asiatic region.

The first major factor was the policy of repression and persecution, which was perpetrated upon the people of this area during the Czarist period and continued by the Soviets. Radical Islam emerged as a reaction to the political marginalisation under the long years of authoritarianism. This was further fed by serious economic stratification, acute social despondency and complex political processes of the Soviet rule. Economic dislocations in the CAR towards the end of the Soviet rule led to the disenchantment of the people with the Communist ideology to a large extent. The pace of economic development in this area led to civic disorders, chronic shortages, mass unemployment, decline in industrial production, and rise in crime rates. Compounded further by the spate of alarming increase in ethnic, clan and religious tensions, the entire prevailing situation throughout the CAR became quite ripe for the Islamic revivalism, which the people considered to be a panacea for all their maladies.

The second major factor behind the emergence of political Islam in the CAR was provided by the impending collapse of communism in the FSU, which left a vacuum in the field of ideology and spiritual life of the Central Asian people. It was during the last phase of *perestroika* that the Islamicists of this area united themselves. During the second phase of *perestroika*, the religious spectacle in Central Asia underwent a sea-change. Thousands and thousands of closed mosques, non-functioning *madrasas*, clandestine prayer houses and *Koranic* schools started functioning openly. Thousands of such religious shrines and institutions were established and repaired with aids from the government, friendly countries and religious trusts. Millions and millions of the copies of *Koran* were smuggled into Central Asia from the neighbouring countries. Several specialised Islamic institutes and research centres were established in all the five republics where special courses were developed regarding Islamic history, civilization and culture. Due emphasis was given to the study of *Shariat* and *Hadith* as well as the preponderance of the *Umma*. The extent of the transformation of Islam may be gauged from the fact that the Islamicists of Tajikistan seized the Presidential Palace in Dushanbe, the TV station, airport, and part of the capital and demanded the establishment of an Islamic state. The two Muslim clerics turned themselves into 'Generals' appended the epithet of the 'Ghazi' with their names and gave the clarion call of the '*jihad*' against the communist state of Tajikistan.

The third important factor for the propagation of political Islam in Central Asia was the gradual Islamisation of society and politics in this area, which had already registered a good deal of developments during the West-sponsored and Pak-supported *jihad* against the Soviets in Afghanistan. This war had enveloped various parts of the CAR. The US administration had then pumped 8 billion dollars into the 'Afghan pipeline' and allowed the CIA-ISI combine to manage this arsenal. Conscriptions were allowed from the various Muslim countries in the world to take part in the 'Holy War'. The *Mujahideen* were amply funded by the CIA, which loaded this outfit not only with the weapons and money but also with copies of the *Koran* and tape-recordings of the inflammatory anti-Marxist speeches. These materials reached the militant Islamicists in Tajikistan and Uzbekistan.

The professed aim of the US-Pakistani game-plan was no doubt the defeat of the Soviets. But even after their withdrawal, the military hawks of Pakistan and the warlords of Afghanistan seized these lethal weapons and used the available opportunity for suppressing their adversaries and usurping paramount political power in their own countries and the adjoining CAR.

POST-SOVIET ISLAMISATION OF CENTRAL ASIA

Initially by overshadowing the well-established buffer state of Afghanistan and subsequently by proxy through the Taliban militia,[1] Islamabad sought strategic depth in Central Asia. It started exporting Islamic fundamentalism, promoting drug money and spreading terrorism. Gradually, Pakistan and Afghanistan bridged the dividing lines between the two well-defined security zones. In the recent years, they sent a large number of mercenaries from various countries in the Gulf and Arab peninsula into this highly volatile region with their various ulterior motives. Saudi Arabia, Kuwait, Libya and the Emirates funded the subversive activities of Osama Bin Laden, his benefactor Mullah Omar and the military oligarchy of Islamabad. Pakistan used these mercenaries in Kashmir and established scores of terrorist outfits in this Indian state in order to wrest it from the Indian control by forceful means.

During the last twenty years, Pakistan has tried hard to make headway into the volatile zone of Central Asia. A year after the disintegration of the FSU, Pakistan's Prime Minister Nawaz Sharif expressed his happiness with the people of Central Asia, who had been 'held apart by the artificial barriers.'

While the importance of Pakistan as one of the most convenient gateways to Central Asia's growing business with the outside world by both land and sea routes cannot be denied, the ever-increasing interests of the fundamentalist forces of the *Jamaat-e-Islami* is worth mentioning. This *Jamaat* has played the role of an interlocutor between the leaders of the Islamic Renaissance Party in Uzbekistan and Tajikistan as well as the various militant Arab Islamic groups in Afghanistan. It was this party, which trained the Central Asian mercenaries to fight against the Soviets in the Afghan war along with the *Mujahideen*. Even in the recent years the *Jamaat* has been openly accused by the leadership of the CAS of arming, training and abetting the Islamic provocations from their countries against their well-established secular governments. It was at the behest of the *Jamaat* that hundreds of Xinjiang Islamic militants were trained by the Afghan *Mujahideen* for fight against the FSU in the Afghan war. Only recently, the Chinese authorities have confirmed that Abdul Kasim, who had organized the fundamentalist Muslim uprising in Xinjiang, was a leader of the Free East Turkestan Movement and he had been supported by the mercenaries from Afghanistan as well as Pakistan. It is worth mentioning that keeping into consideration Pakistan's clandestine support to trans-border Islamic infiltration into the CAR and the adjoining Xinjiang area, the Chinese authorities used to close the Karakorum Highway. The mix of Islamic militancy and resurgent Pan-Turkic euphoria has been worrisome for Beijing, which has recently warned Islamabad several times that if it would anchor the fundamentalist forces on its territory, People's China would feel constrained to review its ties with the Pakistani Government.

The multiplicity of these factors thus prepared the background for the emergence of the Islamic challenge in Central Asia and Southwest Asia. It was in the years following the Soviet collapse that Islamicism played a vital role in the Tajik Civil War. The Islamic Rebirth Party and several other religious outfits like the *Adolat, Tauba* and *Islam Lashkari* started propagating extremist ideas. Thousands of Uzbek fundamentalists reinforced their base in Afghanistan. The Wahabists of the Ferghana Valley, Namangan and Andijan have come out in the open to wage a bloody war against the state. Attempts in certain quarters have been made to set up the Caliphate and run it according to the Islamic rules. Things are no different in Osh and Jalalabad oblasts of Kyrgystan. In the Chimkent region of Kazakhstan, the Alash National Freedom Party has played a vital role in propagating radical Islamic ideas. The Sunnah Society of Turkestan has also conducted an active campaign in the same direction. Islamic fundamentalism has shown its ugly head in the Caucasus region of the Russian Federation also, more particularly in Chechnya. Radical Islam has affected the life of millions of Muslims living in different parts of Russia.

Various fundamentalist organizations and political parties both in Tajikistan and Uzbekistan have been engaged in extremist activities among the Uighurs. This may have serious implications for political stability across the Central Asian border in Chinese Turkestan, which has recorded phenomenal rise in Islamic fundamentalism.

DRUG TRAFFICKING

Drug trafficking has been abundantly used to promote terrorist activities in the CAR for the ultimate propagation of radical Islam in this area. It has posed one of the biggest challenges to political stability in this area and regional security as well. Someone has aptly called it the 'Columbianisation' of Central Asian economy and polity. Drug routes of the Balkans, the Golden Triangle and the Golden Crescent also pass through this region, which ultimately terminates in the Western markets. Several American drug cartels are also involved in Central Asian transactions.

Among the CAS, Tajikistan is the first leg on the transit for the drug trade. With the opening of the new road between Tajikistan and China in 1998 with access to Pakistan, drug trade has increased in the CAR. Several transportation routes for drugs pass through Uzbekistan where several laboratories have been set up for the manufacture of contraband drugs. Turkmenistan and Kazakhstan continue to be the most popular corridors for drug trafficking. There are several chemical plants in these two countries which manufacture drugs and their well-developed banking systems help the process of the laundering of drug money. The drug corridor of Kyrgyzstan also helps the illicit trade in *hashish* and marijuana.

Russia has also been a major conduit for illicit drug in the Western markets, which reaches the Central Asia.

Drug trade has flourished a good deal in the Xinjiang province of China, which has recently turned into a bridge between the Golden Triangle and the Golden Crescent. The development of railroads in this part has connected the Central Asian drug markets with Myanmar and far-flung destinations in South-East Asia.

Drug trade in Central Asia, which is now globally well connected, is worth billions of dollars in a year. The warlords, criminal gangs, the terrorists and the militant Islamicists in the CAR have been using the drug money. Since drug money has been used in promoting Islamic fundamentalism in Central Asia, it has become linked up with the problem of security in the whole region. There are unimpeachable evidences to testify to the use of drug money in the purchase of arms for the promotion of terrorist and fundamentalist activities.

The USA also has its own share behind the drug trafficking business in this area. It is a well-known fact that it was with the connivance of the US administration that the *Mujahideen* warlords of Afghanistan used drug money to fight their *jihad* against the Soviets almost throughout the eighties. It would not be out of place to mention here that during the long-drawn fighting in Vietnam also, in which nearly 50,000 American soldiers lost their lives, the CIA not only ignored the drug trade of the anti-communist guerrillas, but they profusely funded and armed them also. Similarly, it has been found that the Reagan administration chose to close its eyes to the growing co-operation between the Pakistani drug traffickers, the military hawks of Afghanistan and the Afghan *Mujahideen*.

It was after the fall of the Soviets that the drug-lords of Pakistan started financing the terrorists and the Islamicists of their own country and of Afghanistan, who subsequently forged direct linkages with the Central Asian and the Chechen fundamentalists. Despite the Islamic prohibition on the intoxicants, the Taliban militia collects 20 per cent revenue from the producers and the traffickers as *Zakat*. And the money thus earned is used for promoting terrorism as well as Islamic fundamentalism. One of the world's four major narcotic routes originates from the Pak-Afghan border.

The drug trafficking in Central Asia has become such a huge problem that recently the UNO has held a special session on this illicit trade in this area. In order to forestall the narco-trafficking in this region, the drug control commissions of the Economic Cooperation Organization, the law enforcement agencies of the Shanghai 5, the Kazakh-Russian Conference on anti-narcotics campaign, the UN International Narcotics Control Board, the anti-drug agencies of the Confederation of Independent States and the CAS have also directed their efforts to check drug trafficking. But this trade is going on unabated and it is affecting Central Asian security in a big way.

TERRORISM

The Central Asian security is being affected by the various terrorist groups in this area which support the Islamic movements here. Most notable among them are the Al-Qaida,[2] Islamic Movement of Uzbekistan (IMU)[3] and a few groups in Pakistan, which operate on both sides of the Durrand Line, in the Indian state of Kashmir and in far-flung areas such as Chechnya in Russia and in Xinjiang, the most immediate neighbourhood of China.

The Al-Qaida was set up by Osama Bin Laden, the Saudi Arabian fugitive—an engineer by profession, a terrorist by training and an Islamicist by faith—who has been killed recently by the US forces. Born in Yemen in an affluent family and raised in Saudi Arabia, Osama took active part in the West-sponsored jihad against Red Russia in the 1980s from his base in Afghanistan. He, however, soon became disenchanted with the US policy of withdrawal in the wake of Soviet exit from Afghanistan and its subsequent dismantling. The Al-Qaida was thus set up by him in order to attack on the American bases in Saudi Arabia and root out its ever-increasing influence in West Asia as well as East Africa. There are unimpeachable evidences of its armed operations in Somalia in 1993 and East African bombings in 1998—both aiming at the killing of American citizens and eradication of the US global predominance. Subsequently, the Al-Qaida expanded its militant activities in Pakistan and Afghanistan in collusion with the ISI, which gave unstinted military support to the Taliban.

In the recent years, the Al-Qaida has been working as a proxy for most of the terrorist outfits in Central and Southwest Asia. Its networks have expanded in Bangladesh and Nepal, India, Pakistan, Afghanistan and the CAR, including Chechnya and Xinjiang.

The Islamic Movement of Uzbekistan (IMU), a conglomeration of Muslim militants from Uzbekistan and other CAS, has been in the forefront of terrorist activities in this vast region. For several years, it was led by Juma Namangani, who created this terrorist outfit in 1998 with Tahir's support. Namangani, one of the organisers of the *Toyba,* was helped by Mohammad Sharif, the founder of the Party of Islamic Revival in Tajikistan. Many of the terrorists, caught by the police in Tashkent bombings in 1999, admitted of receiving material, moral and military support from the Afghanistan-based Islamic Council, which was guided by Mullah Omar, Osama Bin Laden and Abu Suhayif of Syria. The range of this Council is gauged from the fact that it has the representation of the terrorist groups from the countries like Iran, Sudan, Lebanon, Egypt, Chechnya, Palestine, Yemen and others. It received huge donations from the Al-Qaida, narcotic trade, militant Muslims and the Uzbek Émigré community in Saudi Arabia.

The aim of the IMU, which is based on militant pan-Islamism, is to topple the duly elected Presidency of Islam Karimov and set up an Islamic state on the basis of the *Shariat*. Listed by the US as a leading terrorist organisation, the IMU led armed incursions into the Batken region of neighbouring Kyrgyzstan. This organization has close linkages with the ISI and the intelligence agencies of Saudi Arabia. The IMU has been trained by the Arab brigade of Osama and enormously financed by him. It has received recruits from the Sipha-e-Shaba and the Harkat-ul-Mujaheddin of Pakistan.

The fact that IMU has recently changed its name to the Islamic Party of Turkestan testifies to the increase in its scope and activities. Several Kazakh, Kirghiz, Tajik, Uighur and Chechen militants have joined the ranks of this movement, which received many-sided assistance of the Taliban including bases and sanctuaries in Mazar-i-Sharif and Kunduz.[4]

Of the various terrorist groups working in Pakistan, the Lashker-e-Taiba and Jaish-e-Mohammad are the most important. In view of the sanctions imposed from time to time by the US Department of State, these groups change names but continue to function largely under the banner of the Al-Qaida and the guidance of the ISI. All these groups, however, work for the political de-stability and economic dislocation in India. Their prime target is the seizure of Kashmir by sheer military might. The various bomb blasts in Mumbai, Kolkata, Jammu as well as Parliament building in New Delhi are their handiwork. In collusion with the warlords, the die-hard Islamicists and the drug barons, the various terrorist groups in Pakistan have practically seized all political initiatives in this trouble-torn country. India has to bear the onslaughts and the two neighbouring countries are ceaselessly engaged in worst possible military confrontation since 1989 when the various terrorist groups started infiltrating into the Indian state of Jammu and Kashmir after their disengagement from the theatre of war on the Soviet front in the wake of Moscow's withdrawal from Afghanistan.

Due to the heavy onrush of the terrorist groups of various hues the security scenario of the vast areas from the CAR to the Southwest Asia has become abnormally messed up. Despite the various attempts to cover up overt and covert nexus between Pakistan-sponsored terrorism and the Taliban, their impact on the grim military situation has been felt. Prince Turki, the former head of Saudi Intelligence, has accused Islamabad of re-creating the Taliban. The well-documented proofs submitted to the Security Council by Russia amply reflect on the role of Pakistan in the various subversive activities across the border. The documents of the Pentagon, FBI and the CIA, which have been made well known to the military hawks of Pakistan up to January 2012, fully testify to the complete complicity of Islamabad in the promotion of the new Taliban in and out of Pakistan.

INDIA'S CONCERN ON SECURITY ISSUES IN CENTRAL ASIA

The discussion in the foregoing pages makes it clear that the various international actors operating on the far and wide spectrum of Central Asia have redefined its ever-increasing strategic significance in the fast changing regional as well as global context. On the multiplicity of geopolitical, strategic, cultural and economic grounds, the players have been trying to seek legitimacy in this part of the world. The current ongoing debate on Central Asia and the diverse sorts of dynamisms evolving in this region, however, are inextricably linked up with India's deep concern which has yet to take proper shape despite this country's multi-faceted politico-cultural and civilisational ties spread over millennia.

Being strategically located both in continental Asia and the Indian Ocean region, the CAR matters quite a lot for India which naturally falls in this area of super power rivalry. In view of the expanse of the far-flung Nicobar Islands in the Bay of Bengal in the East, India is closer to South East Asia. In view of peninsular India being so close to the sea routes of the Arabian Sea, it faces West Asia from the point of view of its maritime activities as well as commercial ties. In this strategic location, India looks towards Central Asia in its North and West where the constant threat from Pakistan is increasing day by day.

Pakistan has long been an epicentre of international terrorism. It is interested in a weak Afghanistan having a medieval, reactionary and fundamentalist regime. Pakistan meddles enormously in the internal affairs of this trouble-torn country. With its terrorist camps trenched deeply on both sides of the border in Kashmir, it has been staging a *jehad* against India. By helping the terrorist outfits in Bangladesh and Nepal, Pakistan has escalated the theatre of its proxy war against India through the ISI. Pakistan's proximity with China and the latter's postures towards India are also quite disturbing. China's help to the insurgent groups in the north-east of India has also added to the forces of destabilization in this country.

The People's Republic of China is growing as an economic and military power. It is in occupation of 38,000 sq. km of India's territory in the Aksai Chin area. It is not relentless in its claim of 90,000 sq. km. in the Eastern Sector. Already it is in possession of 5,100 sq. km. of territory in the Pak-occupied territory of Kashmir which was illegally ceded to it by Pakistan in 1963. As on today, every major city of India is well within the reach of Chinese ballistic missiles. It can counter the US Missiles Defense Programme. China is in possession of Submarine Launched Ballistic Missiles. Despite vocal support in both India and China to the *Panchsheel*, their Confidence Building Measures, several joint working group meetings and dialogue in the SCO, India-China mechanism on counter terrorism has failed to record any tangible success.

Pakistan's strong and manifold politico-military ties with China will always remain an irritant in Beijing-Delhi relations with their reverberations on India's attitude towards the CAR in many ways.

The US-led coalition war in Afghanistan and Iraq has distracted its attention from Pakistani behaviour against Afghanistan and India. Washington's policy has thus suffered hugely on this count. Pakistan has been practically taken over by its military junta. Instances like the rigged elections, fake referendum, legal framework order, institutionalised role of the army, powers of the National Security Council of Pakistan, and the involvements of the Pakistani leaders in the recent Memo gate have converted this country into a failed state. Despite India's firm commitments to the Tashkent Declaration, Shimla Agreement and Lahore Declaration, Pakistan is not relenting on the supply of cross border terrorism into India.

Seen in the backdrop of the aforesaid facts, the CAR holds quite significant place in the strategic calculations of India in many ways.

The energy resources of Central Asia are of vital importance for India in view of the shrinking supplies of gas and oil from the traditional sources in West Asia. The open society, secularism and democracy of India have caught the attention of the five countries in Central Asia which have deep underlying geopolitical, cultural and historical linkages.

Hundreds of joint ventures between India and the five CAS, several bilateral and multi-lateral projects in the hydro-carbon energy sector between them, several state visits of leaders of these countries, India's formal application for full-time membership of the SCO, New Delhi is committed to expanding its multi-faceted ties in this sprawling area. This will augur well for regional peace, offer fillip to counter-terrorism and contribute to the weakening of fundamentalist forces in this vast area.

India can be a security provider and stabilizer in Central Asia. Its strong economic and military ties with both Russia and the USA may also contribute to this process. The recent Indo-Russian dialogues for New Delhi's possible participation in the Collective Security Treaty Organisation open up great vista.

THE US PERCEPTION

As regards the US response to the grim situation in this resource-rich and strategically significant region, Washington has only recently engaged itself in this area—bilaterally, multilaterally, militarily, economically and diplomatically. It is, however, worth mentioning that the American engagement in Central Asia began with the dissolution of the FSU. This area occupied the lowest rung on the ladder of the strategic concern of the US administration. On the chessboard of diplomatic games, it remained a remote region of little concern for the defence policy community of this country.

As everywhere, Washington's concern for democracy, human rights and civic society remained peripheral in Central Asia. Constitutions have been usurped and elections rigged in this vast area. But the US administration either kept on blind-folded pampering the despotic regimes or closing its eyes to the developments taking place in this region. Whatever little concern the US had, it was represented through Turkey, a trusted Mediterranean ally and NATO partner. In the absence of readily available alternative to the intensely entrenched Islamicists, the US policy-makers preferred to close their eyes to the excesses of the former communist turn-coasts who had instantly converted themselves into democrats. For no valid reasons, Iran's role in Central Asia was laboriously overblown by the US foreign policy makers in the wake of the Soviet collapse.

Just after the disintegration of the FSU, the NATO chief warned Moscow of the impending dangers of the emergence of Islamic fundamentalism in the CAR. It was widely propagated by the leading academic community that the descendants of the Mongols and the Turks would soon stand at the gates of the 'End of History'. Samuel Huntington's thesis of 'Clash of Civilisation' came into wide circulation. It was made to believe that Central Asia would soon join the Islamic world. Celebrities like Bernard Lewis, Stephen Blank and Oliver Roy widely propagated the views that this area would soon be connected with the Middle East. The BBC and the VOA, and NATO Bulletins and the Reuters correspondents referred at length to the impending threats from the forces of radical Islam. "The United States is terrified by the Mullah", and "Kazakhstan would soon degenerate into one thousand Yugoslavia"—such wild were the insinuations.

With the fast changing security scenario in the CAR in the wake of the rise of Taliban and the discoveries of the 'New Kuwait' in this area, the US reversed its earlier policy. It carefully stage-managed the entry of the CAS into the North Atlantic Cooperation Council (NAAC) in order to integrate them within the security structure of West Europe. As such, all these countries obtained the right to interact with the full members of the NATO partners. They were entitled to consult them on the various political and security issues including regional conflicts.

In the recent years preceding the 11 September raids, the American interests in both the Central and Southwest Asian regions evidently started coinciding with those of the CAS and other chief actors such as Russia, China and India. Washington half-heartedly tried to distance itself from Pakistan and seek closer ties with New Delhi. It became seized of the nuclear confrontation in South Asia. Its defence forces participated in joint military exercises with the troops of the CAR. The US administration supported the various efforts of the NAAC,

Partnership for Peace, EU, CIS, Conference on the Confidence Building Measures in Asia, Organisation for Security and Cooperation in Europe, Six-Plus Two, Shanghai Cooperation Organisation, G-7, UN Security Council and a host of other organisations, which tried to bring peace in this fractious region.

The 11th September Attack and Security Implications for the Region

The Al-Qaida attacks on the twin towers of the World Trade Centre (WTC) in New York exposed America's military might, its ill-preparedness and its foreign policy bankruptcy.[5] The giant was grievously slapped by the pigmy. The targets of the terrorists were iconic. The magnificent structures, which were the symbol of America's greatness and grandeur, were reduced into rubble within 90 minutes. It was, however, not the economy of the USA, rather the domineering position of this country and its absolute abrogation of global authority, which the Al-Qaida terrorists had invaded at the date, time and place of their choosing.

The attack had global ramifications. It generated unprecedented political upheaval, economic meltdown, military challenges and ideological fluctuations which impacted the whole world. Within one melodramatic jerk, the whole dynamics of world security underwent a sea-change.

The implications of the 11 September attack for the regional security in Central and Southwest Asia have been enormous. This inroad led to the formation of the 'first' international coalition, which waged the 'first' war of the twenty-first century. The 'first' war of its type was fought between the richest as well as the strongest countries combined and the poorest state of Afghanistan.

Beginning on 7 October 2001, the US-led 'Operation Enduring Freedom' lasted just two months. The 'desert-storm' of Kuwait was certainly less bold in respect of performance than the impressive and masterful feet of the quickest possible military action. Only 30 soldiers of the international coalition lost their lives whereas 8000-12000 Taliban troops died in this regional conflict. All the NATO allies stood by the side of America, which dropped more smart bombs on Afghanistan than dropped on Serbia in 1999. The theatre of this conflict enveloped in its train the air bases of some of the CAS, a few naval installations in the Persian Gulf and Diego Garcia. Re-supply needs to the US marines were met by the Pakistani bases.

The war in Afghanistan was no doubt half-heartedly won, but peace was eventually lost. The Al-Qaida leaders, including Osama and Mullah Omar, chief of the Taliban emirate of Afghanistan, remained untraced. Pakistan-sponsored terrorist attacks continued to rock the state's assembly in Srinagar and the Indian Parliament at the most critical juncture when America was spearheading the war in Afghanistan. Washington, however, remained grossly engaged in making the best of both the worlds. It managed total support from the CAS on the one hand and all the countries in the Southwest Asian region on the other. To cap it all, it embraced Islamabad again to which was instantly pledged more than a billion dollar aid in the name of humanitarian assistance which was diverted on the war front.. The American candles thus no doubt shone brilliantly on the entire vast region, but the problems of security in this part of the world escalated manifold in real sense of the term.

The 11 September has entered the contemporary history of the world as a landmark date. It has been rightly observed that the post-cold war security bubble finally burst on that day.[6] Michael Cox has described this attack as 'the most devastating terrorist atrocity in the history and the first really serious mainland attack on the USA since the British burnt the White House in 1812.[7] Although wrongly, comparison of the terrorist attack on America's financial capital and the seat of its military strength was drawn with Japan's surprise attack on the Pearl Harbour in the Hawaii islands in 1941. The site of Japanese attack is at least one thousand kilometres away from the mainland and only 2,403 American lives were lost in this misadventure, whereas the Al-Qaida targeted the greatest show-piece of America in its very mainland in which some six to seven thousand lives are feared lost.[8]

The twin towers of the WTC in New York, symbol of America's greatness and grandeur, had taken seven years to construct at a cost of $30 billion. The iconic targets of the Al-Qaida attacks reduced the magnificent structure to rubble within 90 minutes. The Pentagon was slashed open. The targets were slightly missed. The White House stood enormously threatened. The US President had to hide himself motionless in a bunker. His whereabouts were the topmost secret of the sole super power. The CIA, custodian of America's security with its $30 billion annual budget, global reach, mastery over numerous spy satellites and world-wide espionage network of at least 100,000 well trained and fully equipped staff drew total blank. The failure of the US intelligence was monumental. What a great irony that even a secret office of the CIA was destroyed in the attack, temporarily disturbing normal intelligence operations.[9]

"The CIA was asleep at the switch", observes Richard K. Belts.[10] While writing in the *New York Times* on 7 October 2001, Tim Weiner asked: "What will the nation's intelligence sources have to change to fight this war?" The short answer is: almost everything.[11] Both the CIA and the FBI abruptly failed to tail the movements of Bin Laden's operations. It has been revealed recently that the intelligence supplied to President Bush at least a month before the Al-Qaida attack was ignored by the administration.[12]

The terrorist attacks exposed America's military might, its foreign policy bankruptcy along with its unilateralist postures and expansionist designs which it had continuously nourished since the collapse of the USSR. What a great paradox is contained in the fact that even after the termination of the Cold War, the US kept on continuously spending forty per cent of the world's total military expenditure which accounted for sixteen per cent of the US budget.

The US Defense Review holds that it was all set to maintain its dominance in the post-Cold War world.[13] But the 11 September attacks shattered the military preponderance of America, dashed its economic might and questioned its political authority in ways which will continue to be analysed for all time to come.

It is estimated that total cost of the lost economic growth around the world might have crossed a trillion dollars whereas the Al-Qaida attack itself would have cost hardly a few hundred millions. The enormity of the attacks may further be gauged from the fact that the economic loss to New York City was roughly estimated at $ 83 billion in lost output. Nearly 52,000 jobs were cut immediately. Up to the Christmas, well over 60,000 jobs were slashed. This exceeded all the job cuts for the five year period between 1993 and 1997.[14] The airlines industry in the country had to be provided with $ 15 billion in assistance in order to save it from sinking whereas payouts to insurance policy-holders ranged from $30 to $70 billion.[15]

In point of fact, what was attacked by the Al-Qaida terrorists was not the economy of the USA. It was the domineering position of America, its absolute abrogation of global authority with no accountability and its vanity as well as its arrogance which was invaded on the 11 September. The message of the aggressor was loudly heard throughout the world that henceforth the world and America shall not be the same again. No doubt, the attack had global ramifications; it generated unprecedented political trauma, economic downslide, military challenges and ideological vibrations. The whole dynamics of world security underwent a sea-change. And all this happened precisely at a time when America was firmly saddled at the pinnacle of its historic glory, economic breakthrough, technological skills, and military capabilities. America stood defenceless, immensely vulnerable, even though it had in its armoury more weapons than the rest of the major powers combined. The hegemony was grievously slapped.

The 11 September had in its train several 'firsts'. The Al-Qaida attack was the most devastating terrorist atrocity in history and the 'first' really serious mainland attack on the USA since the storming of the White House in 1812 by the British. This inroad led to the formation of the 'first' international coalition which waged the 'first' war of the 21st century. Further, it demonstrated the 'first' major failure of the CIA in half a century since its inception in 1947. And to cap it all, it was the 'first' and the only war of its type fought primarily between the most successful country on the one hand, and Afghanistan, the most failed state on the other. Ironically enough, Afghanistan was recognised by only three countries out of which two, Pakistan and Saudi Arabia, they were the most allied allies of America which were engaged by it for long in "running with the hare and hunting with the hound". The war fought between patron Pakistan and protege Emirate of Mullah Omar was indeed 'first' of its type.

It was the 'first war' between the creator of the proverbial monster and the monster itself. The 11 September was indeed the 'first most horrifying single day in American history', it unravelled several painful surprises of which the 'first' and foremost was this war between the satellite state of Afghanistan and its sponsor's (Pakistan's) sponsor—the USA. Last but not the least; it was for the 'first' time in its history that clause V of the NATO was invoked for the first time to wage really the 'first' international war in the post-Second World War period.

The Al-Qaida inroads made it possible for the USA to lead the alliance of states in the ill-defined war against Afghanistan. With the most unanticipated speed, America accomplished the task within a few weeks. It was feared by many critics that the military impasse in the inaccessible mountain terrain of Afghanistan will prove yet another Vietnam, a Balkan or a Korea. Many pundits surmised that the embers of the battle-ground would percolate down to the Indian Subcontinent and envelop even the volatile CAR. Fears of the escalation of the crisis in the Middle East were also expressed.

The war, however, proved all the guesswork totally wrong. The Gulliver won in the land of Lilliputs. All the allies of the NATO stood by the side of America. The USA dropped more smart bombs on Afghanistan that the NATO dropped on Serbia in 1999. The Taliban forces, estimated at 50,000 to 60,000 strong and a few thousand Al-Qaida fighters were crushed by the US troops numbering around 60,000 and the allied forces numbering approximately 15,000. War-ships of Japan, Italy, Britain and the Netherlands were deployed in the Arabian Sea. The bombs of the US armed forces operated in and out of Diego Garcia. Land-based aircrafts flew from Oman and planes from the American aircraft carriers, based in Arabian Sea, provided for the rest of the combat punch. From the air bases of some of the CAS came some air support whereas bases in the Persian Gulf region as well as Diego Garcia were used for reconnaissance and refuelling. Re-supply needs of the units of US marines were met with by using Pakistani bases. The cost of the Afghanistan War reached $ 3.8 billion, whereas the military cost of the Homeland Security efforts in the USA was $ 2.6 billion.[16]

Beginning on 7th October, the 'Operation Enduring Freedom' lasted just two months. It is said to be 'masterful' in both design and execution. The 'Desert Storm' is said to be 'less bold' in terms of performance. The US forces, which have claimed to have staged 'impressive' feat of quickest possible military action, lost about only 30 personnel whereas 8,000 to 12,000 Taliban troops are believed to have died. The war was no doubt won, because the Taliban emirate collapsed. Peace, however, was lost.

Top Al-Qaida leaders like Osama Bin Laden, al Zawahiri and Abu Zubaydah could not be liquidated. Mullah Omar remained traceless. Pak-sponsored terrorist attacks rocked the state's assembly in Srinagar and the Indian parliament at the most critical time when America was spearheading the war. All along, Washington remained a passive spectator, but grossly engaged in making the best of both the worlds. It embraced Islamabad again, offered it much more than a billion dollar humanitarian aid, needless to mention unaccounted military assistance to the re-appointed frontline state of Pakistan and massive aid package from the IMF. All nuclear-explosion related sanctions were also lifted.

America's most allied ally was thus totally absolved of all the responsibilities behind the decade old terrorist activities in South Asia. The largest democracy of the world was ignored by the strongest democracy, which preferred Pakistan's oligarchy and theocracy even though it had repeatedly deposed the duly elected heads of the state by means which have been terrorist out and out. Despite assurances to New Delhi about the inclusion of terrorism in Kashmir in America's fight against international terrorism, nothing substantial came out. Nobody less than the father of President Bush in his capacity as the US President had threatened Pakistan that it might be declared a state-sponsor of terrorism and be kept on the watch-list. The US administration had itself admitted early in 2000 that the centre of gravity of terrorism had shifted from the West to South Asia. America's list of the rogue-states however remained unchanged since 1993. Neither Pakistan nor Afghanistan was included in it, even though in April 2000, the State Department's annual terrorism report for the first time severely accused these two countries for making South Asia a major hub of international terrorism. While admitting that Pakistan was harbouring and aiding the terrorists many of whom were fighting in Kashmir at its behest, America kept this country out of the list.

The reason of America's benevolence towards Pakistan is very easy to understand. It was through this state that the US administration had wilfully pumped in $ 8 billion into the Afghan pipe line when the 'jihad' against the godless soviets was being waged in the 1980s. Growth of Islamic fundamentalism, terrorism and drug-trafficking was fully promoted by the CIA and ISI combine with the sole aim of crippling the so-called 'evil empire' of the former USSR and entering into its backyard in the CAR for the purpose of getting the much-needed 'strategic depth'. The CIA thus used the Mujahideen as the strategic weapon and the ISI played the role of the priest in this marriage of convenience. The Taliban is the consequent product of the toils of these two god fathers who offered all types of patronage to Osama bin Laden and his cohorts during the holy war. In short to say, the American administration thoughtfully didn't address itself to the Kashmir issue. It went on harping on the old tune of negotiated and bilateral political settlement. Pakistan was fed to the brim and armed to the teeth. Dreadful clouds of a nuclear confrontation and a shooting war in South Asia started emanating not from mere words but from the actual deeds of Islamabad at a time when the USA, patron of the military junta in Pakistan, was recording heroic victory in the theatre of the Afghan War. The

American candles were shining brightest in Pakistan, but the Indian candle was burning at both the ends. India was kept totally in the dark about the war ends by the descendants of Gorge Washington, Thomas Jefferson, Woodrow Wilson and Franklin Roosevelt. The Generals of Pakistan always carried the day.

The American candles shone brilliantly even in the CAR. It left no time in plain the role of the regional arbiter in the most immediate neighbourhood of Russia and ironically enough, with the latter's consent. Washington acquired several military bases in this part of the world, some of which were most adjacent to China and furthest from the war-zone. Within ten days of Al-Qaida attack, the *Wall Street Journal* (Europe) observed, "Three Central Asian nations seem open to US military".[17]

The wings of America's eagle were clipped at home in the wake of the Al-Qaida inroads, but it soared loftily on the Central Asian horizon.

In the aftermath of the 11 September attack, the CAR entered into the spotlight of international focus. The five CAS, which appeared to slide into oblivion into the late 1990s, came out to be the most dramatically affected parts of the world by the chain of the events which followed. Time without number, the CAS were lectured by the US administration for their human rights deficits. They were never allowed to eat the American cake and hence this area was forced to come under the umbrella of the Russian-Chinese monopoly on the region's chief exports of oil and gas. The internally fragile, economically crippled, politically instable and ethnically divergent CAS had remained enormously endangered after coming out of the 'prison' of the soviet nationalities. The Afghan situation had further worsened the socio-economic condition of these resource-rich countries which were engaged in the task of nation-building. Central Asia was threatened by Taliban-Pakistan combine, which was continuously aiding and abetting the IMU in its terrorist activities in the area.

The 11 September attacks proved major windfall to America in the CAR. First, it brought in an overwilling Karimov government in Tashkent who at once became a key player in Washington's war efforts. The Uzbek President had double-edged weapons in his hands which he used to silence dissidence at home and the Islamicists inside Central Asia and Afghanistan. Karimov offered military bases to the USA in the name of humanitarian aid as well as search and rescue purposes in order to save himself from domestic criticism. He, however, did not mind the stationing of 1,000 strong US troops on the Uzbek territory. Even, the French troops were allowed not only transit facilities but also the use of Khanabad military air base. The US administration reciprocated by fiercely retaliating against the IMU, freezing its assets and attacking its training camps inside Afghanistan. It extended security guarantees to Uzbekistan which grabbed the opportunity of sliding it out of Russia's security orbit and establishing strategic partnership with the USA. Right since mid-1990s, military relations were slowly developing between Tashkent and Washington. In return for its offer of military bases, Uzbekistan was given $ 150 million in grants and loans.[18]

In December 2001, Tajikistan also welcomed stationing of the American troops on its territory and allowed them the use of their air bases. Kazakhstan and Kyrgyzstan also did accordingly. Turkmenistan however, preferred to remain neutral. This republic had not been a member of the Russia-sponsored Collective Security Treaty (CST) and hence it was not committed to any collective military action against the Taliban. Its engagement with the Confederation of Independent States (CIS) also did not warrant any such step. Turkmenistan's negotiation with Taliban for the construction of a pipeline is also a well known fact. Despite all these facts, President Niyazov finally agreed to allow the US to use its airspace for humanitarian purposes.

One major tangible impact of the coalition-led war against the Taliban on the CAR was the removal of this terrorist regime which had occupied the whole Afghanistan in association with the Al-Qaida. It resulted in the waning of the activities of the IMU in the CAR, more particularly in Uzbekistan and Kyrgyzstan.

The hope of using of prevailing peace for the re-opening of the trade routes to South Asia via Afghanistan and Pakistan has been completely belied due to the Indo-Pak standoff. It was expected further that the US commitment to the democratization, rule of law and human rights in the CAR would be kept up. The record of the CAS testifies to the further strengthening of the authoritarian rule in the newly independent states (NIS). Islam Karimov got himself elected life-President by the Uzbek Parliament in the midst of the war on the pattern of his Turkmen counterpart. Elsewhere in the CAR, the war was used to intensify repression.

America, however, reaped most of the harvests. Its success against Taliban slackened the hold of Russian-Chinese condominium which was spread over the whole region in various ways. America put an end to the isolation of the CAS. For quite some time Moscow and Beijing had strengthened their grip on the energy resources of this area. None of them, however, had opted to tame the Taliban even though they had nuclear warheads in their arsenals and their territorial integrity was being openly challenged in Chechnya and Xingjian. It was by no means an achievement for America to enter into Russia's traditional sphere of influence in Central Asia and station its troops in the most sensitive areas bordering the Russian and Chinese territories.

INTERNATIONAL PERSPECTIVES

In the recent years, the Taliban has threatened the Shiite regime of Iran and affected the security of Xinjiang. Russia is also deeply concerned with developments taking place in the Caucasus where its territorial integrity is being threatened by the Muslim separatists. Islamic fundamentalism has affected the security mechanisms of the CIS. If not restrained in time, the further successes of the fundamentalist forces in the sprawling CAR may have transnational impact on events in the Balkans where the complex ethnic mix has been at a highly vulnerable pitch. The European Union (EU) is gradually feeling concerned.

Central Asia is situated on the junction of Asia and Europe as well as on the intersection of the two age-old civilisations—Christendom in the north and the world of Islam in the south. In view of the spread of political Islam and its various far-reaching consequences, it has been considered to be an extension of the Middle East, and hence at the root of the 'Clash of Civilisations'. It has the potential of adding to the simmering configuration in the Balkans and to endangering the strong socio-economic and political fabric of the EU as well.

Looked at from the ethnic standpoint, Central Asia is a sort of bridge between Turkey and Iran. These two countries have been clamouring again for an exclusive role in this area on the basis of their ethnic, linguistic and cultural connections in the past and sizeable economic participation in the present.

The strategic implications of the recent manifestations of political Islam in the two neighbouring regions across the Asiatic continent have immeasurably shot up in terms of the global fallout and extra-territorial portents of purely local conflict-situation. This area is enormously imbued with vital human and natural resources. But it has yet to attain political stability, democratic traditions and the marketisation of economy. Its geo-strategic significance has recently increased due to complete power-vacuum and the consequent emergence of the centrifugal forces which have affected the traditional balance of powers on a large scale.

NEW SECURITY CHALLENGES

The Islamicists of the CAR have caused the virtual destabilisation of the buffer state of Afghanistan and bridged the two distinctly separated geo-political as well as strategic regions into one 'arc of crisis'. They have exported Islamic fundamentalism in all the directions. With the help of drug-money and cross-border terrorists, they have seriously menaced several well-established secular regimes in this sprawling region. The territorial integrity of Russia in the adjoining areas has also been increasingly threatened. These very elements have fought the decade-long proxy war in the Indian state of Kashmir also. The army of Islam has practically seized by force almost half of this state.

The highly complex conflict issues and the mercurial role of the various regional actors have turned this vast region into murky battleground. These forces have impinged upon the security scenario of the vast areas from Central Asia to Southwest Asia, Caucasus to Kashmir, Xinjiang to Afghanistan and Iran to Pakistan. Everywhere their prime purpose is the complete Islamisation of this area.

The aggressive postures of Islam in this wide region and the consequent problems of various hues have converged with other significant contentious issues in the area such as the safe passage of the trans-continental energy and communication routes. Due to geographical proximity, the development of energy resources in the Caspian basin as well as the Black Sea has also been greatly affected.

The extra-territorial inputs of the main conflict and its ramifications beyond the precincts of this zone of crisis are indeed too crucial to be ignored by the strategic thinkers, policy-planners and students of contemporary politics.

Serious domestic demands for ethno-nationalism, separatism, new processes of political plurality, social-engineering, democratisation, market reforms and human rights protection in the entire area under review are also indelibly linked with the solutions to the aforesaid problems. The problems of political Islam are sometimes deliberately magnified by the authoritarian regimes in this area to suppress the opposition, which has been forced to take to the mosques and exploit the grinding poverty, immense improvisation and international security.

The centrality of Central Asian security actually lies in its geo-strategic situation. The three countries of Southwest Asia (India, Pakistan and Afghanistan) and the five new states of the CAR are standing today at the geographic nexus of a host of potential upheavals of various varieties, which have been confronted by them from their hoary past. The complex current situation has further exacerbated the prevailing alarming situation. As a result of the serious internal convulsions and other external factors, the entire regional and strategic dimensions of the challenges from the forces of political Islam in this vast region have thus undergone a sea-change.

While functioning both operationally and ideologically at local, regional and global levels, the Al-Qaida has enormously threatened the Southeast Asian security in the recent years. The various international intelligence agencies, led predominantly by the CIA and the FBI, are engaged in confronting the biggest ever challenges to this far-flung region, which have been thrown up by the first multinational and the most feared terrorist outfit of the 21st century. Having a global reach across the entire continent, this group has catapulted terrorism as an integral part of the most coherently organised international instrument with avowed commitment to the substitution of corrupt Western influence in the Muslim-populated Southeast Asian region. After the world's most devastating terrorist outrage of the 11 September, it has been acknowledged as the pioneering vanguard of the worst variety of global Islamist threat. The Al-Qaida, the shadowy body of the Islamicists, and its other associate terrorist groups have been alleged by the CIA to have infiltrated one-fifth of all the Islamic NGOs sprinkled all over the world in general and the Southeast region in particular. The Al-Qaida has managed the strategic depth even among the European, North American and Australian Muslims.

The Al-Qaida aims at the replacement of the existing Muslim regimes with Islamic polity in accordance with the tenets of the *Shariat*. Its associate groups in West, Central and Southeast Asia have been acting in concert with British, German, French, Spanish, Belgian, Canadian, Italian, Albanian, Bosnian and US cells. The Al-Qaida has developed indelible connections with Abu Sayyaf Group (in Malaysia and the Philippines), Palestinian Islamic Jihad, Islamic Jihad (in Egypt), Jemaah Islamiah (in Indonesia), Islamic Army of Aden, National Islamic Front (in Sudan), IMU, Salafist Group and Armed Islamic Group (in Algeria), Lashkar-e-Toiba and Jaish-e-Mohammed (in Kashmir), and various terrorist outfits in West and Central Asian countries.

The multinational, multiethnic and multilingual Al-Qaida groups predominantly share Sunni Muslim fundamentalist groups, but after the Afghanistan debacle, they have steeped up co-operation with Hezbollah, the minority Shiite militia from Lebanon with the backing of Iran. Over the years, it has cut across sectarian classes and has drawn followers from all strata of society.

In recent years, the Al-Qaida has concentrated its operations in various parts of Southeast Asia. After the 11 September, which was like a wake-up call to the USA and its traditional allies, experts have been continuously unearthing unimpeachable evidences testifying to the existence of numerous locally trained separatists and terrorist groups in the Southeast Asian region, having long running connections—both locally and globally. The various Islamic terrorist organisations in this area are aiming at creating Islamic Super State consisting of Indonesia, Singapore, the Sultanate of Brunei and parts of the southern most areas of the Philippines, Thailand and even Cambodia.

The Al-Qaida made first inroad into Southeast Asia with the dispatch of Muhammad Jamal Khalifa to this region as far back as in 1988. Osama bin Laden deputed Ramzi Ahmad Yousef to the Philippines after he bombed the World Trade Center in February 1993. Khalifa backed him in training the Abu Sayyaf Group (ASG) in terrorist techniques.

The Philippines

It was in the course of the trial of Yousef in the USA after his detention in the aforesaid bombing case that the details of Al-Qaida network in the Philippines during 1988-89 came to be known to the world.[19]

In 1994, the Al-Qaida plotted to kill Pope John Paul II during his visit to Manila and a year later, it made an abortive attempt to assassinate President Bill Clinton during his state visit to the Philippines. As a part of the Al-Qaida-sponsored *Oplan Bojinka* in 1994, which was plotted by Yousef, Philippines President Fidel Ramos, his two aids, numerous foreign envoys along with several top defence and police personnel were to be killed.

Yousef's plot was aimed at bombing chief business offices, departmental sources, churches, main government buildings and the US Embassy in Manila. The Al-Qaeda had also gone to the limits of plotting to bomb 11 US Airplanes over the pacific. Due to Yousef's timely detention, however, series of the well-planned mishaps, including the one to crash an explosive-laden aircraft on to the Pentagon and CIA headquarters, were averted.

It is worth mentioning here that Jamal Khalifa, one of Laden's top associates and his brother-in-law, subsequently led the ASG in the southern part of the Philippines.[20]

Initially the ASG was led by Abdurajah Janjalani, a native Muslim, who fought in Afghanistan as a Mujahideen. Osama is said to have forged links with Janjalani and introduced him to Yousef in Peshawar. It is believed, says Gunaratna, that the ASG's organisation, ideology, target selection and tactics are deeply influenced by the Al-Qaida.[21] The ASG has taken leading role in bombing the churches, murdering the missionaries and the foreign priests as well as abducting the American tourists in the Philippines.

In addition to the ASG, members of the Moro Islamic Liberation Front (MILF) are also believed to have been trained in the Al-Qaida camps in Afghanistan. The MILF has been reported to have arranged for the huge collection of weapons as well as explosives which were used in attacking on the US, Australian, Israeli and British targets in Singapore.[22]

The Al-Qaida, which had earlier formed a special Moro sub-brigade in Afghanistan for fighting against the Soviets, later picked up a few hundred Moros from the Mindanao region in southern Philippines. Those Moros were organized and trained for fighting a Jihad in order to set up an independent Islamic state.

In order to ward off the close connections of the Al-Qaida with both the ASG and the MILF, the Bush Administration has shared armed forces intelligence with the Philippines Government and provided it with training assistance as well as two hundred military advisers also as far back as in February 2002.

Recently, the Philippines government arrested Rahman al Ghazi, an Indonesia explosive expert for forging linkage between Islamiah of Indonesia and the MILF, which has threatened to attack any joint Philippines-US forces. While committing all out support to the US led global campaign against terrorism, the President of the Philippines has offered logistical support, the country's air space, intelligence reports and the two former American Navel Bases Clark, Air Force Base and the Pubic Way.

In addition to clearing the anti-money laundering legislation to forestall the flow of terrorist and drug-money, Manila has called for a tri-nation anti-terrorist coalition with Malaysia and Indonesia. Recently, they have agreed to draft an agreement, which would facilitate the various measures required to combat terrorism and border crimes. The Philippines government has further agreed to receive advice and logistical support from the US troops in its fight against the ASG.

The Philippines is the only country besides Afghanistan to receive US troops in the global fight against terrorism. In addition to the 500 support and technical personnel, the US contingent consists of 160 special operation forces including Navy SEALS, the armies green berates, marines armed special forces. The US forces, while providing only technical support, advice and training, will not participate in combat. Since 31 January 2004, however, joint training exercises have been conducted for the "Balikitan' (shoulder-to-shoulder) operations against the Al-Qaida and allied terrorist groups in the Philippines.

Indonesia

There have become available several evidences of clandestine Al-Qaida operations in Indonesia, which has been continuously marred by violence, terrorism and separatism perpetrated primarily by numerous radical Islamic groups of this country. The Jemaah Islamia (JI) is alleged to be involved in several bombings in Indonesia and in the Philippines, including explosions in Jakarta as well as Manila in December 2000, which took 35 lives.[23] The JI is said to have expanded the Al-Qaida network in the entire Southeast Asian region in association with the Kumpulan Mujahidin Malaysia (KMM)). It is alleged to have executed the terrorist attack on nightclubs in Bali in 2003 which was reportedly plotted by Khalid Saikh Mohammad.[24] Abu Bakr Bassy is said to have led the JI. Bakr was detained on complaints from Singapore and Malaysia but was released for want of concrete evidences of involvement in the terrorist activities. It is alleged that the Indonesian government is soft on him for fear of Muslim backlash in the country. Critics maintain that in July 2003 five Al-Qaida terrorists sneaked into this country with a view to blowing up the US Embassy in Jakarta. The US officials, however, hold that they were allowed safe passage by the Indonesian authorities to slip away from the country in order to escape from the resultant terrorist crackdown in the event of their detention.

Initial denials notwithstanding, the Indonesian government acknowledged in December 2003 the presence of Al-Qaida training camps on its soil. Engaged in the killing of several Christians, this group is led by Jaffar Umar Thalib, who is believed to have interacted closely with Laden in the 1980s, though he has denied any such ties including receiving monetary assistance from the Al-Qaida. The country's Foreign Minister has also denied any ties of local Muslim outfit with any international terrorist network. Another militant Muslim group named Lashker-e-Jihad has been set up in Indonesia with the sole agenda of funding an Islamic state on its soil. There are reports that Indonesian Islamic Liberation Front (IILF) has received direct training from the Al-Qaida in Afghanistan as well as from the trainers in some pockets in the Philippines.

Just a few months ago, the Bush administration dispatched a secret Delta force to the Indonesian capital to bolster its feeble security arrangement. The US Congress has passed a bill in December 2003, which has permitted the Indonesian security personnel to take part in counter-terrorism-training programmes. In addition to the sanction of non-military assistance to Indonesia, the Bush administration has granted a sum of $ 10 million to this country for the training of its police, customs and bank officials. It has proposed intelligence sharing.

Indonesian response to anti-terrorist activities amounts to loud rhetoric but no substantial action. Critical of Indonesia's feeble response, the neighbouring countries have mounted their pressures on it. It is true that this enormously poor, largest Muslim but hugely scattered country has long been embroiled in bloody secessionist movement and recurrent sectarian violence between the Muslim majority as well as Christian minority. President Megawati Sukarnoputri has, no doubt, chosen to support George Bush in his global attack on terrorism. She was one of the first heads of state to meet Bush, offer condolence and pledge support to the USA in the post 9/11 period. Back home, however, she was dissuaded by some of the largest protests denouncing US military campaign in Afghanistan. The violent reaction of the country's 176 million Muslim did not allow her to respond positively.

Malaysia

Some recent evidences have revealed that numerous Al-Qaida related terrorists have been filtering in and out of Malaysia, which has been used as a staging ground for a couple of abduction cases by the Abu Sayyaf terrorist group of the Philippines. According to the recent report of the FBI, Malaysia has been a primary operational launch pad for 9/11 attacks. This tiny country has caught the attention of strategic thinkers. Although critical of the FBI reports, Prime Minister Mahathir Mohammad has acknowledged the identification of 50 natives with Al-Qaida ties.

Yazid Sufaat, an important suspect, has been recently detained under the controversial Internal Security Act. This Malaysian chemist has been associated with the Jemaah Islamiaah of Indonesia and Hambuli, the notorious terrorist, who has been the leader of the Kumpulen Mujahidin Malaysia (KMM). This terrorist organization seeks to establish an Islamic state composed of Malaysia, Indonesia and the Muslim dominated Philippines.

In December 2003, the government of Mahathir has taken strong measures against Al Maunah, an Islamist sect of Malaysia, and has ordered the hanging of three of this group and life imprisonment for its 16 members on the charges of treason. He, however, has been critical of creating 'more terror' through the US-led coalition. Mahathir tried to impress upon the world leaders at the World Economic Forum in February 2004 that they should try to understand

Muslim grievances and "listen to the views of others". Sufaat is alleged by the US officials to have known at least two of the hijackers on board the ill-fated planes on 9/11. He helped Bin Laden, both financially and organisationally, in the expansion of Al-Qaida's network throughout Southeast Asia.

Singapore

Of late, the activities of the Al-Qaida in the affluent city-state of Singapore have triggered off alarm bells in the entire Southeast region. While blaming Abu Bakr of the Jemaah Islamiaah for plotting to bomb the American Embassy including other Western installations in Singapore, the intelligence community of this country has unearthed numerous evidences testifying to direct linkages between this group and the Al-Qaida. Along with the Philippines, Singapore has also fully supported the anti-terrorist coalition with the US. Since 9/11, it has set up a national security secretariat within its defence ministry in order to oversee counter terrorist measures. By way of tightening its border security, it has made it necessary for the citizens of Iran, Saudi Arabia, Sudan, Pakistan and Egypt to obtain visas before entering Singapore.

From the foregoing account of the activities of the Al-Qaida and its associate Islamist groups, sprinkled over the Southeast Asian countries, it becomes obvious that these elements are deeply entrenched in this volatile region. The intricacy of the working of the various terrorist conflicts, their elaborate networking, elusive nature of the native partners, clandestine activities of the perpetration of terrorism and the complicities of their involvement in the drug-trafficking as well as money laundering businesses have contributed enormously to the consolidation of Al-Qaida in this remote region. It augurs well for all the countries in this area that all the governments of this vast region have acknowledged the need of cooperation for further enhancement of legal, military and political arrangements. Although the words of the heads of state are not matching with their deeds, it is worth noting that Indonesia, Malaysia and the Philippines have agreed to finalize an accord with a vow to combating terrorism. This may lead further to the creation of a Rapid Response Force. The long existing Forum of the Association of Southeast Asian Nations is already available for coordination among them in the field of security arrangements. It was at the Brunei Summit in November 2003, the ASEAN Declaration on joint action to counter terrorism was adopted. Procedures for collaborative efforts are being finalized. The ASEAN initiative has earned high credibility in the anti-terrorism global coalition. Its success will further pave the way for stronger and broad anti-terrorism framework through the collaboration efforts of ASEAN-Plus-Three (Japan, South Korea and the USA), ASEAN-China summits, ASEAN Regional Forum as well as the US-ASEAN Dialogue. All this augurs well for the progression of the global fight against terrorism.

CONCLUSIONS

Our study thus shows that the strategic and regional implications of political Islam in the two regions across the Eurasian continent along with the extra-territorial portents of the conflict situation and its global fallout have become inordinately significant at the present critical juncture.

The CAR is very vast, more than the size of the USA and almost of the size of whole Europe. This area is directly sandwiched by the two nuclear powers—Russia and China. It falls within the closest possible neighbourhood of the two South Asian adversaries like India and Pakistan, which have fought three bitterest wars and have now turned into nuclear states. Neighbouring Iran, which has made its presence enormously felt in Central Asia for millennia, is believed to have nuclear potential. Israel has expanded its military ties with some countries in this area. It has hugely invested in several key-commercial enterprises in this region. Very antagonistic to Iran, Afghanistan and Pakistan, Israel is also believed to have serious nuclear ambitions. In the Central and Southwest Asian regions, where world's nearly half the population resides in and around the periphery of this area, and where some of the contending powers are so deeply entrenched against each other, the impending dangers of political Islam have no doubt tremendously impacted the security scenario of these two regions and the vast areas beyond them which fall in the sprawling Southeast Asian areas.

The significance of the resource-rich CAR has further shot up due to the recent construction of the various trans-continental energy and communication routes, which have linked up this area with destinations in Eurasia, China, Persian Gulf and West Europe with tremendous possibilities of expansion up to the Indian subcontinent.

The fast changing politico-military dynamics as well as economic implications of political Islam in the CAR and Southwest Asia have influenced the regional balance of powers. They are bound to affect the European, Middle Eastern and Southeast Asian geo-politics as well economics in the foreseeable future.

ACKNOWLEDGEMENTS

The author fervently expresses his deep sense of gratitude to Dr. Ranjit Sinha, Member Secretary of the Indian Council of Social Science Research, and Prof. Shaumian Tatyna of the Institute of Oriental Studies of the Russian Academy of Sciences for having facilitated his visit to Moscow where this paper was revised. He is beholden to Prof. TCA Anant, Member of the Executive Council of the ICSSR, who took keen interest in the product of the author's field trip. Prof. DN Tripathi, formerly Chairman of the ICHR and the Editor of the Proceedings of the Indo-Russian International Seminar as well as Prof. Ishrat Alam, the present Member Secretary of the ICHR are thanked profusely for reviving several deadlines for the publication of this volume.

This paper has turned into the brief summary of UGC Major Research Project which the author has undertaken at the Centre for Russian & Central Asian Studies, JNU. He gratefully acknowledges support from Prof. Ajay Patnaik, Prof. Tulsiram and Prof. Arun Mohanty of this Centre.

NOTES AND REFERENCES

1. For the details regarding the Taliban, see (i) William Marley, *Fundamentalism Reborn? Afghanistan and the Taliban*, London, 1998, (ii) Peter Marsden, *The Taliban: War, Religion and the New Order in Afghanistan*, London, 1999, (iii) Matinuddin, *The Taliban Phenomenon*, Karachi, 1999, (iv) M.J. Gohari, *Taliban: Ascent to Power*, Oxford, 1999, (v) Ahmed Rashid, *Taliban, Islam, Oil and New States of Central Asia*, London, 2000.
2. For the details regarding the terrorist activities of the Al-Qaida and the role of Osama, see (i) Ahmed Rashid, *Taliban, Islam, Oil and New States of Central Asia*, London, 2000, (ii) V.D. Chopra (ed.), *Rise of Terrorism and Secessionism in Eurasia*, New Delhi, 2001, (iii) Rohan Gunaratna, *Inside Al-Qaida*, London, 2002, (iv) *International Terrorist Support Networks: The Dynamics of Ethno-nationalist Campaigns*, London, 2002.
3. For the details regarding the IMU, see Poonam Mann, *Strategic Analysis*, New Delhi, April-June 2002, pp. 194-203.
4. For the details regarding India's relations with the CAS, see Report on (i) *Reconnecting India and Central Asia: Emerging Security and Economic Dimensions,* (ed.) Nirmala Joshi, *Central Asia*, Caucasus Institute, Silk Road Studies Programme, (ii) *Strategic Environment in Central Asia and India,* Arun Sahgal and Vinod Anand, (iii) *Energy Security in Asia: China, India, Oil and Peace* – Report on the Norwegian Ministry of Foreign Affairs, Stein Tonnesson and Ashild Kolas, International Peace Research Institute, Oslow, April 2006. (iv) *Inside Central Asia*, Dilip Hiro, Harper Collins, July, 2010, (v) Congressional Research Service, *Central Asia's Security: Issues and Implications for US Interests,* Jim Nichol, March 11, 2010, (vi) *The Journal of International Security Affairs*, India's Stake in Afghanistan, Spring-Summer 2011, (vii) *Mapping Central Asia, India's Perceptions and Strategies,* (eds.) Marlene Laurelle and Sebastien Peyronse, August 2011, (viii) East Asia Forum, May 9, 2011, Challenge of Energy Security, (ix) Under the Shrinking US Security Umbrella: India's End Game in Afghanistan, Washington Quarterly, Spring 2011, (x) Asia Report, N. 225, 24 May 2011, 1 August, 2011, (xi) Debate: SCO, 13 June 2011, China Daily, August 17, 2011.
5. For the details regarding 11 September events, see (i) *Foreign Affairs*, Washington, January-February 2002, (ii) *Foreign Policy*, Washington, January-February, 2002, (iii) *Orbis,* Philadelphia, Spring 2002, (iv) *International Studies Perspectives,* Oxford, February 2002, (v) *International Affairs*, London, 78(2), 2002, (vi) *International Security*, Washington, Winter 2001, (vii) *Financial Times*, London, 17 December 2001 (viii) *New York Times*, 2 December 2001, and (ix) *Asian Affairs*, London, February 2002.
6. Ashton B. Carter, 'The Architecture of Government in the Face of Terrorism', *International Security* (Washington), Winter 2001/2, p. 5.
7. 'September 11th and US Hegemony – Or Will the 21 Century Be American Too', *International Studies Perspectives* (Oxford), February 2002, p.53.

8. *New York Times*, 2 December 2001, see also Michael Radu, 'Terrorism after the Cold War: Trends and Challenges', *Orbis* (Philadelphia), Spring 2002, p. 290.
9. Thomas Homar-Dixon, 'The Rise of Complex Terrorism', *Foreign Policy* (Washington), Jan.-Feb. 2002, p. 57.
10. 'Fixing Intelligence', *Foreign Affairs* (Washington), Jan.-Feb. 2002, p. 43.
11. *Ibid.*
12. *Regional Studies* (Islamabad), Summer, 2002, p. 40
13. Michael Cox, 'American Power before and after 11 September: Dizzy with Success?' *International Affairs* (London), 17 December 2001.
14. Op. cit., see also *Financial Times* (London), 17 December 2001.
15. Radu, op. cit.
16. Michael E. O'Hanlon, 'A Flawed Masterpiece', *Foreign Affairs*, May-June 2002, pp. 48-50, 60.
17. *New York*, 21-22 September 2001.
18. Michael Dennison, 'Central Asian Politics After the Taliban: New Risks, New Opportunities', *Asian Affairs* (London), February 2002, p. 83.
19. Simon Reeve, *The New Jackals: Ramzi Yousef, Osama bin Laden and the Future of Terrorism*, London, 1999, p 157. See also *Ramzi Ahmad Yousef*, Intelligence Report, Kuwait, 1996.
20. See Muhammad *Jamal Khalifa*, Biographical Profile, Directorate for Intelligence, Philippines National Police, Manila, n.d.
21. Gunaratna, Rohan, *Inside Al Qaeda: Global Network of Terrorism*, New Delhi, 2002, p. 174.
22. *Ibid.*
23. 'Muslims Groups Hunt for the Americans', *The Jakarta Post*, 24 September 2001.
24. 'Anti-US Plots', *Los Angeles Times*, 7 February 2002.

26

Russian-Indian Strategic Partnership as a Historical Necessity

Andrei Volodin

The issue of Russian-Indian strategic partnership should be positioned in a broader historical context, particularly that of the late 80s and the early 90s of the previous century. We all know that the disintegration of the bipolar model world politics after the demise of the former Soviet Union has not transformed into emergence of new international network based on horizontal relationships among the states and harmonious interaction between various cultures and civilisations.

> As is known, relationships based on horizontal interactions (coordination) are better equipped to manage world politics today than principles of subordination, i.e., the vestiges of neocolonialism.

The latest developments, and the events of September 11 in particular, have demonstrated convincingly that the hegemony of the so-called 'core' area is unrealistic if not counter-productive. It is not an exaggeration to state that these events have been instrumental to shatter the psychological foundations of the superpower/superiority mental complex, existing within the American society. We can easily make reference to the Balkan peace settlement, Mr. Saddam Hussein's staying in power, the international oil market 'regulation', etc. as vivid examples of Western hegemony's inefficiency.[1]

Writers of a variety of political persuasions have pointed out that the world economy in general and the most advanced segments of this entity in particular had already slipped into recession that will result in a number of unintended geostrategic consequences. Only 35 percent of the electorate in the 'core' economy of Germany favour the eastward extension of the European community. Given decline in the United States and the difficulty of reversing it as well as a weakening of growth in Germany and Japan, a noted American economic historian, Charles P. Kindleberger, wrote prophetically in the mid-90s:

> I happen not to be prophet or the son of a prophet, but I predict muddle. Many problems will be dealt with one at a time, others will persist and produce conflicts that linger and mildly poison international economic and political relations. Some agreements reached will not be carried out. On occasion unsolvable disagreements will gradually fade into unimportance. There will be some regionalism, some cooperation among great powers, some persistent low-level conflict. In sum, muddle is indicated. In due course a country will emerge from the muddle for a time as the primary world economic power. The United States again? Japan? Germany? The European Community as a whole? Perhaps a dark horse like Australia or Brazil or China? Who knows? Not I.[2]

The fragility of contemporary world order is the natural outcome of disrupted international networks formerly based on three pillars (1) Accumulation regulated in the West by Keynesian national politics, consistent with a coherence between openness to the world market and the historic capital/labour compromose. (2) Modernization in the newly independent peripheries (the so-called Bandung Project). (3) The Soviet project, catching up with the West by means of state ownership and the centralisation of political and economic power in the hands of 'a new bourgeoisie-information, the nomenclature of the communist parties'.[3] This tripolar system constituted the basis of a sustainable economic expansion in each of the three regions.

After the demise of what was referred to as the 'World Socialist System' a kind of a vacuum emerged in the international set-up. Nevertheless, the inability of the West to materialise its hegemony in the world order raises the issue of new pillars for the international system. The only solution to this problem is to build a principally different international network functioning on the basis of horizontal relations and taking into consideration the interests of the overwhelming majority of world politics.

It is logically relevant to suggest that in a newly emerging community of horizontal ties, a significant role belongs to the so-called 'superlarge' states entities, namely Brazil, China, India and Russia.

So far as Russia is concerned, its ruling elite has to maximize the factor of new 'gravitation poles' in world politics and exploit to the fullest extent the possibilities opened by a realignment of international forces that has already started. Putting it differently, the strategic partnership is a mode of relations designed and shaped by common geopolitical perspectives. For India and

Russia, the common geopolitical perspective is by at least three long-term trends. These trends are mentioned below:

1. India and Russia are 'underdeveloped' and tentatively gigantic markets potentially capable to digest the most up-to-date manufacturing and technologies. Both India and Russia acquire a huge intellectual and scientific potential that can be best utilised in the conditions of reciprocity and complementarity. The 'horizontal' relationships are very much relevant to solve the problems of the new millennium like prevention of environment degradation, ecological reconstruction of 'traditional' industries, development of transportation system, creation of new materials and sources of energy, etc.
2. The 'superlarge' states like India and Russia are now facing a number of problems engendered by globalisation, and these issues are better tackled by joint efforts. First, the crucial role of the state as an instrument mitigating the consequences of globalization for the overwhelming majority of the people should be maintained and protected. Furthermore, the national state is the primary agent of a coherent and a long-term strategy of employment: the functioning of spontaneous market regulators could result in massive unemployment and widespread public unrest. Second, for modernisation to be supported by the people, this process should be complemented with a gradual, non-violent transformation of society's national identity. The maintenance of the cultural matrix, as the experience of the earlier modernisers like Japan and Germany demonstrates, is instrumental in strengthening a given country's position in the world economic and political hierarchy. Third, one of the by-products of globalization, the so-called 'mass culture' has done a lot to dismantle indigenous values, orientations and modes of behaviour of non-Western societies. To prevent this negative chain of events, in my humble opinion, India and Russia should elaborate on an efficient educational and scientific policy and a strategy in science and technology aimed at enlarged reproduction of our nations' intellectual potential.
3. The chaotic trends in world politics, the dismemberment of Yugoslavia, the Middle East imbroglio, the public unrest in Africa and Southeast Asia in particular, cannot be reversed by unipolar structures. The G7 institutions have been proved inefficient to counter the parametric challenges of the twenty first century. The inadequacy of the Western 'gravitation pole' will objectively stimulate such nations as India, China, Russia and Brazil to seek meaningful institutions and forces in a fast changing international set-up. One of the pillars of a new international system is allegedly a

renovated United Nations Organization stripped of former ideological disputes and entitled to solve the aggravating problems of an unevenly developed world.

Potentially promising is the cooperation between India and Russia in the sphere of national security. Such kind of collaboration was emphasised during Prime Minister A.B. Vajpayee's last visit to Russia.

I will point to the four pillars of the India's concept of national security that may be of significant relevance for the Russian Federation.

1. *Food security:* Both the countries have already experienced the political pressure of the West, exerted under the most unfavourable circumstances: India was blackmailed by the Johnson administration in the mid-sixties, while Russia/Soviet Union was the target of the American sanctions after the invasion of Afghanistan, in December 1979. So, the Russian ruling elite's goal is complete self-reliance in food supplies that has distinctive political repercussions.

It is highly instructive that the American political establishment, in the late 70s and early 80s, seriously considered grain as a weapon potentially more effective than a nuclear bomb.

2. *Energy security:* India, having a limited amount of energy resources, actively and consciously develops alternative sources including nuclear and solar energy. This approach widely shared by the main segments of Indian public opinion envisages a policy of self-reliance, also in the area of energy supply minimising the role of the so-called energy factor in foreign policy implementation.
3. *Economic security:* The Indian Government, tracing the basic trends in world economy, encourages the flow of national resources to the industries based on progress in science and technology. The development of the indigenous support for the 'New Economy' will naturally strengthen the country's position in the world economic and political hierarchy and will allow India to compete on equal footing with the nations' leaders of world economy.
4. *Military security:* To maintain its dominant position in the Indian Ocean basin and to repel the potential threats coming from both inside and outside of the region, India has resolutely chosen the policy of sophisticated weaponry employment. In this area, Russian-Indian co-operation remains absolutely essential.

In my humble view, Russian-Indian strategic partnership is not to be transformed into a kind of the 'Axis'. Nevertheless, the co-operation of our two nations (plus China and Brazil) in areas of economy and foreign policy could eventually convert Russian-Indian strategic partnership into a new 'gravitation pole' in the international system.

Let me conclude by saying that strategic partnership between India and Russia, with tentative subsequent involvement of China and Brazil, will ultimately pave the way for a new international order to be established on the basis of human values, sustainable development and harmonious relationship of nature and society.

NOTES AND REFERENCES

1. The seminar where this paper was presented was held in 2001, before the US invasion of Iraq.
2. Charles P. Kindleberger, *World Economic Primacy: 1500 to 1990*, Oxford, 1996, p. 228.
3. S. Amin, *Capitalism in the Age of Globalization: The Management of Contemporary Society*, London, 1997, p. 46.

Bibliography

BOOKS

Abas, M.H., *All about the Khilafat,* Calcutta, 1923.

Abu'l Fazl, *Ain-i-Akbari,* ed. by H. Blochman, *Bib. Indica,* Calcutta, 1867-77.

Abu'l Fadi Bayhaqi, *Tarikh-I-Miasudi (1030-1041),* Russian tr. A.K. Arends, Moscow, 1969.

Abu'l-Fadl' Allami, *Akbarnama,* English tr. by H. Beverdge, 3 vols., Calcutta, 1897-1921.

Adamec, Ludwing W. (ed.), *Historical and Political Gazetteer of Afghanistan,* Vol. 3, Graz, Akademisch Druck-u-verlagsnstat, 1975.

Adhikari, G. (ed.), *Documents of the History of Communist Party of India,* New Delhi, 1971.

Adshead, S.A.M., *Central Asia in World History,* New York, 1993.

Ahmad, Qeyamuddin, *The Wahabi Movement in India,* Calcutta, 1966.

Ahmad, Tasneem (tr.), *Tarikh-I-Akbari (Muhamad Arif Qandhari),* New Delhi, Pragati Publication, 1993.

Ahmad, Aziz, *Studies in Islamic Culture in the Indian Environment,* Oxford University Press, 1964.

Aini Sadriddin, *Pages from My Own Story, Memoirs,* trans. by George H. Hauna, Moscow, Foreign Language Pub. House, 1958.

——, *Yada Sht-ha (Memoirs),* The Complete 5 volumes, in one, ed. by Said Serjani, Tehran, 1983.

Aitchison, Charles, *A Collection of Treaties, Engagements and Sanads Relating to India and Neighbouring Countries,* Calcutta, 1909.

Akbar, Muhammad, *The Punjab under the Mughals,* Delhi, Idarah-i-Adabayat, Delhi, 1974.

Akiner, Shirin (ed.), *Cultural Change and Continuity in Central Asia,* London, Kegan Paul International, 1991.

——, *Political and Economic Trends in Central Asia,* London, 1994.

——, *Tradition and Change in Central Asia,* London, 1991.

Alam Khan, Iqtidar, *Coming of Gunpowder and the Response of Indian Polity,* Calcutta, Centre for Studies in Social Science, 1981.

Alam, M. and S. Sanjay (eds.), *The Mughal State 1526-1570*, Delhi, 1998.

Al-Biruni, *India*, English tr. by E. Sachau, 2 vols., London, 1910.

Al-Bundari, *Zubdat al-nusra*, (ed.) M.T. Houtsma, Leiden, 1889.

Allchin, B. and Raymond Allchin, *The Birth of Indian Civilization*, Penguin, 1968.

Alder, G.J., *British India's Northern Frontier, 1865-1895*, London, 1963.

Algar, Hamid, *Religion and State in Iran, 1785-906: The Role of the Ulama in the Qajar Period*, Berkeley, University of California Press, 1969.

Al-Kufi, Ali B. Hamid, *Chach-Nama*, English tr. by K. Mirza, Karachi, 1960-62.

Allen, Charles, *A Mountain in Tibet: The Search for Mount Kailas and the Sources of the Great River of India*, Macmillan, 1982.

Al Nawabkhti, *Firaqal-Shia*, ed. by H. Ritter, Istanbul, 1931.

Alonso, M.E. (ed.), *China's Inner Asian Frontier*, Historical Text by Joseph Fletcher, Cambridge Mass., Peabody Museum, 1979.

Al-Utbi, *Al-Tarikh al-yamini*, with Commentary by Shyakh Ahmad l-Manini, Cairo, 1869.

Allworth, Edword, *Central Asia, A Century of Russian Rule*, New York, Columbia University Press, 1967.

——, *Uzbek Literary Politics*, The Hague, Mouton, 1964.

Amfroz, Oton, *Realignment of World Power: The Russo-Chinese Schism*, 2 vols., New York, 1972.

Andrew, W.P., *The Euphrates Valley Railway*, London, 1870.

——, *The Euphrates Valley Route to India in Connection with the Central Asia and Egyptian Question*, 2nd edn., London, 1882.

Antonius, George, *The Arab Awakening*, London, 1938.

Arberry, A.J. (ed.), *The Legacy of Persia*, Oxford, 1953.

Arnold, T.W., *The Caliphate*, Oxford University Press, 1924.

Atiya, Aziz, S., *A History of Eastern Christianity*, London, Methuen, 1981.

Atkien, Muriel, *The Subtle Battle: Islam in Soviet Tajikistan*, Philadelphia, Foreign Policy Research Institute, 1989.

Attarchand, *Bibliography of Indo-Soviet Relations*, New Delhi, Sterling, 1978.

——, *India, Pakistan and Afghanistan, A Study of Freedom Struggle and Abdul Ghaffar Khan*, New Delhi, Commonwealth, 1989.

——, *Revolutionary and Arabs*, Delhi, Hamdard Pub., 1981.

Azeem, Anwar, *Deep are the Roots*, New Delhi, PPH, 1969.

Azizuddin, M.M., *Tarikhi Chitral*, Rawalpindi, 1987.

Bacon, Elizabeth, E., *Central Asia under Russian Rule: A Study in Cultural Change*, New York, Cornell University Press, 1968.

Baddeley, J.F., *Russia, Mongolia, China*, 2 vols., London, 1919, reprinted in New York, 1969.

Bag, A.K., *Science and Civilization in India*, Vol. I., Delhi, Navrang, 1985.

——, *History of Technology in India*, vol. I, New Delhi, Indian National Science Academy, 1997.

Bagchi, P.C., *India and Central Asia*, Jadavpur, National Council of Education, 1955.

——, *India and China: A Thousand Years of Sino-Indian Cultural Contacts,* Calcutta, China Press, 1944.

Baha, Lal, *North-West Frontier Province: Administration under British Rule*, Islamabad, National Commission on Historical & Cultural Research, 1978.

Bailey, F.M., *Mission to Tashkent,* London, 1946.

Bain, S.K., *Afghanistan will not Die: An Authentic Account of How the Afghan Crisis has Developed Crisis for the World*, Calcutta, 1982.

Baker, Valentine, *Clouds in the East: Travels and Adventures on the Perso-Turkhan Frontier,* London, 1878.

Balubushevich, V.V. and Bimal Prasad (eds.), *India and the Soviet Union—A Symposium,* New Delhi, PPH, 1969.

Baloch, N.A., *Fatehnamah-i-Sind, Being the Original Record of the Arab Conquest of Sind,* Islamabad, 1983.

Bamzai, P.N.K., *A History of Kashmir: Political, Social and Cultural,* Delhi, 1962.

Banerji, S.K., *Humayun Badshah,* Vol. I, OUP, 938; Vol. II, Lucknow, 1941.

Baqir, Muhammad, *Lahore, Past & Present,* Lahore, 1952.

Barber, A. Colborne, *Travels and Research in Western China,* London, Murray, 1982.

Barhebraeus, *Chronology,* English tr. by E.A. Wallis Budge, London, 1932.

Barnes, John Robert, *An Introduction to Religious Foundations in Ottoman Empire,* Leiden, 1987.

Barni, Diya' Al-Din, *Fatawa-Ji jahandari*, (ed.) Afsar Saleem Khan, Lahore, 1972.

——, *Tarikh-I-Firuz-Shahi,* (ed.) Sayyid Ahmad Khan, Calcutta, 1862.

Barret, D. and B. Gray, *The Paintings of India*, Lusanne, 1963.

Barthold, Wilhelmm, *Turkestan Down to the Mongol Invasion,* 3rd ed., London, 1968.

——, 'A History of the Turkman People', in *Four Studies on the History of Central Asia,* English tr. by V. and T. Minorsky, Vol. 3, pp. 73-170, Leiden, 1962.

Basham, A.L., *The Wonder That Was India,* New York, Grove, 1954.

Bales, E.S., *Soviet Asia: Progress and Problems,* London, 1942.

Bawden, C.R., *The Modern History of Mongolia,* London, 1968.

Bayly, C.A., *Rulers, Towns and Bazaars, North Indian Society in the Age of British Expansion 1770-1870,* Cambridge, Cambridge University Press, 1982.

Beal, Samuel, *Buddhist Records of the Western World,* Reprint, Delhi, 1969.

—— *The Life of Hiuentsiang,* London, 1885.

Beames, John, *History, Folk Lore & Culture of the Races of North-Western Provinces*, Vol. I & II, Reprint, Delhi, 1978.

Becker, Seynour, *Russian Protectorates in Central Asia, Bukhara and Khiva, 1865-1924,* USA, 1968.

Beckwith, Christopher J., *The Tibetan Empire in Central Asian Frontier,* Princeton University Press, 1987.

Begley, W.E. and A.A. Desai, *The Shahjahanama,* Oxford University Press, 1990.

Belenitsky, A., *The Ancient Civilization of Central Asia,* London, 1969.

Benjamin, R., *The Wall Paintings of India, Central Asia and Ceylon—A Comparative Study*, Boston, 1938.

Benord, Cheryl and Zalmay Khalizad, *The Govt. of God, Iran's Islamic Republic*, New York, Columbia Univ. Press, 1984.

Beni Prasad, *History of Jahangir*, 2nd edn., Allahabad, 1930, 5th edn., 1962.

Benningben, Alexandre, *Muslims of the Soviet Empire: A Guide*, Bloomington, Indiana University, 1986.

——, 'The Turks under Tsarist and Soviet Rule', in *Central Asia*, ed. by Gavin Hambly, London, Weidenfield and Nicolson, 1969, pp. 187-207.

Bernier, Francois, *Travels in the Mogul Empire* AD *1656-1668*, London, 1934.

Beverige, A.S., *The Baburnama in English*, 2 vols., London, Luzac, 1922.

Bhattacharya, Chaya, *Art of Central Asia*, Delhi, 1969.

Bialer, Seweryn (ed.), *Stalin and his Generals*, Pegasus Press, 1969.

Biddulph, J., *Tribes of the Hindookoosh*, Reprint, Karachi, 1977.

Bilgrami, *Ashgar Husain, Afghanistan and British India 1793-1907: A Study in Foreign Relations*, New Delhi, 1973.

Bindra, S.S., *India and her Neighbours: A Study of Political, Economic and Cultural Relations and Interactions*, New Delhi, Deep & Deep, 1984.

Bongard-Levin, G.M. and A. Vigasin , *Ancient Indian Civilization*, Arnold-Heinemann, 1985.

——, *The Image of India: The Study of Ancient Civilization in the USSR*, Moscow, Progress Publishers, 1984.

Boorman, H.L. *et al.*, *Moscow-Peking Axis, Strengths and Strains*, New York, 1975.

Bose, Ashish, *India and the Asian Population Perspective*, Delhi, BRPC, 1993.

Bosworth, C.E., *The Ghaznavis—Their Empire in Afghanistan and Eastern Iran 994-1040*, Edinburgh, 2nd edn., Beirut, 1973.

——, *The Later Ghaznavis, Splendour and Decay. The Dynasty in Afghanistan and Northern India 1040-1186*, Edinburgh, 1977.

——, *The History of the Saffarids and the Maliks of Nirmruz (247/861 to 949/1542-3)*, New York, 1994.

——, *The Interaction of Arabic and Persian Literature and Culture in the Tenth and Early Eleventh Centuries Reprinted in Medieval Arabic Culture and Administration*, No. VIII, London, 1982.

——, *The Medieval History of Iran, Afghanistan and Central Asia*, London, 1977.

——, *The New Islamic Dynasties: A Chronological and Genealogical Manual*, New York, 1996.

——, *Sistan under the Arabs, From the Islamic Conquest to the Rise of Saffarids (30-250/ 651-864)*, Rome, 1968.

Bougler, Demetrius Charles, *Central Asian Questions: Essay on Afghanistan, China and Central Asia*, London, 1885.

——, *England and Russia in Central Asia*, Vol. 1, London, 1879.

Boyle, J.A. (ed.), *The Cambridge History of Iran*, Vol. V, Cambridge, Cambridge University Press, 1968.

——, (tr.), *The Success of Genghis Khan*, by Rashid al-Din Talib, Columbia University Press, 1971.

Brermmer, Lan and Ray Taras (eds.), *Nations and Politics in the Soviet Successor States*, Cambridge, 1993.

Bretschneider, E., *Medieval Researches from Eastern Asiatic Sources*, 2 vols., London, 1911.

Brown, C.J., *The Coins of India*, Calcutta, 1922.

Brown, Percy, *Indian Architecture: The Islamic Period*, Bombay, 1928.

——, *Indian Painting under Mughals*, Oxford, 1924.

Browne, E.G., *A Literary History of Persian*, Vol. III, *1226-1502*, Vol. IV, *Modern Times 1500-1924*, Cambridge, 1928.

——, *The Persian Constitutional Revolution*, Cambridge, Cambridge University Press, 1910.

Brydges, Harfod Jones, *Dynasty of the Kajars, London*, J. Bohn, 1833, Reprinted in 1973 by Arno Press, New York.

Bulliet, Richord W., *The Camel and the Wheel (Cambridge Mass.)*, Harvard University Press, 1975.

Burn, Capt. A.H., *Troublous Times, Experiences in Bolshevik Russia and Turkestan*, London, 1931.

Burnes, Alexander, *Travels in Bukhara*, 3 vols., London, 1836.

Burrow, T., *The Languages of the Kharosthi Documents from Chinese Turkestan*, Cambridge, 1937.

——, *A Translation of the Kharosthi Documents from Chinese Turkestan*, London, 1940.

Bussagali, M., *Paintings of Central Asia*, Geneva, 1963.

Butt, G.M. (ed.), *Central Asia and Eastern Himalayas: A Forgotten Link*, Jodhpur Scientific Pub., 1985.

Caroe, Olaf, *Soviet Empire, The Turks of Central Asia and Stalinism*, London, Macmillan, 1967.

Carr, E.H., *The Bolshevik Revolution 1917-23*, London, 1960.

Carrere, D'Encause H., *Islam and the Russian Empire: Reform and Revolution in Central Asia*, London, 1988.

Castells, Mannel, *City, Clan and Power*, London, 1878.

Cazalet, Edward, *The Berlin Congress and the Anglo-Turkish Convention*, London, 1978.

Chakraberti, Kanchan, *Society, Religion and Art of the Kushana Period*, Calcutta, K.P. Bagchi & Co., 1981.

Chakravarti, N.P., *India and Central Asia*, Calcutta, Prabasi Press, 1928.

Chakravarty, Suhash, *From Khyber to Oxus—A Study in Imperial Expansion*, Delhi, Orient Longman, 1976.

Chamay, Francois-Bernard, *Expedition de Timour-I-lenk (Tamerlane) Contre Toqtamiche en 1391 de J.C., St. Petersburg 1834-35*, Amsterdam, Philo Press Reprint, 1975.

Chandra, Lokesh and Devendra Swarup (eds.), *India's Contribution to World Thought and Culture*, Madras, Vivekanand Rock Memorial Committee, 1971.

Chandra, Satish, *Parties and Politics at the Mughal Court 1707-1740*, Aligarh, 1959.

Charak, Sukhdev Singh (tr.), *Rajdarshini (A Persian History of North-Western India from Earliest Times to* AD *1847)*, Jammu, J.K. Book House, 1991.

Chatterjee, Basant, *Indo-Soviet Friendship—An Analytical Study*, New Delhi, S. Chand & Co., 1974.

Chopra, Pran, *Before and After the Indo-Soviet Treaty*, New Delhi, S. Chand & Co., 1974.

Chopra, V.D. (ed.), *Studies in Indo-Soviet Relations*, New Delhi Publishers, 1986.

Clubb, O. Edmund, *China and Russia—The Great Game*, New York, 1971.

Cole, Juan Ricard Irfan, *Imami Shi 'ism from Iran to North India 1722-1856: State, Society and Clerical Ideology in Awadh*, Ph.D.. dissertation, Univ. of California, Los Angeles, 1984.

Creswell, K.A.C., *Early Muslim Architecture*, 2 vols., London, 1940.

Crooke, W., *The North-Western Provinces of India: Their History, Ethnology and Administration*, Reprint, Delhi, 1971.

Czaplica, M.A., *The Turks of Central Asia in History and the Present Day*, Oxford, 1918.

Dabbs, J.A., *The History of the Discovery and Exploration of Chinese Turkestan*, The Hague, 1963.

Dallin, D.J., *The Rise of Russia in Asia*, London, 1950.

Dalton, O.M., *The Treasure of Oxus*, London, 1926, 3rd edn., 1964.

Dange, S.A., *Gandhi Versus Lenin*, Bombay, 1921.

Dani, A.H., *History of Northern Areas of Pakistan*, Islamabad, 1989.

——, *Islamic Architecture: The Wooden Style of Northern Pakistan*, Islamabad, 1989.

——, *New Light on Central Asia*, Delhi Renaissance Publishing House, Reprint, 1993.

Daniel, Elton, *The Political and Social History of Khurasan under Abbasid Rule 747-820*, Minneapolis and Chicago, 1979.

Danziger, Nick, *Danziger's Travels: Beyond Forbidden Frontiers*, London, Grafton, 1987.

Dash, P.L. (ed.), *Russian Dilemma: The Ethnic Aftermath*, Cuttack, Arya Prakashan, 1994.

Dashpurev, D. and S.K. Soni, *Reign of Terror in Mongolia: 1920-1990*, New Delhi, South Asian Publishers, 1992.

Davies, C.C., *The Problem of the North-West Frontier 1890-1908*, London, 1974.

Demko, George J., *The Russian Colonization of Kazakhstan 1896-1916*, Bloomington, Indiana University Press, 1967.

Denison, Ross E. (tr.), *A History of the Moguls of Central Asia* (in 2 vols.) Reprint, New Delhi, ABI Prints & Publication Co., 1998.

Deshpande, M.M. and Peter Edwin Hook (eds.), *Aryan and Non-Aryan in India*, University of Michigan Press, 1979.

Dhavalikar, M.K., *Cultural Imperialism (Indus Civilization) in Western India*, New Delhi, Books & Books, 1995.

Dichter, David, *The North-West Frontier of West Pakistan: A Study in Regional Geography*, Oxford, 1967.

Dmytryshyn, Basil (ed.), *Imperial Russia: A Source Book 1700-1917*, 2nd edn., Illinois, The Dryden Press, 1974.

Donie, Sir James, *The Punjab, North-West Frontier Province and Kashmir*, Reprint, Delhi, Seema Publishers, 1974.

Druthe, David, *Soviet Russia and Indian Communism, 1917-1947*, New York, 1959.

Drew, F., *The Northern Barrier of India*, London, 1877.

Dugersuren, M., *The Mongolian People's Republic & International Relations,* Ulan Bator, 1981.

Dughalta, Mirza Muhammad Haydar, *Tarikh-I-Rashidi*, ed. & English tr. N. Elias and Denis Ross, *A History of the Moghuls of Central Asia,* London, 1895.

Du Jarric, Pierre, *Akbar and the Jesuits,* London, 1926.

Dunlop, M.D., *The History of the Jewish Khazars,* New York, 1954.

Dutt, J.C., *Kings of Kashmir,* 3 vols., Calcutta, 1879-98.

Dutta, R.P., *India Today,* Calcutta, 1970.

Eaton, Richard Maxwell, *Sufis of Bijapur, 1300-1700: Social Roles in Medieval India,* Princeton University Press, 1978.

Elias, N. and E. Dennison Ross, *A History of the Moghuls of Central Asia,* London, 1895.

Elliot, Sir H. and Dowson J., *A History of India as Told by its Own Historians,* 8 vols., London, 1867-75.

Elphinstone, Mountstuart, *An Account of the Kingdom of Caubul,* 2 vols., London and New York, 1815, 1972.

Engels, Donald W., *Alexander The Great and the Macedonian Army,* Berkeley, University of California Press, 1978.

Etherton, P.T., *In the Heart of Asia,* London, 1925.

Fakhr Al-Din Mubarakshah, *Tarikh,* (ed.) R.D. Ross, London, 1927.

Fedorova, T.E. Goroda, *Tajikistana Problemy Rostai Razbilia,* in Russian, Dushanbe, 1981.

Fennels, John, *The Crisis of Medieval Russia 1200-1304,* London, Longmans, 1983.

Fergusson, James, *History of India and Eastern Architecture,* (ed.) James Burgess and Pheni Spiers, London, 1910.

Firdausi, *The Epic of the Kings, Shah-Nama,* trans. by Reuben Levy, London, Routledge & Kegan Paul, 1965.

Firishta, *Tarikhi-I-Firishtra,* abridged English tr. by John Briggs, *A History of Rise of the Mohammedan Power in India till in Year* AD *1612,* Vol. I, London, 1829.

Fischel, Walter J., *Ibn Khaldun and Tamerlane,* Berkeley, University of California Press, 1952.

Fitzgerald, W.F.V., *The Suez Canal, The Eastern Question and Abyssinia,* London, 1867.

Fletcher, Joseph, 'China and Central Asia', in John F. Fairbank (ed.), *The Chinese World Order,* Cambridge Mass., Harvard University Press, 1968.

Forbes, Andrew D.W., *Warlords and Muslims in Chinese Central Asia,* Cambridge, Cambridge University Press, 1986.

Forsyth, T.D., *Memorandum on the Routes from the Punjab to Eastern Turkestan,* Lahore, 1868.

——, (ed.), *Report of a Mission to Yarkand,* Calcutta, 1875.

Foster, W. (ed.), *The Embassy of Sir Thames Roe to the Great Mogal 1615-19* (as narrated in his Journal and Correspondence) (in 2 vols.), Hakluyt Society, 1899.

Frazer-Tyller, W.K., *Afghanistan: A Study of Political Development in Central Asia,* London, 1950.

Friters, Gerald M., *Outer Mongolia and its International Position,* Baltimore, 1949.

Frye, R.N., *The Golden Age of Persia: The Arabs in the East,* London, 1975.

——, *Bukhara, The Medieval Achievement,* Norman, University of Oklahoma Press, 1965.

——, *The History of Bukhara*, Cambridge, 1954.

Fusfeld, Warren, *The Shaping of Sufi Leadership in Delhi: The Naqshbandiyya Mujaddidiyya, 1750 to 1920* (Ph.D. dissertation), University of Pennsylvania, 1981.

Gafurov, B.G., Bongard Levin *et. al.*, *Central Asia in the Kushana Period*, 2 vols., Published under UNESCO, Moscow, 1974-75.

Gandhi, M.K. (ed.), *Young India 1919-22*, Madras, 1924.

Ganjoo, Satish, *Afghanistan, Strugle for Resurgence*, Delhi, Akashdeep, 1985.

Gaur, R.B., *Afghanistan: Expanding Social Base of Revolution*, New Delhi, Allied, 1987.

Gaury, Gerald de and H.V.F. Winstone (eds.), *The Road to Kabul: An Anthology*, New York, Macmillan, 1982.

Gerald, M.G., *Report on the Proceedings of the Pamir Boundary Commission*, Calcutta, 1897.

Ghafoor, M.A., *Two Lost Inscriptions Relating to the Arab Conquest of Kabul and the North-West Region of West Pakistan, Ancient Pakistan*, Vol. 2, Peshawar, 1959.

Ghani, Abdul, *A Review of Political Situation in Central Asia*, Lahore, 1921.

Ghirshman, R., *The Art of Ancient Persia*, Paris, 1964.

——, *Iran, Parthians and Sassanians*, London, 1962.

Ghosh, D.K., *England and Afghanistan*, Calcutta, 1960.

Gibb, H.A.R., *The Arab Conquests in Central Asia*, London, 1923.

——, (ed.), *The Encyclopedia of Islam*, London, 1960.

Gidadhubli, R.G. (ed.), *Socio-Economic Transformation of Soviet Central Asia*, New Delhi, Patriot Publishers, 1987.

Gilard, David, *The Struggle for Asia 1828-1914*, London, Methuen, 1977.

Gilsenan, Michael, *Recognizing Islam: Religion and Society in the Modern Arab World*, New York, 1982.

Giradet, Edward, *Afghanistan: The Soviet-War*, New Delhi, Select Book Service, 1986.

Goetz, H., *The Crisis of Indian Civilization in the Eighteenth and Early Nineteenth Centuries*, Calcutta, Calcutta University Press, 1938.

Good, Byron J., *The Art of What is the Matter: The Structure of Medical Discourse in a Provincial Iranian Town* (Ph.D. dissertation), University of Chicago, 1977.

Gopal, Surendra, *Indians in Russia in Seventeenth-Eighteenth Centuries*, Calcutta, Noya Prakash, 1986.

Gorbunova, N.G., *The Culture of Ancient Ferghana*, Oxford, B.A.R., 1986.

Grant-Duff, M.E., *The Afghan Policy of the Beaconsfield Government and its Results*, London, 1886.

Grantovsky, E.A. and G.M. Bongard-Levin, *The Origins of Aryans from Scythia to India*, New Delhi, Arnold-Heinemann, 1980.

Gray, B., *The Art of India and Pakistan*, London, 1950.

Greaves, R.L., *Persia and the Defence of India*, London, 1959.

Griffith, Ralph T.H. (tr.), *The Hymns of the Rigveda*, 2nd edn., Benares, 1976.

Grousset, Rene, *The Empire of the Steppes: A History of Central Asia, 1939*, tr. by Naomi, Walford, 1970.

Guha, Amalendu (ed.), *Central Asia: Movement of Peoples and Ideas from Prehistoric to Modern*, New Delhi, ICCR, 1970.

Guha, Pradyot, *Russia's Second Revolution: An Inquiry into the Roots of Perestroika*, Calcutta, Firma K.L. Mukhopadhaya, 1990.

Gupta, Hari Ram, *Panjab, Central Asia and the First Afghan War*, Chandigarh, Panjab University, 1940.

Gupta, S.P., *Archaeology of Soviet Central Asia and the Indian Border Lands*, 2 vols., Delhi, B.R. Publishing Corporation, 1979.

——, *The Lost Sarasvati and the Indus Civilization*, Jodhpur, Kusumanjali Prakashan, 1995.

——, *Roots of Indian Art*, New Delhi, B.R. Publishing Corporation, 1983.

Habib, Irfan, *An Atlas of the Mughal Empire*, New Delhi, Oxford University Press, 1982.

——, *The Agrarian System of Mughal India 1556-1707*, rev. edn., New Delhi, 1999.

Habib, M., *Collected Works: Politics and Society during the Early Medieval Period*, Vol. 2, ed. by K.A. Nizami, 1981.

——, *Sultan Mahmud of Ghazni*, 2nd edn., Delhi, 1951.

Habib, M. and K.A. Nizami (eds.), *A Comprehensive History of India*, Vol. 5, *The Delhi Sultanate* (*AD 1206-1526*), New Delhi, 1970.

Habibullah, A.B.M., *The Foundations of Muslim Rule in India*, 2nd edn., Allahabad, 1961.

HacKin, J., *Buddhist Art in Central Asia*, London, 1937.

Hafiz Muhammad Fazil Khan, *Tarikh-I-Manasil-I-Bukhara* (Persian Text), ed. by I.H. Siddiqui, Patna, K.B.O.P. Library, Patna, 1993.

Halim, Abdul, *History of the Lodi Sultans of Delhi and Agra*, Dacca, 1961.

Hambly, Gavin (ed.), *Central Asia*, London, 1969.

Hardy, P., *Historians of Medieval India, Studies of Indo-Muslim Historical Writing*, London, 1960.

Harmatta, J., 'The Emergence of the Indo-Aryan Languages', in A.H. Dani and V.M. Mason (eds.) *History of Civilizations of Central Asia*, Vol. I, Paris, UNESCO Publication, 1982.

Harmstone, T.R., *Russia and Nationalism in Central Asia: The Case of Tadjikestan*, Baltimore, Johns Hopkins Press, 1970.

Harris, David, *A Diplomatic History of the Balkan Crisis of 1875-1878*, California, 1936.

Hasan, Mohibul, *Kashmir under the Sultan*, Calcutta, 1959.

Haunuer, Milan, *What is Asia to US: Russia's Asian Heartland Yesterday and Today*, Boston, Unwin Hyman, 1990.

Hazard, John J., *Communists and their Law*, University of Chicago Press, 1969.

Heden, Sven, *Central Asia and Tibet: Towards the Holy City of Lossa*, 2 vols., Delhi, Classics India.

He-Dong, Kim, *The Muslim Rebellion and the Kashgar Emirate in Chinese Central Asia 1886-1877*, Harvard, University of M.I., 1988.

Hirlekar, K.S., *Soviet Asia: The Power Behind USSR*, Bombay, 1945.

Hodivala, S.H., *Studies in Indo-Muslim History* (supplement, Vol. II), Bombay, 1957.

———, *Studies in Indo-Muslim History*, Bombay, 1939.

Holdich, Col. Sir T. Hungerford, *The Indian Borderland, 1880-1900,* Reprint, Delhi, Gian, 1987.

Hozier, H.M. (ed.), *The Russo-Turkish War Including an Account of the Rise and Decline of the Ottoman Empire and the History of Eastern Questions,* 5 vols., London, 1877-79.

Hughes-Butler, *Baluchistan District Gazetteer,* Vol. V, *Quetta-Pishin District,* Ajmer, 1907.

Huloewe, A.F.P., *China in Central Asia—The Early Age,* Leiden, 1979.

Husain, Agha Mahdi, *Rise and Fall of Muhammad bin Tughlaq,* London, 1938.

Huttington, Ellsworth, *Pulse of Asia,* London, 1971.

Hutton, John, *Central Asia,* London, 1875.

Hyman, Anthony, *Afghanistan under Soviet Domination 1964-81,* New Delhi, Macmillan, 1982.

Ibn Al-Adim, *Bughyat al Lalab fitarikh Halab* (Partial Turkish, tr. Ali Sevim) , Ankara, 1976.

Ibn Battuta, *Travels,* English tr. by A.R. Gibb, Vol. 3, Cambridge, 1976.

Imam, Zafar, *Colonialism in East-West Relations,* New Delhi, 1969.

———, *The Effects of Russian Revolution on India 1917-20,* London, 1968.

Inghott, H., *Gandharva Art in Pakistan,* New York, 1937.

Islam, Riazul, *Indo-Persian Relations: A Study of the Political and Diplomatic Relations between the Mughal Empire and Iran,* Teheran, Iranian Cultural Centre, 1970.

Jackson, Peter and Lawrence Lockhart, *The Cambridge History of Iran, The Timurid and Safavid Periods,* Vol. 6, Cambridge University Press, 1986.

Jagchid, Sechini, *Peace, War and Trade between North Asian Nomadic Peoples and the Agricultural Chinese,*Taipei, 1972.

——, 'The Rise and Fall of Buddhism in Inner Mongolia', in A.K. Narain (ed.), *Studies in the History of Buddhism,* Delhi, B.R. Publishing Corporation, 1980.

Jagchid Sechini and Paul Hyer, *Mongolia's Culture and Society,* Boulder Colorado, Westview, 1979.

Jarring, G., *On the Distribution of Turk Tribes in Afghanistan,* Leipzig, 1939.

Jelavich, C. (ed.), *Russia in the East 1876-82,* Leiden, 1959.

Joshi, Nirmala, *Foundations of Indo-Soviet Relations,* New Delhi, Radiant Publishers, 1975.

——, *Foundations of Indo-Soviet Relations: A Study of Non-Official Attitudes and Contacts, 1917-1947,* New Delhi, Radiant Publishers, 1979.

Joshi, P.C., *et al., Lenin in Contemporary Indian Press,* New Delhi, 1970.

Justi, F., *Central and Eastern Asia in Antiquity,* London, 1902.

Juvaini, Ata-malik, *The History of the World Conqueror,* (tr.) John Andrew Boyle, 2 vols., Cambridge, Harvard University Press, 1959.

Kachroo, P., *Central Asia and Kashmir: Archaeology and Florislias,* Jodhpur, Scientific Publishers, 1995.

Kahn, Paul, *The Secret History of Mongols,* San Francisco, North Point, 1984.

Kalhana, *Rajatarangini,* English tr. by M.A. Stein, London, 1900.

Kapur, Harish, *Soviet Russia and Asia, 1917-27,* Geneva, 1965.

Karunakaran, K.P., *India in the World Affairs,* London, Oxford, 1958.

Karimev, I.A., *Uzbekistan: The Road to Independence and Progress,* Tashkent, 1992.

Kaser, Michael and Santosh Mehrotra (eds.), *The Central Asian Economies after Independence*, London, 1992.

Kaul Deambi, B.K., *History & Culture of Ancient Gandhara and Western Himalayas*, New Delhi, Asiana Pub. House, 1985.

Kaul, T.N. *et al.*, *Indo-Soviet Relations, Prospects and Problems*, New Delhi Publishers, 1991.

———, *India and Asia*, Delhi, Lancer, 1991.

——, *Stalin to Gorbachev and Beyond*, New Delhi, Lancer International, 1991.

Kaushik, Devendra, *India and Central Asia in Modern Times: A Study in Historical, Cultural Contacts from the Early XIXth Century*, New Delhi, Satvahan, 1985.

——, *Socialism in Central Asia*, New Delhi, Vikas, 1976.

——, *Soviet Relations with India and Pakistan*, New Delhi, Vikas, 1971.

Kaushik, Devendra and Leonid Mitrokhin (eds.), *Lenin: His Image in India*, New Delhi, 1970.

Keene, H.G., *Turks in India*, Delhi, Oriental Publishers, 1972.

Kent, R., *Old Persian*, New Haven, American Oriental Society, 1953.

Khalfin, N.A., *Russia's Policy in Central Asia 1957-68*, London, 1968.

Khan, A.N., *Al-Mansurah: A Forgotten Arab Metropolis in Pakistan*, Karachi, 1990.

Khan, Azizpur Rahman and Dharam Ghai, *Collective Agriculture and Rural Development in Soviet Central Asia*, London, 1979.

Khan, F.A., *Banbhore*, (3rd edn.), Karachi, 1969.

Khan, Hashmatullah, *Tarikh-I-Jammu*, 2nd edn., Lahore, 1942.

Khan, Rasheedudin (ed.), *India and the Soviet Union*, New Delhi, Allied Publishers, 1975.

Khanikoff, *Bukhara: Its Amir and Its People*, London, 1845.

Kirby, Stuart, *Siberia and the Soviet Far East: Resources for the Future*, The Economist Intelligence Unit, Spl. Report No. 117, London, 1984.

Knobloch, Edgar, *Beyond the Oxus: Art and Architecture of Central Asia*, London, Ernest Benn Ltd., 1972.

Kochar, Rajesh, *The Vedic People: Their History and Geography*, Hyderabad, 2000.

Kohl, Philip L., *Central Asia: Paleolithic Beginnings to the Iron Age*, Paris, 1984.

Komarov, E.N., *Indo-Soviet Cooperation: Historical Background and Present Day Developments*, New Delhi, Allied, 1976.

Konow, Stein, *Corpus Inscription Indicarum*, Vol. II, Pt. I, Calcutta, 1929.

Kosentko, L.F., *The Turkestan Region*, in 3 vols., trans., Simla, 1882.

Krader, Lawrence, *Peoples of Central Asia*, Bloomington, 1996.

Kulkarni, Maya, *Indo-Soviet Relations*, Bombay, 1968.

Kumar, Baldev, *The Early Kushanas*, New Delhi, Sterling Publishers, 1973.

Kumar, Dharma (ed.), *Cambridge Economic History of India*, Vol. 2, Cambridge University Press, 1982.

Kumar, Ravinder, *India and the Persian Gulf Region 1858-1907*, Bombay, 1965.

Kuniholm, Bruce R., *The Origins of the Cold War in Near East: Great Power Conflict and Diplomacy in Iran, Turkey & Greece*, Princeton, Princeton Univ. Press, 1980.

Kuntiz, Joshua, *Dawn Over Samarkand—The Rebirth of Central Asia*, Calcutta, 1943.

Lal, K.S., *Growth of Muslim Population in Medieval India*, New Delhi, Research Publications, 1973.

——, *History of the Khaljis*, rev. edn., Delhi, 1980.

——, *Twilight of the Sultanate: A Political, Social and Cultural History of Sultanate of Delhi from the Invasion of Timur to the Conquest of Babur 1398-1526*, London, 1963.

Lambton, A.K.S., *Landlord and Peasant in Persia: A Study of Land Tenure and Land Revenue Administration*, London, 1953.

Lane-Poole, R., *The Coins of Mohammedan Dynasties in the British Museum*, Vol. 2, London, 1876.

Langlois, John D. (ed.), *China under Mongol Rule*, Princeton University Press, 1981.

Laski, H., *Communism*, London, 1927.

Lecoq, A. Von, *Buried Treasure of Chinese Turkestan*, London, 1928.

Lentz, Thomas W. and Glen D. Lowry, *Timur and the Princely Vision, Persian Art and Culture in the Fifteenth Century*, Los Angels, County Museum of Art, 1989.

Le Strange, Guy, *Clavijo, Embassy to Tamerlane 1403-1406*, London, Routledge, 1928.

Lettner, G.W., *Results of a Tour in Dardistan, Kashmir, Little Tibet, Ladak, etc*, London, 1868-73.

Lobanov-Rostovsky, A., *Russia and Asia*, Michigan, 1951.

Longworth, M. (tr.), *The Baloch Race*, London, 1954.

Lowich, N.M., *Coinage and History of the Islamic Worlds*, Variorium Reprints, London, 1990,

Lubin, Nancy, *Labour and Nationality in Soviet Central Asia: An Easy Compromise*, No. VI, London, 1984.

Ma'aroof, Mohd. Khalid, *Afghanistan and Super Powers*, New Delhi, Commonwealth, 1990.

Macdonell, A.A. and A.B. Keith, *Vedic Index of Names and Subjects*, Delhi, Motilal Banarsidass, 1967.

Mackay, Ernest, *Early Indus Civilization*, Clay and Sons, London, 1935.

Maclean, Fitzroy, *To the Back of Beyond: An Illustrated Companion to Central Asia and Mongolia*, Boston, 1975.

Maclagon, E.D., *Gazetteer of the Multan District*, Lahore, 1902.

Madelung, W., *Religious Trends in Early Islamic Iran*, Albany, New York, 1988.

Mallreoy, J.P., *In Search of the Indo-European Languages: Archaeology & Myth*, London, Thames & Hudson, 1991.

Malleson, Col. G.B., *History of Afghanistan*, London, 1878.

Mandel, W., *Soviet Far East and Central Asia*, New York, 1944.

Mangait, A.L., *Archaeology in the USSR*, Moscow, 1959.

Manik, S.S. and A. Chandel, *The Aryans and the Indian or Indus Civilization*, Dhaka, 1995.

Manrique, Fray Sebastian, *Travels 1629-43*, Hakluyt Society, 1926-27.

Manucci, Niccolo V., *Storia do Mogor 1653-1708*, tr. by William Irvine, London, 1907.

Manz, Beatrice F., *Central Asia in Historical Perspective*, Oxford, Westview Press, 1994.

Manz, Beatrice Forbes, *The Rise and Rule of Tamerlane*, Cambridge University Press, 1989.

Marshall, John *et al.*, *Mohenjodaro and the Indus Civilization*, London, 1931.

Marshall, Sir John, *Taxila*, 3 vols., Cambridge, 1951.

——, *The Buddhists of Gandhara*, Cambridge, 1960.

Masani, M.R., *The Communist Party of India*, London, 1954.

Masson, V.M., *Central Asia and the Ancient East*, Moscow, 1964.

Martin, Mike, *Afghanistan: Inside a Rebel Stronghold*, New Delhi, Heritage, 1985.

Mazumdar, R.C. (gen. ed.), *The History & Culture of the Indian People*, Vol. 4: *The Age of Imperial Kanauj*, Vol. 5: *The Struggle for Empire*, Vol. 6: *The Delhi Sultanate*, Bombay, 1955-60.

McGovern, M.W., *The Early Empires of Central Asia*, Chapel Hill, N.C., 1939.

Miller, W., *The Ottoman Empire and Its Successors 1801-1927*, 3rd edn., Cambridge, 1927.

Mills, Margaret, *Oral Narrative in Afghanistan: The Individual in Tradition* (Ph.D. thesis, unpublished), Harvard University, 1978.

Minorsky, V., *Sharaf al-Zaman Tahir Marvazi on China, the Turks and India*, London, 1942.

Mishra, Yogendra, *The Hindu Sahis of Afghanistan and the Punjab* AD *865-1026*, Patna, Vaishali Bhawan, 1972.

Misra, A.S., *Nana Saheb Peshwa and the Fight for Freedom*, Lucknow, 1961.

Misra, K.P. (ed.), *Afghanistan in Crisis*, New Delhi, Vikas, 1981.

Mitchiner, M., *The Multiple Dirhems of Medieval Afghanistan*, Surrey, Sanderstead, 1973.

Mittal, K.V. (ed.), *History of Technology in India*, Vol. III (from Antiquity to AD 1200, Modern Period), New Delhi, Indian National Service Academy, 2001.

Mohanlal, *Travel in the Punjab, Afghanistan, and Turkestan to Balk, Bukhara and Herat*, Calcutta, K.P. Bagchi & Co., 2nd rev. edn., 1977.

Monalt, Alexander, *Archaeology in the USSR*, Moscow, Foreign Languages Publishing House, 1959.

Monserrate, *The Commentary of Father Monserrate, or His Journey to the Court of Akbar*, tr. by J.S. Hoyland and annotated by S.N. Banerjee, Oxford University Press, 1922.

Morgan, D.O., *The Mongols*, Oxford, 1986.

Moynihan, Elizabeth B., *Paradise as a Garden in Persia and Mughal India*, London, Scholar Press, 1980.

Muhammad Abdul Ghani, *A History of Persian Language and Literature at the Mughal Court* (Babur to Akbar), in 3 parts, Allahabad, 1930.

Mukherjee, B.N., *An Agrippan Source: A Study in Indo-Parthian History*, Calcutta, Pilgrim Publishers, 1969.

——, *The Economic Factors in Kushana History*, Calcutta, Pilgrim Publishers, 1970.

——, *The Kushanas and the Deccan*, Calcutta, Pilgrim Publishers, 1968.

——, *The Kushana Genealogy*, Calcutta, Sanskrit College, 1969.

——, *The Rise and Fall of the Kushana Empire*, Calcutta, 1988.

Mukherjee, Sadhan, *Afghanistan from Tragedy to Triumph*, New Delhi, Sterling, 1984.

Murphy, Georges S., *Soviet Mongolia: A Study of the Oldest Satellite*, Berkeley, 1966.

Murtaza, Mirza Ghulam, *Tarikh-I-Chitral*, Peshawar, 1962.

Naik, J.A., *Russia's Policy Towards India: from Stalin to Yeltsin*, New Delhi, M.D. Publication, 1995.

——, (ed.), *Russia in Asia and Africa Documents 1972-75,* Kolhapur, Avinash Ref. Publication, 1980.

Nair, S.V., *Afghanistan: Perspectives for Reconciliation and Peace,* New Delhi, Panchsheel Publication, 1988.

Nalle, David, *Conference on the Study of Central Asia,* Washington DC, Kennan Institute for Adv. Russian Studies, and the Woodrow Wilson Institutional Centre for Scholars, 1983.

Nanda, B.R., *Socialism in India,* New Delhi, 1972.

——, (ed.), *Indian Foreign Policy: The Nehru Years,* New Delhi, Viva, 1976.

Narain, A.K., *The Indo-Greeks,* Oxford, 1957.

Narshakhi, *Tarikh-I-Bukhara,* English tr. and Commentary by R.N. Frye, *The History of Bukhara,* Cambridge, Mass., 1954.

Nazarli, M.D., *Cosmogony and Creation, Safavids Painting of the Sixteenth Century,* Moscow, 1993.

Nazim, M., *The Life and Times of Sultan Mohammed of Ghazni,* Cambridge, 1931.

Needham, Joseph, *Science and Civilization in China,* Cambridge University Press, 1954.

Nehru, Jawaharlal, *The Discovery of India,* London, *1947.*

Newell, Richard and Nancy Newell, *The Struggle for Afghanistan,* London, Cornell University Press, 1981.

Nicholson, Reynold Alleyne (ed. and tr.), *Selected Odes from Divan-i-Shamsi-I-Tabriz,* Cambridge, Cambridge University Press, 1898.

Nizam Al-Mulk, *Siyar al-Muluk (Siyasat-nama),* English tr. by H. Darke, *The Book of Government or Rules for Kings,* 2nd edn., London, 1978.

Nizami, Farhan Ahmad, *Madrasas, Scholars and Saints: Muslim Response to the British Presence in the Delhi and the Upper Doab 1803-1857,* Ph.D. dissertation, Oxford University, 1983.

Nizami, K.A., *Akbar and Religion,* Delhi, 1989.

——, *The Life and Times of Shaikh Nizam-ud-Din Auliya,* Delhi, 1992.

——, *Religion and Politics in India During the Thirteenth Century,* Bombay, 1961.

——, *State and Culture in Medieval India,* Delhi, 1985.

——, *Supplement to Elliot & Downson's History of India,* Vol. 2; *The Ghaznavids and Ghurids,* New Delhi, 1981.

Noble, Jojannes, *Central Asia: The Connecting Link Between East & West and other Lectures,* Nagpur, International Academy of Indian Culture, 1952.

Noorani, A.G., *Brezhnev Plan for Asian Security,* Bombay, Jaico, Punjab House, 1975.

Nove, Alec and J.A. Neweth, *The Soviet Middle East: A Model for Development,* London, 1967.

Olschki, L., *Marco Polo's Asia,* Berkeley, University of California Press, 1962.

Onon, Urgunge (ed. & tr.), *Mongolia Heroes of the Twentieth Century,* New York, 1976.

Padmore, George, *How Russia Transformed her Colonial Empire: A Challenge to Imperialist Power,* London, 1946.

Paksoy, H.B. (ed.), *Central Asia Reader: The Rediscovery of History,* New York, M.E. Sharpe, 1994.

Palat, Madhavan K. and Geeti Sen (eds.), *Rethinking Russia*, New Delhi, India International Centre, 1994.

Pandey, Deen Bandhu, *Sahis of Afghanistan and Punjab*, Delhi, Oriental Publications, 1972.

Pandit, R.S., *Kalhana's Rajatarangini*, New Delhi, Sahitya Akademi, 1968.

Park, A.G., *Bolshevism* in *Turkestan 1917-27*, New York, 1957.

Parker, E.H., *A Thousand Years of the Tartars*, London, Kegan Paul, 1895.

Parmu, R.K., *A History of Muslim Rule in Kashmir*, New Delhi, 1967.

Patnaik, Ajay, *Central Asia Between Modernity and Tradition*, New Delhi, Konark, 1996.

——, *Perestroika and Women Labour Force in Soviet Central Asia*, New Delhi, 1989.

Pennar, Jaan, *The USSR and the Arabs: The Ideological Dimension*, London, C. Hurst & Co., 1973.

Penrose, Boies, *Sherleian Odyssey, Being a Record of the Trends and Adventures of the Three Famous Brothers*, England, Taunton , 1938.

Pepys, Samuel, *The Diary of Samuel Pepys*, ed. by Henry P. Wheatley, London, Bell, 1920.

Petrov, Victor P., *Mongolia: A Profile*, New York, 1970.

Pierce, R.A., *Russian Central Asia 1867-1917: A Study in Colonial Rule*, Berkeley, 1960.

Pipes, Richards, *Moslems of Soviet Central Asia*, Cambridge, 1954.

Polo, Marco, *The Travels of Marco Polo*, tr. by R.E. Latham, Harmondsworth Penguin, 1958.

Pope, A.U., *A Survey of Persian Art*, 6 vols., London, 1938-39, 1964.

Popowski, Josef, *The Rival Powers in Central Asia or the Struggle between England and Russia in the East*, Westminster, 1893.

Possehl, Gregory L., *Indus Age – The Beginnings*, New Delhi, Oxford & IBH, 1999.

Prasad, Bimal, *The Origins of Indian Foreign Policy*, Calcutta, 1960.

Prasad, Bisheshwar, *The Foundation of India's Foreign Policy 1860-82*, Calcutta, 1955.

Premdev, Jai Prakash, *Indo-Soviet Relations*, Meerut, Meenakshi Prakashan, 1984.

Pugachenkova, G.A., *Ancient Monuments of Samarkhand and Bukhara*, 2nd edn., Moscow, 1968.

Pumpelly, R., *Explorations in Turkestan, Expedition of 1904*, Washington DC, 1908.

Puri, Baij Nath, *Kusana Bibliography*, Calcutta, Naya Prokash, 1977.

——, *India under the Kushanas*, Bombay, 1950.

——, *Buddhism in Central Asia*, Delhi, Motilal Banarsidass, 1987.

Puryear, V.J., *England, Russia and the Straits Question 1844-1856*, Calcutta, 1931.

Qamaruddin, *The Mahdavi Movement in India*, Delhi, 1985.

Quelquejay, C.L. *et al.* (eds.), *Turko-Tatar Past, Soviet Present*, Paris, 1986.

Quereshi, I.H., *The Administration of the Mughal Empire*, Karachi, 1966.

Rachelwiltz, I. de, *Papal Envoys to the Great Khans*, London, Faber & Faber, 1971.

Rafiqi, A.Q., *Sufism in Kashmir from the Fourteenth to the Sixteenth Century*, Delhi, 1972.

Rahman Abdur, *The Last Two Dynasties of the Sahis: An Analysis (of Their History, Archaeology and Paleography)*, Islamabad, 1979.

Rahul, Ram, *Afghanistan, Mongolia and USSR*, New Delhi, 1987.

——, *Central Asia: An Outline History*, New Delhi, Concept, 1997.

——, *Central Asia: Major Perspectives*, New Delhi, 1993.

——, *China, Russia and Central Asia*, New Delhi, 1993.

——, *Mangolia between China and USSR*, New Delhi, 1989.

——, *Struggle for Central Asia*, Delhi, Vikas, 1982.

Rai Chaudhuri, T. and Habib Irfan (eds.), *The Cambridge Economic History of India*, Vol. I, Cambridge, 1982.

Randhava, M.S., *Paintings of Babur-Nama*, New Delhi, 1983.

Rao, S.R., *Lothal and the Indus Civilization*, Bombay, Asia Publishing House, 1973.

Ratnam, Perala, *Afghanistan's Uncertain Future*, New Delhi, Tulsi Publication House, 1984.

Raverty, H.G. (tr.), *Tabaqati Nasiri*, 2 vols., London, 1981-97.

Rees, E.A., *State Control in Soviet Russia*, London, Macmillan, 1987.

Renfrew, Colin, *Archaeology and Language: The Puzzle of Indo-European Origins*, London, Cape, 1987.

——, *Towards an Archaeology of Mind*, Cambridge University Press, 1982.

Ricci, A., *The Travels of Marco Polo*, London, 1931.

Rizvi, Saiyid Athar Abbas, *The Wonder that Was India*, Vol. 2, London, Sidgwick & Jackson, 1987.

Rizvi, S.A.A., *Rawshaniya Movement*, Leiden, Abu Nahrein, 1968.

——, *Shah Wali-Allah and his Time: A Study of Eighteenth Century Islam, Politics and Society*, Canberra, 1980.

Rishi, W.R., *India and Russia: Linguistic and Cultural Affinity*, Chandigarh, Rama Publications, 1982.

Rodgers, C.J., *Catalogue of the Coins Collected by Charles J. Rodgers in the Lahore Museum*, Part-2, Calcutta, 1894.

Rorlich, Azada-Ayse, *The Volga Tatars: A Profile in National Resilience*, Stanford California, Hoover, 1986.

Ross, Sir E.D., *Sir Anthony Sherley and his Persian Adventure*, London, 1933.

Rossabi, Morris (ed.), *China Among Equals. The Middle Kingdom and its Neighbours.Tenth-Fourteenth Centuries*, 1988.

——, *China and Inner Asia from 1360 to the Present Day*, New York, 1975.

Rowland, B., *Ancient Art of Afghanistan, Treasures of Kabul Museum*, New York, 1968.

Rowland, Benjamin, *Art in Afghanistan*, London, 1971.

Roy, M.N., *India in Transition*, Bombay, 1964.

——, *Russian Revolution*, Calcutta, 1948.

Roy, Oliver, *Islam and Resistance in Afghanistan*, Cambridge University Press, 1986.

Rumer Boris, Z., *Soviet Central Asia: A Tragic Experiment*, Boston, 1989.

Rypka, J. *et al.*, *History of Iranian Literature*, Dordrecht, 1968.

Rywkin, Michael, *Moscow's Muslim Challenge: Soviet Central Asia*, London, 1982.

Sachau, E., *Alberuni's India*, 2 vols., London, 1910.

Sadiq, Mohd., *Turkish Revolution: A Perspective on Ideological Change in Turkey*, New Delhi, Macmillan, 1997.

Saguchi, Toro, *The Eastern Trade of the Khoqand Khanate*, Toyo Junko, 1965.

Saha, Panchanan, *Russian Revolution and the Indian Patriots*, Calcutta, Manisha Granthalaya, 1987.

Samra, Chattar Singh, *India and the Anglo-Soviet Relations, 1917-47*, Bombay, 1959.

Sanaullah, M.F., *The Decline of the Saljuqid Empire*, Calcutta, 1938.

Sankalia, H.D., *Prehistory and Protohistory of India and Pakistan*, Pune, Deccan Postgraduate College and Research Institute, 1974.

Sardesai, G.S., *India and the Russian Revolution*, New Delhi, 1967.

Sareen, Anuradha, *India and Afghanistan*, Delhi, Seema Publication, 1981.

Sareen, T.R., *British Intervention in Central Asia and Trans-Caucasia*, New Delhi, Anmol, 1989.

——, *Russian Revolution and India, 1917-21*, New Delhi, Sterling, 1977.

——, *Russian Revolution and India: A Study of Soviet Policy Towards Indian National Movement 1922-29*, New Delhi, Sterling, 1978.

Sandorji, M. Manchu, *Chinese Colonial Rule in Northern Mongolia*, New York, St. Martin Press, 1980.

Sarkar, Jadunath (tr.), *Masir-I-Alamgiri*, Calcutta, Royal Asiatic Society of Bengal, 1947.

Sarkar, Indunath, *Nadir Shah in India*, Patna, 1925.

Sanders, A.J.K., *The People's Republic of Mongolia*, London, 1968.

Saunders, J.J., *The History of the Mongol Conquests*, London, Routledge & Kegan Paul, 1971.

Schafer Edward, H., *The Golden Peaches of Samarkand*, Berkeley, University of California Press, 1963.

Schuyler, Eugene, *Turkestan, Notes of a Journey in Russian Turkestan Kokand, Bukhara, and Kuldja*, 2 vols., London, 1876.

Setan-Watson, H., *The Decline of Imperial Russia 1855-1914*, London, 1956.

Shahab, Qudratullah, *Pathans*, Karachi, 1964.

Shaban, M.A., *The Abbasid Revolution*, Cambridge, 1970.

Shahrani, M. Nazif and Rober L. Canfield (eds.), *Revolutions and Rebellions in Afghanistan and Anthropological Perspectives*, Berkeley, Institute of International Studies, University of California, 1984.

Shahrani, M. Nazif, *The Kirghiz and Wakhi of Afghanistan: Adaptation to Closed Frontiers*, Seattle, University of Washigton Press, 1979.

Shames-ud-Din (ed.), *Perestroika and the Nationality Question in the USSR*, New Delhi, Vikas, 1990.

——, *Secularism in the USSR*, New Delhi, Vikas, 1982.

Sharar, Abdul Halim, *Lucknow: The Last Phase of an Oriental Culture*, tr. & ed. by E.S. Harcourt and Fakhir Hussain, London, 1974.

Sharma, C.S., *India and Anglo-Soviet Relation 1917-1947*, Asia Publication, 1959.

Sharma, R.A., *Technology and Material Life of Central Asia: From Chalcolithic Period to Mauryan Period*, Delhi, Agam Kala Prakashan, 1991.

Sharma, R.R., *A Marxist Model of Social Change: Soviet Asia 1917-1940*, Delhi, 1979.

Sharma, R.S., *Advent of the Aryans in India*, New Delhi, Orient Longman, 1995.

——, *Looking for the Aryans*, Delhi, Orient Longman, 1995.

——, *Urban Decay in India*, New Delhi, Munshiram Manoharlal, 1987.

Shastitko, P.M., *Russia and India: Ancient Links Between India and Central Asia*, Calcutta, 1992.

Shaw, Robert, *Visits to High Tartary, Yarkand and Kashgar*, London, 1871.

Shaw Stanford, J., *Between Old and New, The Ottoman Empire under Sultan Selim III 1789-1807*, Cambridge, Harvard University Press, 1971.

——, *History of the Ottoman Empire and Modern Turkey*, Vol. I., *Empire of the Gazis: The Rise and Decline of the Ottoman Empire 1280-1808*, Cambridge, Cambridge University Press, 1976.

Shukla, R.L., *Britain, India and the Turkish Empire 1853-1882*, New Delhi, Peoples Publishing House, 1973.

Shukla, Vivekanand, *Soviet Revolution and the Indian National Movement*, New Delhi, H.K. Publishers, 1989.

Sidi Ali Reis, *The Travels and Adventures of the Turkish Admiral Sidi Ali Reis in India: Afghanistan, Central Asia, Persia during the Years 1953-56*, London, 1899.

Simon, J.L., *The Ultimate Resource*, Princeton, Princeton University Press, 1981.

Singh, Khushwant, *A History of the Sikhs*, 2 vols., London, Princeton University Press.

Singh, Patwant, *The Struggle for Power in Asia*, New Delhi, B.I. Publication, 1971.

Singhal, C.R., *Bibliography of Indian Coins*, Pt. 2, *Muhammadan and Later Series*, Numismatic Society of India, Bombay, 1952.

Singhal, D.P., *India and Afghanistan 1876-1907*, Queensland, 1963.

Sinha, P.B., *Indian National Liberation Movement and Russia (1905-1917)*, New Delhi, 1975.

Sinor, Denis, *Inner Asia, A Syllabus*, Indiana University Press, 1969.

Sirhindi, Y.A., *Tarikh-I-Mubark Shahi*, (ed.) M. Hidayat Husain, Calcutta, 1931.

Skrine, F.H., *The Expansion of Russia 1815-1900*, Cambridge University Press, 1915.

Skrine, F.H. and E.D. Rose, *The Heart of Asia. A History of Russian Turkestan and the Central Asian Khanates from the Earliest Times*, London, 1899.

Slobin, Mark, *Music in the Culture of Northern Afghanistan*, Tuescon, University of Arizona, 1976.

Snesarev, A.N., *Afghanistan*, Moscow, 1921.

Spain, W. James, *The Pathan Borderland*, Hague, 1963.

Spate, O.H.K., *India and Pakistan: A General and Regional Geography*, London, 1954.

Srivastava, A.L., *The Mughal Empire 1526-1803*, 3rd rev. edn., Agra, 1959.

——, *The Sultanate of Delhi*, Agra, 1959.

Starr, L.A., *Frontier Folk of the Afghan Border & Beyond*, London, 1920.

Stein, M.A., *Ancient Khotan*, Oxford, 1907.

——, *Archaeological Reconnaissances*, London, 1937.

——, *Serindia*, Oxford, 1921.

——, 'The Ancient Geography of Kashmir', *Journal of the Asiatic Society of Bengal*, Calcutta, 1989.

——, *The Thousand Buddhas: Ancient Buddhist Paintings from the Cave-temples of Tun-huang*, London, 1921-22.

Sufi, G.N.D., *Kasher: Being a History of Kashmir*, 2 vols., New Delhi, Light and Life Publishers, 1974.

Sukhareva, O.A., *Bukhara XIX*, Moscow, Nauka, 1966.

Sumner, B.H., *Russia and the Balkans 1870-80*, Oxford, 1937.

Swinton, Arthur, *The North-West Frontier 1839-1947*, London, 1967.

Tagore, Rabindranath, *Letters from Russia*, Calcutta, 1960.

Tarachand, *Material and Ideological Factors in Indian History*, Allahabad University, 1966.

Tan, Tennyson, *The Political States of Mongolia*, Shanghai, 1932.

——, *Tarikh-I-Sistan*, English tr. by Milton R. Gold, *The Tarikh-e-sistan*, Rome, 1976.

Tarn, W.W., *The Greeks in Bactria and India*, 2nd edn., Cambridge, 1975.

Thaden Edward, C., *Russia Since 1801: The Making of a New Society*, New York, John Wiley & Sons, 1971.

Thakur, A.K., *India and the Afghans: A Study of a Neglected Region 1370-1576*, Patna, Janaki Prakashan, 1992.

Tendulkar, G.B., *Abdul Ghaffar Khan: Faith Is a Battle*, Bombay, Popular Prakashan, 1967.

Thevenot, *Indian Travels of Thevenot and Careri*, ed. by S.N. Sen, New Delhi, 1949.

Thomas, F.W., *Tibetan Library Texts and Documents Concerning Chinese Turkestan*, London, 1935.

Tirmizi, S.A.I. (ed.), *Persian Letters of Ghalib*, New Delhi, Ghalib Academy, 1969.

Titley Norah, M., *Persian Miniature Painting and its Influence in the Art of Turkey and India*, Austin, University of Texas, 1983.

Toynbee, A.J., *Civilization on Trial*, London, Oxford University Press, 1953.

——, *A Survey of History*, London, 1954.

——, *Survey of International Affairs*, Oxford University Press, 1925.

Trench, Charles Chenevix, *The Frontier Scouts*, London, Jonathan Cape, 1985.

Trimingham, J.S., *The Sufi Orders in Islam*, Oxford, 1971.

Turner, R.L., *A Comparative Dictionary of the Indo-Aryan Languages*, Oxford University Press, 1966.

Tuzmuhamedov, R., *How the National Question was Solved in Soviet Central Asaia?* Moscow, 1973.

Tyulayev, S.I., *Miniatures of Babur Namah*, Moscow, 1960.

Ure, John, *The Trail of Tamerlane*, London, Corestable, 1980.

Usmani, Shaukat, *Peshawar to Moscow*, Benares, 1957.

Vafa, A., *Soviet Scholars on Mohandas Karamchand Gandhi*, New Delhi, 1971.

Vaidynath, R., *Formation of Soviet Central Asian Republics, 1917-36*, New Delhi, PPH, 1967.

Vambery, Arminius, *Sketches of Central Asia*, London, Alien, 1968.

——, *Travels in Central Asia*, London, 1864.

Van Bruinessen, M.M., *Agha, Shaikh and State: On the Social and Political Organisation of Kurdistan*, Ph.D. Dissertation, University of Utrecht, 1978.

Vats, M.S., *Excavations at Harappa*, 2 vols., Delhi, Govt. of India, 1940.

Venkatasubhaiah, F., *India and Asia*, Delhi, Patriot.

Venyukov, M.J., *The Progress of Russia in Central Asia*, St. Petersburg, 1877.

Verma, Birendra, *English East India Co. and the Afghans*, Calcutta, Punthi, 1968.

Verma, N.P., *India's Problems in Progressive Russian Social Thought 1857-1890*, New Delhi, Janaki Prakashan, 1986.

Verma, S.P., *Struggle for Himalayas: A Study in Sino-Indian Relations*, New Delhi, 1971.

Vernadsky, G., *The Mongols and the Russia*, London, 1953.

Vighne, G.T., *Travels in Kashmir, Ladakh and Ishkavdo*, London, 1842.

Vitkovich, Victor, *A Tour of Soviet Uzbekistan*, Moscow, *1954*.

Von Mohrenschildt, Dimitri, *The Russian Revolution of 1917: Contemporary Accounts*, Oxford University Press, London, 1971.

Vohra, N.N. (ed.), *Culture, Society and Politics in Central Asia and India*, New Delhi, India International Centre, 1999.

Wakman, Mohd. Amin, *Afghanistan at the Cross-Roads*, New Delhi, ABC Publishing House, 1985.

——, *Afghanistan, Non-aligned and the Super Power*, New Delhi, Radiant, 1985.

Walker, J., *A Catalogue of the Arab-Sasanian Coins in the British Museum*, Vol. 1, London, 1941.

Warikoo, K., *Central Asia: Emerging New Order*, Delhi, Har Anand, 1995.

——, *Central Asia and Kashmir: A Study in Context of Anglo-Russian Rivalry*, New Delhi, Gian, 1989.

——, *Ethnicity and Politics in Central Asia*, New Delhi, 1992.

——, *Himalayan Frontiers of India*. London, Routledge, 2009.

Walters, Thomas, *On Hiuen Tsiang Travels in India*, Reprint, Delhi, 1961.

Well Robert, S.R., *A Forgotten Empire, Vijayanagar*, New Delhi, Pub. Division, 1962.

Wessels, Cornelius, *Early Jesuit Travellers in Central Asia 1603-1721*, The Hague, Nijhoff, 1924.

Wheeler, Geoffrey, *The Modern History of Soviet Central Asia*, New York, 1964.

——, *The Peoples of Soviet Central Asia*, London, 1966.

Wheeler, Mortimer, *The Indus Civilization*, Cambridge, 1953.

William of Rubruck, *The Mission of Friar William of Rubruck: His Journey to the Court of the Great Khan Mongkee 1253-1255*, tr. by P. Jackson, comm. and notes by P. Jackson and D.O. Morgan, London, The Hakluyt Society, 1990.

Wilson, A.T., *The Persian Gulf*, Oxford, 1928.

Wink, *Al-Hind, The Making of the Indo-Islamic World*, Vol. 1, *Early Medieval India and the Expansion of Islam, 7th-eleventh Centuries*, Leiden, 1990.

Wolff, Joseph, *A Mission to Bukhara*, Introduction by Guy Wint, New York, 1969.

Wright, H.N., *The Coinage and Metrology of the Sultans of Delhi*, Delhi, 1931.

Yapp Malcome, E., *Strategies of Britain, Iran and Afghanistan, 1798-1850*, Oxford, 1981.

Yule, Sir Henry, *Cathay and the Way Thither*, 4 vols., 2nd Series, No. XXXVIII, London, Haklyut Society, 1915.

Zenkovsky, Serge A., *Pan-Tourism and Islam in Russia*, Cambridge (Mass), 1960.

ARTICLES

Aalto P., 'On the Role of Central Asia in the Spread of Indian Cultural Influence', *Vivekanand Commemorative Volume*, Madras, 1970, pp. 249-62.

Adrnov, I., 'The Awaking East', *New Times*, USSR, March 1967.

Adrnov, I.N.Z., 'Bravin (1881-1919) Soviet Diplomats in Iran and Afghnistan', *New Times*, February 1967.

Agrawal, R.C., 'Form of Taxation in the Kharosthi Documents', *Indian Historical Quarterly*, 1953, pp. 340-53.

——, 'Numismatic Data from Kharosthi Documents', *Journal of Numismatics*, 1953, pp. 103-06.

——, 'Position of Slaves/Serfs in the Kharosthi Documents', *Indian Historical Quarterly*, 1953, pp. 97-110.

——, 'Some Aspects of Indian Culture in the Kharosthi Documents from Chinese Turkestan', *Vivekanand Commemorative Volume*, Madras, 1970, pp. 275-81.

Ahmad, S.H., 'Sino-Soviet Dispute and India', *China Report*, New Delhi, August-September 1967.

Algar, Hamid, 'The Naqshbandi Order: A Preliminary Survey of its History and Significance, *Studia Islamica*, 44, 1976, pp. 123-32.

——, 'The Oppositional Role of the Ulama in the 20th Century Iran', in *Scholars, Saints and Sufis in Muslim Relgious Institutes Since 1500*, ed. by N.R. Keddie, Berkeley, University of California Press, 1979.

Altekar, A.S., 'A Bull and Horse Man Type of Coin of the Abbasid Capliph al Muqtadir Billah Jafar', *Journal of the Numismatic Society of India*, Vol. 8, 1948, pp. 75-81.

Ansari, Md. Azhar, *Jawed Ashraf and Tasneem Ahmad Geographical Glimpses of Medieval India*, in 3 vols., Delhi Idarah-i-Adabiyati, Delhi, 1989.

Arjomand, Said Amir, 'Religious Extremism: Sufism and Sunnism in Safavid Iran: 1501-1722', *Journal and Asian History*, Vol. 15, No. 1-35, p. 1981.

Baker, Hans, 'The Implications of the Islamic Question for Soviet Domestic and Foreign Policy', *Central Asian Survey*, Vol. 2, No. 1, 1983, pp. 110-20.

Beeka, Jiri, 'Islamic Schools in Central Asia', *New Orient*, Vol. 5, 1966, pp. 1186-90.

Beekinth, C.I., 'Aspects of the Early History of Central Asian Guard Corps', *Islam Archivum Eurasiae Medie Aevi*, Vol. 4, 1984, pp. 29-43.

Benerji, P., 'Hindu Deities in Central Asia', *Vivekanand Commemorative Volume*, Madras, 1970, pp. 81-118.

Bosworth, C.E., 'The Early Islamic History of Ghur', *Central Asiatic Journal*, 6, 1961, pp. 116-33.

——, 'The Political and Dynastic History of the Iranian World (AD 1000-1217)', in *The Cambridge History of Iran*, V, Cambridge University Press, 1975, pp. 1-202.

——, 'Rules of the Makran and Qusdar in the Early Islamic Period', *Studies Iranica*, Vol. 23, 1994, pp. 199-209.

——, 'The Tahirids and Saffarids', in *The Cambridge History of Iran*, Vol. 4, pp. 90-135, 1975.

——, 'The Rise of the Karamiyyah in Khurasan, Muslim World', *Hartfird Commemorative Volume*, 50, 1960, pp. 5-14.

——, 'The Imperial Policy of the Early Ghaznavids', *Islamic Studies, Journal of the Central Institute of Islamic Research*, Karachi, Vol. 1, No. 3, 1962, pp. 49-82.

—— 'The Titulature of the Early Ghaznavids', *Oriens*, Vol. 15, 1962, pp. 210-33.

Boughler, D.C., 'Our Relations with Afghanistan', *Contemporary Review*, Vol. CXVI, 1919.

——, 'A Russian Representative at Cabul', *Contemporary Review*, LXXXIII, 1903.

Brand, Michael, 'Akbar and Fatehpur-Sikri', *Marg*, Vol. XXXVIII, No. 2, Bombay, p. 99.

Bregel, Yuri, 'Nomadic and Sedentary Elements among the Turkmenes', *Central Asiatic Journal*, Vol. 25, No. 1-2, 1981, pp. 5-37.

——, *The Role of Central Asia in the History of the Muslim East*, New York, The Asia Society Afghanistan Council, Occasional Paper No. 20, 1980.

Buell, P.D., 'Early Mughal Expansion in Western Siberia and Turkestan (1207-1219): A Reconstruction', *Central Asiatic Journal*, The Hague, 1992.

Buell, P.D., 'Sino-Khitan Administration in Mughal Bukhara', *Journal of Asian History*, Vol. 13, 1971, pp. 121-51.

Case Frank, B., 'Decisive Battles of the World: The Kirghiz Steppe 2002 AD', *Military Review*, (Fort Leavenworth) November 1959.

Canfield Robert, L., 'Faction and Conversion: Religious Alignment in Hindu Kush', Ann Arbor Museum of Anthropology, University of Michigan, Anthropological, 1973, p. 50.

——, 'Soviet Gambit in Central Asia', *Journal of South Asian and Middle Eastern Studies*, Vol. 5, No. 1, 1981, pp. 10-30.

——, 'Western Stakes in the Afghanistan War', *Central Asian Survey*, Vol. 4, No. 1, pp. 121-35.

Carley Patricia, M., 'The Price of the Plan: Perception of Cotton and Health in Uzbekistan and Turkestan', *Central Asian Survey*, Vol. 8, No. 4., pp. 1-38.

Chakrabarti Dilip, K., 'Colonial Indology and Identity', *Antiquity*, Vol. 74, No. 285, September 2000, pp. 667-71.

Chertena, Z.S., 'The Bourgeois Theory of Modernization and the Real Development of the Peoples of Soviet Central Asia', *Soviet Review*, Vol. XXII, No. 2, 1981.

Chokaiev, M., 'Fifteen Years of Bolshevik Rule in Turkestan', *Journal of the Royal Asian Society*, 20, London, 1933.

——, 'Turkestan and the Soviet Regime', *Journal of the Royal Central Asian Society*, 28, 1931.

Cleaves, F.M., 'The Sino-Mongolian Inscription of 1346', *Harvard Journal of Asiatic Studies*, Cambridge, Mass, Vol. 15, 1952.

Colquhoun, A.R., 'Afghanistan: The Key to India', *Asiatic Quarterly Review*, 1900.

Colvin, A., 'Indian Frontiers and Indian Finance', *Nineteenth Century Magazine*, 1895.

——, 'The Problem Beyond Indian Frontier', *Nineteenth Century Magazine*, 1887.

Curzon, G.N., 'The Fluctuating Frontier of Russia in Asia', *Nineteenth Century Magazine*, 1889.

Dani, A.H., 'Lakor, Qa-Gaur or Nagor', *Journal of the Numismatic Society of India*, Vol. 16, Pt. 2, 1955.

Dikshit, K.N., 'Buddhist Centres in Afghanistan', *Vivekanand Commemorative Volume*, Madras, 1970, pp. 229-38.

Dupree, Louis, 'Islam in Politics: Afghanistan', *The Muslim World*, 56, Vol. 4, 1966, pp. 269-76.

Fairservice (Jr), Walter A., 'Central Asia & the Rgveda, The Archaeological Evidence', in George Erdosy (ed.), *The Indo-Aryans of Ancient South Asia*, New Delhi, Munshiram, 1997.

Feshbach, Murray and Stephen Rapaway, 'Prospects for out migration from Central Asia and Kazakistan in the next decade, in Soviet Economy in a time of Change', Joint Economic Committee of the U.S. Congress, Washington DC, Govt. Printing Office, 1979.

——, 'Soviet Population and Manpower Trends and Politics, Soviet Economy in a New Perspective', U.S. Congress Joint Economic Committee, Washington, DC, 1973.

Frechtling, L.E., 'Anglo-Russian Rivalry in Eastern Turkestan 1863-81', *Journal of the Royal Central Asian Society*, XXVI (1939), p. 471.

Frye, R.N., 'The Samanids', in *The Cambridge History of Iran*, IV, Cambridge University Press, 1975.

Frye, R.N. and A.M. Sayili, 'Turks in the Middle East before the Saljuqs', *Journal of American Oriental Society*, Vol. 63, 1943, pp. 194-207.

Gentelle, P., 'Landscapes, Environmental and Irrigation for the Study of the 3rd and 2nd Millennium (BC)', *Man and Environment*, X, 1986, p. 105.

Gleason, Gregory, 'Uzbekistan from Statehood to Nationhood', in Ian, Bremmer and Raj Taras (eds.), *Nation and Politics in Soviet Successor States*, Cambridge, 1993.

Grievson, G.A., 'On the Languages Spoken beyond the North-West Frontier of India', *Journal of Royal Asiatic Society*, London, 1900.

Gupta, S.P., 'Prehistoric Indian Cultures in Soviet Central Asia', *Vivekanand Commemorative Volume*, Madras, 1970.

Habib, Irfan, 'Imaging River Sarasvati: A Defence of Commonsense', *Social Scientist*, New Delhi, Nos. 332-333, Vol. 29, Jan-Feb, 2001.

——, 'The Historical Geography of India', *Proceedings of the Indian History Congress*, New Delhi, 1992.

Habberton, W., 'Anglo-Russian Relations Concerning Afghanistan 1837-1907', University of Illinois Studies in the Soviet Sciences, XXI, No. 4. 1937.

Hailder, M., 'The Mongol Traditions and their Survival in Central Asia, XIVth-XVIth Centuries', *Central Asiatic Journal*, Vol. 29, The Hague, 1984, pp. 57-59.

Hayword, G.W., 'Journey from Leh, Yarkand and Kashar', *Journal of the Royal Geographical Society*, XL, 1870, p. 33.

Hearsey, Maj (ed.), Moorcrafts 'Journey to Balkh and Bukhara', *Asiatic Journal*, XVIII, 1853, pt. 1, pp. 105-71 and 208.

Holdich, T.H., 'The Arabs of Our Indian Frontier', *Journal of Anthropological Institute*, 1899.

——, 'The Influences of Bolshevism in Afghanistan', *New Europe*, 1919.

Husain, Iqbal, 'Hindu Shrines and Practices as Described by a Central Asian Traveller in the First Half of the Seventeenth Century', in Irfan, Habib (ed.), *Medieval India, Research in History*, Oxford University Press, 1992.

Imshchenetskiy, A.I., 'Some Aspects of the Development and Location of Industry in Central Asian Economic Region', *Soviet Geography Review and Translations*, Vol. 13, No. 10, 1972.

Jarring Gunnar, 'Materials to the Knowledge of Eastern Turki', Parts 1, 2, 3 & 4, *Lunds Universitets Arsskrift*, 1938-1946,1948 and 1951.

——, 'A Tall Tale from Central Asia', *Script Minora, 3, 1972-73.*

Joyle, T.A., 'Notes on the Physical Anthropology of Chinese Turkestan and the Pamirs', *Journal Anthropological Institute,* Vol. XLII.

Kakharov, A., 'The Outlook for the Economic Development of Tadzhikistan', *Problems of Economics,* Vol. II, No. 1, 1959, New York.

Kalandarov, G., 'Tajik Cotton', *Current Digest of the Soviet Press*, Vol. XXV, No. 43, 1973.

Kamilov, R.T., 'Growth of the Working Class of Uzbekistan (1953-58)', Part I, *Soviet Society*, Vol. II, No. 4, 1964.

Kapadia, E.R., 'Alexander Burne's Mission to Kabul', *Journal of Indian History*, XLIV, 1944.

Kara, G., 'The Kitan Scripts' in, P.T. Daniels and W. Bright (eds.), *The World's Writing Systems,* Oxford, 1996, pp. 230-35.

Khan, G.M., 'A History of Bahrain Shah of Ghaznin', *Islamic Culture*, Hyderabad, 1949, pp. 62-91.

Khan, Iqtidar Alam, 'Fire-arms in Central Asia and Iran during the Fifteenth Century, etc.', *Proceedings of the Indian History Congress*, New Delhi, 1992.

——, 'Nature of Handguns in Mughal India, Sixteenth and Seventeenth Centuries', *Proceedings of Indian History Congress*, New Delhi, 1992.

Khan, Ahsan Raza, 'Gradation of Nobility under Babar', *Islamic Culture*, Hyderabad, January 1986.

Kiernan, V.G., 'Kashgar and the Politics of Central Asia', *Cambridge Historical Journal*, XI, 1953-55.

Kingsmill, T.W., 'The Intercourse of China in the Eastern Turkestan', *Journal of Royal Asiatic Society*, 1882.

Lal, B.B., 'The Indo-Aryan Hypothesis vis-a-vis Indian Archaeology', *Journal of Central Asia,* Vol. 1, No. 1, July 1978, pp. 21-41.

Lambton, A.K.S., 'The Internal Structure of the Salijuq Empire', in *The Cambridge History of Iran*, Vol. 5, 1975, pp. 203-82.

Lattimore, O., 'The Geography of Chengeskhan', *Geographical Journal,* Vol. 129, No. 1, 1963, pp. 1-7.

Lewis, B., 'The Mongols, the Turks and the Muslim Policy' in *Islam in History*, ed. B. Lewis, London, 1973.

Lewis, Robert A., H. Richard and Rowland, and Ralph S. Clem, 'Modernization, Population Change in Nationality in Soviet Central Asia and Kazakhstan', Canadian Slavonic Papers, Vol. XVII, Nos. 2-3, 1975.

Litvinsky, B.A. and L.T. Pastrol, 'Tribes of the Bronze Age in the Pyankova Oxus Valley', in *History of Civilization of Central Asia,* Vol. 1, UNESCO Pub., Paris, 1992.

Labanoff-Rostovsky, 'The Soviet Muslim Republics in Central Asia', *Journal of Royal Institute of International Affairs,* London, 1928.

Lowick, N.M., 'An Early Tenth Century Hoard from Isfahan', *Numismatic Chronicle,* 7th Series, Vol. 15, 1975, pp. 110-54.

——, 'On the Dating of Samanid Outsize Dirhams, Spinks', *Numismatic Circular,* London, 1977, pp. 204-07.

Mackerras, C., 'Sino-Uighur Diplomatic and Trade Contacts', *Central Asiatic Journal,* Vol. 13, pp. 215-40, 1969.

MacMunn, G., 'The North-West Frontier of India Today', *Journal of Royal Artillery Institute,* 1924.

Mahan, Alfred T., 'The Persian Gulf and International Relations', *National Review,* Vol. 40, No. 140, 1902.

Maleson, Maj General Sir Wilford, 'British Millitary Mission to Turkestan 1918-1920', *Journal of Royal Central Asian Society,* 1922.

Marnie, Sheila and Erick Whitlockle, 'Central Asia and Economic Integration', *REE/RL Research Report,* Vol. 2, No. 14, 2nd April 1993.

Marx, Karl, 'The Future Results of British Rule in India', *New York Tribune,* 22 July 1853.

Michell, R., 'The Region of the Upper Oxus', *Proceedings of the Royal Geographical Society,* Vol. 1884, p. 419.

Mills, Margaret, '*Cupid and Psyche in Afghanistan: An International Tale in Cultural Context,* New York, Afghanistan Council of Asia Society, Occasional Paper No. 14, 1978.

Millward, W.G., 'Iran', in *Introduction to Islamic Civilization,* ed. by R.H. Savory, pp. 169-77, Cambridge University Press, 1976.

Mirkhasilov, S.M., 'Socio-Cultural Changes as Reflected in the Contemporary Rural Family in Uzbekistan', *Soviet Society,* Vol. XVIII, No. 4, 1980.

Mitrokhin, L.V. and A.V. Raikov, 'Impact of October Revolution on Ghadar Party', *Soviet Review,* Vol. X, 23 May 1973.

Montgomerie, T.G., 'On the Geographical Position on Yarkand and Some Other Places in Central Asia', *Journal of the Royal Geographical Society,* XXXVI, 1866, p. 157.

——, 'Report of the Mirza's Exploration from Cabul to Kashgar', *Journal of the Royal Geographical Society,* Vol. XLI, No. 1871, p. 132.

Morgan, D.O., 'The Mongol Armies in Persia', *Der Islam,* Vol. 56, No. 1, 81, 96, 1979.

Morgan, E.D., 'Faiz Baksh's Journey via Badakhsan and Wakhan to Yarkand', *Journal of the Royal Geographical Society,* Vol. XLII, No. 1872, p. 320.

——, 'The Old Channels of the Lower Oxus', *Journal of the Royal Asiatic Society,* Vol. XL VII, No. 1878, p. 201.

——, 'Pandit Manpul's Report on Badakshan', *Journal of the Royal Geographical Society,* XLII, (1872), p. 322.

——, 'Recent Geography of Central Asia from Russian Sources', *Royal Geographical Society,* Supplementary Paper No. 1882-83.

Mottahedeh, R., 'The Abbasid Caliphate in Iran', in *The Cambridge History of Iran*, Vol. 4, 1975, pp. 57-89.

Naby, Eden, 'Ethnicity and Islam in Central Asia', *Central Asian Survey*, Vol. 12, No. 2, 1993.

——, 'The Uzbeks in Afghanistan', *Central Asian Survey*, Vol. 3, No. 1, pp. 1-21.

Nandi, R.N., 'Aryan Settlements in Rigveda', *Indian Historical Review*, Vol. XXI, No. 1-2, July 1994-January 1995, pp. 9-36.

Nath, R., 'Scrutiny of the Persian Data Related to the Builders of Taj Mahal', *Indo Iranica*, 32, 1-18, 1979.

Newell, R.S., 'The Government of Muhammad Moussa Shafiqi, the Last Chapter of Afghan Liberalism', *Central Asian Survey*, Vol. 1, No. 1, pp. 53-64.

——, 'The Shattari Saints and their Attitude towards the State', *Medieval India Quarterly*, Vol. 1, 1950, pp. 56-70.

——, 'The Suhrawardi Silsila and its Influence on Medieval Indian Politics', *Medieval India Quarterly*, Vol. 3, 1957, pp. 109-49.

Noorzay, M. Siddiq, 'Soviet Economic Interest in Afghanistan', *Problems of Communism*, May-June, pp. 43-54.

Paksoy, H.B., 'Central Asia's New Dustan', *Central Asian Survey*, Vol. 6, No. 1, pp. 75-92, 1987.

Parpola, Asko, 'The Coming of the Aryans to Iran and India and the Culture and Ethnic Identity to Daises', *International Journal of Dravidian Linguistics*, Vol. XVII, No. 2, pp. 85-228.

Patnaik, Ajay, 'Modernization, Change and Nationality Process in the USSR', in Shams-ud-din (ed.), *Perestroika and the Nationality Question in the USSR*, New Delhi, 1999.

——, 'Restructuring Soviet Central Asia', in Zafar Imam (ed.), *Restructuring in the USSR*, New Delhi, 1986.

——, 'Women and Economic Change in Central Asia'. Paper presented at the International Seminar on "Women and Economic Change in Central Asia" organized by Central Asia Research Forum and UNESCO at SOAS, University of London, 6-9 July 1992.

Pennel, T.L., 'Tribes on Our N.W. Frontier', *Asiatic Quarterly Review*, XXX, 1910.

Perevedentser, V., 'Population Movement in Central Asia', *Current Digest of the Soviet Press*, Vol. XXVIII, No. 4, 1976.

Persits, M., 'Transition of Indian National Revolution to Marxist-Leninism', *Soviet Review*, Vol. XI, 16 May 1974.

Pervi, T.N., 'Coins of the Early Muslim Period from Bambhore', *Pakistan Archaeology*, No. 6, pp. 117-81.

Petrushevsky, I.P., 'The Socio-Economic Condition of Iran under the Ilkhans', in *The Cambridge History of India*, Vol. 5, 1968, pp. 483-537.

Popkhsishevsky, V.V., 'Prospectus of Population Inflation in the USSR', *Soviet Geography Review and Translation*, Vol. 4, No. 1, 1963.

Pulleyblank, E.G., 'A Sogdian Colony in Inner Mongolia', *T'oung-Pao*, Leiden, Vol. 41, 1952, pp. 317-56.

——, 'The Name of the Kirghiz', *Central Asiatic Journal*, The Hague, Vol. 34, 1960, pp. 98-99.

Puri, B.N., 'Geographical Information from Rajasekhara 's Works', *Journal of Indian History*, 1962.

Rawlinson, H.G., 'Afghan Wazirs and their Country', *Asiatic Quarterly Review*, January 1895.

——, 'The Independent Afghan or Pathan Tribes', *Asiatic Quarterly Review*, Vol. VIII, 1893-94.

Rawlinson, H., 'The Afghan Crisis', *Nineteenth Century Magazine*, 1877.

Rawlinson, H.C., 'On Bada-Kshan and Wakhan', *Proceedings of the Royal Geographical Society*, XVII (1872-73), p. 108.

Regel, A., 'Dr. Albert Regel's Journey to Karategin and Darowaz', *Proceedings of the Royal Geographical Society*, IV, 1882, p. 412.

Riasanovsky, Nicholas V., 'The Emergence of Eurasianism', *Slavic Studies*, 4: 39-72, 1967.

Roemer, H.R., 'The Sucessors of Timur and the Turkemen Dynasties', in *The Cambridge History of Iran*, Vol. 6, pp. 98-188, 1986.

Roy, Olivier, 'The Origins of the Islamic Movement in Afghanistan', *Central Asian Review*, Vol. 3, No. 2, 1984, pp. 117-27.

——, 'Sufism and the Afghan Resistance', *Central Asian Survey*, Vol. 2, No. 4, 1983, pp. 61-79.

——, 'What is Afghanistan Really Like?' *Dissent* (Winter): 47-54, 1981.

Rywkin, Michael, 'Religion, Modern Nationalism and Political Power in Soviet Central Asia', *Canadian Slavonic Papers*, Vol. XVII, 1975, pp. 2-3.

Sahrani, M. Nazif, 'Afghanistan's Kirghiz in Turkey', *Cultural Survival Quarterly*, Vol. 8, 1984, pp. 31-34.

Saryyev, B., 'Crimes Against Women in 1961 Turkmen Criminal Code', *Central Asian Review*, Vol. 13, No. 3, 1965.

Senga, T., 'The Toquz Oghuz Problem and the Origin on the Kahzars', *Journal of Asian History*, Vol. 24, pp. 57-69.

Sharma, R.R., 'Class and Social-Agrarian Transformation in Soviet Central Asia—A Historical Cultural Context', *Man and Development*, New Delhi, September 1986.

——, 'Social Parameters of the Agarian Transformation of Soviet Central Asia: The Historical Cultural Context', *International Studies*, Vol. 24, No. 2, New Delhi, 1987.

Sheehy, Ann, 'Labour Problems and Employment in Kazakhstan and Central Asia', *Central Asian Review*, Vol. 14, No. 2, 1966.

——, 'Primary and Secondary Education in Central Asia and Kazakhstan', *Central Asian Review*, Vol. 16, No. 3, 1968.

Shister, G.A., 'The Current Stage of Development of the Working Class of Uzbekistan', *Soviet Sociology*, Vol. 14, No. 1, 1975.

Siddiqui, I.H., 'Social Mobility in the Delhi Sultanate', in Irfan Habib (ed.), *Medieval India*, Vol. I; *Researches in the History of India 1200-1750*, pp. 22-48, Delhi, 1992.

Siren, O., 'Central Asian Influences in Chinese Paintings of the Tang Period', *Arts Asiatique*, III, 1956, pp. 3-4.

Smith, Johan Masson, 'Mongol and Nomadic Taxation', *Harvard Journal of Asiatic Studies* Vol. 30, 1970, pp. 46-85.

Smith, J.M., 'Ayn Jalut: Mamluck Success or Mongol Empire', *Harvard Oriental Journal of Asiatic Studies*, Vol. 44, 1984, pp. 307-45.

——, 'Mongol Manpower and Persian Population', *Journal of the Economic and Social History of the Orient*, Vol. 43, No. 3, 1975, pp. 271-99.

Spring, Derek W., 'The Trans-Persian Railway Project and Anglo-Russian Relations', *Slavonic and East European Review*, Vol. 54, No. 1, 1976, pp. 60-82.

Srivastava, K.M., 'The Myth of Aryan Invasion of Harappan Towns', in B.B. Lal and S.P. Gupta (ed.), *Frontiers of the Indus Civilization*, Book & Book, New Delhi, 1984.

Stein, Awul, 'Archaeological Discovery in the Neighbourhood of Niya', *Journal of Royal Asiatic Society*, 1901, pp. 569-72.

——, 'Ancient Manuscripts from Khatan', *Journal of Royal Asiatic Society*, 1906, pp. 695 ff.

Storn, S.M., 'The Early Ismaili Missionaries in the North-West Persia and in Khurasan and Transoxania', *BSOAS*, Vol. 23, pp. 56-90.

Sykes, H.R., 'Our Recent Progress in Southern Persia and Its Possibilities', *Proceedings of the Central Asian Society*, London, 1905, pp. 1-20.

Tahir, Mahmud, 'Abunasir Kursavi, 1776-1862', *Central Asian Survey*, Vol. 8, No. 2, pp. 158 ff.

Tett, Gillian, 'Women and Islam in Tazikistan'. Paper presented at the International Seminar on "Women and Economic Change in Central Asia", Organized by Central Research Forum and UNESCO at SOAS, University of London, 6-9 July 1992.

Thomas, E., 'Complimentary Contribution to the Series of the Coins of the Kings of Ghazni', *Journal of the Royal Asiatic Society*, London, Vol. 17, 1860, pp. 138-208.

——, 'On the Coins of the Hindu Kings of Kabul', *Journal of the Royal Asiatic Society*, London, Vol. 9, pp. 117-88.

——, 'On the Coins of the Kings of Ghazni', *Journal of the Royal Asiatic Society*, London, Vol. 9, pp. 267-386.

Thomas, F.W., 'Glimpses of Life Under Tibetan Rule in Chinese Turkestan', *Man*, Vol. XXXVI, pp. 1010 ff.

Thornton, A.P., 'Afghanistan in Anglo-Russian Diplomacy, 1869-73', *Cambridge Historical Journal*, Vol. XI, 1953-55, pp. 204 ff.

——, 'British Policy in Persia 1858-90', *English Historical Review*, Vol. LXIX, 1954-55, pp. 504 and 601.

——, 'The Reopening of the Central Asian Question, 1864-9', *History*, Vol. XLI, 1956, p. 122.

Trotter, H., 'On the Geographical Results of the Mission to Kashgar under Sir T.D. Forsyth in 1873-4', *Journal of the Royal Geographical Society*, Vol. XLVIII, 1878, p. 113.

Umarov, H., 'Development and Socio-Cultural Transformation'. Paper presented at the Seminar on "Socio-Economic Transformation of Soviet Central Asia" in the Centre for Soviet Studies, University of Bombay in 1985.

Valiev, A., 'Central Asian Republics' Creation of National Intelligentsia', *Socialism, Theory and Practice*, Vol. 1, No. 42, Moscow, 1977.

Vinikov, I.A.R., 'National and Ethnographic Groups in Central Asia as Reflected in Ethnic Statistics (Pt. I)', *Soviet Society*, Vol. XIX, No. 2, 1980.

Wheeler, G.E., 'Cultural Developments in Soviet Central Asia', *Journal of Royal Central Asian Society*, 41, 1954.

White-King, L., 'History and Coinage of the Barakzai Dynasty of Afghanistan', *Numismatic Chronicle*, 1896.

Yarshater, Ehsan, 'The Development of Iranian Literature', ed. by Ehsan Yarshater, *Columbia Lecture on Iranian Studies*, no. 3, New York, 1988, pp.3-37.

Yarshater, E., 'Mazdakism', in *The Cambridge History of Iran*, Vol. 2, 1983, pp. 991-1024.

Yate, A.C., 'The Proposed Trans-Persian Railway', *Proceedings of the Royal Central Asia Society*, February 8, 1911.

——, 'The Visit to India of Amir Habibullah Khan', *Asiatic Quarterly Review*, 1907.

Younghusband, G.J., 'The Permanent Pacification of the Indian Frontier', *Nineteenth Century Magazine*, 1998.

Zadykhina, K.L., 'Ethnographic Data on the Mode of Life of the Uzbek Workers of Tashkent and Andizhan', *Soviet Society*, Vol. 1, No. 4, 1963.

Zarrinkub, Abid Al-Hussain, 'The Arab Conquest of Iran and its Aftermath', in *The Cambridge History of Iran*, Vol. 4, pp. 1-56, 1975.

Zurcher, E., 'The Yueh-chi and Kanisks in Chinese Sources', in *Papers on Date of Kaniska*, A.L. Basham (ed.), Leiden, E.J.Brill, 1967.

Index

AVPRI 222
Abbas, Shaikh 100
Abdullahnama 115
Afghan *Mujahideen* 265, 267
Afghanistan 4, 14-15, 19, 22, 24, 31, 46-51, 67, 97, 139-40, 152-53, 155-56, 158, 164, 171-78, 185, 187-88, 192-93, 196, 198, 213, 215-18, 226, 231-32, 236-38, 248-49, 263-71, 273-74, 276-85, 287, 293
Agathocles 49
Age of imperialism 214
Agnostic ideas 84
Ahlae Sunna 134
Ahlekufr 135
Airyanem Vaejo 24
Al-Beruni/Al-Biruni 6, 47-48
Al Hind 56
Al-Khwārizmī 106
Al-Qaida 268-69, 273-79, 281-86
Alash National Freedom Party 266
Alexander 6, 36, 44, 65, 148, 164, 168, 180, 185-86, 189, 192, 197-99, 203-04
Aligrama in Swat Valley 18
Aliyev, Igrar 24
Almagest 105
Altai 33
Amantia muscarita 39
Amour-propre 14
Andronovo culture 21
Anglo-Russian rivalry 187, 205, 210, 221, 222
Apara-Godana 16
Āpastamba 9
Apianus 10
Arjabhar 103
Armenia 4-5, 31, 83, 85, 113
Āryabhaṭa 10, 12, 103
Āryavarta 57
Ashraf, K.M. 82
Asiatic civilization 221
Asoka 48, 180
Aśokaḥ Brāhmaṇa 61
Athar Ali, K.M. 82, 87
Atharvaveda 15, 39
Auqaf 132
Avestan 5
Axis 294
Azerbaijan 4, 83, 85, 239

Babur 111, 114-15, 121-22, 132, 184, 245
Bactria 3, 6, 15, 21, 25, 39, 45-47, 65-67
Baqam 112
Bahlikas 15
Bailey, H.W. 39
Balkan Peace settlement 290
Baltistan 40, 57, 188, 201, 231, 249
Bandar Abbas 192-93, 247
Banished Princes 123

Bārhut 60
Barmakiyan 140
Barthold, V.V. 93, 199
Baudhāyana 9
Bazaars 97
Bhāskara 10, 104
Bhaṭapusvāmi 61
Big siege 158
Bilateral agreements 247-48
Black Sea 3-4, 31-34, 36-37, 142, 181, 189, 215, 232, 235, 281
Board of Trade 175
Bombay 150, 152, 189-90, 192, 225, 232, 235-36, 256, 260
Bradenstein, Wilnelm 21
Brāhmaṇas 61
Brāhmasphuṭasiddānta 102
Brāhmī 59
Bre ye yogo 40
Britain/British 148-49, 151-58, 161, 163-65, 167, 169, 171-75, 177, 181, 183, 186-92, 198, 201, 203-10, 213-19, 221-29, 231, 235-39, 251-56, 274-75, 282-83
British Empire 217, 224, 228
Buddha 48-49, 56, 59-60, 62-63, 72-73, 140-41
Buddhist council 49
Bukhara 6, 83, 87, 96, 97, 98, 111, 112, 113, 114, 115, 116, 117, 118, 119, 120, 121, 122, 124, 131, 138, 141, 142, 148, 155, 162, 163, 166, 171, 172, 173, 174, 175, 176, 177, 182, 183, 184, 185, 186, 188, 190, 191, 192, 195, 196, 197, 198, 199, 202, 204, 205, 206, 207, 208, 215, 232, 233, 234, 235, 236, 238
Bukhari, Khwaja Fared 134
Burnes, Alexander 197-99

CAR 262, 264-72, 276, 277-81, 287
Cāe 5
Caliphs 140
Capitalist industrialisation 188
Cappadocia 35
Caravanserais 97, 111
Carmakhandikas 17
Catel Huyuk 3
Caucasus 3-4, 6, 19, 33-34, 81, 113, 215, 239, 263, 266, 280-81
Chatterjee, Bina 105
Chaudhary, Azam 62
Cherniaev, Maj. Gen. M.G. 205
China 3-14, 18, 30, 34, 46-51, 55, 65-69, 71, 87, 100, 110-12, 121, 131, 162-65, 167-68, 177, 190, 196, 213, 217, 221-22, 226-27, 229, 249, 259, 266-68, 270-72, 278, 287, 291-92, 294
Chingiz Khan 245
Chumbi Valley 227-28
Cimmerians 30
Clavijo 110
Clerics 246, 264
Colonialism 192, 238
Columbianisation 266
Commercial transaction 110, 116, 120, 171
Communist Party 238, 251-54
Constantinople 239
Cosmic concept 103
Cossacks 148
Cotton cloth 111-12, 171, 191, 196
Culikas 17
Cuneiform tablets 13
Curzon, Lord 55, 221-22, 225

Daeva 38
Dalai Lama 221-24, 229
Dandamaev, M.A. 31
Danibegov, Rafail 190-91
Dānu 4
Dardic culture 22
Darius 35
Darul harb 136
Darya 6
Dashli Tepe 19
Days of Sverdlovsk 260
Desperadoes 122
Diakonow 30
Diwan Baksh 167
Dnieper-Donets 3
Dogra chief 204

Dreikaisersbund 216
Drug Trafficking 266-67
Dughlat, Haider 121, 123
Durability of Russian fabric 175
Durand Line 218
Durand, Sir Mortimer 213, 218
Dushanbe 23-24, 141, 248, 264

Early Bronze Age 79
Economic cooperation 192, 268
Edwards, H.B. 204
Ekvilocanas 17
Ethno-nationalism 281
Eriskine 85
Euphrates 3
Eurasian cultural continuum 3

Farman 121
Khan, Hafiz Muhammad Fazil 196, 198
Fertile crescent 3
  oases 6
Fine wool 68, 202
Fire chemical 7
Fitch, Ralph 183
Flotsam 7
Forsyth, Douglas 164-65
Forward Policy 203, 217
Frank, Andre Gunder 81, 89
Free trade 116

Gandhara Grave Culture 41
Gandhi , Mahatma 187, 255
Gates of friendly intercourse 203
Gathas 38
Georgia 4, 202
Gerard, Col. M.G. 218
Ghazi, Ataliq 164-65, 168-69
Ghazni 84, 100
Ghirshman, R. 22
Gilgit 42-43, 57, 67, 188, 201, 217, 249
Gimirrai 34
Gissar culture 180
Godhūma 4
Goes, Bento de 112, 124
Golden Horde 182
Gomal 15
Gomar 34
Gorchakov, A.M. 206
Gotra 157
Gravitation Pole 291-92, 294
Great Game 171, 201, 214, 231
Griffin, Lepel 172
Grigoriev, Prof. V.V. 151, 153
Guṇasena 62

Hallucinogenic mushroom 39
Harappa/Harappan 3, 5, 19, 41, 43, 180-81
Harmata, J. 24
Harmony 13, 169, 197
Harper, Charles 198
Harṣacarita 17
Haumavarga 34
Herat 65, 83, 87, 98, 111, 122, 131, 152, 155, 157, 172, 174, 190, 215
Heretical influence 133
Himalayas 3, 14-15, 39, 57, 164, 206, 221, 223, 226
Hindukush 3, 20, 40, 57, 65, 80, 99, 115, 139, 172, 181, 187-88, 215, 217
Hipea Dhia 50
History of Indo-Aryan Problems 20
Hoama 37
Holy Tribes 131
Homeland 21
Huntington, Ellsworth 55, 67-69

Ibn Battuta 96-100, 110, 113, 115, 122, 182
Imperialist powers 232
Indian National Congress 187
Indo-China 11
Indo-Iranian Line 22
Indonesia 8, 282-86
Interaction 12-14, 18, 20, 56, 68, 140, 169, 180, 204, 209, 249, 290
Intrusion of Islam 82
Iqta 85
Iran 5, 14, 22-25, 30, 35, 38, 43, 79-80, 113, 115, 117, 138-39, 143, 182-84, 186, 190, 192-93, 198, 246-47, 269, 280-82, 286-87
Iron weapons 5
Isfendiyad 47

Iskuza 31, 34
Islamic militancy 266
Issyk-kul lake 33

Jacām 5
Jaihum 98
Jambhagavibhaṭṭa 60
James, Vernon 132-33
Jauvaini, Ata Malik 97
Jaxartes Valley 35
Jaziya 197
Jetsam 7
Jibin 43
Jihad 264, 267, 268, 282, 283, 284
Jones, Sir William 20
Jyā 102

Kabul 15, 46, 51, 66, 99, 100, 114-15, 122, 133, 140, 171-76, 178, 190, 196-99, 202-04, 207-09, 215, 218, 238
Kālakācārya kathanaka 57
Kalhana 83-84, 139-40
Kalmuk 119
Kalmyk Steppe 221
Kambojas 15-16, 48
Kamkhab Baf 131
Kanceya 4
Kandhar 175
Karaghan haven 118
Karakorum Pass 67, 69, 203
Karimov, Islam 248, 269, 279
Kārpasā 4
Kashgar 67, 83, 114, 161-69, 190, 202, 204, 209-10, 239
Kashmir 14, 18, 21, 25, 39, 65, 67, 73, 81, 83-84, 86-87, 115, 140-42, 152, 155-56, 163-64, 187-92, 196, 201-10, 213, 231, 235, 239, 249, 263, 265, 268-70, 277-78, 281-82
Kashmir Durbar 208, 210
Kātyāyana 9
Kauper, R. 58
Kazak detachment 229
Kazakhstan 4-5, 20, 23, 83, 193, 246, 249, 266-67, 272, 279
Kehr, George Jacob 186
Kelteminar 3
Kerpās 4
Khan, Abdurrahman 153, 156, 158
Khan, Kublai 12
Khanates 6, 113, 120, 172, 175, 185, 198, 199, 202, 204, 205
Khanqas 87
Kharoṣṭi/Kharoshthi 48-51, 59-60, 68
Khayyam, Omar 10
Khazanov 30-31
Khiva 6, 97, 116, 119, 141, 163, 172, 174, 184, 198
Khorasan 48
Khubha 46
Khwaja 132
Kiakhta 176
Kiev Rus 182
Kindleberger, Charles P. 291
Kokand 84, 141, 162-63, 172, 198, 202, 204, 206-07, 209, 232, 239
  Envoy 204
Kokcha Valley 39
Komba-Ovaleko 227
Kossovitch, K.A. 152
Kraunchdvipa 16
Kumarajiva 51
Kushanas 49, 51, 56, 65, 69, 80, 85
Kurram 15, 50
Kuwait 265, 272-73
Kyrghystan 4

Ladakh 57, 84, 162, 164, 188, 193, 201-04, 208, 231
Laden, Osama Bin 265, 268-69, 277, 282
Land of Shem 182
Lashkar-e-Toiba 282
Lazurite 180
Lebedev, G.S. 189
Lesseps, F. 192
Lhasa 221, 223-25, 227-29
Liu, Xinru 68
Livshitz, V.A. 24
London Cabinet 223, 225-26

Lunar Zodiac 12
Lyonnet 19

Madineh-e-thani 142
Madrasas 87
Mahabharata 15-17, 39
Mahmandar 166
Mahasanghikas 50
Mahāśradhopāsaka 62
Mahāvastu 65
Maktubat wa asnad 125
Malaysia 282, 284-86
Malenky, Semen 148
Manucci 114-15
Marcanda 44
Marg 40
Market-oriented system 259
Masnawi 132
Masson 18-19, 21, 79
Material culture 22, 31, 41, 80, 180
Mathura 45, 50
Mazar-e-salatin 142
Merv 111
Migration of armymen 163
Mikhailovich, Tsar Aleksei 184
Milindapanho 48, 65
Military oligarchy 265
Ministry of Defence 149
Mlecchas 43
Mobility 19, 31-32, 37, 41, 88
Monarchy 85
Mongolia 6, 34, 122, 221, 226
Moorcroft 202-04
Morier, Sir R. 217
Motherland 152-53, 158, 255
Muhalla(s) 99, 246
Muhtasib 120, 168
Müller, Max 21
Multan 115, 171, 235
Munjan 40
Mutiny 149, 151, 158

Nagna Parbat 57
Nakeen Pelisse 124
Nakhshab 98
Nakṣatara 12
Nallino 103
Nana Sahib 151, 154, 157-58
Naqsh-I-Rustam 36
Naqshbandiyya 131
Narain, A.K. 66
Naśuputra 61
NATO 249, 272-73, 276
Neelfarushan 112
Nehring, Alfons 21
Nehru, Jawaharlal 255
Nei Ching 8
New Delhi 193, 245, 247-48, 269, 271, 273, 277
New Economy 293
Nomadic tribes 22, 31, 183
Novoye Vremiya 174

Omar, Mullah 265, 269, 273, 276-77
Oporrocorra 15
Orthodox Christianity 186
Orusa 4
Ottorokorrha 15
Oxus 3, 18-19, 21, 23, 37, 44, 112, 139-41, 163, 175, 204, 210, 216-18, 232, 235

Paibas 86
Pakistan 3, 43, 57-58, 213, 246, 249, 263, 265-72, 274, 276-79, 281, 286, 288
Pamir 21, 40, 67, 180-81, 188, 217-18
Pancāṅgas 107
Pañcha Siddāntikā 10
Panini 181
Parthia 45-47, 65
Pascal, Blaise 10
Patela melni 7
Path Abad 97
Paul, Tsar 148
Pazyryk burials 33
Penetration 65, 113, 192, 222, 224, 226, 229
Penjdeh crisis 218
Persia 4-6, 10, 47-48, 85, 97, 110, 112-14, 119, 121-22, 152, 154, 156, 177, 183-85, 187, 192, 226

Persian couplet 207
Peshawar 49, 114-15, 124, 172, 174-75, 192, 198, 202, 204-05, 207-09, 283
Peshkash 121
Petersburg 151-53, 155, 157, 174, 177, 186, 189-91, 203, 213, 215-17, 222-24, 261
Phala 9
Pingree, David 106
Pogrebova, M.N. 24
Polaus Arcticus 7
Police surveillance 174, 236
Prakrit 47, 68
Pramāṇa 10
Prophytactic system 8
Prostration 86
Prunes 113-14, 119, 121
Psenica 4
Ptolemy 15, 32, 41, 102, 105, 107
Punjab 14-15, 43-45, 50, 65, 80, 84, 96, 152, 158, 162, 164, 172, 174, 180, 202-04, 208, 210, 231, 235, 240
Purva-Videha 16
Pyotr Ivanovich Sungur 186

Quraishi, Prof. Ishtiaq 133

Racialism 238
Radical Islam 263, 266, 272
Rahman, Abdur 171-72, 174-75, 177-78, 187, 213, 215
Rajatarangini 83
Ramchandra 151-58
Rasail 107
Reasons for decline in Trade 120
Red Army 239
Reinforcements 83
Religious diversity 68
endowment 132
Ribatat 97
Rigveda 5, 14-15, 22, 25, 38-39, 41-43
Robertson, V.R. 226
Romanovsky, D.I. 206
Rude Kausar 135
Rugged Pathans 171
Rupee trading system 259
Russki invalide 177
Russia 3, 6, 13-14, 30, 34, 36, 55, 81, 111-19, 123-24, 147-49, 151-56, 158, 164-65, 167, 171-78, 181-93, 195-99, 202-04, 206-08, 210, 214-19, 221-29, 231-32, 235-36, 238, 248-49, 255, 258-60, 266-69, 271-72, 278-81, 287, 291-94

Safa, Prof. Zabihullah 140
Sakas 20, 30-39, 42-45, 56, 180
Sakadvipa 16
Samarkand 6, 47, 87, 96, 98, 110-14, 119-20, 132, 139, 141-42, 163, 172, 174-75, 182-84, 188, 192, 198-99, 206-08, 215, 217, 232
Sanskrit 4-5, 10, 17-18, 24, 47-48, 83, 103, 108, 139-40, 141, 152, 181, 186
Sarakhs 99, 192-93
Sarianidi 21, 79
Sarvastivadins 50
Saudi Arabia 246, 265, 268-69, 276, 286
Śaṣya 5
Scythians 30-32, 37
Secret deals 113
Secretary of state 165, 224, 227
Semipalatinsk 190, 202
Semirechye 37
Semitic medical systems 8
Serṇi 65
Sexagesimal system 11
Shaw, R.B. 161-62, 166-69
Sharia 131, 134, 197
Sharif, Nawaz 265
Shatial 70
Shih 9
Shir Siyah 99
Siberia 3, 5, 55, 113-14, 117-18, 121, 185, 260
Sijda 86
Silao 124
Silk Route 66, 83, 142, 193, 201
Sind 45, 96, 190, 231, 233, 235
Sine table 102, 104-05, 107
Singapore 282-84, 286

Singh, Maharaja Ranbir 187, 205, 207-10
Singh, Maharaja Ranjit 203
Singh, Mehta Sher 207
Sinor, Denis 81
Sipha-e-shaba 269
Sirghe 4
Sirhindi, Shaikh Ahmed 133
Skobelev, M.D. 155-58
Snesarev, A.E. 188
Sobolev, Col. L.N. 154, 156
Social landscapes 68
  organisation 81
Socialism 255
Socio-economic interaction 209
Soghdiana 140
Solovyev, O.F. 202
Southeast Asia 5, 11, 282, 286, 292
Soviet relations 255
Spalli Tepe 19
Spirit of Camaraderie 69
Spiritual Culture 180-81
Sramana 72
Stagnation 125, 199
Stūpa 70
Sudan 216, 269, 282, 286
Suffimenta 42
Sulba Sūtras 9
Sunni-Wahhabism 246
Sūnya 10
Swastikas 63
Swat 15, 18, 22, 40-43, 49, 56
  Grave Culture 42
Syria 5, 35, 47, 269

Tabulghu 111
Tajikistan 4, 14, 23, 138-39, 141, 143, 180, 213, 232, 235, 239, 246-49, 264-66, 268, 279
Taliban militia 265, 267
Tamgha 118
Tanais 4
Tanish, Hafiz 114
Taoist ideas 47
Tariqate Khwajagan 131
Taskent 84
Tathagata 49
Tenishevo 182
Term Davan 67
Terrorism 248-49, 265, 267-71, 277, 281, 283-86
Textile industry 188-89, 191, 247
Thapar, B.K. 41
Theodama 56
Thewalt, Volkar 58
Tibet 16, 47, 115, 141, 162, 166, 193, 221-29
Tigraxauda 32, 34
Tigris 3
Timur 6, 121, 124, 183, 245
Tirmiz 98, 111
Tokharestan 17
Trade/Traders 6-7, 66, 71, 83, 88, 111-17, 119-25, 162, 165, 169, 176, 183, 190-91, 203, 208, 210, 231-37, 239, 247, 259
Traditions of hospitality 167
Trans-caucasian 217, 232
Transoxiana 80
Trishulas 64
Tsarist administration 192, 210
Tughluq, Muhammad bin 96, 100
Turcoman Khivans 123
Turfan 6
Turkestan 15-16, 46, 49, 67, 83, 87, 89, 97, 111-15, 118-19, 121, 138, 141, 153, 155-56, 158, 161, 163, 166, 171, 174, 176-77, 186, 201, 203-09, 231-33, 235-39, 263, 265-66, 269
Turkey 113, 115, 152-54, 166-67, 191, 246, 259, 263, 272, 280
Turkmenistan 3-4, 14, 18-19, 24, 40, 180, 193, 247, 249, 267, 279

Uighur 47
Ukraine 3, 7, 81
Ulakh 7
Upper lands 139
Urheimat 21, 32
Usman, Arif 137
Utkramajyā 103
Uttara 15

Uzbekistan 4, 6, 14, 24, 239, 246, 248, 264-66, 268, 279
Vajpayee, A.B. 293
Varahamihira 11, 104
Varna 90
Varṣa 16
Veddoid 41
Vedic Aryans 19
Velayat 143
Velayat-e-bala 139
Vihara 48
Vrihi 4

Wheeler, R.E.M. 66

Yarqand 161-62, 164-69
Younghusband 217, 229

Zoroastrianism 48, 231